THE UNITED STATES AND GERMANY

ALSO BY MANFRED JONAS

Die Unabhängigkeitserklärung der Vereinigten Staaten (1964)

Isolationism in America, 1935–1941 (1966)

American Foreign Relations in the Twentieth Century (1967)

Roosevelt and Churchill: Their Secret Wartime Correspondence, with F. L. Loewenheim and H. D. Langley (1975)

New Opportunities in a New Nation: The Development of New York after the Revolution, with R. V. Wells (1982)

The United States and Germany

A DIPLOMATIC HISTORY

MANFRED JONAS

*

Cornell University Press

ITHACA AND LONDON

First published 1984 by Cornell University Press.
Published in the United Kingdom by Cornell University Press Ltd., London.

International Standard Book Number 0-8014-1634-5
Library of Congress Catalog Card Number 83-15278

Printed in the United States of America

*Librarians: Library of Congress cataloging information
appears on the last page of the book.*

*The paper in this book is acid-free and meets the guidelines
for permanence and durability of the Committee on Production
Guidelines for Book Longevity of the Council on Library Resources.*

To Nancy, as ever

Contents

Preface

The United States and Germany have on two occasions been
enemies in war, on many others cooperative partners in peace. They
have both coexisted happily and been active rivals for trade and
power. Their peoples have more than once moved from mutual admiration to mutual hatred and suspicion and back again. At the same
time, Germany has evolved from a geographical concept for which
the Kingdom of Prussia served as the logical surrogate through an
expansionist empire, a diminished and disadvantaged republic, a
demonic dictatorship, and almost total destruction into two states
that represent one of the major divisions in today's world. Changes
in the United States have been less cataclysmic, but they have been
sufficient to transform an infant agricultural republic, geographically
remote from the centers of civilization, into a beleaguered economic
and military giant at the very heart of the world power structure.
The two nations have, separately and jointly, affected profoundly
the course of events over the past two centuries, and an examination
of their relationship during this period sheds light both on their
development and on the nature and scope of international affairs.

Relations between nations, not unlike those between persons, are
enormously complex, and it is hardly surprising that they are most
frequently treated only in limited time frames and in the context of
important world events. While such treatments do much to illumi-
nate these events and the conduct of the participants, they necessarily slight the significant element of historical continuity inherent in
any relationship.

The important studies of American-German relations focus on those moments in which the two nations either interacted in extraordinary and unusual ways or not only impacted upon each other but jointly contributed to major international developments. Thus Alfred Vagts's *Deutschland und die Vereinigten Staaten in der Weltpolitik* (1935) examines the effect of the almost simultaneous appearance of the United States and Germany on the world power stage at the turn of the century. Ernest May's *The World War and American Isolation* (1959) considers America's relationship with Germany (as well as that of Great Britain with both) in the context of the First World War. Werner Link's *Die amerikanische Stabilisierungspolitik in Deutschland* (1970) treats the impact of U.S. policy toward the Weimar Republic on world order in the 1920s, and Arnold Offner's *American Appeasement* (1969) focuses on the alleged failure of the United States to come fully to grips with the problems posed by Hitler's Germany and thus on its failure to work effectively to prevent World War II.

All these works, and others that might equally well be cited, make important contributions to our understanding of the relations between the United States and Germany. None, however, really considers the interaction over time, that is, the effects of mutual perceptions and misperceptions based on historical experience on the relationship in any given set of circumstances, though all imply that such effects were of considerable significance. The only attempt to examine the full sweep of these relations, Hans W. Gatzke's *Germany and the United States* (1980), concentrates so heavily on the period after 1945 that most of what precedes the Nazi period appears simply as a prelude of marginal importance.

It is my basic assumption here that to the extent to which a continuity exists in the development of nations there is continuity in the relations between any two of them and that this continuity affects both the nature of the relationship and the actions that the parties reciprocally take at any particular time. In the effort to prove the validity of this assumption I have attempted to steer a middle course between too much detail and too broad generalizations, to provide a clear picture of the overall relationship with all its twists and turns, but to limit detailed examination to selected instances that serve to clarify the intricacies and complexities informing the relationship at all times. When we focus on the relationship itself, rather than on the world events that were affected by it, transitional periods such as 1902–1908 or 1929–1935, as well as times during which contact between the two nations was limited, take on added significance. At the same time it becomes clear that the span from the American Civil War to the aftermath of World War II most effectively illustrates the dynamics of the relationship and that, in this particular case at least, political and geopolitical factors played a more prominent role than did simple economic ones or the much-discussed cultural interchange and "German element" in the United States.

Although the present book is based on considerable archival research, on an exhaustive study of the voluminous printed sources, and on a careful examination of the secondary literature, all indicated in the Bibliographical Essay, footnoting has been kept to a minimum. To do justice to the frequently contradictory assessments provided by the sources would require a scholarly apparatus so large and so complex as to overshadow the text. Simply to list references would, in most instances, be misleading. Given the basically interpretive nature of this book, the responsibility for all judgments and evaluations must rest with the author in any case.

Over the years during which this volume has been in preparation I have incurred debts to so many individuals that it is impossible to list them all here. I therefore take refuge in a blanket acknowledgment and express my thanks to all whose patience and helpfulness have made this book possible. I must single out, however, those individuals and institutions without whom the project would never have come to fruition at all.

Robert A. Divine first suggested the idea for such a volume to me many years ago, though neither he nor I envisaged the size and scope it would assume. The staffs of the National Archives and the Library of Congress in Washington, the Politisches Archiv des Auswärtigen Amtes in Bonn, the Bundesarchiv in Koblenz, the Franklin D. Roosevelt Library in Hyde Park, the Widener Library of Harvard University, the Stirling Library of Yale University, the Universitätsbibliothek of the University of the Saarland, and the Schaffer Library of Union College, Schenectady, New York, provided invaluable assistance in assembling the necessary materials. The trustees of Union College granted sabbatical leaves that allowed me to devote time to the project, and the Union College Humanities Faculty Development Fund underwrote some of my expenses. A Fulbright-Hays grant made possible the necessary research in Germany, and a fellowship at the Charles Warren Center not only opened to me the immense resources of Harvard University, but also provided invaluable logistical support and inspiration. For all that, I am grateful.

I owe a debt, too, to Bernhard Kendler of Cornell University Press, whose encouragement, support, and unfailing goodwill enabled the manuscript to find its final home, and to Carol Betsch, whose promptly and firmly wielded blue pencil eliminated much awkwardness and ambiguity, though I remain fully responsible for that which may remain. The late Annie F. Sweet typed most of the early version of the manuscript and Rita Michalec spent endless hours on additions and corrections.

Portions of Chapters 2 and 3 previously appeared in "The Major Powers and the United States, 1898–1910: The Case of Germany," in Jules Davids, ed., *Perspectives in American Diplomacy* (New York, 1976), and are reprinted here by permission of The Ayer Company; portions of Chapter 6 previously appeared in "Mutualism in the Relations between the United States and the Early Weimar Republic," in Hans L. Trefousse, ed., *Germany and America: Essays on Problems of International Relations and Immigration* (New York, 1980), and are included here by permission of the Program on Society in Change and Brooklyn College Press.

Last, but in no sense least, I acknowledge the contribution of my wife, Nancy Greene Jonas, who shared the strains and burdens of this enterprise, provided aid and comfort, and deserves a full share of the credit for its completion.

MANFRED JONAS

Schenectady, New York

THE UNITED STATES AND GERMANY

Chapter I

AN ERA OF
GOOD FEELINGS

*

For Liberty and Union

On February 7, 1871, just three weeks after the proclamation of the Second German Empire in the Hall of Mirrors of the palace at Versailles, President Ulysses S. Grant asked the United States Congress to raise the pay of the American minister in Berlin to the level of that of his colleagues in London and Paris. "The union of the States of Germany into a form of government similar in many respects to that of the American Union," he asserted, "is an event that can not fail to touch deeply the sympathies of the people of the United States. . . . The adoption in Europe of the American system of union under the control and the direction of a free people, educated to self-restraint, can not fail to extend popular institutions and to enlarge the peaceful influence of American ideas." In glowing terms he referred to an "intimacy of personal and political intercourse" with Germany, "approaching, if not equal to, that with the country from which the founders of our Government derived their origin."[1]

The admiration for Germany which suffused the president's message and the high hopes that his words expressed were widely shared in the United States and were based, at least in part, on the earlier history of relations between the two countries. To many of the eighteenth-century colonists, Frederick the Great of Prussia had

1. James D. Richardson, *A Compilation of the Messages and Papers of the Presidents, 1789–1902*, 9 vols. (Washington, D.C., 1903), 7: 120.

seemed not only an invaluable ally during the French and Indian War but also the champion of Protestantism—and, therefore, of liberty and enlightenment—on the Continent. His prompt, though temporary, prohibition of the transit of "Hessian" mercenaries bound for America during the Revolution, and his only partially concealed glee at England's discomfiture in these years, had confirmed the founding fathers in their estimate that the German monarch was a friend of America, even though Arthur Lee had had little success during his stay in Berlin in securing assurances of positive support. And, although "Baron" Frederick von Steuben had left the Prussian service long before his arrival in the beleaguered colonies, his contribution to the cause of independence was also credited to Prussia.

Once American independence was achieved, Prussia became one of the first nations to enter into a treaty of amity and commerce with the new republic. The agreement that John Adams, Benjamin Franklin, and Thomas Jefferson concluded on September 10, 1785, in negotiations with the Prussian minister to the Netherlands called not only for "firm, inviolable, and universal peace, and sincere friendship," but also for trade reciprocity and for freedom of the seas for neutral vessels, even in time of war. "It is perfectly original in many of its articles," George Washington delightedly informed Count Jean Baptiste de Rochambeau, the former commander of French troops in America, "and, should its principles be considered hereafter as the basis of connexions between nations, it will operate more fully to produce a general pacification than any measure hitherto attempted amongst mankind."[2] The treaty proved to be durable. It was reenacted with mutually agreeable changes in 1799, when young John Quincy Adams was sent by his father to Berlin to conduct the negotiations, and formed the basis for a new agreement thirty years later. The Treaty of 1828 in its turn lasted for nearly a century and was to regulate commerce between the United States and the German Empire during the period when both nations rose to the status of major trading powers.

The development of a tradition of amity between the United States and Prussia owed less, however, to either the liberality of existing treaties or the memory of Frederick the Great than it did to

2. Jared Sparks, ed., *The Writings of George Washington*, 12 vols. (Boston, 1858), 9: 182.

the happy fact that for nearly a century few, if any, serious problems arose between the two nations. Prussia had limited maritime interests and no overseas possessions, while the United States studiously avoided involvement in purely Continental problems. Under these circumstances, points of contact were few, and points of friction virtually nonexistent. Even trade between the two nations did not reach significant proportions until the 1850s, and the internal contradictions inherent in American efforts to expand commerce while avoiding political ties, contradictions that at various times disturbed relations with both Great Britain and France in the early national period, did not become apparent in dealings with the German kingdom.

Prussia found it unnecessary to maintain a permanent representative in Washington until after the enactment of the Tariff of 1816, and did not appoint a regular chargé d'affaires until 1822. The United States did not reciprocate for more than a decade after that. Only when trade with Prussia, particularly in tobacco, began to increase somewhat and when the immigration of Germans began to attract attention was the need for regular diplomatic representation considered seriously. Even then the initiative was left to Prussia, which, in 1834, appointed Friederich Ludwig von Roenne, a trade expert, minister-resident to Washington and, in the following year, requested that the noted jurist and historian of international law Henry Wheaton, then in Copenhagen, be sent to Berlin to help negotiate commercial agreements with the newly organized Zollverein. Wheaton became the first accredited American diplomat in the Prussian capital since the departure of John Quincy Adams in 1801. "It is gratifying to know," Secretary of State John Forsyth wrote in the letter of appointment, "that not a single point of controversy exists between the two countries calling for adjustment; and that their commercial intercourse, based upon treaty stipulations, is conducted upon those liberal and enlightened principles of reciprocity . . . which are gradually making their way against the narrow prejudices and blighting influences of the prohibitive system."[3] Wheaton's elevation to the rank of minister in 1837, more than half a

3. John Forsyth to Henry Wheaton, April 20, 1835, in "Diplomatic Instructions of the Department of State, 1801–1906: German States, April 30, 1835–July 23, 1869," 2, 53. Microfilm copy 77, roll 65, Record Group 59, National Archives, Washington, D.C. (hereafter cited as NA). Post-1868 "Instructions" are on rolls 66–72. Despatches received from various German states are on Microfilm copy 44.

century after the Declaration of Independence, marked the actual beginning of full diplomatic relations between the United States and Prussia.

Even after that, however, cultural relations with Germany as a whole remained far more important than either diplomatic or commercial dealings with Prussia or other German states. The glowing reports brought back by Americans who began in increasing numbers to study at German universities did much to create admiration for German thought and culture, and the influence of Germany on the New England renaissance was far greater than its effect on American foreign or commercial policy. The debt of Ralph Waldo Emerson to Immanuel Kant and Georg Wilhelm Friedrich Hegel, and of George Bancroft and John Lothrop Motley to German historical scholarship, formed part of a cultural bond that was to leave a permanent impress on American thought and, in particular, on American education. Unencumbered by political or diplomatic friction, German ideas flowed freely to America, where they formed part of a significant cultural exchange. Most informed Americans believed that Germany would be more than repaid for the export of the ideas of her poets and thinkers by the reciprocal flow of political ideas from the United States, and few doubted that these political ideas would find in Germany a particularly fruitful soil.

The great expectations that many Americans had of Germany did not rest on a clear understanding of German history, German politics, or the character of the German people. Instead, they were based on the fact that in certain superficial respects Germany seemed closer to the Jeffersonian ideal than did any of its neighbors and, therefore, more likely than they to establish a government on the American model. Its population had a higher literacy rate than that of Italy, or Austria, or even France. As a predominantly Protestant people, the Germans appeared more likely to free themselves from the reactionary ultramontanism that hampered the democratization of France and slowed political progress everywhere. Moreover, Americans viewed the absence of strong central government in Germany as a major advantage, since it seemed to presage the establishment of a federal system that would serve, there as here, to safeguard individual freedom.

Americans who, like Daniel Webster, believed that liberty and union were essential and inseparable components of the American system and who shared the missionary faith that this system was destined to spread throughout the world came to equate the German desire for unity with that for liberty and were certain that if the one were to be achieved, the other would inevitably follow. In the absence of serious disputes between the United States and any of the states of Germany, such essentially romantic notions could reach full flower and produce a legacy of goodwill which affected relations between the two countries for many years.

The German Revolution of 1848 only encouraged such thinking. "The President," Secretary of State James Buchanan informed Andrew J. Donelson, the minister to Prussia, "has observed with the deepest interest the efforts of the German States and the People to establish an efficient Federal Government for all Germany; and he will hail, with unalloyed pleasure, the accomplishment of this great event." Pointing out that "the sympathies of the American people have ever been warmly enlisted in all that can contribute to the welfare and power of Germany," he expressed the wish for "the final establishment of a Confederacy, which shall secure the liberty and prosperity of the people, without unnecessarily abridging the power of the Sovereign States, of which it is composed." The presumed parallel to the American experience was clear enough, but Buchanan made sure that the point was not missed. "It is under such a system," he concluded, "that we have preserved public order, maintained private rights and enjoyed unexampled liberty and prosperity."[4] Germany, he was certain, was following the American example.

Within three weeks, Donelson was officially designated "Envoy Extraordinary and Minister Plenipotentiary to the Federal Government of Germany," in the full expectation that the Frankfurt parliament would produce a plan of government which would be closely modeled on the American Constitution, and that thereafter Prussia would be "definitely deprived of the power to enter into negotiations with powers beyond the limits of Germany."[5] So convinced was the United States that the work at Frankfurt was deserving of American support and would be crowned with success that President James K. Polk acceded to a request by the new "Central Government" and arranged to have Commodore Foxall A. Parker of the United States Navy given leave so that he might investigate the possibility of

4. James Buchanan to Andrew J. Donelson, July 24, 1848, in "Diplomatic Instructions: German States," 14: 125, RG 59, NA.
5. Buchanan to Donelson, August 3 and 7, 1848, in ibid., 127.

organizing a German Federal Navy with American assistance. Even after the new Whig administration replaced Donelson in Berlin, he remained in Frankfurt as envoy to the new "German Empire" until September 1849, by which time all hopes of German unification had passed. Those Americans who paid attention to matters beyond their own borders persisted even then in the belief that Germany, of all the nations of Europe, was the most likely to follow the American example in due time. "I have more hope of her," John C. Calhoun confided to his brother-in-law, "than of France, or any other of the Continental countries. Indeed, I look to her to save Europe, including France herself."[6]

The increasingly large influx of Germans to the United States encouraged the persistence of that belief. Between 1850 and 1870, the number of German-born residents increased from less than six hundred thousand to nearly 1.7 million—three times as fast as the population as a whole. Half a million Germans came to America between 1852 and 1854 alone. Not only were a substantial portion of the new arrivals political liberals and partisans of German unity, they also made converts to their cause by creating a generally favorable impression in their adopted country. Though nativists criticized them for their clannishness, and orthodox Calvinists took them to task for desecrating the American sabbath by frequenting the beer-gardens more religiously than the churches, the Germans were generally greeted with considerable enthusiasm. Most Americans were inclined to agree with the estimate of the *New York Times* that they constituted "undoubtedly the healthiest element of our foreign immigration," and with James Buchanan's judgment that "we have no more useful citizens,"[7] and to admire their level of education, their thrift, and their industry. These virtues, combined with the fact that they arrived with more capital than most immigrants, enabled the Germans to become substantial citizens after a relatively short period of residence.

Moreover, their politics coincided to a remarkable degree with the mood of native-born Americans, particularly in the North and West, where more than 90 percent of them settled. The Germans generally voted Democratic until the early fifties because they regarded them-

6. J. Franklin Jameson, ed., *Correspondence of John C. Calhoun*, vol. 2 of *Annual Report of the American Historical Association for the Year 1899* (Washington, D.C., 1900), 750.

7. Buchanan to Donelson, August 15, 1848, in "Diplomatic Instructions: German States," 14: 131, RG 59, NA; *New York Times*, January 31, 1869.

selves as small-*d* democrats and believed the party of Jefferson and Jackson to be more interested in the cause of the common man. They switched increasingly to the Republican party after 1854 because they held chattel slavery to be incompatible with the dignity of labor, and they thereby remained accurate indicators of majority sentiment. By adjusting with relative ease to both the political and the economic life of their adopted country, they fostered a feeling of German-American kinship and helped to sustain the American belief that the German people were the most suitable vehicles for the transmission of American political ideas to Europe. They thus increased the sympathy for German efforts to achieve unity and strengthened the expectation that a liberal and democratic nation would emerge.

If Americans were always predisposed toward national unity in general and the unification of Germany in particular, the circumstances under which German unity was achieved only tended to increase American goodwill. The late fifties were, after all, a time during which the continued unity of the United States became a major domestic issue, and by 1861 Lincoln had led America into a war to preserve the Union. Under these conditions it was hardly surprising that both popular sentiment in the North and the official attitude of the U.S. government should become more favorably disposed than ever to strivings for unity in other parts of the world. And it was precisely during the years of the American Civil War that Otto von Bismarck laid the groundwork for the establishment of the German Empire.

Just three months before Confederate batteries opened fire on Fort Sumter, William I ascended the Prussian throne, determined to bring about the unification of Germany under Prussian leadership. When his initial efforts to strengthen the army ran into opposition from the liberals in parliament who refused assent to the annual appropriation bills, the king called on Bismarck to deal with the impasse, and the process of unification got actively under way. American newspapers had generally sided with the parliamentary opposition during the army debate and hardly regarded the new chief minister as a liberal hero. But most Americans, like the liberals of Germany, came eventually to believe that unification—and the liberalization they were certain would follow—was highly desirable, regardless under whose auspices or by what methods it was attained.

Such a conclusion was greatly facilitated by the apparent sympathy that Prussia showed for the Union cause. The Prussian minister for foreign affairs, rejecting all rebellion on principle, issued an immediate declaration against the Confederacy, and assured the American minister in May 1861 that his government "would be one of the last to recognize any de-facto Government of the disaffected States of the American Union."[8] Bismarck showed himself equally cool to a French proposal that called on the United States in effect to recognize the Confederacy by concluding a six-month armistice with it. Prussia, moreover, refused, unlike Great Britain and France, even to issue a declaration of neutrality, on the grounds that such a declaration would suggest that the Union and the Confederacy were belligerents with equal status under international law. The Prussian minister for foreign affairs even instructed Baron Friedrich von Gerolt, the minister in Washington, not to follow the example of his French colleague in approaching the government in Montgomery on the question of neutral rights. He wished, he insisted, "to convince the government of the United States more and more firmly of the loyalty of our attitude and of our intentions."[9] When the seizure of two Confederate commissioners from the British mail steamer *Trent* subsequently outraged all maritime nations and seriously embarrassed the Lincoln administration, it was Prussia that both moderated its own protest and helped produce a face-saving solution.

The German press and public opinion also tended to favor the North, and the American legation at Berlin was flooded with offers of volunteers for the Union army. The stream of German immigrants to the United States continued at a level only slightly below that of the prewar years and contributed not a little to the fact that the proportion of Germans in the Union army greatly exceeded their share in the general population. Gustav Körner, a former lieutenant-governor and friend of Lincoln's, and Friedrich Hecker, a leader of the 1848 revolution in Baden, raised whole regiments in Illinois and Missouri respectively. Hecker's fellow revolutionary Franz Sigel raised and trained an entire federal volunteer corps and commanded it and other units, first as brigadier general and then as major gen-

8. Joseph A. Wright to William H. Seward, May 6, 1861, in "Despatches Received by the Department of State from United States Ministers to: German States and Germany, 1799–1906," 11: 173. Microfilm copy 44, RG 59, NA.

9. Alexander von Schleinitz to Friedrich von Gerolt, June 13, 1861, reprinted in Baldur Eduard Pfeiffer, *Deutschland und der amerikanische Bürgerkrieg, 1861–1865* (Mainz, 1971), 96. This and all subsequent translations are mine.

eral. Carl Schurz, the most politically active of the 48ers, who had led the Wisconsin delegation to the Republican convention of 1860, served for the better part of the war as a major general of volunteers.

Even more significant from the American standpoint, the Germans proved to be the heaviest subscribers to U.S. government bonds. Robert J. Walker's European fund-raising mission in 1862 and 1863 enjoyed little success either in England or the Netherlands, but in Frankfurt, Walker was able to sell some $250,000 worth of securities in a relatively short time. By the war's end, nearly $800,000 in Union securities had been sold through the Frankfurt exchange. Americans naturally interpreted this financial support as a display of German faith in the Union cause, and were prepared to reciprocate by looking with favor on the course of German unification.

They came to look even more warmly on unification under Prussian auspices as the alternatives became clearly defined. Prussia's chief competitor for the leadership of Germany was Catholic Austria, whose reputation remained that of the citadel of reaction in post-Napoleonic Europe. It was Austria that had been most closely identified with the efforts of the Holy Alliance to restore her American colonies to Spain, and it was an Austrian archduke who had come to Mexico during the Civil War as the puppet of Napoleon III. Whatever shortcomings Prussia or Bismarck might have had from the American point of view, these were more than overshadowed by the defects attributed to Austria.

As a result, the United States accepted the outcome of Prussia's war against Denmark in 1864 and of the Austro-Prussian War of 1866 with considerable enthusiasm. An American naval squadron, led by the two-turreted monitor *Miantonomah* and carrying the former assistant secretary of the navy, Gustavus V. Fox, paid the first official visit by units of a foreign fleet to Prussia's newly acquired naval base at Kiel in 1867, and its officers were duly entertained by H.R.H. Prince Adalbert, the commander-in-chief of the navy. Shortly thereafter, the United States moved to cement Prussian-American relations still further by appointing George Bancroft minister to Berlin. The distinguished historian had previously served as secretary of the navy and as minister in London and had thus achieved prominence in the political as well as the cultural field. More significantly, Bancroft was an admirer of Prussia and of all things German. The Roundhill School, which he helped found in 1823, had been the first

American school to introduce the study of the German language, and he had published various studies of German literature before launching on his *History of the United States*. In that, his most famous work, he had heaped fulsome praise on Prussia and on Frederick the Great, and his appointment to Berlin could not fail to be interpreted as a sign of German-American friendship.

The major result of the Austro-Prussian War was the establishment of the Prussian-dominated North German Confederation. Bancroft, who in effect recognized the new political entity on his own initiative by attending the opening of its parliament, called its establishment a "wonderful result" of special interest for America, "because it has sprung from the application of the principles which guided the framers of the Constitution of our United States." Secretary of State William H. Seward not only applauded Bancroft's action but officially recognized what he called "the North German United States" on December 9, 1867. Its flag, he said, "will be hailed with peculiar pleasure" in American waters.[10]

Prussia, looking to a future showdown with France, was equally anxious to cultivate American friendship. Bismarck was not above hoping that war would break out between the United States and France over the continued presence of French troops in the Mexican Empire of Maximilian. Indeed, when Gerolt, acting without instructions, proposed to Seward a plan of action which might secure American objectives without war, he received a stinging rebuke from the chancellor, who at the same time confided to his minister in Paris that "it may well be regarded as unfortunate from a general humanitarian standpoint if France gets into conflict with the United States, *but not from a Prussian one*."[11] But once the Mexican issue resulted in the retreat of France, Bismarck began to cultivate the United States in earnest. As early as April 1867 he inquired of Gerolt whether it would be possible, in case of war with France, to purchase armed vessels in America and to find crews there. Although the minister thought that unlikely, he promised to make inquiries and assured his superior that if war came, "the sympathy of Americans will generally be on the side of Germany, whose sons and

10. Senate Executive Documents, 40th Cong., 2d sess., 1868, 1, no. 9: 13; Seward to George Bancroft, December 9, 1867, in *Foreign Relations of the United States: Diplomatic Papers, 1868*, 2: 40.

11. Otto von Bismarck to Gerolt, December 6, 1865, and Bismarck to Robert von der Goltz, January 5, 1866, in *Die auswärtige Politik Preussens, 1858–1871*, 10 vols. (Oldenburg, 1932–1945), 6: 489, 522. Emphasis added.

daughters and their progeny make up such a significant and respected proportion of the population of the United States."[12]

When that sympathy seemed threatened by American press reports that the commander of the German corvette *Augusta* had attempted to buy or lease territory for a naval station in Costa Rica,
the foreign minister of the new North German Confederation hastened to assure Gerolt that he regarded "maintenance of good relations with the government of the United States as incomparably
more valuable than any territorial acquisitions on the coast or in the
waters of Central America. . . ." Insisting that the naval officer had
acted without instructions, he proclaimed: "It is certain, and I cannot repeat often enough, that the Confederation has no intention to
acquire American territory for the maintenance of a naval station or
for other purposes."[13] When the ex-Confederate captain Raphael
Semmes offered his services to the Prussian navy, Bismarck took
pains to clear the matter with American authorities, and turned
down Semmes's request for a commission when informed he was
"one of the most objectionable men in the whole South." "We want
the respect and good will of the United States at all times," the
Prussian minister declared, "and we will not employ him."[14] At the
same time, Bismarck took the trouble to thank the United States
personally not only for its expression of sympathy on the occasion
of an attempt on his life but also for fifty tons of ice donated by an
American firm for use in Prussian military hospitals.

Even more important, Prussia moved to satisfy a long-standing
American request for the settlement of problems that had arisen
with respect to naturalized Americans who returned to their native
Germany. By the so-called Bancroft Treaties of February 1868, the
North German Confederation recognized a five-year residence in the
United States as sufficient for the acquisition of American citizenship and thus for the voiding of prior military obligations to Germany. Naturalized citizens returning to their homeland were to be
exempted from military service for two years, after which time it
was to be assumed that they had reestablished residence in Germany
and in effect renounced their American citizenship. While the in-

12. Bismarck to Gerolt, April 26, 1867, and Gerolt to Bismarck, May 16, 1867, in
ibid., 740–741; 9: 42–43.

13. Rudolf von Delbrück to Gerolt, July 9, 1868, and August 4, 1868, in ibid., 10:
106–107.

14. Wright to Seward, June 7, 1866, in *Foreign Relations, 1866*, 2: 26.

terpretation of these treaties caused problems for several decades, there can be no doubt that Bismarck regarded the treaties as a serious attempt to accommodate the United States. To Bancroft, they demonstrated "the hereditary disposition of this government, unaltered from the days of the great Frederic and Franklin, to cherish the best relations with us," and William I, on signing the documents, spoke warmly of "two nations closely bound together by commercial interest and family ties."[15] At any rate, the treaties marked an auspicious beginning of relations between the United States and the North German Confederation, and virtually assured further American support for Bismarck's unification plans.

The chief stumbling block in the way of these plans was the determination of Napoleon III to prevent the development of a serious challenge to France's predominance in Europe. In the inevitable showdown between France and Prussia, which was to be decided on the battlefield at Sedan, American sympathies were to be found clearly on the Prussian side. This was the case not only because the United States favored German unification but also because of the low esteem in which it held Napoleon III. Americans had never trusted Napoleon, whom they regarded as the betrayer of the Second Republic, and they had long worried about alleged French ambitions in the Caribbean and in South America. But it was Napoleon's flirtation with the Confederacy and his misguided Mexican policy that clearly marked him a bête-noire in the United States. The empire that French bayonets established south of the Rio Grande in 1862 seemed to be both a blatant effort to flout the Monroe Doctrine and an attempt to turn the troubles of the United States to the advantage of Europe. With Napoleon III as its chief adversary, the cause of Prussia gained additional favor in this country.

When war between the two powers became imminent, President Grant asked the assistant secretary of state, J. C. B. Davis, to remind the French ambassador of the probable attitude of the American people. They would remember, he insisted, that "while the Germans sympathized with the Union and took its bonds freely during the war, the French people had manifested no sympathy for the Union but had negotiated with the Rebels, and the French Gov-

15. Bancroft to Seward, February 22 and March 23, 1868, in *Foreign Relations, 1868*, 2: 48–49, 50.

ernment had sent an expedition to Mexico." Bancroft soon assured Secretary of State Hamilton Fish that the German armies were fighting not only for Germany "but also for the best interests of civilization, of civil and religious liberty and of popular freedom." And Louisa May Alcott wrote to her mother: "I side with the Prussians, for they sympathized with us in our war. Hooray for old Pruss!"[16]

Officially, the United States declared its neutrality on August 22, 1870, but the American course during the war tended, within the limits prescribed by this neutrality, to favor the cause of Prussia. The United States agreed to permit its minister in Paris, Elihu B. Washburne, to represent Prussian interests there and to perform the difficult and often costly job of caring for and eventually repatriating those Germans who had been trapped in France by the outbreak of hostilities. The major cost of this enterprise was borne by Prussia, which negotiated a loan of fifty thousand thalers from the House of Rothschild, but the United States refused reimbursement for the time spent by legation personnel and by extra clerks hired for the purpose. Early attempts by the European powers to include the United States in efforts to save France from utter defeat by mediating the conflict drew the chilling reply from Fish that it was "not the policy of the United States to act jointly with European powers in European questions,"[17] followed by a query to Berlin to ascertain the position of the Prussian government, which, of course, was absolutely opposed to any mediation. Bancroft, meanwhile, lost no opportunity of assuring Bismarck and other German leaders of the goodwill of the United States.

When French naval vessels began hovering near the approaches to American habors in an effort to intercept merchant ships of the North German Confederation, the United States closed both its ports and its territorial waters to belligerent vessels on wartime missions. Less than a month later, Secretary Fish moved to offset French naval superiority in the Far East by proposing that the

16. Bancroft to Hamilton Fish, n.d., quoted in Jeannette Keim, *Forty Years of German-American Political Relations*, (Philadelphia, 1919), p. 14; Louisa May Alcott quoted in Otto, Graf zu Stolberg-Wernigerode, *Deutschland und die Vereinigten Staaten im Zeitalter Bismarcks* (Berlin, 1933), translated by Otto E. Lessing under the title *Germany and the United States of America during the Era of Bismarck* (Reading, Pa., 1937), p. 110.

17. Fish to Elihu B. Washburne, September 8, 1870, in *Foreign Relations, 1870*, pp. 68–69.

French and German China squadrons cooperate with each other rather than fight. The proposal was greeted with enthusiasm in Berlin but firmly rejected in Paris.

Even after the abdication of Napoleon and the proclamation of the Third Republic, the attitude of the American government remained essentially pro-German. The United States recognized the republic but placed little faith in its durability. Moreover, it tended to regard the anarchical tendencies of the Paris Commune with extreme disfavor and to look upon them as bad omens for the future of France. As a result, the United States was less inclined than the European powers to voice opposition to German territorial demands that held up a peace settlement late in 1870. Efforts by the French minister in Washington to persuade the State Department to object to the German demand for Alsace-Lorraine fell on deaf ears. "Ils sont plus Prussien que les Prussiens,"[18] he complained bitterly. In its instructions to Bancroft, the department merely asked him to work for an equitable peace settlement. Under the circumstances it is hardly surprising that the German choice of a mediator to help negotiate an armistice was the American Civil War general Ambrose E. Burnside, who had been present at German military headquarters during the entire siege of Paris. His efforts, however, produced no results.

The astute Bismarck continued to cultivate the goodwill of the United States. He went to extraordinary pains to keep Washington informed of German plans and actions during the war and to thank this country for any and all gestures of friendship. Moreover, he also adopted a remarkably restrained attitude in the case of the one American action that worked to the detriment of Germany. Since the close of the Civil War, the U.S. government had sold surplus war material to private domestic munitions firms. With the outbreak of the Franco-Prussian War, a number of these firms began to trade with France; as a result, rifles and other equipment bearing the imprint of the U.S. government arsenals found their way into the hands of the French army. Although these incidents produced enough controversy to lead to a Congressional investigation, no German protest was ever lodged. Bismarck not only recognized the limitations that the American federal system imposed on the possibilities for the control of private arms traffic, he also rightly judged

18. Jules Berthemy, quoted in Stolberg-Wernigerode, *Germany and the United States*, p. 125.

that the gain that might result from an official protest would be more than offset by the possible damage to good relations with the United States. His sensitivity to American opinion even led him to recall Baron von Gerolt, when that venerable and respected gentleman became too outspoken in his assertion that Germany's real purpose in seeking the annexation of Alsace-Lorraine was not the safeguarding of her borders but the destruction of the power of France.

Bismarck's solicitude reinforced American predispositions. Throughout the winter of 1870/71, Bancroft continued to send his glowing reports of the imminent establishment of "the United States of Germany," which was certain to be the most liberal government in Europe. He hailed the adoption of universal suffrage for elections to the proposed Reichstag, as well as Bismarck's opposition to a hereditary House of Lords, as signs of American influence, and paid little heed to the weakness of the lower house, to the predominance of Prussia with its reactionary three-class system of representation, or to the powerful role of the emperor in the new political arrangements. The federal structure and the end of the "Italian connection," he was certain, would pave the way for the triumph of German liberalism. He reported with pride that more Americans witnessed the triumphal entry of William I into Berlin than nationals of any other foreign country, and saw no reason to revise a prediction he had made early in the war. "If we need the solid, trusty goodwill of any government in Europe," he had told Fish, "we can have it best with Germany, because German institutions and ours most resemble each other. . . . This war will leave Germany the most powerful state in Europe and the most free; its friendship is, therefore, important to us; and has its foundation in history and in nature."[19]

Bancroft's views gained official acceptance. Not only did the United States choose William I as arbitrator in its dispute with Great Britain over the west coast water boundary with Canada in 1871 in the full expectation that a favorable verdict would be rendered, it also reached the conclusion that German and American interests essentially coincided in other parts of the world. "The government of the Emperor of Germany," President Grant happily told Congress, "continues to manifest a friendly feeling toward the United States, and a desire to harmonize with the moderate and just policy

19. Bancroft to Fish, October 18, 1870, quoted in Mark A. DeWolfe Howe, *The Life and Letters of George Bancroft*, 2 vols. (New York, 1908), 2: 246–247.

which this Government maintains in its relations with Asiatic powers, as well as with the South American republics. I have given assurances that the friendly feelings of that government are fully shared by the United States."[20]

Relations between the United States and the German Empire thus began on a high note of cooperation and friendship. The German people, whom most Americans admired, had achieved unity, which was regarded as inseparable from liberty. The new German state would surely concentrate its efforts in Europe, where the United States had long renounced all ambitions, and seemed willing to follow the American lead in Asia and the Western Hemisphere. Under these circumstances, it appeared in 1871 that German-American amity was indeed grounded in history and in nature, and would be likely to endure.

Mutual Admiration and the Bancroft Treaties

For nearly a decade these expectations seemed to approach fulfillment, and relations between the two countries remained harmonious and serene. The United States was occupied with the problems of Reconstruction and less inclined than ever to pay serious attention to matters outside its borders. Germany meanwhile concentrated on securing its new position in Europe by negotiating a series of alliances designed primarily to isolate France. Under the continued guidance of Bismarck, the Reich entertained no colonial ambitions, was not yet embarked on a policy of naval expansion, and was not likely to come into direct conflict with the United States.

Domestic developments in Germany, moreover, continued to win American approval and thus to bolster the prevailing feelings of amity. The so-called Kulturkampf, in which Bismarck cooperated with the anticlerical liberals in an effort to reduce the power and influence of the Catholic church in Germany drew, to be sure, some fire from Catholic groups in the United States, but it was more generally applauded as a step toward liberalism and democracy. "The tendency of Europe," Bancroft reported happily from Berlin,

---

20. Ulysses S. Grant, Annual Message to Congress, December 4, 1871, in *Foreign Relations, 1871*, p. v.

"is toward the American system of separating church and state."[21] The expulsion of the Jesuits from Germany, the curbing of the power of the bishops, the partial secularization of education, and the establishment of compulsory civil marriage were all approvingly reported to Washington. The later dismissal of Adalbert Falk from his post of minister for religious affairs, which marked the effective end of the Kulturkampf, produced some expression of concern.

When Bismarck turned from his attack on Catholics to that on socialists in the late seventies, his actions were once more applauded in America. The Germanophile poet Bayard Taylor, then serving his brief term as minister to Germany, praised the move "inasmuch as the same socialistic movement has already become a disturbing element in the United States." The outlawing of the Socialist party, he assured Secretary of State William F. Evarts, was the work of "prudent, conscientious and patriotic members of the legislative body."[22] Although the cumulative effect of these actions was to strengthen both the Catholic Center party and the Conservatives in the Reichstag at the expense of the National Liberals, American hopes for the future liberalization of Germany remained generally undimmed.

The prevailing German-American friendship was carefully nurtured by Bismarck. The United States, of course, still played a very minor role in Germany's foreign policy calculations, but the astute chancellor went to considerable lengths to avoid offending American sensibilities. When, for example, he became concerned late in 1871 over the harm done to German nationals during political upheavals in Venezuela, Peru, and Brazil, he wisely sounded out the State Department before seriously exploring the possibility of taking joint action with other affected powers. The German minister in Washington rather less wisely put the question in the context of the Monroe Doctrine and received a predictable reply from Secretary Fish. Recalling France's Mexican adventure, Fish declared that the United States would not object to a "remonstrance" by Germany, but would oppose any attempt at coercion by a combination of European powers. When a new German minister, Kurd von Schlözer, assumed his post shortly thereafter, Bismarck instructed him to reopen the discussion with Fish—this time without reference to the

21. Bancroft to Fish, December 1, 1873, in *Foreign Relations, 1874*, p. 474.

22. Bayard Taylor to William F. Evarts, June 10, 1878, in *Foreign Relations, 1878*, p. 216; Taylor to Evarts, November 8, 1878, in *Foreign Relations, 1879*, p. 351.

Monroe Doctrine—and to assure the secretary of state of Germany's desire to follow a common course with the United States in relation to Latin America. "We have no intention whatsoever," he wrote, "of gaining a foothold anywhere in America, and we frankly recognize the paramount influence of the United States on the entire continent as both natural and supportive of our best interests."[23]

Accordingly, Germany abstained from collective schemes of intervention and tried, as best it could, to come to terms with the Latin American states. When this led to a break in diplomatic relations with Peru, the American minister in Lima undertook to represent German interests and to secure an arbitration agreement. Fish acknowledged Bismarck's thanks for American efforts by expressing pleasure over the fact that this country had been "serviceable to a friendly power held in such high esteem as Germany is by the United States."[24] In Haiti in 1872 and in Nicaragua in 1878, the United States raised no protest when Germany moved forcefully to settle the quarrels of its citizens with local authorities. And though a report that Germany was negotiating with Denmark for Saint Thomas or other parts of the Danish West Indies was transmitted by the minister in London in 1874, the State Department, recalling Bismarck's earlier statement, readily accepted Bancroft's assurances that the rumor was wholly without foundation.

If U.S.-German relations thus remained harmonious with respect to Latin America, they were equally undisturbed in Asia, the only other area of the world in which the United States had expressed a substantial interest. Germany had not yet begun to seek territorial acquisitions there and, like the United States, was primarily concerned with retaining trade and access rights in the face of predominant British power. Under these circumstances, German editorial writers, often with at least semiofficial sanction, were prepared to recognize the legitimacy of the American interest in Hawaii and to praise the Far Eastern policy of the United States as working "in the spirit of progress and unfettered freedom." "The East Asiatic policy of the German Government," Bancroft accurately informed Fish, "is identical with that of our own."[25] Indeed, when six years later Great

23. Bismarck to Kurd von Schlözer, December 18, 1871, reprinted in Stolberg-Wernigerode, *Germany and the United States*, pp. 296–297.
24. Fish to Schlözer, December 15, 1875, in *Foreign Relations, 1875*, I: 577.
25. Bancroft to Fish, February 10, and July 19, 1873, in *Foreign Relations, 1873*, I: 277–278, 296.

Britain and France, frustrated in their efforts to penetrate Chinese etiquette in their dealings with the government at Peking, sought German agreement to demanding free access to the provincial authorities, the German minister in Washington was first instructed to get the approval of the American government.

The apparent commonality of interest and viewpoint between the two countries was given additional credence by the decision that William I reached in his role as arbitrator of the dispute over the boundary between British Columbia and Washington Territory. On October 21, 1872, he duly announced that the true interpretation of the Anglo-American treaty of 1846 was "most in accordance" with the American claim that the boundary should run through the Haro Channel. So pleased was the United States with the award that it offered to reimburse the German government for expenses incurred in the arbitration proceedings. The refusal of Germany to accept payment was regarded as still further evidence of friendship and goodwill, and additional, if less tangible, evidence continued to be forthcoming. Both the emperor and Bismarck took the occasion of the one hundredth birthday of the United States to remind President Grant of the undisturbed friendship between the two countries since the days of Frederick the Great and to express their fondest hopes for its continuance; and when Grant visited Berlin in the summer of 1878, he was showered with expressions of esteem and friendship.

For nearly a decade, the only issue that occasionally rippled the smooth surface of German-American relations was the fate of naturalized German-Americans who returned to the country of their birth, only to run afoul of the local authorities. Between five and twelve such persons applied to the legation for assistance every year—the numbers were to grow somewhat in later years—mostly in order to be freed from the obligation of military service. At the root of their troubles lay the sometimes arbitrary actions of provincial governments, the doubtful validity, at least under German law, of their claims to American citizenship, and genuine differences between Germany and the United States over the interpretation of the Bancroft Treaties of 1868. The applicability of these treaties to the "national territory" of Alsace-Lorraine caused the most confusion. The American ministers duly carried complaints to the Foreign Office and noted their resolution in annual reports on "military cases" submitted in Washington. In most instances, the German government proved remarkably accommodating, particularly during the time in which the elder Bernhard von Bülow was in charge of the Foreign Office. "I had rather give the United States two hundred doubtful cases every year," Bülow once told the American minister in Berlin, Andrew Dickson White, "than have the slightest ill-feeling arise between us."[26] Some ill-feeling, of course, did arise, particularly among the persons directly affected by the few adverse decisions that were made, but in more than two-thirds of the cases the American viewpoint prevailed.

By 1877 relations between the United States and Germany were so amicable that J. C. B. Bancroft, then heading the legation in Berlin, found nothing more pressing to do than to send Washington a lengthy report on the history and functions of the Berlin Museum, with the recommendation that a similar institution be established in the United States. In his message to Congress the following year, President Rutherford B. Hayes, who had appointed Carl Schurz as his secretary of the interior, mentioned some dealings with Britain, Spain, and Italy and concluded: "No questions of grave importance have arisen with any other of the European powers."[27]

26. Andrew D. White, *The Autobiography of Andrew Dickson White*, 2 vols. (New York, 1905), 2: 536.

27. Rutherford B. Hayes, Annual Message to Congress, December 2, 1878, in Fred L. Israel, ed., *The State of the Union Messages of the Presidents, 1790–1966*, 3 vols. (New York, 1966), 2: 1359–1360.

Chapter 2

THE GREAT
TRANSFORMATION

*

Trade and Tariff Conflicts

Even while Bancroft basked in the glories of the Berlin Museum, the
first shadows of events that were to darken German-American relations appeared on the horizon. In the 1870s, and with increasing
speed in the two decades that followed, both the United States and
Germany underwent remarkable economic transformations. It is
perhaps ironic that the parallel development of the United States
and Germany came to manifest itself not in the continuing democratization Americans expected, but in headlong industrialization
and a subsequent drive for overseas expansion. Both nations were
characterized in the last third of the nineteenth century by rapidly
increasing population, widespread urbanization, increased well-
being, and the expansion of world trade. Both built their prosperity
on the extraction of coal and the production of iron and steel, in
which they soon came to rival, and eventually to outstrip, Great
Britain, and both engaged in the large-scale production of heavy
machinery, electrical products, and chemicals. These developments
not only laid the basis for conflict in trade and tariff policies and,
initially to a much lesser degree, for rivalry over markets, they also
tended to alter fundamentally the existing balance of power and to
bring both countries into changing relationships with the world
around them. German-American friendship, which had grown when
neither country was truly a world power and when both had at least
tacitly accepted the predominance of Great Britain on the interna-

tional scene, was thereby subjected to severe and ultimately fatal strains.

It quickly became apparent that in the race for economic development the United States possessed definite advantages over Germany. America commanded vastly larger natural resources and could more readily supply the raw materials for its burgeoning industry from domestic sources and, too, it could increase agricultural production sufficiently to maintain its position as an exporter of foodstuffs despite increasing demand at home. Moreover, the United States was able to expand its labor force more rapidly than was Germany, and generally with a smaller amount of internal dislocation. The United States benefited greatly from increased immigration, while Germany, in the years from 1870 to 1890, lost more than two million persons through emigration—the majority of them to the U.S. Concern over the loss of young and skilled workers to America began to mount when the flow reached an all-time high in the early eighties, and Bismarck soon sought ways of making emigration more difficult without, however, actually prohibiting it. The activities of American agents were restricted, the laws governing the military obligations of prospective emigrants more vigorously enforced, and an essentially anti-American press campaign launched in an attempt to make the United States appear less attractive. It did not bode well for the future of German-American relations that particular efforts were made to channel emigration to areas other than the United States, areas where assimilation was assumed to proceed less rapidly.

As early as 1874 the relative conditions under which industrialization proceeded in the two countries had produced a trade balance unfavorable to Germany. Increasingly dependent on the import of food and raw materials, in part from the United States, the Germans became more and more resentful of American tariff policies that not only hampered their trade in manufactured goods but also discriminated against sugar, the one agricultural product they were still in a position to export. By 1879, when large-scale American wheat exports also began to flood the European market, the pressures on German agriculture had become so great that the landowners joined with the industrialists in urging the abandonment of the traditional free-trade policies and the enactment of Germany's first protective tariff. The American chargé d'affaires in Berlin saw this move as an attempt to make up "in a false way" for the loss of capital and labor allegedly produced by the maintenance of a large standing army, but he also recognized it as "a desperate attempt to resist the competition of the cheaper produce and manufacturers of the United States and Great Britain."[1] In any event, the adoption of the Tariff of 1879 was the first major indication of a developing economic conflict between the United States and Germany, a conflict soon to be marked by recriminations and allegations of discrimination on both sides.

The new German law reversed the trade balance between the two countries for nearly a decade, and initially produced the most anguished outcries from American exporters of now heavily taxed lard. Turning a deaf ear to these complaints Germany pointed in turn to the harm done to its sugar producers by recent U.S. policies. The United States had not only raised the duty on sugar in its tariff act of 1875, it had simultaneously negotiated a reciprocity treaty with Hawaii which, by admitting sugar duty-free from the islands to the United States, had greatly stimulated production there to the detriment of European producers. Amid these claims and counterclaims it seemed to many Americans an act of retaliation when Germany in the summer of 1880 barred the import of American pork products other than ham and bacon, allegedly as a health measure designed to stem the spread of trichinosis. While France, Austria-Hungary, Italy, Turkey, Greece, and even England for a time adopted similar measures, it was Germany that persisted longest in this policy and, in the process, gave the greatest offense to the United States.

Germany threatened to extend its ban to all American pork products in 1883, and Secretary of State Theodore Frelinghuysen found it necessary to protest against such "restrictive and unjust measures." Although he was convinced that economic motives and not health reasons underlay the German action, he proposed nevertheless that a commission be sent to inspect American hog raising and packing practices. When Germany ignored that proposal and, over liberal opposition, enacted the total exclusion measure, Aaron A. Sargent, a California politician whom President Chester A. Arthur had recently sent as minister to Berlin, angrily protested to the Foreign Office. In the process, he proved himself to be a singularly undiplomatic diplomat. His note not only was offensive in tone but included the only slightly veiled threat that the United

1. H. Sidney Everett to William M. Evarts, February 15, 1879, in *Foreign Relations of the United States: Diplomatic Papers, 1879*, p. 361.

States might be compelled to look elsewhere for the products it imported "even if Congress did not meet the issue by legislation, under the belief that another motive than the unsoundness of American pork products caused this exclusion."[2]

Bismarck, who had already become disenchanted with Sargent because the American minister, unlike his predecessors, had failed to cultivate the chancellor but had consorted with members of the parliamentary opposition, was incensed. He icily asked his minister in Washington to ascertain "whether the Government of the United States approved and intended to sustain the interference of its representative in the internal affairs and party struggles of the German Reich."[3] Frelinghuysen hastened to reprimand Sargent and to assure the German government that no threat had been implied, but the damage had been done. Not only had an American diplomat for the first time become persona non grata in Berlin, but Congress was prodded into action by Sargent's suggestion. The Committee on Foreign Relations, acting on a resolution of the Senate, recommended that the president be authorized "at his discretion to exclude from the United States, by proclamation, any products of any foreign state which, by unjust discrimination, prohibits the importation into such foreign state of any product of the United States."[4] Though not adopted at this time, the proposal further sharpened the conflict and was ultimately included in the meat inspection law of 1890.

At the height of the pork controversy, Eduard Lasker, the leader of the National Liberal party in the Reichstag and an outspoken critic of Bismarck's domestic policies, chose to embark on a lecture tour of the United States. In a series of well-publicized speeches, he sharply criticized German economic policy, praised the superiority of American civilization, and spoke of the need for organizing a more determined opposition to Bismarck. When he suddenly died here on January 5, 1884, he was both eulogized by Carl Schurz and Andrew Dickson White for his contributions to German liberalism and memorialized by the House of Representatives as a great statesman whose liberal ideas had been of immense benefit to Germany.

2. Aaron A. Sargent to Count Paul von Hatzfeld, February 23, 1883, in *Foreign Relations, 1883*, pp. 341–342.

3. Bismarck to Karl von Eisendecher, March 3, 1883, in Count Otto zu Stolberg-Wernigerode, *Germany and the United States during the Era of Bismarck* (Reading, Pa., 1937), p. 159.

4. *Senate Report No. 345*, 48th Cong., 1st sess., 1884, 2.

Bismarck, already incensed by Sargent's "interference," was out-raged by this praise for his bitter opponent, which he regarded as inspired by his enemies in Germany. When Sargent handed him the resolution, therefore, he promptly rejected it. In a bitter speech to the Reichstag on March 13, he defended this action while pointing to the long-standing friendship with the United States. On the follow-ing day he informed his minister in Washington that he would insist on the recall of the hapless Sargent. Frelinghuysen, who was as wary as the German chancellor of doing permanent damage to Ger-man-American relations, refused the return of the resolution but agreed to replace Sargent with John A. Kasson, a former minister to Austria and a great admirer of Bismarck.

Although the pork crisis thereupon subsided for a time, trade and tariff conflicts between the two countries continued to arise. When, for example, the shipping act of 1884 lowered the tonnage tax im-posed on shipments from Central American ports, Germany claimed a similar privilege for vessels leaving its ports under the most-favored-nation provision of the treaty of 1828. The United States had always insisted that this provision was conditional and required reciprocal concessions, and it did not abandon that stand now. When German pressure persisted, however, President Grover Cleveland reduced the tonnage duties vis-à-vis Germany on the grounds that the nonimposition of such duties by Germany met the requirements of reciprocity. At the same time, however, he recom-mended to Congress that he be granted the authority to prohibit the import of pork from Germany and France, the two nations that still barred the American product.

The Germans were by no means inclined to yield to this new American pressure, but they soon found themselves compelled to do so by the almost simultaneous passage of the Meat Inspection Act of 1890 and the McKinley tariff of the same year. The inspection mea-sure gave the president the authority to bar imports from countries discriminating against American products. The tariff act replaced the sugar duty with a bounty for domestic producers, while authoriz-ing reinstitution of the duty if any country exporting sugar to the United States imposed unreasonable duties of its own. Germany, which in 1889/90 supplied 15.9 percent of United States sugar im-ports, now faced the prospect of serious damage to its American trade and offered to negotiate the issue. Prospects for successful negotiations were improved by the ouster of Bismarck, and by the determination of his successor, Georg Leo, Count Caprivi, to inaugurate a new economic policy less dedicated to the protection of agricultural products. At a meeting between German and American representatives at Saratoga Springs, New York, on August 22, 1891, it was agreed that Germany would accept the new meat inspection law as sufficient grounds for rescinding the ban on American pork and would extend to American agricultural products the tariff concessions about to be granted to several European states. In return, the United States would not bar the importation of German agricultural products or reimpose the duty on sugar. Accordingly, the German pork decree was repealed on September 3, and the American duty, scheduled for implementation on January 1, 1892, was dropped.

The Saratoga agreement settled matters for only a brief time. The Wilson-Gorman Tariff of 1894 not only reimposed the sugar duty but placed an extra tax on refined sugar from countries that, like Germany, paid export bounties to their own producers. The hard-hit Germans once again protested this alleged violation of the most-favored-nation principle and promptly announced their intention to prohibit the import of American beef and cattle because, they claimed, of an outbreak of "Texas fever," a disease unknown to the United States. At the same time, they vigorously objected to a new American duty on salt. Although Cleveland was prepared to back down on the sugar issue, Congress was not, and Germany's implementation of its cattle ban produced new recriminations on both sides of the Atlantic.

It would be a mistake to read into these maneuvers the signs of a serious rift between the two countries, since neither was heavily dependent on trade with the other. The United States showed its continuing goodwill by bringing the descendants of Baron von Steuben to the United States for the centennial celebration of the battle of Yorktown in 1881, by sending the warmest of congratulations to Emperor William I on his ninetieth birthday in 1887, and by numerous similar gestures. Every president from Arthur to Cleveland found occasion at one time or another to report to Congress on the cordiality of relations between the United States and Germany, and such statements and gestures were fully reciprocated. William II, for example, was the only European head of state to congratulate the United States in 1892 on the four hundredth anniversary of Columbus's discovery of America, and for a time even toyed with the idea of visiting the Chicago World's Fair. Nevertheless, it is clear that the simultaneous expansion of the German and American economies produced genuine conflicts of interest between the two nations for the first time, and helped to create an atmosphere in which the traditional feelings of amity became more difficult to maintain.

The conflict of interest was largely confined to trade relations between the two nations themselves. Although voices on both sides of the Atlantic occasionally pointed to at least an incipient trade rivalry between Germany and the United States over world markets, there was little evidence to support such assertions. Even in Latin America, where both countries made substantial efforts to expand their trade, the problems each encountered had little to do with the competition provided by the other. In Asia, Africa, and the Middle East, neither country as yet had a sufficient commercial stake to arouse serious concern. Economic factors were nevertheless beginning to affect German-American relations, while at the same time yet another conflict of interest became apparent in the Far Pacific.

The Samoan Imbroglio

The simultaneous development of the United States and Germany into major world economic powers was accompanied in both countries by moves toward colonial expansion which showed remarkable parallels. Bismarck rejected the idea of colonial expansion until well into the 1880s, and then just favored limited projects in which the flag followed trade. Only after the fall of Bismarck in 1890, when the young, brash William II began his personal regime, did German dreams of glory and world power find reflection in German policy. And it was not until the appointment of Admiral Alfred von Tirpitz as navy minister in 1897 and the decision in 1898 to build a major battle fleet that Germany truly embarked on its transformation from a continental to a world power. In the same years, the forces that produced the Spanish-American War and the outcome of that war led the United States to begin on a similar course, albeit with considerably less bellicosity and fanfare. When that time came, the relations between the two countries with regard to colonial issues had already been disturbed by an earlier controversy over Samoa, a group of islands of such monumental insignificance that most Americans—and most Germans—would have been hard-pressed to describe their whereabouts.

The U.S.-German conflict over Samoa has all the aspects of second-rate musical comedy, yet was undoubtedly important in the deterioration of relations between the two countries. American interest in the islands had been awakened by whalers and naval officers who began calling there in the 1830s. By 1870 private plans to launch a steamship service between San Francisco and New Zealand had heightened American interest and led to various abortive schemes, occasionally abetted by consular and Navy Department officials, to enter into treaty relations with Samoa and to establish a coaling station there. The State Department turned a deaf ear to a petition, allegedly composed by "the chiefs and rulers of Samoa," which in 1872 requested the president to annex the islands, and a treaty establishing a semiprotectorate, which Commander Richard W. Meade of the U.S.S. *Narragansett* had negotiated on his own initiative in the same year, was never approved by the Senate. But the issue did not die.

An American adventurer, Colonel A. B. Steinberger, was sent by the State Department on a fact-finding mission to Samoa in 1873, and was soon engaged in schemes to annex the islands and to enrich himself through participation in the lucrative copra trade. Without official sanction and indeed over the protest of the resident American consul, Steinberger drafted a constitution for Samoa and for more than a year served as prime minister. Such activities naturally brought local difficulties both with the British, the dominant power in the South Pacific, and with Germany, whose interest in Samoa was based on the establishment there in the 1850s of two copra plantations under the direction of the Hamburg trading firm Godeffroy and Sons.

As early as 1871 the German consul in Samoa, completely on his own initiative, had informed the American commercial agent that Germany intended to claim the islands. The State Department immediately asked Bancroft in Berlin whether such was the case and required a long series of assurances that it was not before permitting the matter to rest. But it was primarily concern over the ambitions of Australia and New Zealand which led the State Department in 1878 to accede to the schemes of its consul, Gilderoy W. Griffin, and sign a treaty with Samoa. Griffin had unsuccessfully sought some form of protectorate ever since his arrival in Samoa. He now persuaded

M. K. LeMamea, the local "secretary of state," to go to Washington to try his luck.

The arrival of the tattooed prince created a sensation, and while the State Department continued to ignore pleas for a protectorate, it found itself unable to turn down the offer of a naval base in the superb harbor of Pago Pago. In return the United States agreed to use its good offices if "unhappily, any differences should have arisen or shall arise, between the Samoan Government and any other Government in amity with the United States." The *New York Times* cheerfully claimed that "without 'entangling alliances' or any troublesome pledges, a valuable naval and coaling station has been acquired,"[5] but that estimate was overly optimistic. Given the fact that the "Samoan Government" was a weak and unstable coalition pulled hither and yon by rival consular officials, and that both British and German economic stakes in the islands were far larger than the American, the United States had in fact concluded an alliance of the most entangling kind and was soon to become embroiled in major troubles as a result.

The American-Samoan treaty of 1878 spawned very similar agreements between Samoa and both Great Britain and Germany in the following year. With all three nations now enjoying a legally privileged position, it was soon obvious that matters could be kept under control only through various working agreements among the consuls of the powers. Such agreements were drawn up in September 1879 and, though never officially ratified, tacitly made the United States a party to tripartite control of Samoa. From the beginning, as might be expected, things worked badly. The consuls intrigued against each other and played on the already existing divisions within the native population. A brief civil war broke out, which was ended only by the guns of a German man-of-war, and the situation became even further confused with the failure of the German firm of Godeffroy and Sons, the main prop of the economy of the islands. Bismarck, though not yet convinced of the desirability of launching a colonial policy, attempted to get the Reichstag to approve the setting up of a government-owned South Seas Trading Company, but did not pursue this course when combined Catholic and Liberal opposition defeated the measure.

With Samoa thus in turmoil before either the United States or

5. *New York Times*, April 10, 1878.

Germany had seriously embarked on an imperialist course, it is hardly surprising that Bismarck's decision of 1883 to enter the international competition for colonies should further aggravate matters. Germany moved at once to expand its position in Africa and to acquire some of the Pacific islands not yet under European control. The Marshall, Gilbert, and Solomon islands were obtained, and negotiations begun with Spain over the Carolines and with Great Britain over portions of New Guinea. In Samoa the German consul was instructed to draw up an agreement with the reigning king for a new government, which Germans would dominate. The hapless ruler signed the agreement under duress, but protested to the German emperor and appealed to the British and American consuls for aid. Before the dust had settled, the German consul had seized the territory around the main settlement of Apia and hoisted the German flag there. Bismarck assured the United States that Germany contemplated no change in the status quo, but at the same time made plans to have the new German-Samoan convention ratified.

Secretary of State Thomas F. Bayard, who inherited the problem early in 1885, soon found things in even worse shape. The consul whom he had appointed took it upon himself to raise the American flag over Apia and to declare Samoa to be under American protection. At the same time, the king of Hawaii, prodded by unofficial American advisers, signed a treaty with Samoa and sent a leaky warship there to signify his support. These events in Samoa mirrored only imperfectly the actual intentions of the powers involved. Germany would have liked to annex Samoa, both to safeguard its commercial interests there and to increase its influence in the South Pacific. But Germany did not wish to offend the United States, and was willing to accept any arrangement that would produce a government strong and effective enough to protect German nationals and German property. On repeated occasions Bismarck expressed his sincere regret over conflict with the United States in "those remote and unimportant islands."[6] Great Britain would have been content to leave Samoa to Germany in return for concessions elsewhere, but was pressed by both Australia and New Zealand to remain.

The United States had both the simplest and the least practical position. Fearful of being shut out of the western Pacific through the annexations of the other powers, it attached increasing importance

6. Chapman Coleman to Thomas F. Bayard, November 5, 1887, in *Foreign Relations, 1888,* 1: 578–579.

"to the maintenance of the rights to which the United States had become entitled in any of the few remaining regions now under independent or autonomous native governments in the Pacific Ocean,"[7] and thus to an independent Samoa ruled by a government of its own choosing. The intrusion of the Hawaiian Kingdom was unwelcome to all powers but was embarrassing only to the United States since both Britain and Germany regarded Hawaii as America's client state and directed their protests over its actions to Washington.

As the situation became increasingly more confused and threatening, Secretary Bayard suggested a conference to settle matters, and Germany and Britain agreed to attend. Given the difficulties of communication with Samoa, however, Bismarck proposed that preliminary to any meeting commissioners "be sent by the three powers to Samoa to obtain for their Governments full information respecting the status there."[8] Like the consuls who had preceded them, the commissioners fell to quarreling with each other as soon as they arrived at their destination and ultimately submitted separate and conflicting reports to their respective governments. Far from clarifying matters or providing the basis for a settlement, these reports led to an exasperating exchange of notes among Washington, London, and Berlin and to repeated visits by the German minister, Count Johann von Alvensleben, to the State Department, visits that Bayard found increasingly annoying. The three powers nevertheless succeeded in drawing up proposals, and on June 25, 1887, the first meeting of the Washington Conference on Samoa was held.

During six sessions attended by Bayard, Alvensleben, and the British minister, Sir Lionel Sackville-West, no agreement was reached. Germany proposed the establishment of a strong native government, which was to rule with the aid of an "adviser" representing the power with the predominant commercial interest in Samoa, that is, Germany. The United States countered this thinly disguised version of a protectorate with a plan that called for the Samoan ministries of state, interior, and the treasury to be filled respectively by nationals of Germany, Great Britain, and the United States, and thus for the continuation and formalization of the pa-

7. Bayard to George H. Pendleton, January 17, 1888, in ibid., 599.

8. Coleman to Bayard, June 18, 1886, in "Despatches Received by the Department of State from United States Ministers to: German States and Germany, 1799–1906," 41: 174, Microfilm copy 44, RG 59, NA.

tently unworkable tripartite control. Great Britain supported Germany in these discussions, both because it regarded the tripartite solution as hopeless and because it was at the time trying to shore up Anglo-German relations. Beset by troubles with both France and Russia, Britain hoped to win German support for its policies in Egypt and elsewhere in Africa by seconding the German claim to Samoa. In the opinion of the British prime minister, Lord Salisbury, Great Britain could annex the Tonga Islands as compensation, and the United States could annex Hawaii. The United States, however, was as yet totally unwilling to engage in such imperialist barter and continued to defend the high moral ground of Samoan autonomy. Under the circumstances America found itself for the first time completely and hopelessly at loggerheads with Imperial Germany.

With the failure of the Washington conference, Germany now moved to protect its Samoan interests independently of the other powers. Long dissatisfied with the reigning king, who had been either unwilling or unable to safeguard the German plantations, Germany now declared war on that hapless ruler, deposed him, and set up one of his rivals, supported by a German adviser. The State Department deplored these actions, in particular the landing of seven hundred German marines, but recognized that as long as American interests were not interfered with, the German moves, although morally untenable, were legally valid.

No such compunctions affected the American consul at Apia, however, and he busily plotted with dissident native groups against the Germans. When such activities ultimately led to an ambush in which fifty German soldiers were killed, and when American and British warships were dispatched to Samoa to join the German vessels already there ostensibly to protect life and property, things threatened to get totally out of hand. By January 1889, the New York *World* carried the headline "German Tyranny in Samoa," the *New York Times* told its readers "Germany Grows Insolent," and the New York *Herald* thought the situation in the South Pacific looked "like war."[9] At the same time, Congress amended the consular and diplomatic appropriations bill to provide five hundred thousand dollars for the protection of American interests in Samoa and another hundred thousand for the occupation and improvement of the harbor of Pago Pago.

If the United States was unhappy over the course pursued by

9. New York *World*, January 23, 1889; *New York Times*, January 25, 1889; New York *Herald*, January 21, 1889.

Germany in Samoa, that feeling was fully reciprocated in Berlin. "In view of the so friendly relations which have continued undisturbed for more than a century between Germany and the United States," the deputy minister for foreign affairs, Herbert von Bismarck, complained to the chargé in Washington, "it is remarkable that on that remote realm of islands, where neither America nor Germany has any political interests to defend, we are exposed to the continual ill-will of a series of American representatives."[10] But with matters rapidly approaching a crisis in the islands, it was primarily in Germany's interest to seek a peaceful solution that would safeguard Germany's economic stake. Accordingly, the German government pressed for a resumption of earlier three-power consultations. It requested that the new meetings be held in Berlin, but gave assurances that it wished to imperil neither the independence of Samoa nor the rights of Great Britain and the United States but simply to guarantee the permanent safety of German commercial interests. To give weight to these assurances, Germany ordered the cessation of all military activity on January 12, 1889. It is characteristic of the situation in Samoa that this order was not obeyed for some time, and that the strong possibility of a miniature naval war in the harbor of Apia was eliminated only when a hurricane destroyed all but the British vessel on March 15. The day before, President Benjamin Harrison had nominated the American commissioners to the Berlin conference.

The Berlin conference and the Samoan treaty that emerged from it represented, in a somewhat Pyrrhic sense, a victory for the United States. Certainly the American press generally rejoiced at its terms, the Senate ratified it without serious difficulty, and the German press regarded it with disfavor. From the outset of the conference, Germany had proved highly accommodating. No longer assured of British support for German preponderance and faced with an American position that the new secretary of state, James G. Blaine, stated in terms virtually identical to those advanced by Bayard two years before, Germany's chief negotiator dropped the proposal for a single German adviser, agreed to the restoration of Malietoa, the king whom the Germans had deposed and imprisoned in 1887, and showed his general goodwill by agreeing to let English be the official language of the conference.

The final treaty set up a government for an "independent" Samoa,

10. Herbert von Bismarck to Kurt von Zedwitz, November 18, 1887, in *Foreign Relations, 1888*, 1: 663.

headed by an elected king but including a chief justice, to be named by the king of Norway and Sweden with the consent of the three powers, and a president of the municipal council of Apia, who would also act as adviser to the king. The president of the council was to be appointed by the three powers or, failing agreement among them, from nominees of the chief executives of Sweden, the Netherlands, Switzerland, Mexico, and Brazil. In any event, the president was to act as representative of the three powers and only under joint instructions. Germany thus relinquished its earlier claim that it should, by reason of its economic primacy in the islands, provide the chief adviser to the Samoan government and agreed in essence to the original American proposal for a form of tripartite control.

But the new condominium proved as unworkable as earlier arrangements had been, and in no way lessened the squabbling among the consuls and other representatives of the three powers in Samoa. It thus failed to alleviate the difficulties between the United States and Germany. Within three years, in fact, President Cleveland noted regretfully that "the United States departing from its policy consecrated by a century of observance, entered . . . into the Treaty of Berlin," and expressed the view that renewed troubles in Samoa "signally illustrate the impolicy of entangling alliances with foreign powers."[11] Germany mistakenly interpreted this to mean that the United States might abandon Samoa, and Chancellor Caprivi at once instructed his ambassador in London to determine how the islands might best be split between Germany and Great Britain.

The Samoan imbroglio was America's first real contact with great-power imperialism. Even though it involved a place in which the material and strategic interests of the United States were relatively small, the fact that Germany by chance appeared as the chief antagonist there tended to undermine the traditional amity between the two nations. Just as the simultaneous attempts of the two countries to build up their economies and their foreign trade led to clashes over tariff and trade policies, so the virtually simultaneous efforts of the two countries to break out of their respective continental isolation and to establish their "places in the sun" led to conflict in the Pacific and to suspicion elsewhere. Germany, though it acquiesced in an "American" solution in Samoa, came increasingly to look upon the United States as something of a rival. The United States became fearful that the aggressive policies of Germany in the islands might

11. Grover Cleveland, Annual Message to Congress, December 4, 1893, in *Foreign Relations, 1893*, pp. viii–ix.

soon find their counterpart in the Caribbean or in South America. By the 1890s, therefore, with both Germany and the United States embarked on the road to world power, the traditionally friendly relations between the two countries were in jeopardy.

The Rivalry of Emergent Powers

Although neither government was anxious for a direct confrontation with the other, Germany and the United States had in fact begun to work at cross purposes, at least in certain areas. American tariff policy, in conjunction with the inherent economic superiority of the United States, caused growing alarm in some German circles and created the widespread impression that America was a roadblock to Germany's legitimate economic aspirations. Berlin's ambassador in Washington began to urge economic reprisals in the form of a tariff war and to find a receptive hearing at least on the middle and lower levels of the Foreign Office and the ministries of finance and agriculture. "The only thing that we can do," he insisted, "is to improve our tariff laws and to give the Government the possibility to do as much harm in a tariff war as can be done to us."[12] The kaiser, impulsive as usual, reached a similar conclusion and entertained grandiose plans for an all-European economic agreement directed essentially against the United States. After a visit to the tsar in 1896, he told the Foreign Office of an agreement on "the getting together of Europe in a battle against MacKinley [sic] and America in a joint defensive tariff alliance be it with or without England, howsoever."[13] Though wholly impractical and never implemented, the kaiser's scheme clearly indicated a change in Germany's attitude toward the United States from the ostentatious friendliness of an earlier day.

Concern over American economic competition, both real and imagined, reached a new high when the Dingley Tariff of 1897 not only raised duties in general but doubled those applicable to sugar, the largest single item of German export to the United States. While the bill was still being debated in Congress, the German ambassador urged his government to launch a protest and give force to it by

---

12. Max von Thielmann to Adolf Marschall von Bieberstein, February 23, 1896, quoted in Alfred Vagts, *Deutschland und die Vereinigten Staaten in der Weltpolitik*, 2 vols. (New York, 1935), 1: 302.

13. William II to Foreign Office, September 9, 1896, in *Die grosse Politik der europäischen Kabinette, 1871–1914*, 40 vols. (Berlin, 1922–1927), 11: 360.

threatening to reimpose the pork import prohibition. Senators from the hog-growing states, he thought, might thereby be persuaded to oppose the measure. Official protests, though devoid of threats, were in fact presented to the State Department while the Senate debated the bill and after it had gone into effect. Only Germany's need for raw materials, its shippers' dependence on the American carrying trade, and the fact that the Dingley Tariff proved less harmful in practice than had been anticipated limited to the press and to the internal memoranda of various ministries the evidences of ever greater antagonism. Nevertheless, Germany pressed its exclusion of American life insurance companies from Prussia, arbitrarily raised transportation costs for American lumber, barred the import of some fruit, threatened to bar import of horses, and in other ways demonstrated its concern over economic competition from the New World. The result, of course, was a sharp and unfavorable turn in American public opinion of Germany.

The mutual disenchantment that developed from economic competition was greatly furthered by simultaneous evidence of both German and American expansionism. The Germans had for some time viewed with considerable distress the prospect of American intervention in Cuba. William II, who now played an increasingly large role in shaping German foreign policy, had become particularly alarmed in September 1897 when the United States made strong representations to Spain about the deteriorating situation in Cuba. In order to prevent the kaiser's feelings of monarchical solidarity from leading to another "Kruger Telegram"—William's congratulatory message to the president of the Transvaal the previous year had gratuitously insulted Great Britain and brought international embarrassment for the Reich—Foreign Minister von Bülow had carefully reminded his ruler of Germany's stake in the American market and of the general undesirability of picking a quarrel with the United States.

The largely pro-Spanish attitude of the German press and government was well known and greatly resented in America, however, and that resentment grew as Germany's own conduct on the international scene became more aggressive. When the murder of two German missionaries in southern Shantung led to the landing of naval forces at Kiaochow on November 14 and to demands on China not only for compensation and apologies but also for the lease of territory for a naval base, Americans readily regarded the Germans not only as bullies but as hypocrites. Fear that they also harbored plans for world domination increased when, three weeks later, German armed ships appeared off Port-au-Prince in order to force the government of Haiti to pay an indemnity of twenty thousand dollars to Emil Lüders, a German national who had been imprisoned there. Although the two incidents bore no actual relation to each other, their coincidence was remarkable. The tendency to see both as part of a German expansionist plot was heightened by Bülow's celebrated Reichstag speech of December 6 in support of the naval appropriation. "We wish to put no one in the shade," the foreign minister declared, "but we too demand our place in the sun. In East Asia as in the West Indies, we intend, in accordance with the traditions of German policy and without undue harshness, but also without weakness, to protect our interests."[14]

The Haitian matter was quickly settled and led to no German demands for territory or special privileges. (An American representative secured Lüders's release, and Secretary of State John Sherman played down both the incident and the subsequent Haitian request for protection, declaring that Germany's actions bore no relation to the Monroe Doctrine.) Moreover, the Germans were soon joined in their efforts to establish control over portions of China by all of the other major powers. Nevertheless, American suspicions continued to be directed primarily against Germany and became a permanent and increasingly disturbing feature of German-American relations.

Just as in the case of commercial relations, it was not that either country particularly sought advantages at the expense of the other. But both sought similar advantages at the same time, and their rival ambitions led to conflict over differences, both real and imaginary. Had the United States not harbored expansionist ambitions of its own, it would not likely have opposed those of Germany with such fervor. It is quite evident, for example, that the ardently anti-imperialist ambassador in Berlin, Andrew D. White, found German policy to be both understandable and even desirable, and that the equally anti-imperialist Secretary of State Sherman could applaud even the forceful actions at Kiaochow as instances of beneficial firmness. Theodore Roosevelt and Henry Cabot Lodge, on the other hand, two men who dreamed of the glories of an American Empire,

14. Ibid., 14: 111–112.

were among the first to warn against the alleged German threat to American interests.

The simultaneous efforts of the United States and Germany to establish themselves on the world scene thus not unnaturally led to conflict. If the United States hoped to secure its interests and expand its trade and its influence by building a massive fleet, it could hardly look with equanimity on the similar effort launched by Germany, particularly not when both countries were diligently following the blueprints provided by Captain Alfred Thayer Mahan's treatise *The Influence of Seapower on History*. If the U.S. expected to extend its hegemony over the Caribbean and Latin America, it was bound to become suspicious of increased German trade there and of the attention paid by the German government to emigrants who settled in Brazil, Chile, and elsewhere in those areas. Neither could the government in Washington fail to reach the conclusion that a nation as patently ambitious as Germany would sooner or later seek some territory, at least for a naval base, in the Western Hemisphere when such projects were regularly proposed in the publications of the Kolonialverein, the Alldeutscher Verband, and the Flottenverein.

Likewise, if both the United States and Germany hoped to expand trade and influence in Asia, each necessarily resented the other's similar efforts. When in 1898, for example, the United States sought a railroad concession in China which had already been secretly given to Germany, Friedrich von Holstein, perhaps the most influential official in the Foreign Office, was sufficiently concerned to consider the possibility of a German-American naval war. "It is unavoidable," he wrote to the ambassador in London, "that with our present expansionist colonial policy we should sometimes get into sticky situations." His concern was in part the result of the general paranoia that underlay many of Germany's actions during these years, but it reflected as well that need to build up and maintain prestige which provided much of the rationale for all of the expansionist powers. "A retreat," he insisted, "would be the signal for the conduct of a general campaign of humiliation against us."[15] It did not particularly matter that Germany, despite the tone of its nationalist press and the occasional outbursts of its ruler, was, in most cases, quite solicitous of American interests and certainly anxious to pre-

15. Friedrich von Holstein to Hatzfeld, August 19, 1898, in Norman Rich and M. H. Fisher, eds., *The Holstein Papers*, 4 vols. (Cambridge, 1955–1963), 4: 92.

serve the tradition of German-American friendship, or that the United States did not go out of its way to pick a quarrel with the Wilhelminian Reich. The newly developing world power constellation simply placed the two countries in opposing camps.

A key element, and ultimately the deciding factor, in the German-American equation was undoubtedly Great Britain. In a sense, both Germany and the United States were seeking at the close of the nineteenth century a portion of that world power exercised by Britain since the Napoleonic Wars. To obtain it, it was necessary either to reach an agreement with the British or to wrest power from them by actual or threatened force. The Germans at first sought an accommodation with Great Britain. Yet it proved difficult to achieve, partly because William II did not relish the role of junior partner, partly because German ambition clashed with British holdings in too much of the world, and partly because Germany, in its vulnerable place at the center of Europe, could not afford to add Russia— Britain's rival in the Middle and Far East—to the list of its continental enemies. The German decision to build a large navy finally made such an accommodation impossible, since Great Britain's position was clearly threatened by a country that sought to add a very powerful fleet to its already powerful army.

When the United States began to build a large navy of its own and to show what appeared to be imperialistic ambitions, it was logical from the German viewpoint to seek at least an informal alliance with it. Between them, the United States and Germany would have the requisite naval strength to challenge Great Britain in the race for colonies, without thereby endangering Germany's security on the Continent. Although both the kaiser and the Foreign Office saw most things through a glass, darkly, in the years after 1897, and through only the faintest hint of an actual U.S.-German alliance was ever given, it is difficult to escape the conclusion that some such thoughts, however ineptly put forward, underlay the German approach to the United States in the early years of the twentieth century.

Unfortunately for the Germans, however, any such plans that they may have entertained were foiled by the actions of Great Britain. Faced with the simultaneous challenges of Germany and the United States, Britain decided to accommodate itself to the more localized and apparently less dangerous of the two, and deliberately set out to pacify the United States while seeking to contain Germany. As the aftermath of the Venezuela crisis of 1895 clearly shows, the British reached that decision by 1896, although it was not then apparent just how far they were prepared to go in accepting its consequences. Threatened both by Cleveland's message to Congress of December 17, 1895, in which the president declared himself ready to draw the disputed Venezuela boundary himself and force Britain to abide by that decision, and by the kaiser's telegram to Paul Kruger, president of the Transvaal on January 3, 1896, in which William at least implied that Germany would have been happy to help him ward off the British had he been unable to do it himself, Great Britain made its choice. Unwilling and unable to face both an American and a German challenge, the British government heeded the voices of reason and public opinion and backed down on the Venezuela boundary question. Thereafter, Great Britain worked hard to win over the United States to the Open Door policy for China and proved willing to accommodate the United States in disputes that arose over a Central American canal and the Alaska boundary.

In the face of British readiness to yield to the wishes of the United States in matters of substantial importance, any approach by America to Germany could only prove detrimental. The United States had nothing to gain from a tacit alliance with Germany (which had nothing to give) but stood to lose the new willingness of Britain to give America a free hand, at least in the Western Hemisphere. Even leaving aside the growing sentimental feelings about a common Anglo-Saxonism, the logic of this situation could scarcely escape men like Roosevelt, Lodge, John Hay, Henry White, and the other nationalist imperialists who were instrumental in formulating American policy after 1900. It had been apparent even to their less ambitious predecessors. Britain was a satiated state without ambitions that might prove dangerous to America, and a country, moreover, with whom it seemed possible to negotiate successfully. Germany was ambitious and expansionist and ruled by a man whose public utterances were marked both by a striking lack of diplomatic tact and an equally striking lack of consistency. Given this choice, the gravitation of the United States into the British orbit was virtually inevitable. It was equally inevitable that this gravitation would eventually lead to ever greater difficulties with a Germany doomed to be increasingly frustrated in its global ambitions.

The relationship of the United States to Germany thus became in the late 1890s the obverse of the Anglo-American rapprochement. The U.S. increasingly came to identify its world interests with those of Great Britain and, like the British, to see in Germany the major threat to these interests. The result was an almost complete reversal of the situation two decades earlier, when friendship with Germany had been regarded as axiomatic, and "twisting the lion's tail" a favorite American sport. The positive response of Great Britain to America's new ambitions to play a world role and the haggling over trade and Samoa which had clouded relations with Germany contributed to this transformation. But so did the fact that earlier American expectations of a liberal, democratic Germany were disappointed finally, as the kaiser, with his notions of militarism and autocracy, became the generally accepted symbol of Germany, while Britain, through changes in its franchise, moved progressively toward greater democracy.

The Spanish-American War

The first test of the new relationships came in the Spanish-American War. Although public opinion in Great Britain was generally pro-American while that in Germany was pro-Spanish, there was little difference between British and German actions in the early stages of the conflict. If anything, Germany was even more careful than Britain to do nothing to offend the United States and to preserve a position of strict neutrality. Heeding the advice of his foreign minister, the kaiser repeatedly ignored pleas by Spain that he intervene with the United States in the interests of averting a war and the loss of Spanish colonies. He suggested that Austria-Hungary or the pope might be willing to do something, but insisted that Germany would act only if all of the major powers agreed to do so. When the *Maine* went down in Havana harbor, the kaiser promptly expressed his condolences to President McKinley.

It was Austria that proposed early in April 1898 that the ambassadors of the major powers in Washington send a note to McKinley urging him to preserve the peace, and that the powers simultaneously urge Spain to accede to American demands for a cessation of hostilities in Cuba. Bülow instructed Ambassador Theodor von Holleben to sign what he was certain would be a "platonic" note, but expressed no enthusiasm whatever for the enterprise. On the very day the note was delivered, the German foreign minister wrote to

the kaiser: "I share entirely the view that with respect to the Spanish-American conflict we must avoid anything that might appear like
unnecessary anti-American partisanship, and that we can participate
in mediation efforts by the powers only if all the others precede
us. . . ."[16]

After McKinley asked Congress on April 11 for what amounted to
a declaration of war against Spain, it was the British ambassador, Sir
Julian Pauncefote, who raised the possibility of a second and stronger note. Holleben was greatly surprised and immediately cabled to
Berlin his reservations about such a step. But Pauncefote, acting
without direct authorization from London, prepared a new note,
which was translated by the French ambassador for transmission to
the various governments. Austria at once voiced approval, and
France, Italy, and Great Britain accepted the idea conditionally.
Bülow, however, was cool to the proposal, and the kaiser vetoed it
outright. "I regard it as wholly wrong, pointless, and therefore harmful!" he declared. "We make ourselves look ridiculous before the
Americans, as we did before the Greeks and Turks, who also did not
give a hoot for our joint notes!"[17] When Russia also expressed strong
disapproval, the note was not sent. It is symptomatic of the trend in
German-American relations, however, that four years later the story
gained currency that it had been Great Britain that had foiled German efforts to send a stronger note. The reverse had in fact been
more nearly true.

While the German government thus officially made strenuous efforts to avoid offending the United States, opinion in this country
was affected by other matters. The American public relied primarily
on the transatlantic cable from London and on the British press for
news from Europe. As a result, it was treated to large doses of
British suspicion of German aims, supported by alleged evidence
drawn from the pro-Spanish German press and from chauvinistic
pan-German publications such as the *Deutsche Kolonialzeitung* and
the *Alldeutsche Blätter*. By contrast, public support in England for
American policy was played up, as was the Birmingham speech of
Colonial Secretary Joseph Chamberlain, in which he wistfully spoke
of the Union Jack and the Stars and Stripes waving together over an
Anglo-Saxon alliance.

16. Bernhard von Bülow to William II, April 7, 1898, in *Grosse Politik*, 9: 20–21.
17. William II, marginal notes on Bülow to William II, April 15, 1898, in ibid.,
23, 24.

What might have been passed off, despite America's new suspicions of German objectives, as propaganda was given both credibil-
ity and apparent substance by German blunders in the Philippines.
Dewey's victory in Manila Bay on May 1, 1898, clearly indicated
that Spain would no longer be able to control the archipelago, and,
from the German viewpoint, the islands were therefore fair game.
Germany at no time expected to take over the Philippines itself and
was aware from the outset that any disposition of the islands would
have to meet with the approval of Great Britain, which controlled
the seas, and of the United States, which had destroyed the power of
Spain there. Since Admiral von Tirpitz thought Manila would make
an excellent naval base, however, and the kaiser sympathized with
the ambitions of his navy, the Germans did not give up the hope that
their interests would be considered in any division of the spoils.
When the German consul at Manila sent word that the Filipino insurgents were thinking of setting up an independent state under a German prince, and when this message seemed to be confirmed in a
similar report from Prince Henry of Prussia, who was at that time in
the Far East, the kaiser decided to send Vice-Admiral Otto von
Diederichs with a sizable fleet to Manila in order to establish German presence in the area. Though Diederichs soon informed his
superiors that pro-German sentiment was nonexistent and refused to
take control of Manila when it was offered him by the Spanish
governor-general, his presence in the harbor disturbed Dewey and
outraged American opinion.

Great Britain, France, and Japan, to be sure, had also sent warships to the area, but only the Germans had sent a squadron stronger
than Dewey's under a commander who outranked the American.
Only Germany thus left itself open to a charge of harboring ulterior
motives. By mid-June the German ambassador in Washington was
sending reports of a growing anti-German press campaign, a campaign that increased in volume when the two admirals quarreled
over interpretation of the rules of blockade and when Dewey ac-
cused Diederich's of using his ships to prevent the Filipino insurgents from attacking Manila.

As usual during the Spanish-American War, public reaction was
both swifter and more vigorous than that of the government. Secretary of State William R. Day for a time issued official denials of any
German plot against the Philippines and even cited alleged assurances from Berlin for which he had never asked. By July, however,

suspicion ripened even in Washington. The German Foreign Office had already inquired of Ambassador von Holleben what annexations the United States was planning, what concessions it expected to make to Great Britain, and what agreements about naval bases, coaling stations, and the like it was prepared to reach with Germany in return for German support of American annexations. It was important to know what the United States wanted, Deputy Foreign Minister Oswald von Richthofen explained, so that Germany could set its sights on other things. In a subsequent conversation with Ambassador White in Berlin, Richthofen pursued this theme at great length and pointed out the ostensible advantages the United States would gain by agreeing to divide the spoils of war with Germany. Germany, he announced, wanted only Samoa—the United States had, after all, decided to annex Hawaii—the Spanish Carolines, and one or two bases in the Philippines.

When the anti-imperialist White, who in a July Fourth speech at Leipzig had just called Germany a "second motherland," cabled the gist of his conversation with Richthofen to Washington and ventured the opinion that the United States should be "friendly to German aspirations," even the State Department began to register annoyance. Day cabled back that such discussions were premature, to say the least, since the Philippines and Carolines were still held by Spain and Hawaii had nothing whatever to do with the matter. "The United States," he affirmed, "has the right to expect the friendly neutrality of Germany in accordance with the long-established relations of the governments." Shortly thereafter, he asked White to inquire whether Germany really intended to keep such a large naval force in the Philippines and to stop talking with the Germans about things that were "exclusively between the United States and Spain as parties to the war."[18] At the same time, Holleben informed his government that the United States had little understanding for reciprocity in relation to colonial acquisitions, and added somewhat enigmatically: "The ambition of the Americans is limited only by their vanity."[19]

By the time the war ended with a preliminary peace settlement on August 12 it had become perfectly clear that the German mode of

18. Andrew D. White to William R. Day, July 12, 1898, in "Despatches Received: Germany," 63; Day to White, July 13, 22, 25, 1898, in "Diplomatic Instructions of the Department of State, 1801–1906: Germany," 64, Microfilm copy 77, RG 59. NA.

19. Theodor von Holleben to Foreign Office, arrived July 13, 1898, in *Grosse Politik*, 15: 59–60.

conducting its foreign affairs was meeting with neither sympathy nor understanding in the United States. The American public, whose views were growing increasingly annexationist, came to see the Philippine question simply in terms of whether the United States or Germany would reap the fruits of the American victory. And McKinley, still undecided on what annexations should be made, resented what he regarded as Germany's gratuitous interference. The game of international relations, which the men in the Wilhelmstrasse played according to complex rules that bore less and less relation to reality as time went on, could hardly make sense to a country that had sought to ignore the entire game for over a century. It did not matter that Germany addressed highly conciliatory messages to Washington, relinquished all thought of the Philippines as soon as McKinley had reached his decision for annexation, offered to give the United States a lease for a cable station in the Carolines after the islands were acquired from Spain, gave up all thought of getting the Americans out of Samoa, and even dropped the attempt to gain even a leasehold on one of the islands of the Philippines—all in the interest of maintaining friendly relations. Germany even sent Diederichs out of Manila Bay to the Dutch East Indies—ostensibly to help celebrate the coronation of Queen Wilhelmina—and when it withdrew its last vessel in February 1899 asked the United States to take over the protection of German nationals and property. The fact of the matter was that Great Britain had taken American occupation of the Philippines for granted even before that decision had been made, and no other power had raised any questions about American plans. Only Germany, with its nearly paranoid concern for its rights and privileges, had posed problems and, though it had basically sought only agreement with the United States on these matters, appeared as the most ambitious and the most grasping of the European powers.

It was a serious shortcoming of the men who made German policy that they never understood the effect that their machinations, whatever their ultimate intentions, had in the United States and that they continued their insistence on quid pro quo in the face of mounting American annoyance. When the president of the Dominican Republic, General Ulysseus Heureaux, allegedly fearing the power of the United States in the Caribbean, wanted a European nation (preferably Germany) to give him support by signing a trade treaty and leasing some land for a naval station, Germany wisely refused the offer. But it negated the possibly favorable effect of that refusal on U.S.-German relations by first inquiring what the American reaction to German support for Heureaux might be and expressing the thought that any German self-denial should somehow be rewarded by the United States.

By the time the peace treaty with Spain had been signed on December 10, American suspicions of Germany had reached their highest point, and the future of relations between the two nations seemed far from bright. It did not bode well for possible improvement in these relations that Germany protested its total innocence and blamed the American attitude entirely on malevolent British propaganda, or that the press in the United States, and the Navy Department as well, began to suspect German interest in every beachhead in Latin America and every atoll in the South Pacific. The alleged perfidy of the Germans in the Philippines was told and retold in numerous articles and books and embellished in each new version. As early as 1899 the legend that only the interposition of British vessels had prevented an armed clash between Dewey and Diederichs in Manila had found its way into Henry Cabot Lodge's *War with Spain,* and it remained in similar accounts for nearly two decades, serving the dual purpose of burdening German-American relations and aiding those with Great Britain.

The Shadow of the Hun

The situation was not improved when news reached Washington in January 1899 of new difficulties in Samoa. The trouble had actually begun there the previous August with the death of the reigning king. In true condominium style, the German president of the municipal council of Apia, supported by his country's consul, had backed one candidate for the throne, while the American and British consuls backed another. Both sides found support among the natives, and both claimed that their candidate had been duly elected. Under the terms of the 1889 treaty, such diputes were to be settled by the chief justice, who at the time was an American, William T. Chambers. Chambers promptly ruled for the Anglo-American candidate, and the German representatives with equal promptness organized a revolt, placed their candidate on the throne, and forced the chief justice to flee to the safety of a British warship. When news of these events finally reached the new secretary of state, John Hay, he

immediately protested the German action to Ambassador von Holleben and sent Admiral Albert Kautz and the cruiser *Philadelphia* to
Apia to investigate. Kautz soon insisted that the chief justice be
upheld and the deposed king reinstated. When the Germans encouraged their stonger native faction to hold out, Kautz began shel-
ling the local villages and in this endeavor was promptly joined by a
British vessel.

It was now Germany's turn to protest. But its protests were tempered by Bülow's concern that relations with the United not be
strained even further, a concern that he had strongly expressed in
the Reichstag on February 11. In response to questions about German-American differences over trade and tariff matters, he had not
only played down the significance of the Samoan issue but had gone
to extraordinary pains to try to repair any damage done by what he
insisted was the wholly neutral conduct of Germany during the
Spanish-American War. Maintaining that "the relations between the
German government and the American government are good and
friendly and have never ceased being good and friendly," he recalled
the heritage of Frederick the Great and Prussia's conduct during the
Civil War, invoked the ties of blood between the two nations,
heaped fulsome praise on Ambassador White and on the American
navy, and concluded: "The ties that bind Germany and America
together are too varied in nature, and both materially and spiritually
too valuable, to be lightheartedly dissolved." The German and the
American people, he thought, would continue to maintain "calm,
secure, and friendly relations" on the basis of "full reciprocity,
mutual accomodation, and mutual respect."[20]

In any event, it was now plainly in the interest of all the parties to
end the untenable conditions in Samoa, and after some preliminary
wrangling, commissioners from the three nations were once more
sent out. This time they managed to work in sufficient harmony to
effect pacification, the withdrawal of Admiral Kautz, the temporary
elimination of the Samoan kingship, and the drawing up of a joint
recommendation to end three-power control. Harmony among the
commissioners was made possible largely by the fact that the Germans had selected as their representative Baron Hermann Speck
von Sternburg, who had earlier served as secretary to the legation in
Washington and there became the friend of Theodore Roosevelt and

20. Bernhard, Fürst von Bülow, *Reden*, 2 vols. (Berlin, 1907-1909), I: 47-51.

married an American woman. The appointment of Sternburg was a deliberate attempt by Bülow to wean the United States away from the British on the matter of Samoa and thereby to secure a resolution not unfavorable to Germany. In the same spirit Bülow conceded American retention of Tutuila, with the harbor of Pago Pago, which the American commissioner described as "the Gibraltar of the Pacific," and carried on the final negotiations entirely with Great Britain, which he sought to compensate elsewhere for its agreement to leave most of Samoa to Germany. The German foreign minister even asked the United States to bring pressure on Great Britain for a "just" Samoan settlement. "The Imperial Government," he wrote to Washington, once more with his eye on a quid pro quo, "would regard this as a valuable basis for the further development of the friendly relations with America which now happily exist, and the United States could be assured of compensatory action on our part in other situations."[21]

Needless to say, the State Department did not react to this plea. It regarded Pago Pago as American by right of the treaty of 1878 with Samoa and saw no need either to win German support or to alienate Great Britain. Final agreement between Germany and Great Britain was not reached until November 27, 1899, when, faced with the outbreak of the Boer War, the British tried to put an end to difficulties elsewhere in the world. The United States had no part in these negotiations beyond Hay's statement of September 7 that it agreed to the partition of Samoa and would accept Tutuila as its share. In the final agreement Britain gave up its claim to the islands and Germany to that part conceded to the United States. Germany and the United States thus, in effect, divided Samoa, and Britain was compensated rather handsomely elsewhere. The settlement satisfied both Germany and the United States and removed a source of friction between them which had existed for two decades. But it put an end neither to American suspicions of German aims nor to those German policies that produced the suspicions.

The ink, in fact, was hardly dry on the Samoan treaty when the United States found new reasons to worry about German policies. The outbreak of the Boxer Rebellion in China, and particularly the besieging of foreign embassies in Peking, caused concern to all the

21. Bülow to Alfons Mumm von Schwarzenberg, August 29, 1899, in *Grosse Politik*, 14:628n.

powers, and American naval forces took part in initial efforts to secure lives and property. With the murder of the German ambassador, Baron Klemens von Ketteler, however, William II came to regard the rebellion as a German matter in particular and saw himself called upon to lead a crusade against the "yellow peril" of which he had warned for some time. Not only did he threaten to mobilize an entire army corps for service in China—a project from which Bülow dissuaded him only with difficulty—he also insisted on the appointment of Field Marshal Alfred von Waldersee as commander-in-chief of the international forces to be sent to the relief of Peking. In a series of bellicose speeches to troops leaving for the Far East, the kaiser urged them to mete out exemplary punishment, to raze Peking to the ground, and to take vengeance such as the world had never seen. The most celebrated of these exhortations was delivered at Bremerhaven on July 27, 1900. "You will give no quarter!" he told the departing warriors. "You will take no prisoners! Whoever falls into your hands will be your victim! Just as the Huns under their King Attila made a name for themselves a thousand years ago which still, in saga and tradition, makes them appear powerful, so may the name German be impressed by you on China for a thousand years, that no Chinese will ever dare again look askance at a German."[22]

The kaiser's words were widely publicized throughout the world and greatly added to the alarm over German policies and intentions. Indeed, the equation of Germans with Huns, which William proudly made, colored the future view of many people, particularly in America, toward both Germany and its emperor. The United States accepted Waldersee as commander-in-chief but in fact never placed troops under his command. The relief expedition that captured Peking and in which twenty-five hundred American troops participated was organzied before the German field marshal arrived in the Far East and was led by a Russian general. In Waldersee's subsequent punitive expeditions, U.S. forces ostentatiously took no part. The United States in fact devoted much of its subsequent energies to preventing the partitioning of China in the aftermath of the rebellion and to setting reparations terms that China could meet without falling under the financial dominance of one or more of the powers. In this latter aim, the chief difficulty was once again with Germany,

22. Three versions of his speech are reproduced in Wilhelm Schroeder, *Das persönliche Regiment* (Munich, 1907), pp. 41–43.

which not only had spent the most money on its expedition but also had serious budgetary difficulties at home and needed "adequate" compensation.

By the beginning of the twentieth century, therefore, the transformation of the American image of Germany was nearly complete. The romantic notion of a literate, hardworking people striving for liberty and union under the leadership of men who were thought to resemble Carl Schurz had been replaced by the notion of a nation of modern-day Huns, dominated by a military establishment and led by an autocrat whose ambitions knew no bounds. For the United States, newly arrived on the scene of world politics, the new Germany appeared to be hardly a comfortable neighbor, let alone a desirable and dependable partner. The British, by contrast, were seen as safe and sane and reasonably democratic, and it is hardly surprising that American leaders found it far more desirable to work with them. To be sure, the men who made American foreign policy were aware that the kaiser's more immoderate outbursts did not necessarily reflect German policy, and that American and British interests did not coincide everywhere. But it was clear enough that any future attempts by the Germans to woo the United States away from its British connections and into closer harmony with Germany would not be readily reciprocated.

Chapter 3

A FUTILE COURTSHIP:
THE KAISER AND
THEODORE ROOSEVELT

*

The Second Venezuela Crisis

From the beginning of the twentieth century to the very eve of the First World War, Germany tried hard to reestablish the tradition of German-American friendship and to prevent Anglo-American rapprochement. Dismayed by what they regarded as a wholly unwarranted American response to Germany's actions during the Spanish-American War, both the kaiser and the Foreign Office persistently wooed the United States, but with little success. Even though its war with Spain had catapulted it into the world arena and given it a tangible stake in both the Caribbean and the Far East, the United States was neither willing to participate fully in the prevailing balance-of-power system nor convinced of the need to do so.

To Germany, the arrival of the United States as an activist on the world scene meant simply that it had to be fitted somehow into the context of the alliance system. Like any other nation with colonies and worldwide ambitions, the U.S. had to align itself with those powers with whom it shared common interests or with whom, at least, it had no major quarrel. From the point of view of the Wilhelmstrasse, Germany was such a power. After the settlement of the Samoa question, there was no place in the world where Germany and the United States confronted each other directly, and aside from a continuing tariff problem there was nothing of major consequence on which they seriously disagreed. As far as the Germans were concerned, moreover, the two countries, a land power and a naval power respectively, complemented each other and could be mutually useful. If an Anglo-American alliance were to develop, however, the already difficult German situation would rapidly become worse. Against such a combination, no navy that Germany might conceivably build would be of much value, and the Reich would be either thrown back on the support of a decaying Austria and an unreliable Italy or forced to attempt to win back the alliance of Russia and even of France. The Germans never wholly gave up the latter idea, and made various overtures, particularly to Russia, but the idea of a working agreement with the United States seemed both simpler and more promising during much of the period.

The German courtship of the United States came to nothing, however, not only because America never quite trusted German intentions, but more fundamentally because it did not want an alliance with any of the powers, not even with Great Britain. Even during the most active period of its foreign policy, in the presidency of Theodore Roosevelt, the United States was certain that it could protect its interests through unilateral action and direct negotiation with those powers with whom it encountered difficulties. Alliances or international commitments of any kind were contrary to longstanding American tradition, and there seemed to be no compelling reason to change this policy. Washington had had its way with Spain, with Hawaii, with the Philippines, and with Cuba, and it was soon also to have its way with the isthmian canal, the Alaska boundary, and, to a degree, with the Open Door in the Far East. Under these conditions, there seemed to be no advantage whatsoever in yielding to German blandishments. On the contrary, since it was Germany's intention to draw the United States into an essentially anti-British arrangement, and since a beneficial working relationship with Britain had already been established, such a course could only be harmful to American interests.

There was yet another factor that made the German effort a hopeless one. At the beginning of the century, foreign relations were for the United States, as they had always been, of secondary importance. Domestic reform became the order of the day, and the Progressive movement absorbed American energies to a far greater degree than did considerations of world policy. Even Roosevelt, who liked to dabble in international affairs and who hugely enjoyed his various roles as mediator and peacemaker, was primarily concerned with domestic politics and policy and keenly aware that both the Senate and public opinion posed limits to a president's ability to involve the United States with other nations, limits that he exceeded only at his peril. For Germany, on the other hand, foreign policy was the key not only to its future glory but also, in the eyes of most German statesmen, to its very existence as a nation. Both the kaiser, who had the final voice in all policy and who took an increasingly large role in shaping it, and Bernhard von Bülow, who moved from the Foreign Office to the chancellorship in 1900, therefore threw themselves into foreign policy making with an intensity that was ever more likely to impress the United States simply as overweening ambition and an unwillingness to leave well enough alone. The result was, that though the United States and Germany cooperated in various ways, particularly between 1904 and 1908, it was the far less demanding rapprochement with Britain which became the dominant feature of American policy.

Germany's active courtship of the United States began in the spring of 1899 with the successful request that a German firm be permitted to spend 20 million marks to establish a direct cable link between Emden and New York. The kaiser hoped that this project, designed to decrease American dependence on British news sources and suspectibility to British propaganda, would "help in maintaining and strengthening friendly relations between the two countries."[1] It continued with the long-sought German move to readmit American life insurance companies to doing business in the empire, with a new commercial agreement in 1900 and with various small attentions that exceeded normal diplomatic courtesy. With the accession of Theodore Roosevelt to the presidency in the following year, such efforts were redoubled. The kaiser believed that the new president's feelings paralleled his own, and indeed there were certain superficial similarities. Both men were relatively young and had compensated for physical infirmities by espousing the strenuous life. Both took an active interest in naval construction, and both, above all, had noble visions of the future greatness of their respective countries. But the similarities were more apparent than real. Roosevelt was by far the more able to the two men, the more intelligent and the more realistic. He accepted the kaiser's gestures and flattery with some

1. William II to McKinley, August 30, 1899, in *Foreign Relations of the United States: Diplomatic Papers, 1899*, p. 314.

amusement and returned them freely. Unlike William II, however, he did not see in them the basis for either a personal friendship or for genuine cooperation between the two nations.

William congratulated Roosevelt on his succession, sent him a medal of his own design, and donated a valuable collection of casts to the Germanic Museum of Harvard University, Roosevelt's alma mater. He ordered a yacht built in the United States and asked the president's daughter Alice to christen it. An America Institute was established at the University of Berlin and exchange professorships set up, and the kaiser sent a statue of Frederick the Great to Washington and busts of Frederick and himself to other cities in the U.S. as well. American ships were invited to the Kiel regatta and American observers to German army maneuvers. Most important, perhaps, William II sent his brother, Prince Henry, on a goodwill tour of the United States in February 1902—a tour that, according to Admiral von Tirpitz, who accompanied the prince, was intended "to remove, if possible, the misunderstanding regarding the attitude of Germany occasioned by the presence of German warships at Manila at the time of Admiral Dewey's capture and occupation of that city."[2]

Such a gesture did little to erase the memory of Diederichs's doings in the Philippines or to allay continuing suspicions of Germany's intentions in Latin America. The American press responded negatively when a German vessel took soundings at Santa Marguerita Island off the Venezuelan coast in 1901, and again when reports surfaced that German interests wanted to buy large tracts of land in Lower California, including a fine harbor, as a gift for the kaiser. Although Germany had no real designs on Santa Marguerita and did not succumb to the Mexican schemes of the land speculators, American suspicions were not allayed. They were even increased by rumors, supported by Henry Cabot Lodge in a Senate speech, that Germany was attempting to purchase the Danish West Indies. Secretary of State Hay tried to squelch the rumors by labeling Lodge's remarks a "political eruption," but when the upper house of the Danish parliament blocked an effort by the United States to purchase the islands in 1902 the American press immediately, and falsely, detected the fine hand of the kaiser. Such developments boded ill for German plans for a rapprochement. "The

2. David J. Hill to Elihu Root, December 9, 1908, in State Department Numerical File 16533/39, RG 59, NA.

only power which may be a menace to us in anything like the immediate future," Roosevelt wrote to Lodge, "is Germany." The Germans, he thought, count on American weakness, "so that in a few years they will be in a position to take some step in the West Indies or South America which will make us either put up or shut up on the Monroe Doctrine."[3]

Germany's failure to evoke American goodwill was graphically demonstrated during the Venezuela crisis of 1902. Like Great Britain and various other powers, Germany had considerable difficulty with the corrupt and capricious rule of the Venezuelan dictator Cipriano Castro, who not only failed to make payments on debts his government had contracted, but also made no move to compensate foreign nationals for damages suffered during the almost constant turmoil in his country. On July 16, 1901, Germany offered to submit its claims against Venezuela to the Hague Court for arbitration. When Castro did not reply, tentative plans were made to collect the money by imposing a blockade and perhaps seizing some customs houses. "But we consider it of importance," Ambassador von Holleben explained in a memorandum delivered to Hay on December 11, "to first of all let the Government of the United States know about our purposes so that we can prove that we have nothing else in view than to help our citizens who have suffered damages. . . . We declare especially that under no circumstances do we consider in our proceedings the acquisition or permanent occupation of Venezuelan territory."[4] Roosevelt had in effect already given his approval to the course now proposed by Germany in his State of the Union message the previous week. "We do not guarantee any state against punishment if it misconducts itself," he had declared, "provided that punishment does not take the form of acquisition of territory by any non-American government."[5] Hay simply repeated that sentiment in his reply to Holleben.

The kaiser was not anxious to implement the tentative plan for a "peace blockade" and insisted that in any case all action be postponed until after the visit of Prince Henry. By the time the prince returned, however, it was too late to organize a blockade that would

3. Theodore Roosevelt to Henry Cabot Lodge, March 27, 1901, in *Selections from the Correspondence of Theodore Roosevelt and Henry Cabot Lodge, 1884–1918*, 2 vols. (New York, 1925), 1: 494–495.

4. Holleben to Hay, December 11, 1901, in *Foreign Relations, 1901*, pp. 192–194.

5. Roosevelt, Annual Message to Congress, December 7, 1901, in ibid., pp. xxxvi–xxxvii.

seriously affect Venezuelan trade, and further action was put off until the fall of 1902. In the intervening months, pressure from Castro's German creditors mounted, and Great Britain showed increasing signs of starting its own collection action, as did Italy. From the moment that London showed interest in the venture, the kaiser began to insist that all activity be coordinated with Great Britain, and that the British take the lead in the entire matter. That was precisely what happened. Britain formulated the exact nature of the intervention and sent the first ultimatum to Venezuela on November 10, 1902. When that was rejected on November 19, the British ambassador in Washington informed Hay of his government's intention to proceed with a blockade. He received American approval. On December 9, eight British and four German warships began rounding up the gunboats of the Venezuelan navy, the Germans sinking two that were unseaworthy and could not be towed. On the following day troops were landed at La Guayra.

There can be little doubt that Germany deliberately followed the British lead in these proceedings and played down its own role in a conscious effort to avoid offending the United States. Nevertheless, it was Germany that bore the brunt of American congressional and press criticism during the crisis and that aroused the particular concern of President Roosevelt. Britain, which shared some of the initial blame, was largely exonerated when British public opinion turned against the Venezuelan venture and when King Edward VII also voiced opposition. But the appearance of German warships in the Caribbean, regardless for what reason or in whose company they came, revived earlier American suspicions that Germany harbored territorial ambitions in the Western Hemisphere despite its explicit disclaimers.

Roosevelt, anticipating the desirability of a show of strength, had ordered massive American naval maneuvers in the Caribbean for the fall, and on December 8, as British and German warships were poised to strike at Venezuela, he appointed Admiral Dewey to command the American fleet there—an unprecedented assignment for a four-star admiral. On the same day, the president told Ambassador von Holleben that Germany should submit the whole Venezuelan controversy to the Hague Tribunal for arbitration lest an aroused American public opinion force the sending of the fleet to Maracaibo. Roosevelt's subsequent recounting of his meeting with Holleben was steadily embellished until by 1916 he claimed to have given the kaiser an ultimatum and thereby forced him into arbitration. Neither

Holleben's dispatches to Berlin nor the subsequent course of events, however, reveal any German awareness of such an ultimatum.

It was Castro, finally intimidated by the landing of foreign troops on Venezuelan soil, who first offered to accept arbitration on December 11. That offer was passed without comment by the State Department to London and Berlin. Holleben's message to the Foreign Office on the following day merely warned that American public opinion was growing increasingly hostile to Germany. It reached its destination just as British and German warships were bombarding Puerto Cabello. On December 16 Hay again notified Germany and Britain of Venezuela's willingness to arbitrate, this time urging acceptance, and Holleben for the first time suggested this course, on the grounds that it might be helpful to German-American firms and to trade relations in general. By then, however, unknown to Holleben or Hay, Germany had already reached a decision. Both Britain and Germany formally accepted arbitration in principle by December 20 and asked Roosevelt to serve as arbiter, a privilege that he declined. On the same day they established a blockade in order to maintain pressure on the notoriously undependable Venezuelan dictator.

The blockade prolonged the German presence in the Caribbean and thus the anti-German press campaign, which reached a crescendo in January 1903 when a German warship bombarded the fort and village of San Carlo. It also prolonged the anxiety in Washington, where efforts were made to get arbitration under way. But if Roosevelt had indeed threatened the Germans with use of the American fleet, they remained clearly unaware of it. Holleben informed Bülow on January 2, 1902, that the presence of American naval vessels in the Caribbean had no connection with concern over German intentions, and the chargé d'affaires, Albert von Quadt, labeled as "absolutely correct" on January 29 a *Chicago Tribune* report "that the President and the Administration gave us their fullest confidence, understood the situation completely, and regarded it with great calm."[6]

---

6. Albert von Quadt to Bülow, January 9, 1903, and Holleben to Bülow, January 3, 1903, in "German Foreign Ministry Archives," reel 248, frames 819–820, Microfilm T 149, RG 242, NA. See also Holleben to Bülow, December 16, 1902, in *Die grosse Politik der europäischen Kabinette, 1871–1914,* 40 vols. (Berlin, 1922–1927), 17: 264.

The Foreign Office, in any event, had reached the decision to accept arbitration of its own accord, moved not by ultimata but by genuine concern for maintaining good relations with the United States. It had hesitated even for a few days only because Castro had not accepted the conditions that had been laid down by both Germany and Great Britain. Moreover, Germany steadfastly followed the lead of Britain and proposed Roosevelt himself as arbitrator, a course that, given German sensibilities, would have been ruled out by even the slightest awareness of the kind of threat the president subsequently claimed to have made. When London suggested that the gunboats be returned, Bülow acquiesced. "Out of consideration for the Government of the United States," he told the kaiser, "it is desirable in dealings with Venezuela never to proceed more sharply than England, but to keep in line with it."[7] Accordingly, Germany also agreed to scale down the "non-negotiable" portion of its claim, accepted the American minister in Caracas as Venezuelan representative in preliminary arbitration proceedings, and expressed willingness to submit the entire matter to the Hague Tribunal for final settlement. Far from being an example of Germany's expansionist ambitions, the Venezuela crisis merely demonstrated that at least in the Western Hemisphere it could never proceed with enough care to assuage American concerns. As an ultimate peace offering to the United States, Germany recalled Ambassador von Holleben, whose dispatches had displeased the kaiser as early as January 1902 and who, according to Roosevelt, was not a man with whom the president "could discuss important issues of the day freely and confidentially."[8] Holleben was succeeded by Baron Hermann Speck von Sternburg.

The appointment of Sternburg, whose diplomatic credentials were meager, can be construed as another of the kaiser's friendly gestures that in a sense backfired. William II was pleased to have an ambassador in Washington who was a friend of the president and went riding and played tennis with him. But if he thought this personal friendship could be transformed into German-American friendship, he was mistaken. In the relationship between Roosevelt and Sternburg, the president was the dominant figure, and as a result Sternburg neither represented German views as energetically as he might

7. Bülow to William II, January 23, 1903, in ibid., 275.
8. Hermann Speck von Sternburg to Foreign Office, November 26, 1902, in "German Foreign Ministry Archives," 243/00528, T 149, RG 242, NA.

have nor adequately communicated American reactions to the Foreign Office. When he arrived in New York to take up his new duties, however, Sternburg clearly sought to bring an end to the unhappy Venezuelan business and to revive American confidence in German goodwill. "The Emperor understands the Monroe Doctrine thoroughly, . . ." Sternburg told waiting reporters. "He would no more think of violating that doctrine than he would of colonizing the moon."[9]

The Russo-Japanese War and Algeciras

The Venezuelan debacle confirmed Roosevelt in his opinion that the Dutch and Danish possessions in the Caribbean at least would be a constant temptation to Germany "unless, or until, we take them,"[10] but it in no way discouraged Germany from thinking of future coop- eration with the United States. Developments in the Far East soon provided an opportunity for such cooperation. Throughout the re- mainder of 1903 the presence of Russian troops in Manchuria and the near completion of the Trans-Siberian Railway, which would make it possible to transport more troops and supplies, alarmed Japan. On February 4, 1904, the German chargé in Peking cabled Berlin that war was imminent and inevitable, and the Foreign Office immediately expressed concern. A war that would occupy Russia in the Far East and thereby relieve the pressure on Germany's eastern frontier was not entirely undesirable, particularly if, as expected, Russia were to win and come to look on East Asia rather than the Balkans as its field for future expansion. The diplomats in Berlin, however, feared that the impending war would also mean the divi- sion of China. That, in turn, might lead Russia and Japan to band together with their respective allies, France and Great Britain, to exclude Germany altogether from the Far East. Reluctant to make any overt move for fear of alienating Russia and provoking the other powers who already suspected Germany's motives, the kaiser en- listed the aid of that champion of the Open Door, Theodore Roosevelt.

On February 6, when Japan broke off diplomatic relations with Russia, Ambassador von Sternburg approached the president with

9. New York *Herald*, January 31, 1903.
10. Roosevelt to John Hay, April 27, 1903, in Elting E. Morison et al., eds., *The Letters of Theodore Roosevelt*, 8 vols. (Cambridge, Mass. 1951–1954), 3: 465.

the proposal that the United States ask the powers to use their influence to persuade Russia and Japan to respect the neutrality of China outside Manchuria, the presumable scene of the war. Secretary Hay was at first unimpressed by what he viewed as a German attempt to win international sanction for the Russian conquest of Manchuria, but soon came to see that the German proposal, if broadened substantially, might indeed serve to safeguard the Open Door. On the day that Japan initiated hostilities with a devastating surprise attack on the naval base at Port Arthur, he addressed a circular note to the powers, asking them to prevail upon Russia and Japan "to respect the neutrality of China and in all practical ways her administrative identity." In handing the note to the Foreign Office in Berlin, the U.S. ambassador, Charlemagne Tower, coyly informed the undersecretary that "this circular is sent at the suggestion of the German Government." Bülow now had little choice but to support the American move and to urge agreement on Russia, though he hastened to assure Saint Petersburg that the administrative identity of China need be preserved only "in so far as this may be compatible with the respective interests of the belligerent powers."[11] Since German fears of British and French ambitions were largely unfounded, all of the powers seconded the American initiative and Russia and Japan soon acquiesced. Roosevelt gave full credit to "Bill the Kaiser," and Tower on February 16 conveyed to the emperor "the President's profound appreciation of His Majesty's generous initiative and powerful cooperation in the matter of Chinese neutrality."[12]

William II had approached Roosevelt because the kaiser believed that German and American interests coincided in the Far East, and he regarded the success of the maneuver as confirmation of the wisdom of working together with Washington. But in fact there was no identity of interest beyond the vague one of the Open Door. Germany essentially hoped for a Russian victory, while the United State favored a stand-off. And whereas Germany was suspicious of British and French motives, the United States continued to suspect Germany's. The suspicion of Germany was also shared by Japan, which proceeded to ask Roosevelt to use his influence with the kaiser. "I am inclined to think," the Japanese ambassador in Wash-

11. Hay to Charlemagne Tower, February 8, 1904, and Tower to Hay, January 9, 1904, in *Foreign Relations, 1904,* pp. 309–310.
12. Tower to Oswald von Richthofen, March 16, 1904, in *Grosse Politik,* 19: 109.

ington wrote to Foreign Minister Jutarō Komura, "that the voice of the United States Government may be respected by Germany more than that of any other Government in case she should attempt to meddle with the conclusion of the war."[13]

By this time, however, the president was becoming concerned over the possibility that a smashing Japanese victory might leave it in possession of both Manchuria and Korea, and thus in a dominant and threatening position in the Far East. He began to speculate on how the trust he enjoyed in both Germany and Japan might give him the opportunity to end the war quickly on reasonable terms. The key problem in effecting such an outcome was the future of Manchuria. Russia would certainly not agree to turn this area over to Japan and would be most reluctant even to relinquish its own control. Japan would insist on obtaining Manchuria. Roosevelt's proposed solution was to bribe Germany into persuading Russia to give up that territory and to appease Japan by agreeing to its annexation of Korea instead.

Accordingly, the president confided to Ambassador von Sternburg that he wanted a peace settlement in which Japan would get Korea, and Manchuria would be established as an autonomous Chinese province under a viceroy nominated by Germany. Neither Chancellor von Bülow nor the kaiser were tempted by this proposal, since both believed Russia still had a good chance of keeping Manchuria. Moreover, neither regarded the dubious honor of naming a viceroy sufficient compensation for further straining relations with Saint Petersburg. Bülow, however, saw in Roosevelt's confidences to Sternburg another sign of growing German-American cooperation. In view of the fact that Great Britain and France had launched their Entente Cordiale on April 8, 1904, with an agreement that principally concerned Egypt and Morocco, it was now more essential than ever to expand this cooperation and to secure the United States on the German rather than on the British side. Accordingly, Bülow prevailed upon the kaiser not to reject the American overture by assuring him that "the President is a great admirer of Your Majesty and wishes to rule the world hand in hand with Your Majesty, considering himself, in a sense, an adherent of Your Majesty." Flattered, William accepted the proposal concerning Korea, and agreed to "operate together with Roosefeldt [sic]."[14]

13. Kogoro Takahira to Jutarō Komura, June 27, 1904, quoted in Raymond A. Esthus, *Theodore Roosevelt and Japan* (Seattle, 1967), p. 44.
14. Bülow to William II, August 31, 1904, in *Grosse Politik*, 19: 537.

In an attempt to establish the identity of German with American interest and to arouse suspicion in Washington concerning British plans in the Far East, the German chancellor now began to bombard Roosevelt with messages about Britain's alleged desire to establish control over the Yangtse Valley and to exclude foreign commercial interests from the area. Although Roosevelt privately categorized these charges as a "pipe dream" of the kaiser's, Sternburg gained the impression that the president was not unsympathetic and conveyed this in his dispatches to Berlin. As a result, Bülow was soon talking of "the so important relationship of Your Majesty to the American President and the slowly emerging friendly relations of Germany to America," and speculating on the mutual benefits of a defensive alliance, "despite the well-known aversion of the United States to foreign entanglements."[15] To foster this spirit of cooperation, Germany went so far as to accede to a long-standing American request and signed an arbitration treaty on November 22, 1904, despite often expressed misgivings about the desirability of such arrangements. The Senate refused to ratify this and several similar agreements with other countries on the grounds that their provisions did not leave it the ultimate decision on what matters were to be subject to arbitration. It is a significant commentary on the thinking of the Foreign Office at the time, however, that this was the only occasion on which the German Empire ever signed such a treaty.

By January 1905 Bülow saw yet another opportunity for joint action with the United States. More worried than ever that the powers might seek to carve up China at the end of the war, he wrote to Roosevelt: "You should ask all powers having interest in the Far East, including the minor ones, whether they are prepared to give a pledge not to demand any compensation for themselves" when peace comes.[16] The president, delighted to learn that Germany sought no compensation, promptly agreed, and Hay sent a new circular note to that effect on January 10. When France, Britain, and Italy had joined Germany and the United States in accepting the proposal within a week, Bülow was sure his diplomacy had scored another triumph. "It is, after the neutralization of China, the second time within a year," he happily told Sternburg, "that a confidential agreement between Berlin and Washington has proven useful not only for Germany and America, but also for the securing of world

15. Bülow to William II, December 24, 1904, in ibid., 547–548.
16. Bülow to Hilmar von Bussche-Haddenhausen, January 4, 1905, in ibid., 556–557.

peace. This fact will also not have escaped President Roosevelt."[17] At almost the same moment, he first inquired of his chargé d'affaires in Tangier about American commercial interests in Morocco.

When, early in 1905, France began to make use of the free hand given it by Britain in order to establish effective control over the theoretically independent sultanate of Morocco, Germany felt compelled to challenge this move and, with it, the effectiveness of the Entente Cordiale. Although it was the difficult situation of France's ally Russia which led the Germans to believe the moment was propitious for such a challenge, the Foreign Office's expectation of success also stemmed from the belief that it could count on the cooperation of the United States. America was assumed to have a serious interest in Morocco both because it was a signatory of the Madrid Convention of 1880, which dealt with that country, and because of the strong stand it had taken in the Perdicaris affair the previous summer. At that time, the United States had not only dispatched warships into Moroccan waters to secure the release of Ion Perdicaris, who had been captured by the chieftain Raisuli, but, in a resounding telegram to the American consul at Tangier, had demanded "Perdicaris alive or Raisuli dead."[18] Moreover, the Foreign Office reasoned, the cooperation that the United States had manifested in respect to the Open Door in China could easily be extended to Morocco, if the issue there were also to be defined in terms of equal commercial opportunity for all the powers.

On February 24, Bülow made his first attempt to sound out Roosevelt on the Moroccan question. Although the president was noncommittal, the Foreign Office interpreted as signs of decided interest his mild expression of distrust for French motives and the raising of the American consulate in Tangier to the status of a legation. Bülow promptly assured the sultan that both Germany and the United States would support him in efforts to resist pressure from France. At the same time, he explained to Roosevelt that the Far Eastern and Moroccan questions were closely related, and that confidential and altruistic German-American cooperation in both areas was essential to the preservation of world peace. "The President need never fear," he wrote, "that we will attempt to misuse his confidence for unacknowledged purposes of making gains. If ever, in the future, German policy should seek special benefits in a joint

17. Bülow to Sternburg, January 20, 1905, in ibid., 564.
18. Hay to Samuel R. Gummeré, June 22, 1904, in *Foreign Relations, 1904*, p. 503.

diplomatic venture with the United States which are not clearly apparent, we will confidentially inform the President of them from the beginning."[19] Similar messages followed even after Roosevelt told Sternburg the president could do nothing since Congress barely tolerated his actions with regard to the Far East, opposed his moves in Latin America, and would surely be up in arms over any American intervention in Morocco, particularly because of the dubious outcome of the Perdicaris affair. Perdicaris, it turned out, may well not have been a U.S. citizen, and the United States had unwittingly become involved in Raisuli's quarrel with the sultan.

Since the president also told the German ambassador, however, that he valued German-American friendship and even suggested that the kaiser might help in trying to end the Russo-Japanese War, and since German plans for Morocco did not envisage any American action requiring Congressional approval, Bülow was not at all discouraged. Quite the contrary, when the Foreign Office learned in late March that Russia might be interested in an international conference to end the war, it turned immediately to Roosevelt for help in forestalling what it was certain was a new plot to carve up China. Roosevelt shared Germany's opposition to such a conference and made it clear that the United States would not participate. When the scheme subsequently came to nothing, the German chancellor thought he had detected yet a third example of successful German-American cooperation, and he gained renewed confidence in the hope that the matter of Morocco would provide a fourth.

The Moroccan situation reached crisis proportions on March 31, when the kaiser, then on a Meditteranean cruise, was persuaded by Bülow to stop off at Tangier, where he ostentatiously saluted the independence of Morocco. At the same time, Germany proposed an international conference to settle the future of that country. Through these two maneuvers, Germany not only succeeded in emphasizing the urgency of the situation, but also created a possible avenue for the resolution of the crisis which would involve the United States. To the Foreign Office, it seemed a master stroke. A conference on Morocco promised both to curb French pretensions there and to bring Germany out of the international isolation with which it felt itself threatened.

An important element in this reasoning was the role assigned to the United States. Germany could, from the outset, be certain of the

19. Bülow to Sternburg, February 25, 1905, in ibid., p. 578.

support of Austria-Hungary and of the opposition of France and Spain. If the United States were to support the German cause in the name of an Open Door for Morocco, the Foreign Office believed that Great Britain, Italy, and Russia would do likewise. Britain, the Germans were certain, had given France a free hand in Morocco only in return for similar privileges in the Yangtse Valley. Since the American circular note, inspired by Germany, had now effectively ruled out the supposed Yangtse project, the British would no longer be interested in supporting the French in Morocco, particularly not if it meant incurring the enmity of the United States. If Britain would not oppose Germany, Italy would feel free to support it. Russia, in turn, would realize that no acceptable Far Eastern settlement could follow the war it was rapidly losing without the support of Britain, Germany, and the United States, and would therefore also abandon its ally, France. That this analysis, as subsequent events were to show, bore only the most tenuous relation to reality did not deter the Foreign Office from setting the project in motion by bringing further pressure on Roosevelt.

Germany's American overtures had not escaped attention in London, and in February, Edward VII had thought it necessary to write to the president, "contrasting the fickle nature of Germany's friendship with the constancy of England."[20] Roosevelt needed no such reminder. "The Kaiser," he confided to Hay, "has become a monomaniac about getting into communication with me every time he drinks three pen'orth of conspiracy against his life or power." In the Far East, he conceded, William II "at the moment is playing our game," but the Mediteranean was a different story. "We have other fish to fry," he told William Howard Taft, "and have no real interest in Morocco."[21] Nevertheless, he suggested to the British the possibility of a conference on Morocco, though he did not pursue the matter when London failed to respond.

Roosevelt never shared the kaiser's fear of British aims, but he also did not yet believe that Germany had aggressive designs on England which it was likely to turn into a program of action. He therefore saw no reason to join in the games played by these powers and disliked having to choose between them in international disputes. But there was never any doubt what Roosevelt's choice

20. Roosevelt to Hay, February 27, 1905, in Morison et al., *Letters,* 4: 1128.

21. Roosevelt to Hay, April 2, 1905, and to William Howard Taft, April 18, 1905, in ibid., 1157, 1162.

would be if it became necessary to make one. There was much he admired about the kaiser and even more about the German people. "But," as he made clear to the British ambassador, Cecil Spring-Rice, "the German people are too completely under his rule for me to be able to disassociate them from him, and he himself is altogether too jumpy, too volatile in his policies, too lacking in the power of continuous and sustained thought and action for me to feel that he is in any way such a man as for instance [William Howard] Taft or [Elihu] Root. . . . I should never dream of counting on his friendship for this country."[22] Because of the president's attitude and the widespread American distrust of German motives which had prevailed since the Spanish-American War, not even the substantial degree of German-American cooperation which developed in the summer of 1905 would help to bring about the quasi-alliance that Germany clearly sought.

While Germany was busily trying to involve America in the affairs of Morocco, Roosevelt's primary foreign policy interest remained the war in the Far East. In March he had already offered his services to Japan as mediator in trying to arrange a peace conference, even while urging William II to play that role. By the end of April, Japan showed signs of interest. Russia, however, still hoped to turn the tide and was sending its Baltic fleet to the Far East. The kaiser shared that hope and regarded Roosevelt's efforts as premature. He concentrated instead on efforts to get the Morocco conference under way. The battle of Tsushima on May 28, in which the Russian fleet was utterly destroyed, brought both matters suddenly to a head. For Germany, the now clearly demonstrated weakness of France's ally made it imperative that the confrontation over Morocco be precipitated before Russia had a chance to recover. Accordingly, Bülow sent an urgent message to Washington on May 30, urging Roosevelt to support the conference idea. The alternatives, he insisted disingenuously, were either war with France or German adherence to the Franco-Russian alliance. On the very next day Japan, with its military successes at a high but finding the war an increasing economic strain, officially asked for Roosevelt's mediation in bringing about a peace conference.

The president did not yet take the German threat seriously and turned his attention toward persuading Russia to accept a peace conference. Even before he had a chance to approach Saint Peters-

22. Roosevelt to Cecil Spring-Rice, May 13, 1905, in ibid., 1177.

burg formally, however, the kaiser decided to intervene. Convinced now that Russia was thoroughly beaten and fearful that its continuation in the war might topple the tsar and threaten autocracy everywhere, he grasped what he regarded as an opportunity both to cement ties with the United States and to help Russia and himself, and urged the tsar to accept Roosevelt's assistance. "If anybody in the world is able to influence the Japanese or to induce them to be reasonable in their proposals," he assured Nicholas II on June 3, "it is President Rooseveldt [sic]. Should it meet with your approval, I could easily place myself—privately—en rapport with him, as we are very intimate with each other."[23] When the American ambassador delivered Roosevelt's note on June 6, the Russian government had already taken up the matter and was ready with a positive reply. At the same time, however, the Germans did not neglect Morocco. They induced the sultan to invite the signatories of the Madrid Convention of 1880 to a conference, immediately accepted this invitation themselves, and urged the other powers to do likewise. They laid stress in particular on the importance of American participation.

The increasing stridency of German statements on Morocco now, for the first time, began to worry Roosevelt. He did not understand why Germany wanted the conference in the first place, since he could not see what the Germans could realistically hope to gain. But he now became convinced that the Foreign Office was sufficiently serious about the matter to risk war with France, which seemed to him a highly undesirable outcome. Not only would such a war make the settlement of the Far Eastern conflict more difficult and disrupt world trade, it might also result in a German victory and thus destroy the existing balance of power, to the detriment of the United States. The president therefore told Sternburg that America would not participate in a Moroccan conference unless France first agreed to it, but at the same time suggested to the French ambassador, Jules Jusserand, that France should give in, since most of the participants in such a conference, including the United States, would agree to no settlement that did not safeguard France's interests. When Jusserand informed Roosevelt on June 24 that France no longer objected in principle to a conference, Roosevelt took the occasion to congratulate the kaiser on his success in securing French assent.

The kaiser, though flattered, was also perplexed. France had not

23. William II to Nicholas II, June 3, 1905, in *Grosse Politik*, 19: 419–422.

in fact signified its agreement to Germany and the two countries seemed as far apart as ever on the specific issues with which such a conference might deal. Having come this far, however, Roosevelt now pushed with great determination for a final settlement so that he could proceed with arrangements for the Far Eastern peace conference. He informed the Foreign Office that "the French Government has now done what at His Majesty's request I urged should be done," called it a "genuine triumph for the Emperor's diplomacy," and advised Germany not to raise questions about minor details. At the same time he told Sternburg that if Germany simply agreed, the United States would do the same and urge Great Britain to join in. On the sticky matter of the conference program, he had told Jusserand and now told Sternburg: "Let France and Germany go into the conference without any programme or agreement; but to discuss all questions in regard to Morocco, save of course where either is honor bound by a previous agreement with another power."[24] The maneuver worked, and on July 1 Germany and France officially agreed to a conference on these terms.

There can be little doubt that Roosevelt's efforts were made primarily in the interests of peace, secondarily in those of France, and not at all in those of Germany. Jusserand correctly explained to his government that the president had sought to accommodate "l'orgueil de Guillaume II et nos droits,"[25] and Roosevelt himself repeatedly wrote that his basic interest had been the preservation of Anglo-French unity. Indeed the phrase concerning "previous agreement with another power" clearly suggested that Roosevelt accepted the Moroccan provisions of the Entente Cordiale. But from the viewpoint of the German Foreign Office, the president's action represented intervention on behalf of Germany and therefore a genuine triumph of its policy for winning American support. Bülow had already cabled to Washington on June 26 that "Germany's Emperor and Germany's people, both of equally peaceful disposition," would be forever grateful to Roosevelt for saving them from war, and on the following day he gave expression to his faith in Roosevelt's goodwill toward Germany in a message that was as remarkable as it was unwise. "When France has accepted the con-

24. Sternburg to Foreign Office, June 25, 26, and 27, 1905, in *Grosse Politik,* 20: 473–475, 479–481; Roosevelt to Whitelaw Reid, April 28, 1906, in Morison et al., *Letters,* 5: 230–240.
25. Roosevelt to Reid, loc. cit.

ference and we negotiate with the French," he wrote, "if any differences of opinion should arise, I will always be ready to recommend to His Majesty the Emperor, those decisions which President Roosevelt regards as practical and fair."[26] Bülow, to be sure, was talking about the preliminary negotiations that were then in progress. But Sternburg, in translating the message for Roosevelt, went a good deal further. He told the president, in fact, that the kaiser would always support the position that the United States would take on any disputed question at the forthcoming conference.

Roosevelt considered it extraordinary that William II should "instruct his delegates to vote as the United States delegate does on any point where I consider it desirable," and was wary of availing himself of this offer.[27] Certainly he was not swayed by this expression of trust from his basic belief that right in the Moroccan question was on the side of the French. For Germany, however, Roosevelt's efforts to bring about the Moroccan conference that the Foreign Office had sought for so long, combined with the cooperation of the two powers in bringing Russia and Japan to the conference table, seemed incontrovertible proof that it had broken out of its diplomatic isolation by enlisting the aid of the United States. When he concluded his abortive defensive alliance with Nicholas II at Björkö on July 24, the kaiser not only wished to inform Roosevelt at once, he also dreamed of a wider alliance that would include the United States.

German hopes of continuing cooperation with the United States were to receive still further encouragement during the Portsmouth conference over the summer before being rudely, though not finally, shattered in the following year at the Moroccan conference at Algeciras. The Russo-Japanese peace conference, originally scheduled to take place in Washington, had been transferred to the New Hampshire coast owing to the summer heat in the nation's capital. Despite the pleasant surroundings, however, the conference reached a stalemate late in August over Japan's demands for Sakhalin Island, which it had captured during the war, and a large war indemnity. Russia adamantly refused either to pay money or to cede territory, and the conference came close to breaking up. Roosevelt, hoping for a settlement that would keep a balance of power between Russia and Japan in the Far East, was able to persuade Japan to settle for the southern half of Sakhalin and to accept, instead of an

26. Bülow to Sternburg, April 26, 27, 1905, in *Grosse Politik*, 20: 475, 481.
27. Roosevelt to Lodge, July 11, 1905, Morison et al., *Letters*, 4: 1273.

indemnity, compensation from Russia for returning the northern half. But Russia rejected this plan, and Roosevelt was unable to win further concessions from Japan. Confronted with this impasse, the president once more appealed to the kaiser on August 23, assuring him that he would "be rendering a great service to mankind" if he persuaded Russia to accept. William II received this message as he was finishing a letter to Nicholas II, and quickly added a postscript to the desired effect. Five days later, Roosevelt drafted yet another appeal to the kaiser. It was not sent, however, for on August 29, Russia yielded on the matter of South Sakhalin, Japan withdrew its demand for money, and the Treaty of Portsmouth was signed. Roosevelt and the kaiser promptly exchanged telegrams and congratulations.

The happy state of German-American relations, which the kaiser believed had been attained after the signing of the peace treaty, and the high value that the Foreign Office placed on the continuance of that state are well illustrated by a remarkable occurence in September 1905. So certain was William II of his friendship with Roosevelt that he used the occasion of the return of his naval attaché to Washington to send along some pictures as gifts to the Roosevelt children. Included was one entitled "People of Europe, Guard Your Holy Possessions," one of his favorite depictions of the "yellow peril." Moreover, he sent the president a remarkably frank and open personal letter about this alleged danger from the East and urged Roosevelt to do his utmost to counteract it. When the usually subservient Bülow learned of the letter and the "yellow peril" picture, they were already on their way. Nevertheless, he was so concerned that both might offend Roosevelt and that their publication might adversely affect German-American relations, that he went to extraordinary lengths to persuade the kaiser to agree not to have the letter or the picture delivered, and was extremely relieved when his efforts were successful.

It was in the apparent aura of goodwill which followed this high-echelon cooperation that German-American tariff negotiations were resumed. In response to insistent demands by its agricultural producers, Germany had been raising its duties. While special agreements for lower rates had been negotiated with various European countries, there was strong feeling among German officials that the commercial agreement of 1900, which automatically extended such preferential treatment to the United States, should not be renewed.

Neither the Foreign Office nor Roosevelt, however, wanted a new tariff war, which might well follow cancellation of the agreement. The German notice of cancellation, delivered by Sternburg on November 4, 1905, was therefore preceded by an offer to negotiate unresolved differences. With the imminence of the Algeciras conference, at which Germany hoped for American help and the United States, while supporting France, wished to avoid giving offense to Germany, the tariff negotiations proceeded smoothly. Germany consented to extend the lower rates for a year, while the United States revised its customs procedures to permit exporters a greater voice in the valuation given their products for duty purposes. The correspondence accompanying these negotiations was replete with frequent expressions of German-American friendship.

To the dismay of the Foreign Office, however, neither Roosevelt's aid in arranging the Algeciras conference nor the friendliness and willingness to compromise demonstrated in the tariff negotiations was translated into American support for Germany's Moroccan ambitions when the powers convened in southern Spain in January 1906. The key to the discussions there was the control of the Moroccan police. While the American delegation agreed to modifications of the initial French demands both in this matter and in the question of participation in the establishment of a development bank, it never challenged the essentials of the French demand for predominance in Morocco. In the initial vote on the French plan, Great Britain, Russia, Spain, and Portugal supported France, while Italy and the United States abstained. Only Austria and Morocco joined Germany in voting no. Roosevelt then brought forward what he called a compromise proposal. It was, however, a plan that would give France and Spain control over the police and, therefore, effectively over Morocco, and had already been rejected by Bülow for that reason. When Germany balked once more and opted instead for an Austrian plan that would have prevented French hegemony, Roosevelt denounced the Austrian proposal for carving up Morocco into spheres of influence. He reminded the kaiser of Germany's presumed promise of the previous June to support what the United States regarded as practical and fair, and warned him that world opinion would blame Germany if the conference failed to reach an agreement.

Bülow was in a quandary. He realized that without the support of the United States, Germany could not attain its objectives at Algeciras, and Roosevelt's action had made clear that such support would not be forthcoming. The chancellor could either torpedo the conference and come out of it not only emptyhanded but also with the onus for preventing yet another international settlement, or go along with the American proposal by proclaiming it better than the original French plan and thus a victory for German diplomacy. Encouraged by Roosevelt to move in the second direction, he capitulated on March 19. The final agreement, which was signed on April 7, placed the Moroccan police under the command of the sultan and provided for periodic checks by an Italian inspector-general. It also provided for equal participation by the powers in putting up capital for the state bank and contained an agreement by France and Spain that the Open Door in Morocco would be guaranteed. But, as Roosevelt had proposed, it entrusted the training of the Moroccan police—and thereby effective control over the country—to France and Spain.

The Algeciras conference, which Germany had promoted in the expectation that it would lead, in part through the cooperation of the United States, to a break in the diplomatic isolation with which it felt itself threatened, thus served only to demonstrate the degree of that isolation. It showed as well that the German belief in the essential identity of American interests with its own was in error, and that the quasi-alliance for which it had hoped was not likely to materialize. Bülow nevertheless told the Reichstag, that "Germany and America belong to those nations which, both upon natural and historical grounds, should have mutually good relations with each other." He insisted that the United States had "maintained its neutral position throughout" the Algeciras conference, lauded the efforts of Henry White, the chief U.S. delegate, and called the outcome "the second great service which America has rendered to the peace of the world, the first being the reestablishment of peace between Japan and Russia."[28] By contrast, the American press clearly recognized the results at Algeciras as a German defeat and applauded that fact. The Senate even viewed American participation in the conference as a mistake and balked at ratifying the convention that had emerged from it. When Roosevelt pointed out that a refusal to ratify simply meant denying the United States trading privileges in Morocco, the lawmakers conceded, but added that their assent was not to be construed as a departure from traditional American foreign policy.

28. Tower to Root, November 15, 1906, in State Department Numerical File 2883/1057, RG 59, NA.

Despite the fact that German initiatives had prompted American action in both the Far East and the Mediterranean between 1904 and 1906 and that the Foreign Office regarded this interchange as clear evidence of a significant rapprochment, the United States was in no sense ready for the kind of international cooperation which Germany had in mind. Roosevelt's intervention at Algeciras was more sharply criticized by his domestic opponents than any single act of his administration, and both Congress and the public still regarded alignment with any foreign power as clearly contrary to established American policy. Moreover, despite Bülow's herculean efforts and the kaiser's gestures of goodwill, American distrust of Germany had by no means been overcome. It was even heightened when, during the Second Hague Conference in 1907, the Reich was the most intransigent opponent both of international arbitration procedures and of controlled disarmament. These issues were of particular interest to the United States, which had championed arbitration since the days of the post–Civil War Alabama Claims and had accepted the invitation to The Hague only on the condition that it could raise the disarmament question that Germany had successfully kept off the agenda. That Germany's position on both issues was understandable, given its distrust of the other powers and its reliance on military superiority on the Continent, only underscores the absence of any genuine identity of interest with the United States. Nevertheless, yet another effort to bring about at least a tacit German-American alliance was to be made.

The Abortive Far Eastern Accord

The occasion for such a move was once more presented by the situation in the Far East. Although China was never to be carved up among the great powers to the exclusion of Germany, German fears of such a development were heightened in 1907 by a series of international agreements. The Anglo-Japanese alliance of 1902 had been renewed in 1905 and become a permanent feature of the East Asian scene. On June 10, 1907, a Franco-Japanese agreement was concluded, and a Russo-Japanese one on July 30. With France already allied with both Russia and Great Britain, the network was completed with the negotiation of an Anglo-Russian agreement on August 31. German fears of encirclement and exclusion from the Far East reached new heights, and the situation was further complicated by the fact that all of the powers expected the imminent end of the Manchu dynasty to result in new turmoil.

Clearly, from Germany's point of view the only nation to which it could turn was once again the United States. The moment for such an approach seemed extraordinarily propitious. Japanese-American relations had steadily deteriorated since the Portsmouth conference and had reached a low point late in 1906, when the San Francisco school board, reacting to increasing immigration of orientals, provided for school segregation in the city. When Japan protested this action, William II let it be known that he would make a German naval base in the Far East available to the United States in case of war with Japan. Roosevelt succeeded in getting Japan to curb emigration to America in a series of diplomatic notes known as the "Gentlemen's Agreement," and persuaded the San Francisco board to rescind its order. But these efforts to resolve the difficulties made far less of an impression abroad than the evidences of friction and warnings against "the yellow peril," which began to appear with great regularity in the American press. Moreover, the president's decision to send the American battle fleet around the world could only appear as a move to intimidate the Japanese and thus underlined the seriousness of the dispute. Since the United States was also the only other major power to be excluded from the Far Eastern agreements reached in 1907, it seemed the likeliest ally for the German cause.

Almost immediately after the signing of the Anglo-Russian agreement, the German foreign minister raised with Sternburg the possibility of a German-American accord. At the same time, the German ambassador in Peking entered into conversations with the Chinese strongman, General Yuan Shi-kai. Yuan, fearful of Japanese ambitions, expressed interest in agreements with Germany and the United States, and even raised the possibility of a German-American-Chinese alliance. Roosevelt's reaction to such proposals was largely negative, although as usual he was not overly discouraging to Sternburg, but indicated a desire to "go hand in hand" with the kaiser and speculated on the possibility of a U.S.-Japanese war. The Foreign Office thereupon vigorously pursued the matter. When Yuan Shi-kai was appointed foreign minister late in November, discussions were renewed in Peking. By December 30 the kaiser gave enthusiastic approval to a plan for a three-power alliance, to be proposed by China, in which, among other things, the United States and Germany would be granted new commercial privileges. "We can work on Roosevelt through Sternburg," the kaiser told Bülow, "so that when he gets the proposal he will agree to it happily."[29] Bülow, however, vetoed the idea of a formal alliance—the Senate would never approve—and rejected the granting of commercial concessions because they could not be kept secret. But he encouraged Yuan to seek an informal accord through an exchange of notes among the three powers. By January 1908 the Chinese government had decided to send T'ang Shao-yi, the governor of Fengtien, as special envoy to Washington and Berlin, ostensibly to discuss the Boxer indemnity and other financial matters, but probably also to negotiate a German-American-Chinese agreement. The Foreign Office watched with mounting impatience as the plans for the departure of the mission became ensnared in the labyrinth of Chinese bureaucracy, but urged Sternburg to pave the way for the arrival of T'ang in Washington.

Informed of what was to happen, Roosevelt remained publicly noncommittal. The idea of such an accord held little appeal for him, and privately he called the whole scheme impossible. Unbeknown to Germany, the United States had in fact reached basic agreement with Japan concerning the Far East during the Taft-Katsura talks in Tokyo in July 1905. The President was certain that new discussions with the Japanese would serve American interests far better than would laying down a challenge to the island empire through an alliance with a weak and disintegrating China and a Germany whose reliability Roosevelt came increasingly to doubt during the spring and summer of 1908.

At least three incidents during this time led the president to question ever more strongly the wisdom of doing business with Germany and its erratic ruler. Roosevelt had long been unhappy with his ambassador in Berlin, Charlemagne Tower, and in late 1907 had arranged to replace him with David Jayne Hill, then in the Netherlands. The Foreign Office had given its approval for the change on November 6, and the Hill nomination was awaiting Senate approval when, on March 21, 1980, Tower cabled from Berlin: "The German Emperor has expressed the hope that the President will not appoint David Jayne Hill as Ambassador to Germany when this post shall become vacant. The Emperor has had an unfavorable personal opinion of Mr. Hill which dates from the visit of Prince Henry to

29. William II to Bülow, December 30, 1907, in *Grosse Politik*, 25: 88.

America."[30] Roosevelt was annoyed at the emperor's tactlessness and incensed at Tower, who had somehow leaked the story to the press, creating a great uproar. It hardly helped matters when a series of fumbling statements by the Foreign Office made it apparent that it had forgotten its earlier approval of the Hill appointment. Although the matter was smoothed over and Hill was courteously received by the kaiser when he assumed his duties in June, the incident did not further the cause of German-American understanding. Neither was Roosevelt's estimate of William's political acumen raised when he began to receive letters from the emperor warning him that Japanese soldiers—disguised as farmers(!)—were massing in Mexico with the intention of attacking the Panama Canal in the event of war.

The final cause for concern came in August, when Oscar King Davis of the *New York Times* arrived at the White House seeking guidance about an interview that the kaiser had granted William Bayard Hale. William II, at his most expansive, had not only expressed his dislike of Roosevelt's chosen successor, William Howard Taft, and attacked American Catholics in general and Archbishop John Ireland in particular, but had stated flatly that Germany would soon go to war with England, which had betrayed the white race through its treaty with Japan. Moreover, he had told Hale that he had arranged with the United States to back China against Japan in order to maintain the equilibrium in the Far East, and that a Chinese statesman was on his way to Washington to arrange details. A sobered Roosevelt asked the *Times* not to print the interview and thus prevented such a scandal as was to occur on October 28, when the London *Daily Telegraph* printed another interview with the kaiser, one different in content but similar in tone. Roosevelt also wrote to Ambassador Arthur Lee in England that he was no longer so certain that British fears of the kaiser were exaggerated and asked Lee to communicate this change of heart to Lord Balfour and Sir Edward Grey. Moreover, he asked Secretary of State Elihu Root to continue his conversations with the Japanese ambassador Kogoro Takahira, with the view of resolving the outstanding differences between the two countries.

T'ang, meanwhile, had finally left Peking, but had only reached San Francisco when, on November 21, the State Department sent to Tokyo, Peking, Saint Petersburg, Paris, London, and Berlin the

30. Tower to Root, March 21, 1908, in State Department Numerical File 5515/309, RG 59, NA.

advance text of the Root-Takahira agreements, which were to be published the following week. Tokyo, of course, already knew their contents, and London, Paris, and Saint Petersburg could not have been more delighted. But the situation was different in Peking and Berlin. In a stiff and formal note, the German Foreign Office announced its agreement with the principles expressed and its gratitude for having been informed prior to publication. But it could not fail to see the very existence of the agreement as a blow to German hopes. To the utter amazement of the American ambassador in Peking, Yuah Shi-kai displayed irritation and disappointment when informed of what was, after all, a new guarantee of the territorial integrity of China and expressed the opinion that the United States should have awaited the arrival of T'ang before taking such a step. Within twenty-four hours, however, Yuan accepted the inevitable with as much grace as he could muster. Nevertheless he ordered T'ang to proceed at once to Washington, and told Ambassador William W. Rockhill that he hoped "the Government of the United States will listen in a friendly manner to what the Special Envoy may wish to communicate." "No explanation is given for this remark," added Rockhill, who had no idea of the real nature of the T'ang mission.[31]

The formal signing of the Root-Takahira agreement was delayed until T'ang's arrival in Washington on November 30. The Chinese envoy was shown the document before signing and was treated with special consideration by both Root and Roosevelt. But such overtures as he made were politely rejected. It was one of the first tasks of the new German ambassador, Count Johann von Bernstorff—Sternburg had died of cancer in August—to inform Bülow that the United States could not agree to the plans of the German government because China was too weak, an agreement with it would have meant war with Japan, and American public opinion would not have supported a war in the Far East.

Calm before the Storm

With the failure to obtain a Far Eastern accord, the German courtship of the United States, which had been sustained for the better part of a decade, effectively came to an end. But despite Germany's

31. William W. Rockhill to Root, November 25, December 3, 1908, in ibid., 16533/14 and 46.

lack of success in its efforts to involve America in the European alliance system and despite the new doubts in Roosevelt's mind of German intentions, relations between the two countries had, at least outwardly, attained a level of serenity unequaled since the 1870s. Roosevelt, as his term of office came to a close, sent an effusive farewell letter to the kaiser in December 1908, and not long thereafter appeared in Berlin, where William ostentatiously and publicly called him "my friend." The University of Berlin awarded him an honorary degree and set up a Roosevelt Professorship to further German-American friendship. Columbia's Germanophile political scientist John W. Burgess became its first holder. In 1911 the United States reciprocated the kaiser's earlier gift of a statue of Frederick the Great with a likeness of Baron von Steuben, and the dispatches of Ambassador von Bernstorff were filled with accounts of friendliness and goodwill.

Only the issue of an arbitration treaty, which the United States at that time attempted to negotiate with all of the powers, raised actual difficulties. Despite the strenuous efforts of both Root and Roosevelt and the appeal of Ambassador Hill that "the moral isolation of Germany in the society of sovereign states now striving to organize international justice . . . might be a worse calamity than the sacrifice of some of the purely theoretical inequalities,"[32] the legal experts of the Foreign Office refused assent to a treaty that would leave the final decision on any proposed arbitration to the United States Senate and that failed to include a provision for German claims against individual American states. With monotonous regularity, the German negotiators brought up the case of the Brunswick & Albany Railroad, whose bonds had been guaranteed by the Reconstruction legislature of Georgia in 1869, sold to German investors, and then repudiated in 1877 when the departure of Federal troops brought a change in the state's government. Neither persuasion by the United States nor the advice of Bernstorff served to overcome such objections. Germany remained the only major power with whom no arbitration treaty was negotiated before the outbreak of the First World War.

In the area of commercial relations, however, Germany proved far more accommodating. Although the Imperial government's successful efforts to prevent a group of American firms from circumventing the monopoly of the German potash syndicate muddied the

32. Hill to Root, June 23, 1908, in ibid., 11313/7.

waters for a time, substantial agreements were reached in other areas. A patent convention, which had been sought by the United States for decades, was concluded on February 1, 1909, and the following year complex negotiations produced concord on the thorny tariff issue. America's new Payne-Aldrich Tariff was, from the German viewpoint, even worse than the one it replaced, and Germany's trade balance with the United States was increasingly negative. Still, Germany agreed to continue the preferential rates on agricultural products which the United States had heretofore enjoyed and even to dispense with the demand for microscopic inspection of imported pork products in return merely for the application to Germany of the Payne-Aldrich Tariff's "minimum rates." President Taft duly proclaimed them to be in effect on March 11, 1910.

In the Far East, meanwhile, Secretary of State Philander C. Knox's policy of "dollar diplomacy" found its most consistent friend in the German government. Only Germany supported his plan for an international consortium to operate the railroads of Manchuria, and when that project failed of approval by the other powers, was instrumental in bringing American bankers into the syndicate for railroad construction in the Yangtse Valley. "The Imperial Government...," the Foreign Office informed the State Department, "sees in this a new guarantee for the policy of the Open Door, which the Imperial Government has always followed, and in which it has concurred repeatedly with the aims of American policy."[33]

To be sure, such economic cooperation produced no political results. When the outbreak of the Chinese revolution of 1911 once more raised German fears that the partition of the ancient empire was imminent, the German Foreign Minister approached Knox with the suggestion for a new note on the subject of territorial integrity. The United States did not respond, preferring to place its faith in the hope that quick recognition of the new republic would be a sufficient guarantee of future stability in the area. But political cooperation, which had never been desired by the United States on more than an ad hoc basis, was also no longer high on the list of priorities of the Foreign Office.

With the departure of Roosevelt from the presidency and the almost simultaneous dismissal of Bülow from the chancellorship, the principal participants in the earlier courtship were gone. The dollar diplomacy of the Taft administration was specifically intended as a

33. Wilhelm Eduard von Schoen to Hill, June 15, 1909, in ibid., 5315/309.

substitute for political and military action, and thus was even less likely than earlier policies to lead to intergovernmental commitments. And, too, Germany was increasingly involved in the problems of the Balkans and the Middle East, areas in which the United States could not, even by the widest stretch of the imagination, be regarded as having an interest. When Woodrow Wilson abandoned even dollar diplomacy and concentrated the full efforts of his administration on an ambitious program of domestic reform, America's direct relations with the world in general, and therefore also with Germany, receded to the level of activity shown prior to the Spanish-American war. It was to be the calm before the storm.

Chapter 4

THE ROAD TO WAR

*

The Submarine Issue: Phase I

During the crucial years from 1912 to 1914, as the European states moved at a precipitous pace toward war, the United States remained more aloof from their quarrels than at any time since the beginning of the century. President Wilson, elected as a domestic reformer, concentrated his energies during his first year in office almost entirely on his legislative program. When he did turn to matters outside the nation's borders, his attention remained focused on Mexico. There he responded to revolutionary upheavals that threatened American economic interests with a policy of nonrecognition and "watchful waiting." Wilson's secretary of state, William Jennings Bryan, was a near-pacifist whose formula for the preservation of peace was the negotiation of so-called "cooling-off" treaties, and who had neither an interest in nor an understanding for European power politics.

The only member of the Wilson administration to manifest early concern with the larger aspects of world diplomacy was the president's personal adviser, Colonel Edward M. House. In May 1914 the escalation of the European arms race led House to undertake the first of his trips to major world capitals in the interest of preserving, and later of restoring, peace. The object of this trip, he explained, was "to bring about a sympathetic understanding between England, Germany, and the United States, not only upon the question of disarmament, but upon other matters of equal importance to themselves and to the world at large."[1]

House arrived in Berlin on May 25, and exchanged views amicably but ineffectively with the kaiser, as well as with numerous high-ranking officials, including Arthur Zimmermann, then undersecretary of the Foreign Office. He proceeded from there via Paris to London, where he was when the murder of the Austrian archduke Francis Ferdinand precipitated the crisis that was to bring on the world war. On July 18, 1914, House sent a flattering message to William II, urging him to use his influence to preserve the peace. The kaiser's defensive reply did not come until August 1. By then the war that was to change the face of the world and to put unprecedented strains on the relations between Germany and the United States was for all intents and purposes already under way.

On August 4 President Wilson responded to the outbreak of war in Europe by issuing the first of what would become ten separate proclamations of neutrality. Two weeks later he declared that the United States must be neutral "in fact as well as in name" and told the American people that they "must be impartial in thought as well as in action, must put a curb upon . . . sentiments as well as upon every transaction that might be construed as a preference of one party to the struggle before another."[2] That advice, whatever may have been its wisdom, proved impossible to follow. The course of American development and the alterations in the world power balance which, before the outbreak of war, had drawn the United States closer to Great Britain were not negated by the beginning of hostilities. To be sure, the exigencies of war were soon to place strains on Anglo-American friendship. But the established patterns of American trade which favored Great Britain and its allies, America's cultural affinity for the democracies, and British control of the seas made it virtually inevitable that even a neutral United States would prove helpful to the Allied cause. With equal inevitability, these factors would lead to serious difficulties with Germany.

Germany, however, was initially prepared to accept American neutrality at face value, and worked energetically for a time to preserve it. It asked the United States to represent its interests in Brit-

1. Edward M. House to Walter Hines Page, January 4, 1914, in Burton J. Hendrick, *The Life and Letters of Walter Hines Page*, 3 vols. (Garden City, N.Y., 1922–1925), 1:281.

2. Woodrow Wilson, speech of August 19, 1914, in *Foreign Relations of the United States: Diplomatic Papers, 1914, Supplement*, p. 552.

ain, France, and Russia and was pleased when the U.S. agreed to do so. Germany was even more pleased when the State Department on August 6 asked all belligerents to adhere to the narrow definition of contraband contained in the Declaration of London of 1909, and promptly signified its agreement to that principle. The Foreign Office also moved to establish the German Information Service in New York as a propaganda agency. Headed by Bernhard Dernburg, a former colonial minister who had come to America at the outbreak of the war as representative of the German Red Cross, the agency issued daily news summaries to the American press and provided speakers and articles that reflected the German point of view. It supported George Sylvester Viereck's pro-German weekly, *The Fatherland,* and ultimately also acquired both the *International Monthly* and the New York *Evening Mail* in order to assure Germany of a fair hearing.

The activities of the German Information Service, combined with individual efforts by German political and religious leaders who bombarded American publications with letters and articles throughout 1914, were undertaken in the expectation that they would balance out the effects of British propaganda and hold the United States to its determination to remain neutral. "The people of the United States," Chancellor Theobald von Bethmann Hollweg told the readers of *World's Work* in January 1915, "will best serve the cause of peace and humanity by being not only neutral according the letter of President Wilson's proclamation, but also impartial in the spirit of his further utterances." By contrast, a statement by the British foreign secretary, Sir Edward Grey, in the same issue asked the United States to use its influence on the side of right—that is, of Great Britain.[3]

Such efforts, though they were conducted with skill and perseverance, were doomed to failure almost from the outset. The specter of German militarism and autocracy, which had formed an important part of the American image of Germany since the turn of the century, grew to gigantic proportions as reports of the "rape" of Belgium and the enormous initial successes of the German army reached the United States, largely through British channels. The neutrality of thought for which the president had asked became harder and harder to maintain. If the public soon became worried

3. "How Can the U.S. Best Serve Civilization," *World's Work,* 29 (January 1915): 245–252.

about the effects a German victory might have on the United States, so did the American government. Of the leading figures in the administration, only Bryan, who in September 1914 concluded his cherished "cooling-off" treaties with Great Britain, France, and Russia and tried desperately to conclude one with Germany as well, was genuinely neutral. His undersecretary, Robert Lansing, was predisposed toward the Allies from the beginning, though he struggled for a time to keep an open mind and was determined to abide by the letter of the law in regard to neutrality and neutral rights. Colonel House shared Lansing's views up to a point, but believed even more clearly that close cooperation with the Allies was essential and eventual conflict with Germany probable. Even Wilson, though firm in his desire to keep the country out of war, was fearful of a German victory almost from the beginning. "If they succeed," he told the British ambassador only a month after the outbreak of war, "we shall be forced to take such measures of defense here, as would be fatal to our form of government and American ideals."[4]

Given such attitudes, it was almost a foregone conclusion that the United States would be far less critical of British than of German actions that affected American commerce and, conversely, far more reluctant to adopt a hard line toward the Allies than toward the Reich. Evidence of this fact was not slow in coming. In reply to the American note of August 6, Britain issued an Order in Council which made major modifications in the rules on contraband and blockade contained in the Declaration of London. By greatly expanding the list of contraband articles, neutral trade with Germany would be reduced and the blockade made a more effective weapon. France and Russia followed the British example, while Germany, which had already accepted the American proposal, protested at once. Although Lansing at first called the Allied modification unacceptable, the United States withdrew its insistence on the Declaration of London as early as October 24, and thereafter based its claims on the far vaguer general concept of international law.

This action constituted perhaps the only practical course the United States could follow, but it was representative of a host of decisions that worked, however unintentionally, to the detriment of Germany. By January 1915 the chairman of the Foreign Relations

4. Spring-Rice to Sir Edward Grey, September 3, 1914, in George M. Trevelyan, *Grey of Fallodon* (London, 1937), pp. 355, 356.

Committee, Senator William J. Stone of Missouri, could list in a letter to Bryan twenty ways in which American actions seemed to display favoritism of the Allies. Included were not only such matters as American submission to British violations of the rules of absolute and conditional contraband and to the search of American vessels for German and Austrian nationals, but also the seemingly discriminatory application of regulations dealing with coaling rights in the Canal Zone and the use of U.S. ports by foreign vessels. British warships, Stone charged, had been permitted to lie off American ports, where they sometimes had been secretly—and illegally—provisioned. The regulations on loans had been changed to make it easier for Britain to acquire supplies here, and the United States had submitted to British censorship of mail to this country. It had also allowed cable communication with Great Britain to remain uncensored, while strictly monitoring the wireless communication on which Germany depended for its contacts with the United States. Although Bryan denied some of these allegations and sought to explain away others, he conceded the unfavorable effect on Germany produced by the simple fact that Great Britain controlled the seas. By the following month, German dispatches from the front were recording the capture of weapons made in America.

The outbreak of war, of course, produced a multitude of points of contact and friction between the United States and Germany on matters as diverse as the internment of German vessels in Honolulu, the continuing import of cyanides and dyestuffs, and the fate of American citizens stranded in the Reich. But the major dealings between the two countries in the years from 1914 and 1917 revolved around two issues: the efforts of the Wilson administration to act as peacemaker, and the German counterefforts to the British blockade.

On August 4, 1914, even before England had declared war, President Wilson offered his services as peacemaker under the provisions of Article 3 of the Hague Convention. In response, all of the powers concerned expressed their interest in peace but continued their preparations for war. William II, in a long and confused message, absolved himself of all the responsibility for the war but did not even refer to Wilson's offer. Nevertheless, Washington remained undaunted. On September 6 Oscar Straus, the former ambassador to Turkey, appeared at the house of the secretary of state with the news that Ambassador von Bernstorff, at a private dinner the previous night, had seemed receptive to a suggestion for renewed mediation efforts. Bryan at once instructed James W. Gerard, a New York lawyer and power in the Democratic party of that state, whom Wilson had chosen as ambassador to Germany, to take up the matter with the Foreign Office. Bernstorff had agreed to the suggestion only because he realized that peace sentiment was running high in the United States and that public opinion would surely turn against the country that, by first rejecting peace feelers, would appear to favor prolonging the war. The Foreign Office, less attuned to American opinion and fully aware that the German public had scant interest in peace without victory, showed little hesitation in saying no. Undersecretary Zimmermann informed Gerard that Germany would agree to mediation only if such a request came from its enemies. The same point was raised in the official reply of the German chancellor. "If we accept America's mediation offer now," Bethmann Hollweg insisted, "it would be understood by our enemies as a sign of weakness and not understood by our people at all. . . ."[5]

Despite the fact that equally discouraging replies were received in response to soundings in London and Paris, American peace efforts did not come to an end. Wilson, however, now placed the responsibility for these efforts in the hands of Colonel House, and House was far less sanguine than Bryan about the possibilities for immediate results. His initial scheme was to bring about a meeting among the British, French, and German ambassadors in Washington. To this Bernstorff, despite the absence of any encouragement from Berlin, readily agreed, but Spring-Rice, the next to be contacted, adamantly refused. While Bernstorff and other German propagandists in the United States continued to insist, both publicly and privately, that Germany wanted peace, the British let it be known that they would regard further mediation attempts by the United States as an unfriendly act.

The truth, of course, was that neither side was prepared to end the war without being able to show substantial gains from its efforts, and that no agreement between them could be reached on that basis. As 1914 drew to a close, House was rapidly reaching this conclusion and was prepared to drop his efforts. Certainly he was anxious to avoid friction with Great Britain, and he had little reason to believe that Germany would prove genuinely receptive. But just at this

5. James W. Gerard to William Jennings Bryan, September 14, 1914, in *Foreign Relations, 1914, Supplement*, p. 104.

point, the American peace effort was revived by encouraging news from Berlin.

Soon after the outbreak of war, House had received a note from Zimmerman expressing disappointment that the colonel's efforts to preserve the peace had failed. In reply, House had once more offered his services as mediator. Had this letter arrived in Berlin in early September, it presumably would have been regarded as part of the offer that Gerard communicated to the Foreign Office at that time, and probably would have produced the same negative reply. The vagaries of wartime communications delayed the arrival of the letter until October 20, however, and at that juncture it appeared as a new proposal coming directly from President Wilson. The German chancellor was now in something of a quandary. "We must avoid the appearance of being on principle for a continuation of the war à outrance," he confided to the Austrian foreign minister. "On the other hand, I have no hope of success from American interposition."[6] His solution was to let Zimmerman send an encouraging reply which, without committing Germany to anything, expressed a willingness to have House continue his explorations "in the other camp."

Despite strenuous efforts by Sir Edward Grey to prevent House from pursuing the matter—the military fortunes of the Allies were at a low ebb and no good results could be expected from negotiations—and despite the failure of the Germans to give any indication of the specific terms they might consider as the basis for mediation, the colonel left for England aboard the *Lusitania* on January 30, 1915. The six weeks House spent in London were marked by two developments that were to shape the future course of German-American relations. On the one hand, the president's emissary became convinced in the course of his conversations with Grey, with other British officials, and with the Anglophile American ambassador, Walter Hines Page, that peace on German terms would be detrimental not only to the Allies but also to the United States. Given the Germans' advantageous military position, further efforts of mediation would therefore have to await the Allied military successes that were expected in the spring of 1915. Wilson approved this assessment and agreed to be guided by House's judgment. In so

6. Theobald von Bethmann Hollweg to Count Leopold Berchtold, November 23, 1914, quoted in Ernest R. May, *Imperial Democracy* (New York, 1961), p. 108.

doing, he departed from a stance of strict impartiality and thus reduced his chances of effectively acting as mediator.

At virtually the same time, Germany reached the conclusion that countermeasures against both the British blockade and the swelling stream of supplies reaching England from beyond the Atlantic were urgently required. The idea originated with the German navy, which had been both surprised and delighted when its submarines sank a number of British warships in fall 1914. Within a matter of months, grandiose speculations on the possible effectiveness of a U-boat campaign circulated within the government and found their way into the press through interviews given by Admiral von Tirpitz and others. With the German armies now bogged down in the west and encouraging news from the fronts notable by its absence, the chimera of victory beneath the seas caught the imagination of the German public.

Opposition to the idea came largely from the Foreign Office and the chancellor. As late as December 27, Bethmann Hollweg composed a lengthy position paper opposing submarine attacks on merchant shipping. Although his major objections were to the possible effects of such a policy on Italy and other South European neutrals and on the eventual postwar settlement with England, the position of the United States also influenced his thinking. "Although America, because of insufficient armed forces, can hardly declare war against us," he wrote, "it is nevertheless in a position to impose a trade boycott against us, just like England, and to carry on the delivery of war materials to our enemies, something that President Wilson now opposes, more or less officially."[7] On January 9, 1915, Bethmann was still able to persuade William II to resist the navy's blandishments, but by the end of the month, faced by diminishing support in both the Reichstag and the press, he gave in. With the emperor's approval, the admiralty on February 4 proclaimed a war zone around the British Isles in which all enemy merchant ships would be sunk without warning and all neutral vessels traveled at their peril.

The explanatory memorandum that German Foreign Secretary Gottlieb von Jagow sent to the neutral powers was moderate in tone, and as a result the originally proposed American protest note was considerably toned down. The United States nevertheless still called

7. Bethmann Hollweg, position paper, September 27, 1914, in Alfred von Tirpitz, *Politische Dokumente*, 2 vols. (Berlin, 1924–1926), 2:293.

any possible sinking of American vessels "an indefensible violation of neutral rights which it would be very hard indeed to reconcile with the friendly relations now so happily subsisting between the two Governments," and promised to hold the Imperial government "to a strict accountability for such acts of their naval authorities."[8] The American note produced renewed soul-searching in Berlin and revived the argument between the Foreign Office, which did not wish to alienate the United States, and the navy, which chafed at the thought of possible restrictions on its activities. For the time being, the diplomats prevailed.

Although the specific guarantees for American shipping which the Foreign Office had been prepared to offer were dropped from the German draft reply at the insistence of the admirals, Jagow's answer to Bryan was both temperate and conciliatory in tone. The foreign secretary insisted that Germany was acting in self-defense and could assume no responsibility for "unfortunate accidents" that might occur, but offered to reconsider the entire policy if the United States could persuade Britain to allow food and other nonmilitary supplies to reach Germany. When the United States agreed to attempt to do so, the German Admiralty Order of February 18, which had called for the beginning of "commercial warfare with U-boats," was amended to include the reminder to submarine captains that "in view of the difficult political relationship with the United States and Italy in regard to American and Italian vessels, the greatest care must be used to avoid the unintentional sinking of these vessels."[9]

The secrecy in which the struggle within the German government were shrouded and the incompetence of Ambassador Gerard left Washington almost totally unaware that Germany was by no means impervious to the wishes of the United States, and that those most concerned with maintaining amicable relations including the Imperial chancellor, still had the ear of the emperor. As a result, Wilson acquiesced far too readily in the British decision to strike no bargain with Germany at all but rather to use the German declaration of February 4 as an excuse to stop all neutral trade with Germany. The announcement of this policy in Parliament on March 1, and its official proclamation by an Order in Council on March 11, were

8. Bryan to Gerard, February 10, 1915, in *Foreign Relations, 1915, Supplement*, p. 99.

9. Admiralty Order of February 22, 1915, in Arno Spindler, ed., *Der Handelskrieg mit U-Booten*, 5 vols. (Berlin, 1932–1941), I:138–139.

accepted by House, who was still in London, and by Wilson. Both falsely assumed that submarine warfare was a fact, rather than an ineffective plan still opposed in the highest circles of the German government, and that the new British policy was therefore necessary to bring about the favorable military balance on which they rested their hopes for eventual successful peace mediation.

When House arrived in Berlin on March 19, on the second leg of his ostensible mediation mission, he no longer talked of immediate peace negotiations at all, much to the relief of Bethmann and Zimmermann, who were no more willing than Grey had been to acquaint the American emissary with their actual war aims. In more than a week of extended conversations House also did not mention the submarine issue or the British blockade. Instead, he confined himself to generalities and so hoped to maintain a working relationship with the German officials which would prove useful at some future time—one that the United States, and the British, would consider right for talking peace. Just as House's amiability in London had helped to convince the British that the United States would adopt a tolerant attitude toward further violations of neutrality, so his amiability in Berlin somewhat calmed the Foreign Office's fears concerning American reaction to submarine warfare and weakened its position vis-à-vis the admirals.

The American reply to the British order in Council, far from being a vigorous protestation, showed understanding for the British position. The U.S. merely reserved its right to trade with European neutrals and to seek future compensation from any damage done to American shipping by the new British policy. Submarine warfare by Germany now became a certainty. Not only did the publication of the American note in Berlin on April 7 produce a "hate America" campaign in the press, it also weakened the position of the moderates in the Wilhelmstrasse and strengthened the arguments of the navy that restrictions on its submarine commanders should be removed. Its release in the United States had already moved Bernstorff to deliver to the State Department a blistering memorandum in which he expressed his belief that "the United States Government acquiesces in the violations of international law by Great Britain." The United States, he insisted, must curb its munitions industry and embargo arms exports if it wished to live up to not only the "formal aspect" but also the "spirit" of its neutrality declaration.[10]

10. Bernstorff to Bryan, April 4, 1915, in *Foreign Relations, 1915, Supplement*, p. 157.

Nevertheless, the adverse results were not immediate. Germany was certainly still anxious to avoid needlessly offending the United States and, in any case, had a submarine fleet too small—only twenty-one U-boats had been built and fewer than half of those were at sea at any given time—to make its campaign effective even against enemy vessels. And the United States had not yet determined the degree of "accountability" to which it intended to hold the Reich. Both the death of the first American, when the British liner *Falaba* was torpedoed, and the first, presumably inadvertent, attacks on American vessels produced only a mild response in Washington, which seemed satisfied when the Foreign Office expressed regrets and agreed to pay damages. Then, on May 7, a German U-boat sank the great British liner *Lusitania,* resulting in the loss of 1,198 lives, including 270 women and 94 children. Of the victims 124 were American citizens.

The sinking of the *Lusitania* had a profound effect on American attitudes. Not only had a substantial number of U.S. citizens become war casualties, but the attack on an unarmed passenger liner, albeit one carrying contraband, seemed a new example of German barbarism and inhumanity. For many whose sentiments had always been on the side of Britain, the issue now became one of preserving civilization and thus a duty that the United States could not long evade. For others, the last vestiges of "neutrality of thought" simply vanished. All German efforts to explain and excuse the incident, to shift the blame to the British, who had allowed the *Lusitania* to carry war material, or to those Americans who had insisted on sailing on the vessel despite a warning from the German embassy, fell on deaf ears. Bernhard Dernburg, the chief German propagandist in America, found his position wholly untenable and was sent out of the country to avoid having the American government ask for his recall. "We might as well admit openly," Bernstorff dejectedly informed Bethmann Hollweg, "that our propaganda here has *collapsed completely* under the impact of the Lusitania incident."[11]

The American protest note to Berlin was diplomatic in tone and referred to the "special ties of friendship" between the two countries and to the provisions of the treaty of 1828. But it concluded in sterner tones with the demand that Germany give up its submarine war on merchant shipping:

11. Bernstorff to Bethmann Hollweg, May 17, 1915, quoted in Arthur S. Link, *Wilson* (Princeton, N.J., 1947–1965), vol. 3, *The Struggle for Neutrality, 1914–1915,* 378. Original emphasis.

Expressions of regret and offers of reparation in case of the destruction of neutral ships sunk by mistake, while they may satisfy international obligations, if no loss of life results, can not justify or excuse a practice, the natural and necessary effect of which is to subject neutral nations and neutral persons to new and immeasurable risks.

The Imperial German Government will not expect the Government of the United States to omit any word or any act necessary to the performance of its sacred duty of maintaining the rights of the United States and its citizens and of safeguarding their free exercise and enjoyment.[12]

Neither this note nor Bernstorff's dispatches led the Foreign Office to suspect that a serious crisis had developed. Indeed, the almost simultaneous proposal by Colonel House that Britain consider allowing food shipments to Germany through neutral countries in return for the abandonment of both submarine warfare and the use of poison gas seemed to suggest that the proper answer to the American note was evasion and a play for time. Bethmann nevertheless recognized that the continued sinking of neutral vessels and of passenger liners involved grave risks for Germany and he persuaded the kaiser to issue new and secret orders to the navy cautioning against both.

The second American *Lusitania* note, which was sent on June 9, occasioned the resignation of Secretary of State Bryan and his replacement by Robert Lansing, but in essence did little more than insist once again that Germany abandon submarine warfare on humanitarian grounds or face unspecified consequences. Nevertheless, it served to renew the struggle between the navy and the Foreign Office over the future of German policy. The result was a compromise. Germany did not relinquish its right to conduct submarine warfare, but offered to take special precautions to guarantee the safety of American ships and of American citizens traveling on neutral vessels. If not enough neutral ships were available to carry American passengers, the German reply concluded, four enemy liners would be allowed to sail for the duration of the war under the American flag. This arrangement, which had been worked out in Berlin with the assistance of Ambassador Gerard, seemed to Bethmann the limit to which he could push the navy without risking mounting public opposition and the constant diminution of his in-

12. Bryan to Gerard, May 13, 1915, in *Foreign Relations, 1915, Supplement,* p. 396.

fluence on the kaiser. Given Gerard's role in its formulation, it seemed also the basis for reaching a modus vivendi with the United States.

Wilson recognized that the German note made concessions to American interests, but he was also aware that it did not yield on matters of principle and he was not prepared to accept it as final. As a concession to Germany he dropped his previous insistence on the complete abandonment of submarine warfare, but demanded that submarines should henceforth follow the established rules of cruiser warfare. These prohibited, among other things, the sinking of passenger-carrying vessels without warning. The third *Lusitania* note, which promulgated this new American position, began by calling the German reply "very unsatisfactory" and concluded with a reassertion of neutral rights and the threat "that repetition by the commanders of German naval vessels of acts in contravention of those rights must be regarded by the Government of the United States, when they affect American citizens, as deliberately unfriendly."[13]

William II was angered by this note and the German press began to talk of the threat of war. Bernstorff's dispatches, however, clearly indicated that Wilson, if not Lansing, had meant to be conciliatory and fully intended to press Britain on the issue of neutral rights once he regarded the *Lusitania* affair as settled. Bethmann, acting on his ambassador's advice, left the note unanswered, but indicated in the matter of the *William F. Frye,* an American merchantman that had been torpedoed earlier, that Germany was prepared to pay damages according to the rules of cruiser warfare. He even hinted that Germany might be willing to submit to arbitration the question of indemnity for the loss of American life on the *Lusitania.*

By the middle of 1915, therefore, German-American relations seemed to have weathered their greatest storm. The Foreign Office had not only succeeded in limiting German submarine warfare so as to minimize the chance for incidents, it had also succeeded through its various notes in convincing the United States that it intended to honor American wishes at least to some extent and to respect the rights of neutrals. And it retained the support of the emperor for this course. In the United States, meanwhile, excitement over the *Lusitania* was dying down, and sober second thoughts concerning

13. Lansing to Gerard, July 21, 1915, in ibid., pp. 480, 482.

the undesirable possibility of war were finding their way with greater and greater frequency into the press. Yet, in a matter of weeks, the new calm in relations was shattered and months of diplomatic maneuvering undone by the almost simultaneous revelation of German espionage and sabotage efforts in the United States and the sinking of the British liner *Arabic,* in which forty-four persons, including two Americans, lost their lives.

In mid-August, the publication in the New York *World* of documents taken from a briefcase left on an elevated train by Heinrich F. Albert, commercial attaché in the German embassy, caused a sensation and stirred up a wave of anti-German sentiment. Although they revealed no indictable violations of American law, the documents, given to the *World* by Treasury Secretary William Gibbs MacAdoo on condition that their source not be revealed, gave evidence of widespread German activities designed to slow down the flow of arms to the Allies and to create a climate favorable to the Reich.

Meanwhile, the British arrested Commander Franz Rintelen of the German admiralty's intelligence staff, who had just completed a most secret assignment in the United States. At the time of Rintelen's arrest, his presence and the full extent of his activities in America were just becoming known to Washington. Acting as a kind of superagent, well endowed with both connections and funds, the dashing German naval officer had in fact worked to organize a conspiracy to cut the Saint Lawrence River route to the Midwest by blowing up the Welland Canal and to establish facilities for the manufacture of time bombs to be used in destroying war supplies destined for the Allies. He had also formed a union of longshoremen and engineered a brief strike in protest of the loading of munitions ships, and had spent $12 million in an attempt to finance a Mexican counterrevolution that, he hoped, would bring about hostilities between the United States and Mexico. The activities of Rintelen, even more than those of Albert, seemed to point to the existence of a large German subversive apparatus in the United States. They cast new suspicions on the activities of Ambassador von Bernstorff, who had earlier been involved in the issuance of false passports to German officers seeking to return to their homeland and perhaps also in attempts to have German naval vessels on the high seas supplied from the United States.

Wilson had already expressed his concern to House that "the country is honeycombed with German intrigue and infested with

German spies," and New York newspapers had condemned "the meanness and treachery of the spy system,"[14] when the *Arabic* was torpedoed on August 19. Both Washington and Berlin were now thrown into turmoil. The president knew that his last *Lusitania* note required him to take action, perhaps break diplomatic relations, if Germany could not provide an acceptable explanation for the incident. He also knew, however, that such a course risked war, and he was therefore reluctant to embark on it. On the other side of the Atlantic, Bethmann tangled anew with the admirals. "Unhappily," he told the chief of the Naval Cabinet, "it depends upon the attitude of a single submarine commander whether America will or will not declare war. . . . For my part I see no other solution but . . . [that] submarine war against passenger ships must be conducted like cruiser warfare."[15]

Armed with dispatches from Bernstorff pointing to the seriousness of the situation and supported by the opinion of the commander of the army, General Erich von Falkenhayn, that less was to be gained from submarines than would be lost if America entered the war, Bethmann carried his fight to the emperor and won. On August 30 orders went to the fleet not to sink passenger ships without giving adequate warning and rescuing passengers and crew. Within a week this order was extended to include "mixed passenger and freight ships," and by September 18 U-boat warfare had effectively been halted in the English Channel and along Britain's west coast. Tirpitz, who had resigned in protest only to have his resignation refused, complained to the kaiser that the navy, the backbone of Germany, was being sacrificed. But William II was adamant. "America," he wrote, "had to be prevented from participating in the war against us as an active enemy. . . . The war must first be won, and that requires that we do not make new enemies."[16] Even before matters had run their full course in Germany, Bernstorff, following instructions from both Bethmann and Jagow, gave to the State Department and to the press the so-called "*Arabic* pledge": Germany henceforth would not attack passenger ships without observing the

14. Wilson to House, August 4, 1915, quoted in Link,*Wilson,* 3:563; "Light on German Propaganda," *Literary Digest,* 51 (August 28, 1915): 388.

15. Bethmann Hollweg to Karl Georg von Treutler, August 25, 1915, quoted in Link, *Wilson,* 3:571–572.

16. William II to Alfred von Tirpitz, n.d., in Tirpitz, *Politische Dokumente,* 2:428.

rules of cruiser warfare. The United States had scored a signal diplomatic victory.

The magnitude of that victory was, however, at first somewhat obscured by Germany's refusal to make amends for the *Arabic* sinking—on the grounds that the U-boat captain had acted in self-defense—and by an inaccurate report from Gerard that the Foreign Office was getting ready to bow to the demands of the navy. Nevertheless, Bernstorff reaffirmed the pledge on October 5 in a note in which he disavowed the actions of the submarine commander and offered to pay an indemnity for the lives lost. The Foreign Office was not altogether pleased with Bernstorff's action, since the ambassador had failed to condition the German offer on America's pressuring Great Britain to modify her blockade policy. But it gave its stamp of approval to the spirit, if not to the letter, of his agreement.

The Modus Vivendi

The negotiations over the *Lusitania* and the *Arabic,* though they resulted in Germany's abandonment, for all practical purposes, of the kind of submarine warfare to which the United States had objected, nonetheless placed new strains on Germany-American relations. First, they delayed any American effort to bring real pressure on the British and raised serious doubts in Wilson's mind about the reliability of the Germans. In mid-summer he asked his secretaries of war and of the navy to undertake studies looking toward greater American preparedness, and by September 22 he confided to House that "he had never been sure that we ought not to take part in the conflict and if it seemed evident that Germany and her militaristic ideas were to win, the obligation upon us was greater than ever."[17] Moreover, the prolonged negotiations allowed the number of incidents likely to produce anti-German sentiments to multiply. To the Albert and Rintelen affairs were soon added the indiscretions of the Austrian ambassador, Konstantin T. Dumba, whose plan for the disruption of American munitions production fell into the hands of British agents in late August, and the sabotage activities of the German naval and military attachés, Captains Franz von Papen and Karl Boy-Ed, which led to their expulsion in November. The negoti-

17. House diary, September 22, 1915, in House Collection, Yale University Library, New Haven.

ations also gave the British time to take steps to mollify American objections to their policies, particularly the placing of cotton on the contraband list, and enabled the volume of supplies flowing to the Allied side to increase. The United States finally launched its protest against British policies in a note of October 21, which denounced the Anglo-French blockade as "ineffective, illegal, and indefensible." By that time, it was already abundantly clear that, although the U.S. was taking a strong stand on principle, it would be unlikely to insist on British acceptance of that principle with the same determination it had shown in its dealings with Germany.

Indeed, far from pressing its case against Great Britain, the United States in the last months of 1915 engaged in new negotiations with Germany over the final settlement of the *Lusitania* issue. The Foreign Office, though it had agreed to modifications in the submarine campaign, had never acknowledged its culpability in the sinking of the British liner and had never actually offered compensation for the American victims. Secretary of State Lansing, in particular, brought pressure on Germany as the year came to a close, and at least privately threatened to work for a break in diplomatic relations—which might well lead to war—if no satisfaction were obtained.

The German government, in its turn, found the time inauspicious for yielding to further American pressure. The failure of the United States to secure concessions from Great Britain persuaded even Bethmann that Germany had given in more than enough to the American viewpoint and had obtained little or nothing in return. To do more would be to court opposition both in the Reichstag and from the public, which might well drive the chancellor from office. At the same time, the precarious balance within the German government over the submarine issue was upset by the change of heart in General von Falkenhayn. The army commander's support had been crucial to Bethmann in his successful effort to limit submarine warfare after the *Lusitania* sinking. But Falkenhayn, encouraged by German successes in the Balkans, now concluded that America would be no more dangerous militarily as a belligerent than it was as a so-called neutral. Aware, moreover, that the war had to be ended as quickly as possible, he believed an attack on England to be essential and listened with increasing sympathy to the navy's argument that submarine warfare could bring the British to their knees in short order.

Faced by pressure from all sides, Bethmann proceeded skillfully to score what was perhaps his greatest victory for moderation. On the one hand, he persuaded the emperor that provoking a war with the United States was still not in Germany's interest—William called it "folly" on March 5, 1916—on the other, he persuaded both Gerard and House, who was then in Berlin, that Germany could not yield on a matter of honor and admit that submarine warfare was in itself illegal. "What your Government asks," he told Karl von Wiegand of the New York World, "is an impossible humiliation. I have gone far to maintain those cordially friendly relations which have existed between your country and Germany since the day when, more than 125 years ago, Prussia was the first nation to recognize American's independence in her war with England. . . . But I cannot concede a humiliation of Germany and the German people, or the wrenching of the submarine weapon from our hands, even to placate America."[18] When the kaiser went so far as to ask for the resignation of the submarine's most militant champion, Admiral von Tirpitz, and Bernstorff presented a memorandum to the State Department pleading for understanding, the matter of peace or war between the two countries was placed squarely in Wilson's hands. Aware for the first time, through telegrams sent by House, that American insistence on the letter of international law would play into the hands of the most militant factions in Germany, and convinced that the country overwhelmingly favored peace, Wilson eased his pressure on Germany and agreed tacitly to accept the modus vivendi that had been achieved.

This result, obtained through laborious negotiations between the United States and Germany and through long and often acrimonous discussions within the German and American governments, seemed likely to be of short duration. Not only could the modus vivendi be readily upset by the rash action of a single submarine commander, it also rested solely on Bethmann Hollweg's continuing ability to maintain support for his government and on Wilson's being able to reconcile the arrangement with the more general concept for a postwar settlement which was then forming in his mind.

In early 1916, even while negotiations with Germany seemed to be reaching an acceptable conclusion, the president became convinced that military and naval disarmament and a league of nations designed to prevent aggression and to guarantee freedom of the seas

18. New York World, February 9, 1916.

would be essential in any postwar settlement. Having reached that conclusion, he saw little reason to differ with House's contention that Britain and France would be more likely than Germany to agree to such terms and that the United States might well have to apply pressure on Germany—perhaps only moral pressure, as far as Wilson was concerned, but even military pressure, according to House—to assure a settlement on that basis.

Wilson had allowed House to go on another "peace mission" to London, Paris, and Berlin in January 1916. Convinced by his visit to Berlin of what he already believed before he arrived—that is, that Germany would not willingly agree to mediation on Wilson's terms but would be driven by its extremists into war with the United States if mediation proved unsuccessful—he tried to persuade London and Paris to request American mediation. In accordance with a scheme he had already proposed to Wilson tentatively on October 17, 1915, House in effect offered American intervention in the war if Allied proposals for American mediation were rebuffed by Germany. On February 22, House and Grey agreed to a memorandum that stated in part:

> Colonel House told me that President Wilson was ready, on hearing from France and England that the moment was opportune, to propose that a Conference should be summoned to put an end to the war. Should the Allies accept this proposal, and should Germany refuse it, the United States would probably enter the war against Germany.
> Colonel House expressed the opinion that, if such a Conference met, it would secure peace on terms not unfavourable to the Allies; and, if it failed to secure peace, the United States would leave the Conference as a belligerent on the side of the Allies, if Germany was unreasonable.[19]

Wilson accepted this as an accurate statement of American policy, adding only a second "probably" to the text. It is clear, therefore, that the United States, even while tacitly accepting the modus vivendi on the submarine issue, was committed to "peace terms not unfavourable to the Allies" and regarded Germany essentially as an enemy whose success in the war would be unacceptable. Given the fact that substantial and growing elements in Germany already considered the United States an enemy because of its arms shipments to

19. House-Grey memorandum, February 22, 1916, in Link, *Wilson*, vol. 4, *Confusions and Crises, 1915–1916*, 134–136.

the Allies, actual hostilities between the two countries became increasingly possible.

The United States, certainly, hoped that the Allies would ask for mediation and that these efforts would be successful in ending the conflict. And Bethmann Hollweg, who opposed war with the United States, still held the upper hand in Germany. But the Allies, in fact, had been persuaded by House's maneuvers that American intervention was only a matter of time and would not require prior agreement to American war aims, and Bethmann's position was becoming more precarious day by day. When on March 24, therefore, a German submarine without warning torpedoed the French channel steamer *Sussex* with several Americans on board, the final crisis seemed to have arrived.

Both House and Lansing proposed that the incident be made the occasion for an ultimatum that Germany abandon submarine warfare or face the break in diplomatic relations with the United States. Wilson was not yet prepared to go that far. The note that Gerard handed to the Foreign Office on April 20 did threaten to break diplomatic relations but insisted only that "the Imperial Government should now immediately declare and effect an abandonment of its *present methods* of submarine warfare against passenger and freight-carrying vessels."[20] The president, however, was fully aware of the possible results even of this action and called a joint meeting of both houses of Congress to explain what he had done. Gerard was instructed to let Spain represent American interests should the break come.

Germany, however, yielded once more. Bethmann earlier had argued that stepped-up submarine warfare would mean certain war with the United States and thus represented a gamble "in which the ante would be our existence as a great power and our whole national future, while the chances of winning . . . are very uncertain."[21] At his request now the admiralty issued orders to its submarine commanders to observe the rules of cruiser warfare, pending the emperor's decision on the *Sussex* note. William, although angry at that note, was also fearful of involving his country in an even wider war.

20. Lansing to Gerard, April 18, 1916, in *Foreign Relations, 1916, Supplement,* p. 234. Emphasis added.

21. Bethmann memorandum, Februrary 29, 1916, in *Ursachen und Folgen: Vom deutschen Zusammenbruch 1918 und 1945 bis zur staatlichen Neuordnung Deutschlands in der Gegenwart,* 26 vols., ed. Herbert Michaelis and Ernst Schraepler, (Berlin, 1959[?]–1979), I:112.

He listened with some trepidation to the arguments of Falkenhayn and Tirpitz for ignoring the American protest even at the risk of war, and turned with relief to the position taken by Bethmann, which was now rather surprisingly supported by the head of the admiralty. "This rich and inaccessible country can carry on a war for ten years," wrote Henning von Holtzendorf. "It will bring to our staggering enemies considerable moral and material aid and will strengthen them and prolong their resistance—*and in particular England*. Our goal, which is to obtain the end of the war within a short time, will be frustrated, and Germany will be exposed to exhaustion."[22]

On May 4 Jagow handed Gerard the German reply to the *Sussex* note: submarine warfare would be conducted according to the rules of cruiser warfare; let the United States bring equal pressure on Great Britain so that it too would observe the letter of international law. Wilson accepted the German reply but expressly repudiated the notion that Germany's adherence to its new policy was contingent on America's success in getting Britain to modify its stand. But the condition was in fact a very real one. As Bethmann correctly informed Bernstorff a few days later, unless the United States were able to persuade the British in the near future, the clamor in Germany for the resumption of unrestricted submarine warfare would prove irresistible.

Peace Offensives

By midsummer 1916 Bethmann had become convinced that prolongation of the war would bring disaster to Germany. A new Russian offensive in the east, the demonstrated weakness of Turkey, and the entry of Romania into the war made it more likely that the emperor would be persuaded to gamble on the submarine. In this predicament, the chancellor began at least to consider the possible usefulness of the American president in bringing the war to a speedy end. He certainly did not trust Wilson, whom he characterized in early June as "too inclined to the English standpoint and, moreover, a naive statesmen" who would probably try to reestablish the status quo ante, which Germany could not accept.[23] Indeed, Bethmann had

22. Henning von Holtzendorff memorandum, n.d., in Spindler, *Der Handelskrieg,* 3:196. Original emphasis.

23. Bethmann Hollweg, instructions to Bernstorff, June 7, 1916, in *Ursachen und Folgen,* 1:119.

instructed Bernstorff to prevent the president from approaching Germany with any proposal that seemed acceptable to Britain. By August, however, with pressure for the resumption of unrestricted submarine warfare rapidly rising in Germany, Bethmann had changed his mind, at least in part. He now indicated that he would welcome an effort by Wilson to bring about negotiations among the belligerents and might even be willing to accept a more broadly based international conference once such negotiations had been successful. "Of course," he added, "we cannot be expected to commit ourselves, on the acceptance of such mediation, to any concrete peace terms."[24]

Less than two weeks later, the hopelessness of Bethmann's battle against the use of the submarine became fully apparent. A conference of Germany's military and civilian leaders on August 31 not only demonstrated the continuing fundamental split within the government, but also showed that the admiralty had changed its mind since April and now favored unrestricted submarine warfare. Even more ominously, Field Marshal Paul von Hindenburg, the new chief of the General Staff, seemed as agreeable to this as Falkenhayn had become, and asked only for a brief delay in implementation until certain precautions could be taken. It was symptomatic of the flight from reality which increasingly characterized German decision making that the field marshal's hesitation was prompted not by the expected entry of the United States into the war but rather by the possibility of an attack by or through Holland and Denmark.

Bethmann seconded Hindenburg's request for a delay as the best option available, but he immediately cabled Bernstorff to inquire about the possibility of a peace move by Wilson, offering as bait the conditional restoration of Belgium. In late September Bethmann issued new detailed instructions to the ambassador in Washington, expressing even greater interest in an American peace move and stressing that delay until near or after the presidential election would make it too late. Although the kaiser regarded Bethmann's approach as too plaintive and added to the instructions a veiled threat that Wilson's failure to act promptly would result in the unleashing of the submarine, he too now wanted the president to arrange a conference among the belligerents. "The mediation," he indicated, "must seek to bring about an armistice of limited duration—as short as possible—during which the preliminary peace would be concluded at

24. Bethmann Hollweg to Bernstorff, August 18, 1916, in ibid., 1:122.

once."[25] Indeed, William himself drafted a parallel appeal in English, which he intended to send with Ambassador Gerard to Washington.

Although the word "mediation" was used on occasion both by the kaiser and by the Foreign Office, the various messages from Germany made it clear that what was asked of Wilson was not mediation at all but simply a move to bring the belligerents together for negotiations among themselves. The Germans correctly assumed that the presence of the president at any such conference would not work in the interests of the Reich, and indeed Wilson was committed by the House-Grey memorandum to "peace terms not unfavourable to the Allies." But, on its own terms, the German peace offensive was both genuine and relatively risk-free. If Wilson were to succeed in bringing about the conference, the Germans believed that terms favorable to Germany might be obtained. If they were not, it might at least be possible to foster disunity among the Allies and thus permit Germany to resume the fighting under more favorable conditions. Even if no conference could be arranged, the onus for the continuation of the war would be shifted to the Allies, and increasing dissatisfaction in liberal circles in Britain and France could be expected to weaken those countries and their war effort. In that case the United States might even be persuaded to depart from its pro-Allied stance sufficiently to accept the resumption of unrestricted submarine warfare as a justified tactic. That some German leaders from the beginning preferred the last of these alternatives does not alter the fact that Bethmann had found a strategy for which he could win support within Germany and which might yet prevent the unrestricted submarine warfare that he regarded as disastrous. Neither does it change the fact that that strategy depended on the intervention of the American president.

When Bethmann learned on October 1 that Hindenburg had agreed with the naval leaders that the submarine could be unleashed by mid-October, he once more urged postponement, largely on the grounds that the results of the effort to bring about an American peace action were not yet known. When the kaiser supported delay, the chancellor again informed Bernstorff that, while Wilson could not be asked to mediate because of his "previous favoritism of the Entente," a "spontaneous peace appeal," perhaps in conjunction

25. Kaiser's note on Bethmann Hollweg's draft instructions to Bernstorff, September 23, 1916, quoted in Karl E. Birnbaum, *Peace Moves and U-Boat Warfare* (Stockholm, 1958), p. 157.

with the Pope, the King of Spain and other neutrals, would be more than welcome.[26]

The president, engaged in a bitter campaign for reelection and unaware of the struggles within the German government, took no action. But as the fall wore on, he found himself in a radically altered situation. His assumption, implicit in the House-Grey memorandum, had always been that Germany would resist any peace moves and that an Allied proposal for mediation would best serve the interests of peace and of the United States. Now Germany seemed at least to be asking for a conference while the British, fearful that a negotiated peace would only postpone a final showdown with Germany, were unalterably opposed, despite their increasing dependence on money and supplies from America. After the election, Wilson nevertheless determined to use the opportunity to serve as peacemaker. He responded with great restraint to the evidence of new German depredations in Belgium and to sinkings occasioned by a stepped-up German submarine campaign within the terms of the *Sussex* pledge. By November 25 he had completed the first draft of his peace note. Shortly thereafter he informed Bethmann of his desire for "practical cooperation on the part of the German authorities in creating a favorable opportunity for some affirmative action . . . in the interest of an early restoration of peace."[27]

In Berlin, however, the "peace offensive" had meanwhile taken a different turn. Bethmann had been told repeatedly by Bernstorff that Wilson would not act until after the election and was convinced that delay was undesirable because Germany's military situation might deteriorate and the pressure to use the submarine become unstoppable. He had, therefore, listened with interest to the suggestion by the Austrian foreign minister, Baron Burian, that the Central Powers come forward with a peace offer of their own. Burian, who feared the collapse of the Habsburg monarchy if the war continued for long and who also regarded the resumption of unrestricted submarine warfare as a recipe for disaster, proposed on October 18 that such an offer be made in early winter after the Romanian campaign had been finished, and that it include a clear statement of what he regarded as moderate war aims. Bethmann had already insisted in his dispatches

26. Bethmann Hollweg to Bernstorff, October 14, 1916, in *Ursachen und Folgen*, 1:59.

27. Lansing to Joseph C. Grew, November 29, 1916, in *Foreign Relations 1916, Supplement*, pp. 70–71.

to Washington that a statement of war aims was undesirable because no agreement on aims could be reached in Germany and any statement was certain to weaken support for the government. Thus he rejected this aspect of the Austrian proposal but took up the rest with alacrity. In less than two weeks Bethmann had secured the kaiser's consent to an immediate German peace proposal, without, however, a war aims statement. On November 5, even Hindenburg gave his conditional approval.

Although the proposal for a direct peace appeal by the Central Powers had certain advantages with respect to timing, it could not, if rejected by the Allies, bring the same benefits that a proposal by Wilson might. Bernstorff was therefore also encouraged to continue his efforts in Washington. But when the fall of Bucharest to German troops on December 6 seemed to offer a possibility for negotiation from a position of strength, when pressure for the immediate resumption of submarine warfare rose once more, and when Wilson still gave no clear indication when he was prepared to make his peace move, Bethmann decided to act. On December 12 he appeared before a special session of the Reichstag and proclaimed the willingness of the Central Powers to enter into immediate negotiations with their enemies. A note to that effect was transmitted through neutral capitals, including Washington, on the same day. "The Chancellor wishes me to inform you," Bernstorff wrote to House, "that the steps he is taking today are intended to meet the wishes of the President, and that he, therefore, hopes for the President's cooperation."[28]

Wilson did indeed cooperate and on December 16 forwarded the German note to London with an expression of deep interest. Even before he did so, however, reports reached him that the Allies would reject the proposal of the Central Powers and that Germany would thereupon resume unrestricted submarine warfare at once. Since such an eventuality would negate all possibilities for a negotiated peace, Wilson, despite House's contrary views, decided to send his own "peace note" as well. In his message of December 18, he proposed that the belligerents clearly and explicitly state their war aims as a prelude to ending the conflict. All of the powers, he explained, had already stated their desire to assure the security of all other nations and their preference for a single league of nations over a

28. Bernstorff to House, December 12, 1916, in Link, *Wilson*, vol. 5, *Campaigns for Progressivism and Peace, 1915–1916*, 214.

system of rival alliances. The time had now come for them to spell out the specific terms on which they were ready to make peace. The American note made it clear that Wilson was not following the German initiative but acting independently of the Central Powers. The president, in fact, believed that Bethmann's action would make it more difficult for both Germany and the Allies to reject the American proposal and he instructed his ambassadors to inform the respective governments "that it would be very hard for the Government of the United States to understand a negative reply."[29]

Wilson's note produced public and official consternation in the Allied capitals, as well as in Berlin. The British and French were particularly dismayed by the president's assertion that all belligerents shared, in general terms, the same war aims and tended at least initially to see the note as an adjunct to Bethmann's. The German chancellor, on the other hand, was placed in a wholly untenable position by Wilson's insistence that specific war aims be stated. Bethmann had been able to maintain his position and influence only by leading the various German factions to believe that he shared their differing views on this issue, and any statement now was certain to shatter his support. Indeed, Bethmann's Reichstag speech had already been criticized both by Socialist members, on the grounds that it did not renounce all thought of annexations, and by Conservatives, because it did not indicate clearly what tangible benefits Germany expected from any peace treaty.

The Foreign Office's reply of December 26, temporized by agreeing with the spirit of Wilson's proposal but ignoring the request for a statement of aims. Arthur Zimmerman, now foreign secretary, told Bernstorff confidentially, moreover, that Germany wanted only a conference of belligerents at some neutral site in Europe and under no circumstances wished Wilson to get involved in negotiations over aims. The German response in turn made it easier for the Allies to formulate their official position. While rejecting the American contention that the aims of both sides were equally valid and insisting that only an Allied victory could produce the results Wilson envisaged, the Allies were nevertheless able to appear as the more cooperative of the two sides by including a statement of war aims specifically formulated to please the United States and largely based

29. Lansing to Page et. al., December 18, 1916, in *Foreign Relations, 1916, Supplement*, p. 98.

on suggestions that Lansing had earlier made to both Jusserand and Spring-Rice.

Wilson, unaware of the actual meaning of the German note, found its text sufficiently encouraging to suggest that Berlin might perhaps be willing to state its peace terms privately to him and to House. When Bernstorff agreed to pass that suggestion on to Berlin, the president began to work on a major policy statement calling for a negotiated peace and a postwar association of nations as a guarantor of international right and justice. The arrival of the Allied reply sustained the president's optimism, as did Berlin's reply to Bernstorff, at least in the form in which it was communicated by the ambassador to Colonel House. In actuality, Zimmermann had emphasized in his telegram of January 7 that Germany wanted no mediation and intended to win the war. He had asked Bernstorff to employ dilatory tactics in any discussion of war aims and, in view of the decisions then being made in Germany, even inquired how unrestricted submarine warfare could be carried on without causing a break with the United States. Bernstorff apparently told House nothing of this. Instead, he emphasized Zimmermann's agreement to a discussion of such matters as freedom of the seas, arbitration treaties, and a league of nations, and his suggestion of moderate, if vague peace terms, which did not include the annexation of Belgium. With even House now thoroughly convinced that secret mediation efforts were likely to bear fruit, Wilson delivered his "Peace without Victory" speech to the Senate on January 22.

That speech, one of the finest American political utterances, genuinely reflected the president's aspirations, as well as his expectation of what might be attained. On the latter count he was clearly mistaken. By January 1917 Germany and the Allies had already expended too much in blood and treasure to allow their governments to settle for anything but victory, and most leaders on both sides still believed that victory was possible. For the Germans, this victory was to be won by unleashing the submarine. Even as Wilson drafted his speech and House carried on private negotiations with Bernstorff, the Germans decided on this fateful step.

Unleashing the Submarine

Confronted by the failure of Wilson's peace note to meet his wishes and by the Allied rejection of the German peace offer on December

30, and pressed both by the admirals and by Generals von Hinden-burg and Erich Ludendorff, in whom he had the greatest confidence, the kaiser issued a secret imperial order on January 9 calling for the beginning of unrestricted submarine warfare on February 1. Beth-mann, opposed by both the army and the navy, left nearly without support in the government and with dwindling support in the Reichs-tag, had acquiesced. Given the kaiser's decision, which was made in the full realization that it would almost certainly mean war with the United States, the apparently conciliatory messages sent by the Foreign Office to Washington during the following weeks reflected no interest whatever in a negotiated peace but only a forlorn attempt to still keep the U.S. out of war. Indeed, the Zimmermann telegram, which offered Mexico an alliance with Germany in case of a U.S.-German war and agreed to the reannexation of Texas, New Mexico, and Arizona, was composed on January 16 and sent on January 19. It began by informing the German ambassador in Mexico City: "It is our purpose on the 1st of February to commence the unrestricted U-Boat war. The attempt will be made to keep America neutral in spite of it all."[30]

When Bernstorff, who genuinely desired to promote negotiations, urged on January 27 that implementation of the submarine campaign be postponed in order to give Wilson's efforts a chance, William II shrugged off the suggestion by remarking that the president's desire for negotiations arose from the fear that submarine warfare would be successful. Bethmann, by now thoroughly defeated, proposed merely that the possibility of further negotiations not be totally foreclosed. On January 29 the chancellor wrote to Wilson for the last time. While stating disingenuously that it was now too late to stop the submarine commanders, he indicated, for the first time in specific terms, what German terms *"would have been"* in December. "We beg the President, in spite of all," he concluded, "to take up and continue his efforts; and we declare ourselves ready to discontinue the intensive U-Boat warfare as soon as we receive satisfactory assurances that the efforts of the President will lead to a peace which would be acceptable to us."[31] The message was delivered to a

30. Zimmermann to Heinrich von Eckhardt, January 19, 1917, in *Official German Documents Relating to the World War*, (2 vols., translated under the supervision of the Carnegie Endowment for International Peace (New York, 1923), 2:1337.

31. Bethmann Hollweg to Bernstorff, January 29, 1917, ibid., 1048–1059. Original emphasis.

shocked and surprised Wilson on January 31, together with the announcement that, from the following day on, all ships would be sunk without warning in a wide zone around Great Britain and France, as well as in the central and eastern Mediterranean.

The sweeping nature of the German decree left Wilson no choice but to take counteraction, although the president was by no means reconciled to the prospect of war. On February 3, after consultation with his cabinet and with Congressional leaders, he announced that diplomatic relations with Germany had been broken. But he also indicated that the United States would, in effect, accept the new submarine policy so long as no American ships were sunk or American lives lost. His aim, it soon appeared, was to put his country into a state of armed neutrality as an alternative to war. He sought Congressional authorization for the arming of merchant ships, and instructed the secretaries of war and of the navy to proceed with contingency plans. He also told them, however, to avoid displaying outward signs of incipient mobilization. Wilson continued, moreover, to follow up various feelers concerning possible peace negotiations, particularly those put out by the new Austro-Hungarian foreign minister, Count Ottokar Czernin. To all of this Germany remained totally unresponsive.

Then, on February 24, the British turned over a copy of the intercepted Zimmermann telegram to Ambassador Page, who immediately cabled it to Washington. The German foreign secretary's message caused a furor when it was released to the press on March 1, and was undoubtedly a major factor in preparing the U.S. psychologically for war. But it was even more significant in its effect on Woodrow Wilson. Sensitive as the president was in matters concerning Mexico and staunchly committed to the notion of a negotiated peace as a prelude to a more rational world order, he could not fail to see in this incredibly inept German maneuver conclusive evidence that Germany wanted no negotiated peace, already looked on the United States as an enemy, and could not be counted on to contribute toward an equitable postwar settlement.

Only Wilson's personal horror of war and his fear of what involvement in the conflict would do to America postponed the inevitable. But when German submarines sank three American ships between March 16 and 18, and when the success of the Russian Revolution on March 17 removed the necessity of fighting on the side of the tsar, Wilson made up his mind. The decision for war was effectively reached at a cabinet meeting on March 20, with only the timing of the request for a declaration left open for discussion. On April 2 the president addressed a joint session of Congress.

> With a profound sense of the solemn and even tragical character of the step I am taking and of the grave responsibilities which it involves, but in unhesitating obedience to what I deem my constitutional duty, I advise that the Congress declare the recent course of the Imperial German Government to be in fact nothing less than war against the Government and people of the United States; that it formally accept the status of belligerent which has thus been thrust upon it; that it take immediate steps not only to put the country in a more thorough state of defense but also to exert all its power and employ all its resources to bring the Government of the German Empire to terms and end the war.[32]

32. Address of the President, *Congressional Record,* 65th Cong., 1st sess., April 2, 1917, 102.

Chapter 5

WAR AND PEACE

*

The Fourteen Points and the Armistice

From April 6, 1917, when war was officially declared, until October 3, 1918, when the German chancellor, Prince Max of Baden, first proposed to Woodrow Wilson that he arrange for an armistice to be followed by peace negotiations based on the Fourteen Points, German-American relations were essentially carried on in the shipping lanes of the Atlantic and on the battlefields of France. Yet, under a president who had led his country into war in large measure because he hoped to give it a major voice in the conclusion of the peace, it was inevitable that even in wartime consideration would be given to the future role of Germany and the means to get Germany to play that role. In a sense, German-American relations during the eighteen months of America's belligerency became a crucial element in the larger context of Wilson's efforts to define and shape the postwar world.

The definition of its war aims and the question of how these aims might be most effectively implemented at the eventual peace conference became a major concern of the American government almost as soon as the United States entered the war. Petitions offering proposals were received from peace societies and other groups, resolutions were introduced in Congress, and plans were laid, both in the State Department and outside it, for the formation of study groups to take up these questions. By September, the Inquiry, a task force with which some one hundred fifty experts were at one time or another associated, was set up under the general supervision of the ubiquitous Colonel House. Its function was to gather information for the guidance of American representatives to the peace conference. The Inquiry was not a policy making body, but its activities both influenced policy and reflected the general interests of American policy makers. Of some 894 reports that found their way into its files, 174 pertained directly to Germany, including 47 produced by members of the Inquiry itself. More than half of these reports dealt with commerce, tariffs, and finance, or with the key question of the future of Alsace-Lorraine. But there were others on such diverse subjects as politics and government, education, public opinion, militarism, and social welfare.

The conclusions reached by the Inquiry were not wholly consistent, but they were indicative of the attitudes that shaped American policy. Many of them clearly reflected the view of Secretary Lansing that "the German people will never change their code of morals or be worthy of trust and confidence," and that "any means would be justified [which] would render powerless the physical might of the nation which is responsible for this awful crime against humanity."[1] In this spirit, some Inquiry reports favored stripping Germany not only of Alsace-Lorraine but also of the Saar and all of Schleswig, including the Kiel Canal, even if such a disposition of territory would violate the principle of national self-determination. In a similar vein, discussion of the future status of the peoples of the Austro-Hungarian Empire was affected by the fear of many members of the Inquiry that self-determination and the establishment of independent states would lead to German economic control of the entire area. But the conclusions also held the thought that a democratized and demilitarized viable Germany was to be readmitted to full partnership in the family of nations.

The formation of the Inquiry was only one of the steps taken to assure the United States an effective role at the peace conference. More significant in many ways were Wilson's continuing efforts to gain the agreement of all belligerents on a set of war aims which might form the basis for future discussions. A number of events during 1917 persuaded the president that another attempt to secure such agreement not only was necessary but might even prove successful. The first of these was increasing evidence of dissatisfaction

1. Lansing memorandum, October 24, 1917, quoted in Lawrence E. Gelfand, *The Inquiry* (New Haven, 1963), pp. 190–191.

and disunity within Germany, which became apparent during the summer.

The failure of Germany's military leaders and their right-wing supporters to bring the war to a successful conclusion and the entrance of the United States, which made such a denouement even more remote, sparked serious criticism of the government in the Reichstag. Proposals to increase the German lower house's influence on policy through various democratic reforms, particularly in the government of Prussia, were put forward. And, as evidence mounted that the submarine campaign would not attain its promised objective, the demand was heard with increasing frequency that extravagant German war aims that served to prolong the conflict be dropped. The Socialists had long urged such a course and were now joined by substantial elements of the parties of the center. One of the results of this coalescing of sentiment was the adoption of a resolution on July 19, which read in part: "The Reichstag strives for a peace of understanding and the permanent reconciliation of nations. With such a peace, forced concessions of territory and political, economic, and financial acts of force are incompatible." The resolution also called for freedom of the seas, for economic peace, and for the establishment of international organizations for the settlement of disputes.[2]

Ironically, the passage of this resolution produced the ouster of Bethmann Hollweg, a long-time supporter of at least relatively moderate war aims, and demonstrated not merely the growing war weariness of the Germans but also the increasing dominance of the Supreme Army Command. Bethmann's capitulation to the military leaders on the submarine issue had won him no friends, neither among the military nor in the Reichstag. With respect to the peace resolution, the generals now blamed him for being unable or unwilling to stop what they regarded as a damaging public announcement of German weakness, while the Reichstag majority, with few exceptions, considered his position too far compromised to allow him to carry out the terms of the resolution. The kaiser, increasingly uncertain and confused, rejected the chancellor's offer to resign on July 11. But when his rejection produced a threat of resignation from Ludendorff, still regarded as an indispensable architect of eventual victory, William changed his mind. Bethmann was replaced by the

2. Peace resolution, July 19, 1917, in *Verhandlungen des Reichstags: Stenographische Berichte*, 13th legislative period, 2d sess. (Berlin, 1917–1918), 310: 3573.

weak and inexperienced Georg Michaelis, who was subservient to the wishes of the Supreme Army Command and did not enjoy the confidence of the Reichstag, which had not even been consulted on the appointment. The new chancellor began his tenure in office with a public promise to implement the peace resolution, but qualified it with a highly significant "as I understand it."

With both German Socialists and Catholics increasingly talking of peace, however, new impetus was given to efforts to organize a Socialist peace congress in which delegates from both the Central and Allied powers could present their views. At the same time, Eugenio Cardinal Pacelli, the nuncio to Bavaria, suggested to Pope Benedict XV that a peace appeal from the Vatican might prove useful, since a speedy end to the war was necessary to save the Catholic Austro-Hungarian dual monarchy from imminent collapse. The pontiff's proposal for peace on the basis of the restoration of occupied territory, disarmament, and international arbitration was made on August 1. The Socialist Peace Congress convened in Stockholm on September 5.

Although Wilson took a dim view of the Socialist congress—Americans who had been selected as delegates were denied passports—and regarded the pope's appeal as inadequate and basically inspired by Germany, he nevertheless saw these activities as creating an improved climate for his own peace efforts. Increasingly, however, he tied the possibility of peace to a change in the government of Germany. In a Flag Day speech he had already distinguished the German people from "their military masters," and he indicated in his response to Benedict XV that he would not take "the word of the present rulers of Germany" as representing the will and purpose of the ordinary German. He returned to the same theme in his message to Congress on December 4.

If the time seemed right for bringing pressure on Germany, it was also right for persuading the Allies to change course. The Russo-German peace negotiations at Brest-Litovsk, which proceeded through the month of December, produced two developments of particular concern to the American president. In the first place, they led to the publication by the Bolsheviks of hitherto secret inter-Allied treaties that contained provisions wholly incompatible with Wilson's notions of a just peace. Second, they revealed Germany's intention to impose a harsh settlement on Russia. By setting forth his own view of the postwar order for which the United States was

fighting, Wilson hoped to persuade Russia not to make peace but to
keep fighting on the Allied side for terms far more in keeping with its
interests, to persuade the Allies to renounce the objectionable portions of their secret treaties, and, last but not least, to encourage
liberal elements within Germany to increase their pressure for peace
and a change in government. The "Fourteen Points" speech delivered before Congress on January 8, 1918, though an enormous popular and psychological success, failed signally to effect either of the
first two objectives. But it did have repercussions in Germany which
tended to bring the president's overall goal nearer to realization.

To be sure, yet another new German chancellor, the venerable
Count Georg von Hertling, in a speech before the Reichstag on
January 24 disparaged most of the Wilsonian program as providing
insufficient guarantees for the integrity, security, and dignity of Germany. Actual power within the empire, moreover, gravitated even
further into the hands of the army commanders, Hindenburg and
Ludendorff. But four hundred thousand workers went on a one-
week strike in Berlin on January 28 to indicate their desire, among
other things, for a swift peace without annexations, and dissatisfaction within the Reichstag over the government's policies mounted
steadily. Wilson's speech of February 11, in which he outlined the
four principles essential to a just peace, drew a more positive though
still evasive reply from Hertling, who, in concord with the thinking
of the Supreme Army Command, pinned his own hopes for a satisfactory peace on the expected success of the German spring offensive. Launched on March 21, that offensive had failed beyond
doubt, however, by August 8. With that failure the Germans were
left with little alternative but to try for peace on the best terms
available. For the first time, in German eyes, Wilson's proposals
now seemed to provide those terms.

Throughout much of the summer, rumors of a new German
"peace offensive" had been communicated to Washington by diplomatic officials in Europe. To the extent that these rumors suggested
official German policy, they were false. Privately, however, numerous influential German citizens within and outside of the government had been seeking ways to extricate Germany from an
increasingly untenable position. Even Hertling, though his public
utterances remained bellicose and patriotic even while the victory
promises of the generals proved hollow, privately acknowledged a
willingness to negotiate on the basis of Wilson's four principles. The

new foreign secretary, Richard von Kühlmann, went so far as to try to establish secret contacts with Great Britain. Kühlmann, however, was unceremoniously dismissed when his actions became known, and not until the final failure of the German offensive could peace sentiments be officially expressed. So long as Hindenburg and Ludendorff still spoke of victory, they effectively controlled Germany. The Hertling government was too weak and too confused to oppose them openly, and the Reichstag, where peace sentiment was strongest, was effectively ignored by both the military and the ministry.

By August 8, however, the German offensive had clearly spent its force, and twelve days later an Allied counteroffensive began. Shortly thereafter, the Allies launched campaigns that were to bring Bulgaria and Turkey to their knees by the end of September. As early as August 14 Germany's military and civilian leaders, meeting at Spa, had agreed that discussions possibly leading to peace negotiations should be inaugurated as soon as practicable. On September 16 the Reich's major ally, Austria-Hungary, officially asked for peace, and on September 29 Ludendorff, having been rudely awakened from his dream of victory, suddenly informed the kaiser that "the condition of the army demands an immediate armistice in order to avoid catastrophe."[3] He urged that a peace proposal be sent to Washington via Switzerland at once. Ludendorff hoped, certainly, that terms might be secured which would leave Germany in possession of at least its gains in the East, and counted on a rekindling of patriotic fervor to allow the fighting to be resumed if such terms were not forthcoming. But his admission of failure effectively undercut the power of the generals and strengthened the position of the Reichstag and thus of the proponents of both peace and democratic reform.

On September 27, Wilson had delivered a speech at the Metropolitan Opera House in New York in which he had once again given eloquent voice to his vision of the future international order, of which the League of Nations was to be keystone. He had reasserted his conviction that "there can be no peace obtained by any kind of bargain with the governments of the Central Empires, because . . .

3. Ludendorff to Paul von Hintze, September 29, 1918, in *Ursachen und Folgen: Vom deutschen Zusammenbruch 1918 und 1945 bis zur staatlichen Neuordnung Deutschlands in der Gegenwart*, 26 vols., ed. Herbert Michaelis and Ernst Schraepler (Berlin, 1959[?]–1979), 1: 112.

we cannot accept the word of those who forced this war upon us."[4] Wilson's words and Ludendorff's panic combined to produce a change in the government of Germany. Chancellor Hertling, unwilling and unable to face the prospect of reform, resigned. William II, encouraged now by the generals, who hoped to forestall revolution and were unwilling to accept full responsibility for their failure, decreed that elected representatives of the people were henceforth to participate actively in the government of Germany. Autocracy was virtually at an end. The relatively liberal Prince Max of Baden, a long-time advocate of a conciliatory peace, became chancellor on October 3 and accepted into his cabinet leading representatives of the majority parties in the Reichstag, including the Socialists.

It was the intention of the new chancellor to rally support for the reformed monarchy, which he hoped to save, and to impress on Wilson and the world that the preconditions for a negotiated peace now existed in Germany. But Germany's military leaders, who had pushed the country to the edge of disaster with their insistence that victory was in their grasp, failed their people once more. For Ludendorff, the clearly frustrated expectation of victory had been replaced by a premonition of imminent disaster. Accordingly, he insisted that an armistice request be sent immediately, lest even the western front collapse and Germany be invaded. Though Prince Max regarded such a precipitous move as politically counterproductive, he could not risk the disaster of which Ludendorff warned. His first official act, therefore, taken during the night of October 3, was to dispatch to Washington a request for peace negotiations based on both the Fourteen Points and Wilson's September 27 speech that had called for changes in the government of Germany: an immediate armistice was to be arranged.

Wilson received the German peace overture with favor but also with caution. He was not convinced that governmental changes in Germany had really shaken the authority of the emperor and the armed forces—Prince Max, the heir to the throne of Baden, was not convincing as a democrat—and he suspected that the request for an armistice might be nothing but an effort to allow the German armies to regroup. Concern that Germany hoped to win through negotiation what it had been unable to win on the battlefield was voiced in Congress and in the American press and communicated to the White

4. Wilson, speech of September 27, 1918, in *Foreign Relations of the United States: Diplomatic Papers, 1918, Supplement 1*, 1: 317–318.

House in telegrams from various business, civic, and labor leaders. Moreover, none of the Allies had formally accepted the Fourteen Points as the basis for negotiations and they were not anxious to treat with Germany at all, now that complete victory apparently lay within their grasp.

Wilson, however, was committed to peace at the earliest possible moment and could not seriously consider rejecting the German request outright. He therefore proceeded on his own initiative to ask for clarification. Did Germany fully accept the Fourteen Points? Was it prepared to evacuate all occupied territory at once? And, above all, did the request for peace come merely from "the consituted authorities" with whom the Allies were unwilling to negotiate? The German reply of October 12 gave satisfaction on all items and in particular stressed that the peace proposal had the support of the Reichstag majority and thus of the German people.

Wilson meanwhile had received comments from the various Allied governments and listened to the views of the military leaders. He had also noted the repeated demands in Congress for the unconditional surrender of Germany and the strong opposition there to the concept of a negotiated peace. In his letter of October 14 Wilson brought further pressure on Germany. He insisted that arrangements for the evacuation of occupied territory be made under conditions laid down by the Allied military commanders and that the supremacy achieved by these commanders be maintained. In addition, Germany had to stop unlimited submarine warfare at once and to desist from further depredations in Flanders and France before an armistice could even be considered. Wilson reminded the Germans, moreover, that his speech of July 4, 1918, had called for "the destruction of every arbitrary power anywhere that can separately, secretly, and of its single choice disturb the peace of the world," and informed them that "the power which has hitherto controlled the German Nation is of the sort described. It is within the choice of the German Nation to alter it." Such an alteration, he insisted, was "a condition precedent to peace."[5]

Over the objections of Ludendorff, who had recovered his nerve and found acceptance of the new conditions to be incompatible with his "soldier's honor," the government of Prince Max once more sent a basically positive reply to Wilson. To the general's contention that rejection of the note could bring no worse conditions, the chancellor

5. Lansing to Frederick Oederlin, October 14, 1918, in ibid., 358–359.

had pointedly replied: "Oh yes, they [the Allies] will break into Germany and devastate the country."[6] Such a denouement, he was certain, would rob Germany of any possibility for negotiating an acceptable peace or, for that matter, of regaining a position of power and influence in the future.

The president agreed to take up with the Allies the matter of an armistice and peace negotiations. He emphasized again, however, that in his view the German people still had "no means of commanding the acquiescence of the military authorities of the Empire in the popular will; that the power of the King of Prussia to control the policy of the Empire is unimpaired; that the determinating initiative still remains with those who had hitherto been the masters of Germany" and concluded with an ominous warning: "If [the United States government] must deal with the military masters and monarchical autocrats of Germany now . . . it must demand, not peace negotiations, but surrender."[7] While thus attempting to call Germany's bluff, should its overture turn out to have been that, Wilson at the same time sent Colonel House to Europe to sit as his personal representative on the Supreme War Council. House's main task was to secure Allied agreement to the Fourteen Points as the basis for peace negotiations. If such agreement were reached, Wilson believed, an equitable peace settlement would be possible, under which among other things a reformed and repentant but fully sovereign Germany could in time participate actively in that league of nations which would rationalize international relations and guarantee freedom for all.

Wilson's note of October 24 seemed to both Hindenburg and Ludendorff to be a demand for capitulation, and they hastened to Berlin to persuade William II to break off negotiations and to order resistance to the last. The kaiser, thoroughly cowed, referred the generals to the government, where Prince Max firmly believed that further military efforts would prove fruitless and that the war-weariness of the German masses made continued negotiations imperative. The chancellor did not, moreover, entirely share the generals' misgivings over Wilson's demands—he attributed the demands largely to pressure from American "chauvinists" and from the French and the British—and continued to believe that negotia-

6. Minutes of meeting of October 17, 1918, in *Ursachen und Folgen*, 2: 418.
7. Lansing to Oederlin, October 23, 1918, in *Foreign Relations, 1918, Supplement I*, 1: 382–383.

tions could produce an equitable settlement. The chances seemed particularly good if, as was now certain, Germany entered such negotiations with a government clearly responsive to the popular will. As a result, Prince Max forced the dismissal of Ludendorff on October 26 and sent a positive reply to Wilson the following day.

On October 28 major constitutional revisions went into force in Germany. The chancellor henceforth required the confidence of the Reichstag, the secretaries of state were raised to the status of cabinet ministers, questions of war and peace as well as all international treaties now needed the consent of the federal council and the parliament, and the army was brought under civilian control. In Prussia, a bill calling for universal manhood suffrage was approved by the House of Lords. German dissatisfaction with the conduct of the war, a longing for peace, and the prodding of President Wilson thus combined to create a constitutional monarchy. They also produced increasing demands for the abdication of the kaiser, demands that William II still resisted vigorously, although even the chancellor supported them in the interest of saving the monarchy itself.

Constitutional reform, however, did not immediately relieve the distress of the German people or convince them that relief was in sight. The negotiations for an armistice seemed to be proceeding with agonizing slowness, and there was little confidence that the civilian leaders who had bowed for years before the emperor and the army would be able to take effective control. Indeed, the constitutional reforms, though quickly communicated to Wilson, were little publicized within Germany and did not produce visible changes in the leadership of the country. The result was revolution, directed not merely against autocracy and government policy, but against the monarchy itself. Soldiers refused to go to the front and desertions mounted. A revolt broke out in the navy when the High Seas Fleet was ordered to put to sea. By early November, radical elements had overthrown military authority in Hamburg, Brunswick, Hannover, and Cologne. Socialists took over the government of Bavaria, and Berlin's workers made preparations for a general strike. In all areas at least some troops fraternized with the revolutionaries, and the orderly processes of domestic rule came to a standstill.

While internal upheavals thus convulsed Germany, in Paris Colonel House tried to persuade the Allies to agree to Wilson's peace concept. He limited his efforts toward the armistice itself to preventing needless harshness, arguing on occasion that excessive severity might lead to bolshevism in Germany. But his major task was to gain the adherence of the various representatives, particularly of French Premier Georges Clemenceau and British Prime Minister David Lloyd George, to the principles of the Fourteen Points. It was no easy task. Disagreements were numerous, and France and Britain as well as Italy and other of the smaller powers were reluctant to concede any of the possible fruits of victory with that bitterly-fought-for outcome seemingly in sight. House was well aware that lengthy negotiations would shatter any hope of unity among the Allies and thought their talks might well prolong the war and make any future peace settlement even more difficult. He did share the president's view that only acceptance of the Fourteen Points by both sides would provide the basis for a just and lasting settlement, and he therefore applied his not inconsiderable powers of persuasion to secure speedy agreement, at least in general terms.

To achieve final agreement required all of the Texan's diplomatic skills, as well as a threat to make a separate peace if major changes were proposed in Wilson's program—a threat still credible since none of the Allied leaders were fully aware of just how far the German collapse was advanced. Substantial agreement was reached on October 30 when House, subject to the president's approval, consented to a modification of the demand for freedom of the seas and the inclusion of a condition that Germany pay damages for losses incurred by Allied civilians as a result of German aggression, provided that the remainder of the American program be accepted without alteration. Though Wilson and House had thereby apparently obtained their major objective, Allied acceptance, particularly by the French, was far more conditional than it appeared at the time; subsequent events in Germany as well as in the United States tended to strengthen the position of Clemenceau and weaken that of Wilson.

On November 5, 1918, however, agreement to proffer an armistice and to enter into peace negotiations under the terms of the modified Fourteen Points was communicated to the German government in a note from Secretary of State Lansing. Germany was later to claim that this note was a quasi-contractual agreement against which the proposed terms of the Versailles settlement were to be measured and found wanting. But at the time, its specific terms were not even discussed. The note was received with enormous relief by a Germany that had seriously considered the possibility of unconditional surrender if negotiations with Wilson were to break down. Not even the emphasis on the Allied understanding that "compensation will be made by Germany for all damage done to the civilian population of the Allies and their property by the aggression of Germany"[8] or the designation of the French marshal Ferdinand Foch as the "communicator" of the armistice terms caused any discussion. On November 6, a German delegation left for France, surprisingly led not by a general but by Center party leader Matthias Erzberger. The delegation carried instructions from Prince Max to negotiate the best terms possible but, in the end, to agree to an armistice, however harsh. Germany was clearly defeated.

On the same day the German Social Democratic party issued an ultimatum that the kaiser abdicate within seventy-two hours. When hundreds of thousands of workers converged on the center of Berlin on November 9, and when the military leaders convinced William that any attempt to maintain himself on the throne would only lead to civil war, the rule of the Hohenzollern came to an end. A desperate Prince Max, still hoping to save the monarchy, announced the kaiser's abdication even before William had been fully persuaded, and indicated that he would turn over the chancellorship to Friedrich Ebert, a moderate Socialist. It was too late. Leaders of both of Germany's socialist parties proclaimed a republic, and on the morning of November 10, William II left his sanctuary at the army headquarters at Spa and crossed the Dutch border into exile. On the following morning the armistice that sealed Germany's defeat was signed in the forest of Compiègne. Even Hindenburg had agreed that no other course was possible.

For the moment, Woodrow Wilson and America's policy toward Germany seemed triumphant. The Allies had accepted the proposal for a league of nations and, with apparently minor exceptions, all of the president's stated goals. In Germany, militarism and autocracy lay in ruins, and a democratic republic was in the process of formation. The aims for which Wilson had brought his country into war appeared within reach.

It could not be foreseen that the president's position at the Versailles conference would be weaker than it had been before, that the resulting peace treaty would contain numerous punitive provisions not readily compatible with notions of a just peace, and that the

8. Lansing to Oederlin, November 5, 1918, in ibid., 469.

League of Nations, which might in time have established the more equitable and rational world order that Wilson sought, would be fatally weakened at the outset by America's refusal to join. Neither was it altogether clear that the change in the government of Germany would saddle the new republic, rather than the old empire, with the onus for concluding a demeaning peace, and thus relieve the kaiser and the army of much of the responsibility for the consequences of their actions. That, in turn, would lay the basis for a revanchist spirit based on the legend that Germany had not been defeated on the battlefield but stabbed in the back by its new civilian leaders. When Wilson left for Versailles on December 4, 1918, he was a world hero, the supreme peace maker, the savior of mankind. As such he was triumphantly received in the Allied capitals he visited. And he was widely regarded as such even in Berlin.

The Versailles Settlement

The high hopes Wilson held for the Versailles conference and those that the Germans placed in the American president were doomed to disappointment, and these two developments were by no means unrelated. Wilson's effectiveness at the peace conference was diminished by his own preconceptions about Germany, by the erosion of his support at home, and by the very manner in which the war had come to an end. Germany, in turn, was severely handicapped in its efforts to obtain a milder settlement by the failure of its leaders to accept their own position or to understand that of the president.

Although Wilson had obviously abandoned the concept of "peace without victory" after the American declaration of war, his Fourteen Points were still promulgated as the basis for a negotiated rather than imposed settlement. Germany had clearly accepted them as such. The defeat of Germany, evidenced by the signing of the harsh and irreversible armistice and by the increasing turmoil within the country, made such an arrangement impossible. Under the circumstances, Wilson could not play his envisioned role as mediator among at least approximate equals but could merely try to moderate the demands of France and the other victorious Allies in the general spirit of the Fourteen Points.

Further weakened by the Democratic defeat in the Congressional elections of 1918 and by increasing criticism of his own decision to go to Versailles and of the composition of the American delegation, Wilson could appeal only to the Allies' sense of moderation and fair play—unlikely commodities after four years of a war of unprecedented scope and ferocity. Since he was unwilling in any case to commit the United States permanently to Europe, Wilson was unable to use the possibility of American withdrawal effectively to obtain greater leverage. Just before the armistice, House had still been able to get some agreement on American terms by threatening to make a separate peace, but with Germany prostrate the prospect held no further terror for France and the other Allies. The one remaining mode of persuasion—a possible offer to cancel Allied war debts in return for acquiescence in an "American peace"—neither lay in Wilson's power nor conformed to his sense of right. As a result, Wilson was forced to compromise in ways that did not always agree with his own vision of the desirable world of the future, ways that were nearly always disadvantageous to Germany.

Theoretically, of course, Wilson might have aligned himself with Germany—as some German leaders unrealistically expected him to do—and thus created more nearly a negotiation among equals. But in practice that was impossible. Such a course would have required the president's willingness to enter into an alliance for the indefinite future—an idea he rejected in principle—and called for a confidence in Germany which he had never had. Wilson would have had to reverse those views he had formed in negotiations with the Germans between 1915 and 1917 and had expressed in numerous wartime pronouncements. Or, at the very least, he would have had to believe that the changes in Germany since the middle of 1918 had totally reformed that country. Wilson at Versailles still mistrusted the Germans, however. He had little confidence in the emerging new leadership and at times even overestimated Germany's remaining military potential and willingness to use it. He was, therefore, by no means adverse to various punitive and restrictive measures, and insufficiently concerned that these measures might well discredit in the eyes of its people any German government that agreed to them.

The Germans, for their part, consistently misjudged both the president's temper and the nature of his position at Versailles. They failed to understand that the American declaration of war had ended Wilson's quest for a peace among equals, that thereafter he wished to see Germany defeated, and that his conception of justice demanded that nations accept full responsibility for their actions and pay the price for any wrongdoing. Lacking a leader with the perceptiveness of a Talleyrand, the Germans failed to see, moreover, that Wilson was not in a strong position at Versailles and needed their support almost as much as they needed his if a treaty even moderately satisfactory to Germany were to result. As the Allied leader most committed to an expeditious peace settlement and most opposed to the invasion and dismemberment of Germany, the president was, to a limited degree, on Germany's side. For the same reasons, however, Wilson was the statesman least willing to see the Versailles conference fail, and this further reduced his ability to bring pressure on Clemenceau and the others.

By overplaying their own very weak hand, by challenging Wilson on questions on which he was wholly unsympathetic to their views, and by trying to appear more Wilsonian than the president himself, the Germans aggravated the American leader and aroused his resentment. By insisting, in the final analysis, that both Wilson and the Allies were acting in bad faith, they actually reduced their chances for winning limited, but nonetheless significant, concessions.

The Germans had good reason to expect neither trust nor goodwill from the Allies, particularly the French, and pinned their hopes on Wilson from the outset. The relatively hard line taken by the president toward the initial peace feelers proved to be no permanent discouragement, in part because it was interpreted as merely a necessary maneuver to get the Allies to agree to a cessation of hostilities and in part because only faith in Wilson's goodwill offered any hope for Germany at all. Even before the armistice was concluded, the new German foreign secretary, Wilhelm Solf, citing "common aims and ideals of democracy," appealed directly to the president to use his influence with the Allies to mitigate the proposed terms. On the day the document was signed, Solf asked Wilson to arrange for the immediate commencement of peace negotiations, and, on the following day, Chancellor Friedrich Ebert asked the president whether "the United States is ready to send foodstuffs without delay, if public order is maintained in Germany."[9]

These initial feelers elicited replies positive enough to encourage the Ebert government in its efforts. It rejected Russian offers of food and diplomatic contact, opposed left-wing demands within Germany on the grounds that they imperiled relations with Washington, and

9. Hans Sulzer to Lansing, November 12, 1918, in *Foreign Relations, Paris Peace Conference, 1919*, 2: 629.

played up the danger of "bolshevism" in order to enlist American sympathies. The State Department was generally receptive to such moves. William C. Bullitt, then with the Division of Western European Affairs, warned Lansing on November 25 that "bolshevism in North Germany is inevitable unless we act at once and very wisely." The secretary of state in turn informed Wilson that "the governments of Prussia and Bavaria are in the hands of good men—moderate social democrats—and there are many advantages, it seems to me, in doing what we can at the present time to strengthen these governments."[10]

The president, however, was less convinced of the goodness of these men or of their willingness to eschew both bolshevism and right-wing militarism. Moreover, he was extremely wary of producing a quarrel with the French even before his arrival at Versailles. Clemenceau had bitterly objected to Wilson's earlier unilateral dealings with Germany and had insisted that German messages go to all of the Allied governments. He was certain to be outraged by any American effort to strengthen the regime in Berlin. Even when Wilson limited himself to urging the rapid convening of a constituent assembly, the French premier, who hoped that political turmoil in Germany would weaken that country and perhaps lead to its breakup, voiced strong objections. As a result, no overt sign of support for Ebert came from Washington, and even relief shipments of food were withheld for the time being.

Yet even this failure to help did not dampen German hopes or lower unrealistic expectations. Germany established the *Paxkonferenz* as the agency charged with preparations for peace negotiations and appointed the former ambassador in Washington, Count von Bernstorff, as its director. In a memorandum of November 24 Bernstorff outlined the course that in his view had to be followed:

> Because the decision in the war was brought about by the United States, its position and, in particular, that of President Wilson have become decisive for the future. The whole world will become economically and financially dependent on the United States. For that reason we turned to Mr. Wilson when we were compelled to end this war. For that reason we must also attach ourselves politically to the

10. William C. Bullitt to Lansing and Lansing to Wilson, November 25, 1918, in ibid., 101–102.

United States during the peace negotiations and carry out the future reconstruction of Germany with its help.[11]

Shortly thereafter, Ellis Loring Dresel, the first American diplomatic observer to visit Germany after the war, reported that "there is a strong wish to take up relations again with the United States at the same point where they were before the war, and the hope is cherished that the events of the war will be overlooked and condoned and that by the help of America, Germany will be enabled to rehabilitate herself."[12] At the opening session of Germany's National Assembly on February 6, 1919, Ebert reasserted these sentiments: "Germany laid down her arms trusting in President Wilson's principles. Let them now give us the Wilson peace to which we lay claim."[13]

The German approach, however, rested in large measure on wishful thinking. Not only did it count on genuine negotiations over the terms of the peace treaty, it also misread the temper of the American president. Wilson was by no means prepared either to overlook or to condone, or for that matter to accept as permanent the changes in the government of Germany. Thus he had no objections to a harsh peace settlement—even to one attained with only minimal German participation—so long as that settlement conformed in the aggregate to his notions of justice and left Germany a viable political and economic entity.

Wilson concentrated his major efforts at the Versailles conference, which began on January 18, 1919, on what he regarded as the essential issues for the future—the league and the principle of self-determination. He played little or no role in stripping Germany of much of her merchant fleet and all of her colonies, both without compensation. Wilson considered his desire to avoid high reparations and maintain an economically viable Germany satisfied when the Allies agreed to collect only for civilian damages but not for military costs—even though military pensions were to be added to the bill and no agreement on a fixed sum or on the all-important

11. Bernstorff memorandum for Wilhelm Solf, November 24, 1918, in "Der Weltkrieg," file WK 30, vol. 5, Politisches Archiv des Auswärtigen Amtes, Bonn.

12. Dresel to Joseph C. Grew, January 10, 1919, in *Foreign Relations: Paris Peace Conference*, 2: 318.

13. Walter R. Gherardi to American Mission, February 8, 1919, in State Department Decimal File 184.01202/18, RG 59, N.A.

interest rates had been reached. He obtained his major objectives by placing the covenant of the League of Nations at the head of the proposed treaty and getting the self-determination principle accepted as the primary factor in boundary questions. And having done so, he even allowed some violations of the principle in the interest of providing reasonable borders, particularly for the newly created Slavic states.

Wilson did, however, vigorously and successfully oppose French plans to dismember Germany itself. To prevent the annexation of the Saar to France he went so far as to threaten to leave the conference and publicly summoned the U.S.S. *George Washington* to France on April 7. To forestall French annexation of the Ruhr, Germany's economic heartland, and the establishment of an autonomous "Rhenish Republic," he reluctantly agreed to a guarantee treaty, in accordance with which Great Britain and the United States would render military assistance to France in case of future German aggression. In return, France settled for demilitarization and temporary occupation. Only in the areas of Alsace-Lorraine and the newly reconstituted Polish state, with its corridor to the sea, did Germany lose substantial territory, and both of these cessions had been indicated in principle in the Fourteen Points speech.

Wilson's presence at Versailles worked on the whole to Germany's advantage, but it in no way fulfilled Germany's unrealistic expectations. The Germans had hoped, on the basis of their own interpretation of the Fourteen Points, to be treated as equals in the negotiation of a settlement, and they had counted on the American president to support them. From such negotiations they had expected to emerge with their prewar territory largely intact—even Alsace-Lorraine was not fully conceded—with continued control, if not outright ownership, of their colonies, with an economic settlement that would not seriously weaken their production or trading position, and with immediate membership in the league, which would guarantee them a full voice in all future international decisions.

Instead, the draft treaty was handed to them virtually as a fait accompli on May 7. It deprived the Germans of 13 percent of their territory and 10 percent of their population and weakened them economically through the loss of their colonies and most of their merchant marine, as well as through the temporary occupation of some of their most productive regions. Moreover, it presented them with a virtually open-ended bill for reparations, saddled them with the imputation of war guilt and, most galling of all, urged them to accept such terms without any chance for direct negotiations. For much of this they blamed Wilson. Although Foreign Secretary Count Ulrich von Brockdorf-Rantzau, who led the German delegation at Versailles, castigated all of the Allies in his tactless and arrogant speech of May 7, Chancellor Phillip Scheidemann, who remained behind in Berlin, offered a more representative German reaction. "The people," he declared, "express the deepest disappointment at what they consider the crushing defeat of the President in whom they had placed so much reliance."[14]

Wilson rejected the German charges outright. He had at one time envisaged a process of negotiation with Germany, but, the difficulties in reaching agreement even among the Allies had convinced him that reopening questions in the presence of German delegates would guarantee the failure of the conference and might result in the resumption of hostilities. In that event, even the League of Nations might be lost. Moreover, Wilson believed that in general the Fourteen Points had provided the basis for the treaty, and he greatly resented Germany's sweeping claims to the contrary. He regarded the economic terms as hard but not unjust and was certain in any event that efforts to ease them now would encounter the insuperable opposition at least of the French. If some of the decisions regarding boundaries were problematic, Wilson believed that they could be reviewed far more effectively in the future by the League of Nations than in the heated atmosphere of Versailles. On the most emotionally charged of the issues, that of war guilt, Wilson had no sympathy for the Germans at all. As early as February 1, the State Department had rejected a German request for an impartial study of the origins of the war on the grounds that "the responsibility of Germany for the war has already been established."[15]

The Germans were given no opportunity for oral negotiations but allowed three weeks in which to respond in writing to the peace terms. During this period, considerable differences over strategy developed among the leaders in Berlin, but they unanimously condemned the terms as "unbearable" and "unrealizable," and, except for some of the Independent Socialists, considered them "unaccept-

14. Charles B. Dyar to American Mission, May 10, 1919, in ibid., 184.013202/2.
15. William Phillips to Sulzer, February 2, 1919, in *Foreign Relations: Paris Peace Conference*, 2: 74.

able" as well. Brockdorf-Rantzau, hopeful of concessions if Germany remained firm, sought to mobilize public opinion at home and abroad against the treaty draft through the dispatch of numerous notes and the issuance of various public pronouncements. The cutting edge of this strategy was the determination of the foreign secretary to refuse to sign the treaty without substantial modifications. Given the war weariness of the German people and the likelihood of an Allied invasion if negotiations ended in failure, however, no German government was likely to follow that course for long.

More realistically, Center party leader Matthias Erzberger believed that the Allies would yield on very little and then only if Germany showed a conciliatory attitude. Not so realistically, he tried once more to open an "American connection" for the purpose of winning at least some concessions. On May 16 he telephoned American officers at the army headquarters in Trier in an effort to have Ellis Loring Dresel sent back to the German capital for consultations. Dresel was the German expert on the American peace delegation who had only just returned from a fact-finding mission to Berlin and who was known to advocate less punitive terms. The United States refused to send Dresel or to enter into negotiations with Erzberger. Always wary of appearing to undercut Allied unity, Wilson was now also sufficiently offended by the tone and content of Brockdorf-Rantzau's speech at Versailles and annoyed by the first official responses of the German delegation to the treaty draft to reject out of hand the notion that new risks for the failure of the conference should be assumed on Germany's behalf.

Although there can be no certainty that a different course would have produced better results, the German response to the treaty hardened the attitudes of most Allied leaders and particularly Wilson's. The initial German note of May 9 repeated the assertion that the draft represented in effect a breach of "the promise explicity given to the German people and the whole of mankind." But in addition it offered an alternate covenant for the League of Nations which, if seriously considered, would have negated months of negotiations by Wilson and jeopardized the whole project of the league. Wilson promptly responded that the treaty conformed to the promise and that the Allies could only consider German suggestions "of a practical kind."[16]

16. Ulrich von Brockdorf-Rantzau to Georges Clemenceau, May 9, 1919, and Clemenceau to Brockdorf-Rantzau, May 10, 1919, in ibid., 5: 563–564.

Subsequent German notes nevertheless called for, among other things, the strengthening of the labor provisions of the treaty by incorporating those demands for social justice which "have for the most part been realized in Germany . . . in an exemplary manner." They denied that "there could arise out of a responsibility incurred by the former German Government in regard to the origin of the world war, any right for the Allied and Associated Powers to be indemnified by Germany for losses suffered during the war," and questioned whether the Allied delegates understood the "inevitable consequences" of the economic demands: the "death sentence of many millions of German men, women and children." The notes also charged that the proposed treaty allowed German population and territories to be "made the subject of bargains between one sovereignty and another, as though they were mere chattels and pawns in a game," and in other ways impugned the intelligence, the motives, and the morality of "the adversaries of Germany." "We hoped," it was stated in the cover letter of May 29 to the full German counter-proposals, "for the peace of justice which had been promised us. We were aghast when we read . . . the demands made upon us by the victorious violence of our enemies."[17]

The German posture of righteous indignation had some impact on the British delegation, where Lloyd George had developed his own doubts about the wisdom of yielding too much to the paranoia of the French and had become worried that the Germans would not sign. It also confirmed the judgment of some members of the American contingent such as Lansing, who thought the entire thrust of the treaty was a mistake and had no faith whatsoever in the League of Nations. If the Germans believed that their appeal to justice would move Wilson to support their major claims, however, they were profoundly mistaken. The president had already told South Africa's General Jan Christiaan Smuts, who favored a more liberal treaty, that he wished to treat Germany fairly but could not forget "the very great offense against civilization which the German state committed and the necessity for making it evident once and for all that such things can lead only to the most severe punishment."[18] At a full meeting of the American delegation on June 3, Wilson brought these

17. Brockdorf-Rantzau to Clemenceau, May 10, 13, and 29, 1919, in ibid., 572, 727, 739, 818; 6: 795.
18. Wilson to Jan Christiaan Smuts, May 16, 1919, in W. K. Hancock and Jean van der Poel, eds., *Selections from the Smuts Papers*, 4 vols. (Cambridge, 1966), 4: 161.

sentiments directly to bear on the German counterproposals. "Where have they made their good points?" he asked. "Where have they shown that the arrangements of the treaty are essentially unjust?" The question was not "Where have they merely shown that they are hard?" the president continued, "for they are hard—but the Germans earned that. And I think it is profitable that a nation should learn once and for all what an unjust war means in itself."[19]

Wilson in fact supported a number of Germany's requests, including modification of the terms of the Rhineland occupation and the elimination of a clause that would have required Germany to buy back the Saar even if the future plebiscite should go in Germany's favor. He agreed with Lloyd George that the cession of Upper Silesia should be conditional on a vote of the population, and secured a provision calling for Germany's future admission to the league. On the last point, however, he showed no change from the view, first expressed in his speech of September 27, 1918, that "Germany will have to redeem her character, not by what happens at the peace table but by what follows." Before admitting Germany, he told the American delegation, "we should know that the change in government and the governmental method in Germany is genuine and permanent. We don't know either of them yet."[20]

In all other respects, the original treaty was simply returned to the Germans with an ultimatum: they must accept it within one week or face occupation and possible dismemberment of their country. The German peace delegation, true to Brockdorf-Rantzau's basic strategy, thereupon recommended rejection of the treaty. But in Berlin, the government and the parties were divided, and that split permitted no other course than acceptance of the treaty. The Scheidemann cabinet chose to resign rather than accept the inevitable, however, and the new Socialist-Center coalition, hastily assembled by Gustav Bauer, made a final effort to save face. In an extraordinary Sunday session on June 22, the National Assembly approved the treaty with reservations concerning Articles 227–231 (articles that provided for the trial of William II and the delivery of alleged German war criminals to Allied tribunals and contained the imputation of Germany's war guilt). Of all the possible reservations,

19. Stenographic report of meeting of June 3, 1919, in *Foreign Relations: Paris Peace Conference,* 11: 218.

20. Address of the President, September 27, 1918, in *Foreign Relations, 1918, Supplement I,* 1: 318; stenographic report of meeting of June 3, 1919, in *Foreign Relations: Paris Peace Conference,* 11: 215.

these were among the least likely to win American support. Wilson himself proposed the official reply:

> The Allied and Associated Governments have given the fullest consideration to all of the representations made by the German Government with respect to the Treaty, have replied with complete frankness and have made such concessions as they thought it just to make. . . . They can accept or acknowledge no qualification or reservation and must require of the German representatives an unequivocal decision. . . .[21]

Left without further recourse and faced with the prospect of economic chaos, occupation, and civil war, Germany signed the treaty under protest on June 28. The ceremony was staged by the French in the Hall of Mirrors of the palace of Versailles, where the German Empire had been proclaimed less than half a century before.

Victors Divided

The fact that a peace treaty had been imposed on Germany gave added significance to its enforcement provisions and raised immediate problems for the United States. Wilson's interest in the establishment of a stable, responsible, and viable Germany had arisen in part from his general concept of international relations. But it had also been reenforced by the president's unwillingness to commit the United States to extended policing operations in Europe. Had Germany willingly accepted a truly negotiated settlement, it might have been taken for granted that the country would readily fulfill the terms of agreement and that the United States would have no obligations beyond those assumed as a member of the league. But the Treaty of Versailles saddled Germany with commitments that it was initially unwilling and, it claimed, unable to fulfill. The treaty also provided for the temporary occupation of German territory as a means of forcing compliance. The United States, which had acquiesced in this plan only when France absolutely refused to be dissuaded from it, could not now decline to participate in the enforcement of the treaty without relinquishing its own claims. This it was unwilling to do. American participation was also still regarded as a necessary brake on France, whose continuing interest in permanently separating the Rhineland from Germany had been displayed

21. Reply of same day to Geman note of June 22, 1919, in ibid., 6: 612.

again on June 1, when French generals had connived at Wiesbaden in the proclamation of a "Rhenish Republic."

Wilson still hoped that the occupation would not last the fifteen years specified by the treaty but would be substantially shortened once Germany was admitted to the league, and agreed to provide American troops for the occupation of the area between the Rhine and the borders of France and the Low Countries. They were to make up 5 percent of the 150,000-man force ultimately agreed upon. A special American zone of occupation was to center on the city of Coblenz, and an American was to serve as one of the civilian commissioners charged with the general supervision of the entire enterprise. At the same time, the United States continued its active representation on the Supreme War Council, which, until the formal ratification of the peace treaty, exercised control over the conduct of Germany. It also assisted in the preparatory work for the Reparations Commission, on which it expected to have full membership. And, though always with some reluctance, the U.S. became involved in a variety of other ways in the initial attack on what were seen primarily as Europe's postwar problems.

This already somewhat ambivalent American position was further complicated by the battle over ratification of the Versailles treaty which occupied the U.S. Senate during the summer of 1919. Although it was the commitment to the League of Nations which proved to be the biggest bone of contention, the various other obligations that the United States seemed to assume under the treaty, including the continued presence of troops in Germany, formed part of the general criticism. When, therefore, the Senate rejected the treaty on November 19 and made future ratification highly doubtful, the United States began to curtail its activities. It withdrew its representatives on the Supreme War Council and delegated the ambassador in France as "unofficial observer" to that body. The number of troops in Europe was sharply reduced. Then, on January 20, 1920, the Treaty of Versailles officially went into effect, and the Allies were at peace with Germany.

Since the United States remained technically at war, the German-American relationship became more confused than ever. After the Senate rejected the treaty for the final time on March 19, the American member of the Rhineland Commission was withdrawn, even though troops under Major General Henry T. Allen remained at Coblenz, acting technically still under the terms of the armistice agreement. The United States never joined the Reparations Commission at all, but sent yet another unofficial observer, who quickly became involved in the numerous matters that directly affected the U.S., such as the disposal of the German merchant ships and tankers. Ironically, the American relation to the Reparations Commission became technically the same as that of Germany, which also sent an observer, and the unrealistic nature of the entire arrangement was thus clearly demonstrated. On February 19, 1921, the United States withdrew from the commission altogether, though none of the major problems had been resolved by that time.

The relationship between the United States and Germany in the immediate postwar period was thus the most awkward imaginable. Although American restrictions on trade with Germany had been lifted as early as July 11, 1919, the two countries remained technically at war for more than two years after that and were unable and, at least on the American side, unwilling to enter into direct contacts with each other. Still acting under the terms of the armistice, the United States once again sent Ellis Loring Dresel to Berlin as a "commissioner" charged with maintaining contacts, but resolutely denied Germany's repeated requests to send even "unofficial" representatives to Washington.

All of this did not alter the fact that the renewal of trade brought immediate problems or that the United States still had direct claims on Germany resulting from the war and a continuing interest in the manner in which the Versailles treaty was carried out. America opposed, for example, the French occupation of Frankfurt and Darmstadt in April 1920 in retaliation for Germany's sending troops to quell the separatist movement in the Ruhr. It likewise opposed the French seizure of the Rhine ports of Duisburg, Düsseldorf, and Ruhrort in March 1921, when the Reparations Commission found Germany to be technically in default of its payments. Given its peculiar position, however, the U.S. could neither actively support Germany's objections nor work through the machinery set up by the peace treaty to alter the situation. The objections that it raised with the French, virtually as an outsider, were ineffectual.

Still, the German government continued, *faute de mieux*, to seek the aid of the United States. Dresel, who was sympathetic to such requests, was often sought out by German leaders, who looked to America to exert a moderating influence among the victorious powers. Repeated rebuffs, to be sure, produced occasional pique—at one point the Germans even objected to the appointment of an American to the international commission set up to supervise Germany's inland waterways—but this did not alter the basic thrust of the relationship.

Since the Germans were now wholly disillusioned with Wilson, the Democratic defeat in the election of 1920 ironically provided them with some new hope. The Republicans had on the whole been far more Germanophobic than Wilson and less inclined than the president to commit themselves to an active postwar role. Nevertheless, the Germans soon came to believe, or at least to hope, that the return to power of a party broadly representative of American business would bring to Washington a sense that the restoration of a viable world economy depended on the restoration of a stable and prosperous Germany—and that only an amelioration of the peace terms and a check on the designs of France could produce such a result. That hope grew all the more readily because the German elections of June 1920 had eliminated the Socialists from the government and increased the influence of Germany's businessmen on the policies of the new republic. The basis was thus laid for the cultivation of good relations with the United States and for the increasing quest for American assistance, both moral and economic. Cooperation with America was to become part of that policy of ostensible "fulfillment" through which Germany hoped to rebuild its international respectability and, at least in part, its prewar standing.

Chapter 6

THE FRUITS
OF VERSAILLES

*

The April Action and Peace

The First World War and its outcome drastically changed the international status of both the United States and Germany and altered their relationship. Both before 1880, when the two nations had concentrated on domestic development, and in the three decades before the First World War, when they became rivals for trade and world power, their position had been one of relative equality. If Germany developed a more potent military posture and adopted a more aggressive stance in world affairs, the United States had more abundant resources, a greater potential for industrial development, and a larger population. The two nations thus could and did regard each other essentially as equals.

The First World War changed that dramatically. The Treaty of Versailles not only eliminated Germany as a major military factor by sharply limiting its armed forces, it also reduced the country's population, territory, and resources, and, through the mechanism of reparations, converted Germany into the world's major debtor. At the same time, the war and its outcome enormously strengthened the position of the United States. The conflict provided the first convincing demonstration of America's military prowess and greatly expanded the nation's production and trading capabilities. In response to the wartime and immediate postwar needs of the Allies, the conflict also made the U.S. the world's leading creditor nation. The two countries thus moved far apart in terms of relative power.

It is hardly surprising, therefore, that German-American relations underwent their second major transformation in the postwar period, though the nature of that transformation could not be presupposed. The United States, for example, might well have attempted to exploit its victory and Germany's weakness, as France was to do, by simply moving vigorously into Germany's traditional markets and actively seeking economic domination of Germany itself. Germany, in turn, might have continued to deal with America essentially as a rival and even as an enemy. Although proponents of such a course could be found in both countries after 1920, it quickly became apparent that the long-range interests of neither would thereby be served. As a result, after some initial ambiguity, a new spirit of cooperation and even of friendship began to manifest itself, a spirit unmatched since the days of Bismarck and President Grant. In contrast to the earlier situation, however, the discrepancy in power and status remained acutely apparent and tempered both Germany's expectations and the American response.

Whatever the residue of wartime bitterness and peace conference disappointment, the overriding interest of postwar Germany lay in the establishment of effective government, the rebuilding of a shattered economy, and the recovery of at least some degree of influence in international relations. Although the first of these objectives might be attained largely by Germany's own efforts, success even in this area depended in the long run on visible progress toward attainment of the other two. And Germany could neither restore its economic well-being nor regain international prestige without outside assistance that would either circumvent or modify the burdens imposed by the Versailles treaty.

Since France remained Germany's most determined adversary and almost all other nations were too weak to be of help, the Germans could realistically turn only to the Soviet Union, Great Britain, or the United States. The first of these choices, the joining together of Europe's two postwar pariahs, seemed natural in a sense. It manifested itself in the informal military cooperation that the commander of the *Reichswehr,* General Hans von Seeckt, established with the Red Army as early as 1920, in a trade treaty concluded in May 1921, and, most significantly, in the Rapallo treaty, a Soviet-German friendship pact of April 6, 1922, by which Germany became the first of the major countries to establish formal diplomatic relations with the Bolshevik regime.

This Russo-German rapprochement did not, however, meet the basic needs of either party. Not only were both countries too weak and poor to help each other more than marginally, their cooperation was far more likely to accentuate their outcast status and raise new fears of a Bolshevik menace in the West than it was to gain a greater degree of international acceptance for either. Moreover, the German government had been forced to expend considerable effort in 1920/21 to put down Communist uprisings in both the Ruhr and in eastern Germany and was extremely wary of moving too close to a regime that had covertly supported the revolutionaries. As a result, Soviet-German cooperation was never regarded in Berlin as more than a stopgap arrangement that might bring minor tactical benefits and could, it if did not backfire, persuade at least some of the Western powers that a less punitive stance toward Germany would be the course of wisdom as well as justice.

The attempt to secure better relations with Great Britain seemed far more promising to many of Germany's leaders, who hoped to magnify the policy differences between Britain and France in order to attain, at first, forbearance with regard to the Versailles treaty and, later, revision of the treaty itself. Indeed, a succession of German foreign secretaries strove mightily to split Britain from France, and Viscount d'Abernon, who served as British ambassador in Berlin from 1920 to 1926, frequently assumed a mediating role in German negotiations with the former Allies on reparations and similar matters. In the final analysis, however, neither full implementation nor modification of the Versailles settlement was possible without the participation of the United States. German efforts were consequently directed toward securing the goodwill and cooperation of the government in Washington.

As wartime Germanophobia began to ebb, the United States began to reveal a certain willingness to reciprocate. The predominant influence in America during much of the 1920s was exerted by those who had always opposed what they regarded as meddling in European affairs and by disillusioned Wilsonians, who looked on the Versailles treaty as a recipe for renewed war and wanted no part in its enforcement. Logically, both groups would have preferred a policy of isolation marked by American withdrawal from world affairs, yet both recognized the impossibility of such a course. Given the now dominant position of the United States in world trade and the international money market, which neither group was prepared to relinquish, and given the development of postwar economic problems whose solution depended on international stability and order, another approach had to be found.

Under a series of Republican administrations attuned to a business leadership with such world views, the United States embarked in the 1920s upon a policy of involvement without commitment. Through this policy it tried to stabilize the international situation without accepting the formal responsibilities of membership in the League of Nations or other alliances. In promoting disarmament and the outlawry of war and seeking, however unofficially, to resolve the war debts–reparations tangle that threatened the world economy and the stability of all nations, the United States found itself increasingly interested in a stable and prosperous Germany. As a result, it also came to favor the de facto modification of the Versailles settlement. Renewed cooperation between the two countries could thus begin to flourish, particularly since Germany could not make serious demands that might undermine the highly prized "independence" of American foreign policy.

The most pressing issue facing the Germans at the end of 1920 was the settlement of the reparations question. The Versailles treaty had laid down the principles to be applied, but the Allies had been unable to agree on a fixed sum and left the matter to further negotiations among themselves. May 1, 1921, had been set as the deadline for a final decision. With the failure of the United States to ratify the peace treaty, American participation in the process of determining the extent of Germany's obligations had effectively ceased and the influence of France increased correspondingly. Germany meanwhile was obligated to make interim payments and had encountered difficulties in making them to the satisfaction of the Allies. Without a clear notion of what the ultimate bill might be, it was impossible for the Germans to engage in meaningful planning for the fulfillment of their obligations, even to the extent that they were prepared to do so, and equally impossible to negotiate the all-important terms of payment intelligently.

Despite the importance of a clearcut decision, the government in Berlin for a time sought to postpone it in hopes that a dissipation of wartime emotions would improve Germany's chance for a reasonable settlement. The possibility of such a development seemed to grow after the American elections of 1920 guaranteed a new administration in Washington which might, so Germany hoped, resume American involvement with the reparations question and thus serve to check France's more immoderate demands. This strategy received a setback on January 29, 1921, when the Supreme Council—it was no longer a war council—presented Germany with a staggering bill for 226 billion gold marks, plus 12 percent of the annual value of its exports, to be paid over a forty-two-year period. The Germans thereupon offered 50 billion marks to be paid over five years. They knew this proposal would be rejected but hoped it would lead to the constitution of a new committee of experts which the United States might be persuaded to join. The immediate result was not further postponement, however, but the imposition of sanctions by the infuriated Allies. French troops were ordered to occupy three Rhine ports on March 8, and the High Commission in Coblenz was empowered to collect tariffs in the Rhineland and impose special customs duties on the eastern boundary of that territory. If Germany refused to meet willingly the reparations demands of the Allies, payments would be collected by force.

Faced with this new contingency, the German government decided to make a direct appeal to the new American administration. Initially, it took the form of a lengthy memorandum that Foreign Secretary Walther Simons passed on to Dresel for communication to Washington. The memorandum did not specifically ask for American intervention but stressed the reasonableness of Germany's position by indicating the country's willingness to pay reparations to the limits of its ability and to have these limits set by a committee of impartial experts. The new secretary of state, Charles Evans Hughes, was as wary as his predecessors had been of allowing the United States to be maneuvered into supporting the cause of Germany against that of the Allies, and even more wary than they of entering into any binding commitments. He therefore stressed in his reply to Dresel that "this Government stands with the Governments of the Allies in holding Germany responsible for the war and therefore morally bound to make reparation. . . ." At the same time, however, he responded positively to the German initiative. The United States, he declared, "recognizes in the memorandum of Dr. Simons a sincere desire on the part of the German Government to reopen negotiations with the Allies on a new basis and hopes that such negotiations, once resumed, may lead to a prompt settlement which will at the same time satisfy the just claims of the Allies *and permit Germany hopefully to renew its productive activities.*"[1]

It is indicative both of the German government's more rational attitude and of its greater recognition of its own weakness that Simons chose to ignore the renewed imputation of war guilt and instead placed importance on Hughes's expressed interest in new negotiations. Accordingly, Berlin formally asked President Warren G. Harding on April 20 to serve as arbitrator in the reparations dispute, and announced that "the German Government is ready and willing to agree without qualification and reservation to pay to the Allied powers as reparation such a sum as the President after examination and investigation may find just and right."[2] The United States had been approached in this fashion, Simons explained to the Reichstag, not merely because of the decisive influence it had exerted on the outcome of the war, but also because "she is the only power with the financial strength to contribute something meaningful to the solution of the reparation problem," a power, moreover, whose perception of the matter might be expected to be "less clouded by passion and self-interest" than that of the others.[3]

The United States could not, of course, accept the German offer without creating insurmountable problems with the Allies and involving itself further in Europe's affairs than even league membership would have done. Given its interest in international stability, however, the U.S. was prepared to be of some assistance. Hughes, even at this early date, believed a reasonable settlement of the reparations question to be a matter of importance for the United States and was more than willing to have America participate in the search for a solution. Any such participation, however, would have to come on the technical-economic rather than the political level and could be effective only if it were requested by all parties, not merely by Germany. The secretary of state, in short, hoped to be able to maneuver the United States into the position of "honest broker." The official American reply to the German request therefore turned down the arbitrator role for Harding but expressed a desire for "an immediate resumption of negotiations" and offered to transmit to the

1. Charles Evans Hughes to Dresel, March 29, 1921, in *Foreign Relations of the United States: Diplomatic Papers, 1921,* 2: 40. Emphasis added.
2. Dresel to Hughes, April 20, 1921, in ibid., 41.
3. Walter Simons, remarks of April 22, 1921, in *Verhandlungen des Reichstags: Stenographische Berichte,* 1st election period (Berlin, 1920–1924), 349: 3377.

Allies any proposals Germany might wish to make. Unofficially, Hughes was prepared to go even further. "You may tell Simons informally and confidentially," he cabled to Dresel, "that although the Government will not act as umpire in settlement of reparations problem, it would be willing *with concurrence of Allied Governments* to take part in the negotiations."[4]

Despite such evidence of American interest and goodwill, no immediate results were forthcoming. Germany, as it turned out, was not acting entirely in good faith, and the Allies, particularly France, were not yet ready to grant the United States a potentially decisive role. The German counterproposals submitted to Washington on April 24 did not go substantially beyond those the Allies had already rejected in early March and thus did not provide an adequate basis for new negotiations. In any event, they could not be seriously considered before the May 1 deadline for fixing the "final" reparations sum, a deadline the Allies were unwilling to postpone. On April 27 the Reparations Commission—to which the new administration had, despite Senate objections and much to Germany's delight, once more sent an "unofficial observer"—agreed to set the indemnity demanded of Germany at 132 billion mark. This was a substantial reduction from the January figure but still far in excess of what the Germans claimed they could reasonably pay. The Berlin government refused even to discuss this new figure on the wholly specious ground that no reply had been received from Washington to its proposal of April 24.

The United States was thereby placed in the position where pushing for further negotiations effectively meant taking the side of Germany against the Allies. This Hughes remained wholly unwilling to do. Having established that France vehemently opposed further negotiations on the basis proposed by the Germans, on May 2 he rejected the German conterproposals as inadequate. He urged Berlin instead to come forward immediately with clear, definitive, and adequate proposals to be made directly to the Allies. The Allies, however, were unwilling to wait even for that. On May 5 they demanded unconditional acceptance within one week of the sum proposed by the Reparations Commission and of a new, demanding repayment schedule. They made clear their intention to occupy the Ruhr if such acceptance were not forthcoming. The German cabinet

4. Hughes to Dresel, April 21, 1921, in *Foreign Relations, 1921*, 2: 44, 45. Emphasis added.

resigned in the face of this ultimatum and of the failure of its "April Action" toward the United States, but the new government bowed to inevitable. Chancellor Joseph Wirth accepted the terms and declared his intention of setting Germany on a course toward fulfilling them.

The involvement of the United States in the reparations discussion, however tentative and cautious, reemphasized the country's anomalous position. On the one hand, America had a clear stake in these discussions by virtue of its predominant financial and trading position and of its own claims against Germany, particularly with respect to occupation costs. On the other, it had refused to ratify the Versailles treaty, which dealt with these matters, and was in fact still technically at war with Germany. Congress now addressed itself to the latter problem.

After the final rejection of the peace treaty by the Senate, Philander C. Knox, Republican of Pennsylvania, had proposed making peace with Germany by the simple expedient of repealing the declaration of war. A resolution to that effect had been adopted on May 27, 1920, with an added proviso allowing the United States to retain German property seized during the war until war claims had been satisfactorily settled. Wilson had indignantly vetoed this measure as unworthy of a great nation, and the attempt to override the veto had failed. When Harding, in his first speech to Congress on April 12, 1921, indicated a willingness to sign a Congressional resolution ending the war, Knox promptly reintroduced his measure.

What emerged from the ensuing debates was the Knox-Porter Resolution, which the president signed on July 2. This measure not only unilaterally declared the war between the United States and Germany to be at an end but also claimed for America all rights, privileges, indemnities, reparations, and advantages arising from the armistice, the Versailles treaty, and the fact of American participation in the war. The United States also arrogated to itself the right to secure its claims by force and again expressed its determination to retain seized German property until all claims had been met. In short, the U.S. insisted on all of the benefits of the peace settlement without assuming attendant obligations, such as league membership or participation in the enforcement of the Versailles treaty.

However much such a declaration might have pleased the leaders of Congress, it did not of itself reestablish a condition of peace between the United States and Germany. At the very least, it was necessary to persuade Germany to accept this arrangement formally and to agree to abide by its terms, and this the Germans were reluctant to do. The Versailles treaty, with all of its shortcomings, at least spelled out some limits, both in quantity and in time, to Germany's obligations, while the Knox-Porter Resolution, if taken literally, recognized no such limits. Moreover, the Germans hoped to join with the United States in the genuine peace negotiations they had been denied at Versailles and to emerge with a separate treaty that might in some respects serve to undermine the Versailles settlement. The United States was in no mood to further the latter objective, but it did recognize certain advantages in a treaty that Germany would willingly sign and thus presumably fulfill. Despite the rhetoric of the Congressional resolution, it was after all impossible for the United States to embark on enforcement action separate from that of the Allies, who rightly claimed that the Versailles treaty already constituted a first mortgage on all of Germany's assets.

The American request for a protocol of agreement was met by Germany's suggestion for a bilateral document that would spell out both the rights and the duties of the United States under the proposed settlement. Hughes thereupon began to talk in terms of an actual treaty that would incorporate those portions of the Versailles settlement—section 1 of part 4 and all of parts 5, 6, 8–12, 14, and 15—from which America's rights and privileges could be derived. He refused to make the terms more precise, on the grounds that doing so "would amount to an attempt to insert a commentary upon the Treaty of Versailles," something that could only lead to trouble in the Senate. But he agreed to the addition of a clause indicating "that the United States, in availing itself of the rights and advantages stipulated in the provisions of that Treaty . . . will do so in a manner consistent with the rights accorded to Germany under such provisions."[5] As an inducement to Germany to sign this "Treaty between the United States and Germany Restoring Friendly Relations," Hughes offered the immediate resumption of diplomatic relations.

Although the Foreign Office initially opposed this proposal and urged that the apparent American interest be used to win far-reaching concessions, wiser opinions soon prevailed. While sharing the illogical view of the Foreign Office and of Walther Rathenau, the minister for reconstruction, that the Americans "wanted a favor" from Germany for domestic reasons, representatives of the minis-

5. Hughes to Dresel, July 28, 1921, in ibid., 10.

tries of finance and economic affairs nevertheless argued that much needed loans would not be forthcoming so long as a state of war formally existed and that trade and tourism would also suffer if no treaty were signed. The new foreign secretary, Friedrich Rosen, accepted this reasoning and was also influenced by Dresel's argument that a negative attitude toward American proposals would be interpreted by both Congress and the public as a rejection of "the proffered hand of peace." Given the possibility that Germany would be unable to fulfill the reparations obligations it had just assumed and thus once more face the prospect of a Ruhr occupation, the possible loss of American sympathies constituted too grave a risk. "Germany must," Rosen told the cabinet, "look to the United States. Whether they would help is certainly an open question; but this last and only chance should not be destroyed."[6] Chancellor Wirth was moved by similar considerations and, in the final analysis, accepted the view of the American secretary of state. "It should be clearly understood," Hughes had written to Dresel, "that opposition to the Treaty or delay in connection with its signing or ratification by Germany cannot in any possible contingency be helpful to Germany."[7] Acceptance might be.

Although the German government thereupon decided to accept the terms as offered and obtained the agreement of all non-Communist parties to ratification, it asked for further clarification and for a formal promise that diplomatic relations would be resumed at once and questions of trade and of seized German property negotiated. Hughes remained unwilling to go beyond the Knox-Porter Resolution in spelling out terms for fear that Congressional approval would then be unlikely. He readily promised, however, "to resume diplomatic relations at once upon exchange of ratifications and then to undertake any negotiations that may be desired by either Germany or the United States with relation to commerce or other matters." As an added inducement for prompt German approval, he indicated that ways would be found to settle the issue of seized

6. Minutes of meetings of July 20 and August 12, 1921, in *Akten der Reichskanzlei: Die Kabinette Wirth I und II*, 2 vols. (Boppard am Rhein, 1973), I: 145, 195–197; "Akten der Reichskanzlei," file R43, vol. 1, document 95, in Bundesarchiv, Koblenz; meetings of August 12 and 13, 1921, in files of Political Division III (United States of America), Politics 2, Supplement "Friedenschluss," vol. 2, in Politisches Archiv des Auswärtigen Amtes, Bonn.

7. Hughes to Dresel, August 11, 1921, in State Department Decimal File 711.62119/29, RG 59, NA.

German property, "which the President desires to be dealt with upon the most fair and righteous basis."[8]

The so-called Treaty of Berlin was signed on August 25, 1921. It was approved by the Reichstag on September 30 without debate and with only the Communist deputies voicing opposition. Although the arrangement theoretically reaffirmed the hated Versailles treaty and thus offered no direct tangible benefits to Germany, it had, unlike the Versailles treaty itself, resulted from some genuine negotiations and it specifically recognized the existence of German rights as well as obligations. Acceptance, moreover, was likely to increase American goodwill toward Germany, which in turn might prove helpful in future dealings with the Allies.

The U.S. Senate gave its approval by a large margin on October 18. Only the old "Irreconcilables" voted no, on the grounds that the settlement incorporated portions of the Treaty of Versailles. They were mollified neither by the exclusion of the League Covenant and of all other sections of the treaty which might have committed the United States to some form of international cooperation, nor by the Senate's reservation that reaffirmed America's independent position by insisting that "the United States shall not be represented or participate in any body, agency or commission . . . in which the United States is authorized to participate by this treaty, unless and until an Act of the Congress of the United States shall provide for such representation or participation."[9] The vast majority of the senators, however, shared the administration's belief that the Treaty of Berlin, by normalizing relations with Germany without either relinquishing American claims or assuming the international obligations that had been rejected in 1919 and 1920, was in accord with an independent foreign policy designed to serve America's particular interests. Ratifications were formally exchanged on November 11, three full years after the fighting had stopped. Formal diplomatic relations between the two countries were resumed five days later.

A Mutuality of Interests

The primary postwar concerns of both the United States and Germany in their dealings with each other were economic in nature, and this was clearly reflected in the first exchange of ambassadors. The

8. Hughes to Dresel, August 20, 1921 in *Foreign Relations, 1921*, 2: 19–20.
9. Treaty of August 25, 1921, between the U.S. and Germany, in ibid., 33.

Germans appointed Otto Wiedfeldt, a director of the giant Krupp corporation, whose ties to Hugo Stinnes and other leading German industrialists were strong and of long standing. The United States reciprocated by sending to Berlin Representative Alanson B. Houghton of New York, the board chairman of Corning Glass, whose studies at various German universities were among his fondest recollections. For several years their major concerns were to be the settlement of American claims against Germany and the disposition of seized German property in the United States, the negotiation of a trade treaty between the two countries, and American involvement, in one form or another, in the increasingly complex reparations muddle. In the working out of these issues it became abundantly clear that the United States, operating from its position of great strength, could determine its own policy toward Germany without serious opposition from Berlin, which recognized its weakness and in every case eventually accommodated the wishes of the United States. At the same time, however, it was apparent that the U.S., for reasons of its own, was nearly as interested as Germany in a revision of the economic terms of the Versailles settlement, and that increasing American efforts to secure such revision would redound to Germany's benefit. The result was the development of a relationship between patently unequal powers which, at least in broad terms, was satisfactory to both and could be regarded by both as an indicator of the success of their policies.

Germany initially hoped that the resumption of diplomatic relations with the United States would bring about the immediate revival, with such modifications as might be necessitated by postwar conditions, of all of the treaties in force between the two countries in 1914. These included the Extradition Convention of 1852, the Bancroft Treaties of 1868 on the rights of naturalized Americans of German birth, the Consular Convention of 1871, the Copyright Agreement of 1892, and the Patent Convention of 1909. Most important to the Germans, however, was the revival in some form of the Treaty of Commerce and Navigation of 1828, which would have reinstituted trade between the two countries on the basis of the conditional most-favored-nation principle.

The United States readily agreed to revive the patent agreement, which, of course, protected American interests, and agreed informally to abide by existing copyright arrangements that did the same. But it was not interested in returning automatically to the status quo ante, and most particularly not interested either in immediately re-viving the old trade treaty or in negotiating a new one. Though Dresel, much to his subsequent embarrassment, had led the Foreign Office to think otherwise, the United States was perfectly happy to continue for the time being to enjoy unilaterally the most-favored-nation treatment, which under the terms of the Versailles treaty Germany was required to extend to all of the victorious powers until 1925. America was, in any event, already planning to shift its entire trade policy to take advantage of its new dominance in world markets.

The divergence in views over these matters simply demonstrates the differing status of the two countries. For Germany, the return to prewar arrangements with the United States meant overcoming, at least in part, the disabilities her defeat had brought. America, on the other hand, wished to protect and consolidate the gains it had made and thus had no interest in pre-1914 conditions per se. Nevertheless, the aims of both German and American policy turned out to have a common denominator. As the United States encountered increasing economic difficulties during the severe postwar recession of 1921/22, the reestablishment of economic equilibrium on a worldwide basis and the revival of world trade became central objectives of Ameri-can foreign policy. First, however, currencies had to be stabilized, and this in turn seemed to require attention to the basic problems of Germany. "Currencies cannot be stabilized," Secretary of Com-merce Herbert Hoover explained to Harding on January 2, 1922, "until inflation has stopped, and inflation cannot be stopped until government budgets are balanced, and government budgets of Europe cannot be balanced until there is a proper settlement of reparations. . . ." A "proper settlement" clearly required breaking the impasse on the reparations issue that existed primarily between France and Germany, "for chaos here is defeat everywhere."[10] Hoover's views were strongly seconded by leaders of the American business and banking communities.

For a brief time the possibility of acting on such advice was lim-ited by concern over Congressional attitudes. In the first place, the administration was worried about ratification of the treaties on naval limitations and Great Power relationships in the Far East, which had

10. Memorandum attached to letter, Hoover to Harding, January 2, 1922, quoted in Werner Link, *Die amerikanische Stabilisierungspolitik in Deutschland, 1921–1932* (Düsseldorf, 1970), p. 107.

come out of the Washington conference of 1921, and wary of arousing isolationist ire that might prevent Senate approval. The appearance of wishing to meddle in European affairs therefore had to be avoided. In addition, the sensitive issue of Allied war debts, which provided some diplomatic leverage and suggested possible solutions to the reparations tangle, remained unresolved. On February 9, however, the World War Foreign Debt Commission was established by Congress through a bill that categorically forbade the cancellation of war debts, their extension beyond 1947, or the reduction of the interest rate below 4½ percent. The possibility of mutual adjustments in war debts and reparations was thus ruled out, but the Commission and the administration were left with some influence on funding proposals and therefore with some room in the negotiations on other economic matters, including reparations. At the end of March, moreover, the Senate ratified the Washington treaties.

Reduced to its simplest terms, the reparations problem in 1922 was caused by Germany's apparent inability to meet the payment requirements imposed upon it. The obligation for payments in kind and the restrictions placed on German trade made it impossible for Germany to earn sufficient foreign exchange to make cash payments of the order required. Mounting inflation in Germany ruled out the payment in marks. Germany's inability to pay in turn slowed reconstruction particularly in France, Belgium, and Italy, caused economic difficulties in those nations, and made them reluctant to meet their obligations to the United States. The most obvious way out of the immediate dilemma was to support the German economy with foreign loans that would have a stabilizing effect and permit the resumption of that cash flow on which most of the other economic difficulties hinged. Any infusion of capital into Germany, however, depended primarily on the United States. Given both Congressional attitudes and the general American reluctance to run the risk of even greater entanglement through government loans, this infusion depended particularly on American bankers. The bankers, who were clearly interested in a revival of the world economy, were willing enough to lend money to Germany. But they were interested in such an action only if Germany's reparations obligations were reduced to a sum that the Germans were willing and able to pay and Germany thus put in a position to repay the new loans.

Acting from such considerations, the United States sought informally to persuade the Reparations Commission to establish a committee of experts, on which both Germany and the United States were to be represented, which was to explore the possibility of international loans to be applied to the redemption of part of the reparations debt. When Great Britain made such a proposal formally in mid-March and saw it adopted on April 4, the United States appointed no less a personage than J. P. Morgan as its representative on the committee. In so doing, it embarked on a course it was to follow in broad outline for the remainder of the 1920s. Without entering into any formal, governmental commitments and without joining the Reparations Commission itself (an action that Congress would have had to approve), the United States brought its powerful international position and its unmatched financial resources to bear on the solution of the reparations problem in an effort to restore world economic stability and prosperity.

The initial attempt failed because even the redoubtable J. P. Morgan proved unable to persuade French Premier Raymond Poincaré of the necessity for reducing the demands on Germany. France still believed that the Germans were less unable than unwilling to pay and that further sanctions, especially the occupation of the Ruhr, would change their attitude. Poincaré also still hoped that American loans would eventually be forthcoming even without any yielding on the part of France. The Germans, of course, regretted the failure of the American action, for which they largely blamed the French. Germany's industrial leaders in particular, among them Ambassador Wiedfeldt, were now more convinced than ever that only Germany's actual bankruptcy would be sufficient to overcome French intransigence and produce a bearable settlement.

The government in Berlin was not yet prepared for such a cold-blooded conclusion. It had hoped that America would provide loans at least on an interim basis even without French concessions so that the occupation of the Ruhr and the enormous hardships that bankruptcy would bring to the German people might be avoided. The hard line taken by American bankers was therefore a disappointment. Still, the German government could only welcome the fact of U.S. intervention, the increasing isolation of the French, and what seemed to be a greater American awareness of Germany's dilemma. It could therefore embark confidently on a policy of accommodating the United States in other matters, on the assumption that this policy would in the long run help Germany with the reparations issue as well.

The characteristics of this policy were demonstrated most dramatically around the issue of claims against Germany by American individuals and firms, and even by the federal government itself, arising from damages sustained prior to American entry into the war. Congress was particularly anxious for a prompt settlement, and the State Department wanted a satisfactory solution before either the question of the return of seized German property or a new trade agreement was broached. Hughes therefore politely ignored a German request for trade negotiations in April 1922, but countered with the proposal to set up a mixed claims commission. When Ambassador Houghton discussed this matter fully and frankly with Foreign Office officials on May 5, he raised the question of the composition of such a commission. He readily conceded, much to Germany's relief, that there should be a German as well as an American member, but insisted on a third person who could act if the others failed to reach agreement. Houghton, moreover, suggested the appointment of a second American "of high position" and, adding insult to injury, indicated that a request by Germany for such an appointment would have a favorable effect on the attitude of Congress.

Given the desperate need of the Germans to win American approval and support, this extraordinary proposal was readily accepted. Praising Houghton's "valuable suggestion" and claiming, however disingenuously, that "as early an understanding as is possible [on the claims issue] lies especially near my heart also," Walther Rathenau, now foreign secretary, agreed to the establishment of a commission and on June 2 proposed formally, on behalf of the German government, "that the President of the United States be requested . . . to cause a prominent American citizen whose capabilities and character are beyond criticism to take over the honorary chairmanship of the commission mentioned."[11] In subsequent negotiations, a draft agreement proposed by the United States on June 22 was modified only slightly, with Germany yielding quickly on all counterproposals that proved unacceptable to the United States. The role of the "honorary chairman" was clearly defined as that of an umpire whose decision would be final, and the ultimate responsibility for determining both the extent of Germany's obligations and the manner in which these were to be met thus fell to Associate Justice William Rufus Day of the United States Supreme Court, whom Harding initially appointed, and to his successors over the nearly nineteen-year life of the commission.

11. Rathenau to Houghton, June 2, 1922, in *Foreign Relations, 1922*, 2: 244–245.

Germany's formal acceptance on August 22, 1922, of such an arrangement, which not only was patently inequitable but also contravened Article 304 of the Versailles treaty, clearly indicates the parameters within which German foreign policy then operated. The government of Chancellor Wirth obviously believed that no better scheme was possible, since under existing circumstances no technically neutral umpire would be more likely than an American to honor the arguments put forward by Germany. The suggested arrangement at least had the virtue of allowing the Germans a full voice in the settlement of claims. That even the United States might, in the absence of German agreement to a mixed commission of the sort proposed, resort to the kind of unilateral settlement that the Allies had imposed had been graphically demonstrated in late July, when Senator Oscar W. Underwood of Alabama introduced a bill to set up a commission composed entirely of Americans who would determine the validity of the claims and settle them through the sale of seized German property. Even a small portion of a loaf thus seemed better than none.

More important, however, Germany saw its acquiescence in the American scheme as part of a larger strategy. Given the new evidence of American interest in a revised reparations settlement and Hughes's insistence that without a claims agreement no trade negotiations were possible, Germany hoped that yielding on the smaller issue would pay dividends on the larger ones. American help was essential if the reparations burden were ever to be reduced, and negotiation of a trade agreement on the basis of equality with the world's leading industrial nation was the key to ending existing trade discrimination and discrediting the idea of continuing economic exploitation. To further these objectives, concessions on a claims settlement seemed a small price to pay. Nevertheless, the extent of the German capitulation to American demands was sufficiently great to prompt a handwritten memorandum from President Harding: "In making the announcement, please *emphasize* the request to us to name umpire. It is so unusual that its significance is worth bringing to the fore."[12]

Although no actual cause-and-effect relationship existed, subsequent events could be interpreted as demonstrating the accuracy of Germany's calculations and the wisdom of its policy. The Mixed

12. Harding to Hughes, n.d., received August 10, 1922, in ibid., 262. Original emphasis.

Claims Commission carried on its work conscientiously and with much concern for both moral and legal niceties until 1941. It approved only 7,025 of the 20,000 American claims, and the $181 million plus interest awarded was only a minor addition to Germany's total indebtedness. Moreover, the United States released, by the Winslow Act of 1923, all items of seized German property valued at under $10,000 and returned most of the rest five years later. Less than a year after the setting up of the Mixed Claims Commission, negotiations for a new trade treaty got under way and were successfully concluded before the end of 1923. Even before then, the United States had dramatically renewed its efforts to bring order out of the reparations tangle and, however incidentally, to lighten the load that Germany had to bear.

The reparations situation assumed crisis proportions in the second half of 1922, as the political and economic situation of Germany deteriorated rapidly. On June 24, 1922, Walther Rathenau, then the most prominent and most able proponent of the fulfillment policy, was assassinated by right-wing extremists, and potentially revolutionary rumblings from both the right and the left began to be heard with increasing frequency. At the same time, the already eroded mark began to fall rapidly, so that by the end of the year it traded at seven thousand to the dollar. With Germany at this point also falling further behind in some of its payments, the French increased their threats to strengthen control over the occupied Rhineland and to extend this control over the Ruhr as well.

The German government attempted to resolve this situation in a variety of ways. It prevailed upon Great Britain to convince France of the necessity for a moratorium on reparations payments to give the German economy the chance to recover, and even supported the efforts of Hugo Stinnes to negotiate with French industrialists about the possible establishment of joint Franco-German enterprises as part of a general reparations settlement. In the final analysis, however, the Wirth administration and the government headed by Wilhelm Cuno, which replaced it in November 1922, continued to appeal for help to the United States because, as Wiedfeldt told Hughes, "the situation was so critical and there was so much distrust that there was no Power but the United States that could command confidence and bring about a solution."[13]

13. Hughes memorandum of conversation with Wiedfeldt, October 9, 1922, in ibid., 164.

The United States was certainly concerned and by no means unwilling to help. Various proposals and possibilities were discussed in the State Department, informal discussions held both with Wiedfeldt and with French Ambassador Jules Jusserand, and equally informal suggestions made through Myron T. Herrick, the American ambassador in Paris. James A. Logan, America's "unofficial observer" with the Reparations Commission, was also actively engaged in seeking an acceptable solution. Since France continued to oppose all suggestions that might possibly lead to a reduction in reparations, however, little progress was made. The United States remained unwilling to place itself at the center of the controversy by coming forward with specific, substantive proposals of its own and was limited in its ability to put pressure on France both because it still hoped to collect payments on the French war debt and because it wanted French ratification of the treaties concerning the Far East that had resulted from the Washington conference of 1921.

Neither did the Germans prove particularly helpful. In response to repeated suggestions that matters might be more easily resolved if Germany worked out a proposal that forthrightly assessed both the justified claims of the Allies and its own ability to pay, only vague and unacceptable replies were forthcoming. With the policy of "fulfillment" increasingly under attack within the country, the Berlin government found it impossible to volunteer to pay the maximum of which it was capable or even to spell out precisely what that maximum was. Any such proposal, Finance Minister Andreas Hermes confessed, "would arouse indignation in Germany, since concessions would have to be made to the other side which would be regarded as too far-reaching by a large part of the German population, but which would be unavoidable in view of the existing political constellation and the oppressive provisions of the peace treaty."[14] As the situation became ever more critical, the only substantive move made by the new Cuno administration owed something to the prompting of Ambassador Houghton but demonstrated a highly unrealistic expectation of American political, rather than economic, intervention in the resolution of European problems.

On December 15 Ambassador Wiedfeldt approached Hughes with the suggestion that France's security concerns might be assuaged and its attitude toward Germany and reparations thereby softened if

14. Quoted in Link, *Stabilisierungspolitik*, p. 160.

the Berlin government agreed in advance to adhere to a "Rhine Peace Pact." Although the German origin of the proposal was not necessarily to be a secret, the major task of promoting the idea among the countries concerned was to be performed by the American government, which was also to serve as trustee of the agreement. The instructions the ambassador had received showed even more clearly than the version he ultimately passed on to the State Department how actively Germany wished to involve the United States. "If the Government and People of the United States," Berlin had cabled, "in order to save Europe were to come forward with the proposal that the Powers with interests on the Rhine, that is, France, England, Italy, Germany, should solemnly promise each other, and the United States as trustee, not to go to war with each other for one generation without special authorization by plebiscite, Germany would not hesitate to accept such an obligation."[15]

This proposal, though welcome as an indication of Germany's peaceful intent, was unhelpful. France could have regarded it as significant only if the United States had actually been willing to underwrite German compliance and thus to assume, in effect, obligations it had specifically rejected when it failed to ratify the guarantee treaty to which Wilson had agreed at Versailles. But Hughes, who passed the idea on to the French as a German suggestion, vigorously denied that it involved the assumption of any obligation by the United States. The French, in turn, were unwilling to trust the word of the Germans, all the more because they were certain that plebiscitary agreement on a war of revenge could be obtained by any German government that sought it.

By the end of 1922 the United States was thus in something of a dilemma. Hughes's secret, informal diplomacy had produced no tangible results, and the threat of worldwide economic disaster was more acute than ever. The secretary of state remained convinced that the United States needed a solution that did not involve unwanted political entanglements and continued to believe that the path to such a solution ran through a committee of independent financial experts. The findings of such a committee, on which Americans might well serve, could provide the basis for intergovernmental discussions among the European powers in which the United States could play a mediating role. The French had, of course, frus-

15. Minutes of cabinet meeting of December 31, 1922, in *Akten der Reichskanzlei: Das Kabinett Cuno* (Boppard am Rhein, 1968), pp. 109–110 n. 9.

trated this approach in July by their refusal to give the experts a free hand with possible recommendations. Thus the initial problem of even this "objectively economic and businesslike approach" remained the political one of convincing the French to modify their views. "If politicians, feeling themselves incompetent, request intervention of private parties," J. P. Morgan had bluntly told Hughes, then these private parties "must be given complete freedom to arrive at their conclusions and report to the politicians, leaving the latter to act or not as they see fit upon such recommendations."[16]

The crisis deepened. France moved closer to a Ruhr occupation, and Hughes came under increased criticism for alleged inaction (on December 22, for example, Senator William E. Borah of Idaho introduced an amendment to the naval appropriations bill which would have empowered the president to call an international conference on European economic and financial problems). The secretary of state now moved to make public his concerns and his proposal. In order to maintain the official American posture of impartiality and to avoid the appearance of undue pressure that France would resent, Hughes chose to offer his views in an address to the American Historical Association which he was scheduled to make in New Haven on December 29.

The New Haven speech reflected the policy of involvement without commitment which the United States pursued during most of the 1920s. While denying American responsibilities, it emphasized American concerns, and it made unmistakably clear that the desired solutions to the world's economic problems would, however incidentally, be beneficial to Germany. "The economic conditions in Europe," Hughes pointed out, "give us the greatest concern . . . for we are deeply interested from an economic standpoint, as our credits and markets are involved, and from a humanitarian standpoint, as the heart of the American people goes out to those who are in distress. We cannot dispose of these problems by calling them European, for they are world problems and we cannot escape the injurious consequences of a failure to settle them." The crux of the situation, he insisted moreover, "lies in the settlement of reparations." Hughes rejected any connection between reparations and war debts and maintained that the United States could not assume the role of arbiter except in the unlikely event that it would be freely

16. Morgan to Hughes, November 6, 1922, in State Department Decimal File 462.00 R296/7, RG 59, NA.

asked to do so by all parties concerned. But he proposed, for the first time publicly, an agreement by the governments concerned to set up a committee of independent—that is, nongovernmental—experts. "Why," he asked, "should they not invite men of the highest authority in finance in their respective countries—men of such prestige, experience and honor that their agreement upon the amount to be paid, and upon a financial plan to work out the payments, would be accepted throughout the world as the most authoritative expression obtainable? . . . I have no doubt that distinguished Americans would be willing to serve on such a commission."

Although the secretary of state did not speculate on the conclusions that such a commission might reach and conceded that its recommendations would not be binding in any case, he addressed himself to the substance of the matter insofar as it related to Germany. In an unmistakable reference to France's plans for further sanctions in the Ruhr and Rhineland—the Reparations Commission had once more found Germany to be in default on December 27—he indicated that the United States "would view with disfavor measures which instead of producing reparations would threaten disaster," and expressed the American position as follows:

> We have no desire to see Germany relieved of her responsibility for the war or of her just obligations to make reparation for the injuries due to her aggression. There is not the slightest desire that France shall lose any part of her just claims. On the other hand, we do not wish to see a prostrate Germany. There can be no economic recuperation in Europe unless Germany recuperates. There will be no permanent peace unless economic satisfactions are enjoyed.

The establishment of a committee of experts, he concluded, would "open a broad avenue of opportunity if those whose voluntary action is indispensable are willing to take advantage of it. And, once this is done, the avenues of American helpfulness cannot fail to open hopefully."[17]

Although the public announcement of the Hughes Plan did not prevent the French occupation of the Ruhr, which began on January 11, 1923, the plan did in time form the basis for a reparations settle-

17. Those portions of the advance text of Hughes's New Haven speech which were called to the particular attention of the ambassadors in France, Great Britain, Belgium, Italy, Switzerland, and Germany are in Phillips to Herrick, December 29, 1922, in *Foreign Relations, 1922*, 2: 199–202.

ment. The combined effects of the occupation, of the German response, which consisted of passive resistance and a cessation of reparations payments, and of the French counterresponse, which amounted to a virtual blockade of Germany in the west, were devastating. In Germany, inflation on an unprecedented scale set in, sharply reducing the income of the workers and wiping out the savings of the middle class. The value of the mark sank to 160,000 to the dollar by July 1, and by November, the German currency had become almost totally worthless. As a result of the crisis and of French agitation, separatist tendencies began to make themselves felt once more in the Rhineland and the Palatinate, and revolutionary movements of both the left and the right gained new strength. Communists acquired control of the governments of Saxony and Thuringia and led a rising in Hamburg. An extreme right-wing government in Bavaria defied the authorities in Berlin. In November, Adolf Hitler led his unsuccessful "Beerhall Putsch." The French economy was temporarily weakened by the cessation of reparations payments and a shortage of coal, and the franc dropped in value on world markets throughout 1923. World trade suffered a severe setback, and the potential for even further damage increased.

The very seriousness of the crisis, however, made the urgent need for a solution more apparent. The critical situation increased the possibility that all of the powers would become more receptive to America's participation on its own terms in the search for such a solution, and thus brought Hughes's hopes closer to realization. Germany, whose problems were greatest, made the first move. Responding to a speech by British Foreign Secretary Lord Curzon, it offered on May 2 to resume reparations payments to the limit of its ability once the Ruhr occupation had ended and made some suggestions as to how it might meet its obligations. But the proposal fell far short of offering a reasonable basis for discussion. Prodded by Curzon and encouraged by Hughes as well as by Houghton in Berlin, the Germans now for the first time tried to meet the Allied objections. In a new note of June 7 they not only offered to let a committee of experts determine their capacity to pay, they agreed to mortgage their railroads and all of their industrial and landed property to secure foreign capital that would be needed for reparations payments. They also promised to make available the proceeds from various excise taxes and to enter into negotiations with France and the other powers on all disputed questions.

Without taking any position on the details of the German offer, though much of it accorded with his own views, Hughes now proceeded with infinite care, skill, and patience to promote at least informal negotiations that would lead to the establishment of a committee of independent financial experts. He deliberately avoided all appearance of seeking to pressure France and repeatedly reasserted that the United States had no interest in relieving Germany of its legitimate obligations. By doing so, he effectively promoted his views that pushing Germany into total collapse and possible disintegration would hurt the world economy and thereby all nations and that the new German proposals were responsible and offered a basis for independent investigation by financial experts—and thus for a resolution in which the United States might play the role of the honest and helpful broker. At the same time, he did not neglect Germany itself.

Within six weeks of the receipt of the June 7 note, the United States offered the Germans not merely the trade agreement they had so long desired, but a full-fledged "treaty of friendship as well as of commerce and of consular rights." "It is designed," Hughes told Wiedfeldt at the very height of the Ruhr crisis, "to promote the friendly intercourse between the peoples of the United States and Germany. . . . [and] to lay the foundation for a comprehensive agreement responsive to the modern and exacting requirements of important maritime states."[18] The apparent concern for Germany's status and interests implied by this offer was in some ways deceiving. Indeed, the primary motivation of the United States was to launch its new trade policy based on the unconditional most-favored-nation principle. It was a policy deemed to be most beneficial in the light of America's new economic dominance and which, according to the chairman of the Tariff Commission, "with certain safeguards can be made to support an open-door policy . . . throughout the world."[19] The safeguards had already been taken with the passage of the Fordney-McCumber Tariff of 1922 and with the authorization given the president to raise these tariffs even further against any country that adopted retaliatory measures.

Germany was an ideal initial target for such a policy. Not only was the Weimar Republic likely to become an increasingly important market for American exports, it was also faced with the necessity of negotiating new trade treaties with the other powers, through which

18. Hughes to Wiedfeldt, July 25, 1923, in *Foreign Relations, 1923*, 2: 23.
19. W. S. Culbertson to Hughes, December 14, 1922, in ibid., 1: 126.

the unconditional most-favored-nation principle would be extended. It was, in addition, in no position to insist on concessions from the United States in the form of tariff reductions. Nonetheless, the American offer, particularly because of its timing, gave the Germans a much needed psychological lift by promising not only equality of treatment with the world's leading trading nation but greatly improved opportunities for increasing exports to the United States as well. The American draft was therefore approved with very minor changes after only ten hours of actual negotiations. The U.S. did yield to Germany's greatest concern by agreeing that most-favored-nation treatment should not extend to the special concessions made to the Allies under the Versailles treaty. The agreement was signed on December 8.

The Dawes Plan

Even while the negotiations over the German-American trade treaty were approaching their successful conclusion, notable progress was made on the reparations issue. This progress was due in considerable measure to the accession to power in Germany of Gustav Stresemann in August 1923. Stresemann headed the government for only three months but remained in office as foreign secretary continuously until his death in October 1929 and became the key figure in Germany's international rehabilitation. He ended passive resistance in the Ruhr in September, as Hughes had advised and the Allies insisted on, and restored the authority of his government in Saxony, Thuringia, Bavaria, and Hamburg. By reinforcing, with vigorous efforts to stabilize the currency, yet another expression of German willingness to resume reparations payments once the Ruhr occupation was ended he both appeased the French to a certain extent and lent additional credence to Hughes's contention that a viable Germany, willing and able to meet its obligations, was the best guarantee of prosperity and security for all nations. On October 13 Great Britain officially inquired whether the United States still supported the plan Hughes had outlined in his New Haven speech. The positive American reply led to increasing pressure on the French to modify their stand.

By November 30 France had found a formula by which it might escape the diplomatic isolation that now threatened it and test the possibilities of the course proposed by Britain and the United States without appearing to surrender its previous position. On that day, the Reparations Commission approved the formation of two committees of financial experts. The charges given these committees, while by no means providing the total freedom on which J. P. Morgan had earlier insisted, were sufficiently broad and vague to permit recommendations to be made on virtually all issues affecting Germany. Moreover, the request of the commission that American experts serve on the committees and that an American chair the most important of them was formally seconded by all of the governments involved, including Germany's, which was not to be represented, and France's, which still refused to commit itself to anything the committees might recommend. The unanimous request for American participation in reparations discussions, which Hughes had sought for over a year, thus became a reality. The secretary of state, of course, rejected official American representation, which would have required Congressional approval and constituted a formal commitment. His reply to the Reparations Commission was highly positive, however, and indicated that invitations should go out to Charles G. Dawes, the former director of the Bureau of the Budget and a leading Chicago banker, to Owen D. Young, chairman of the board of the General Electric Company, and to Harry M. Robinson, president of the First National Bank of Los Angeles, all of whom would accept.

The first and most important of the committees of experts met in Paris under the chairmanship of Dawes from January 24 to April 9, 1924, including a two-week visit to Berlin. Although formally charged only with "seeking means for balancing Germany's budget and measures to be taken in order to stabilize its currency," the committee produced the basic recommendations for what was to become the Dawes Plan for the comprehensive settlement of the reparations question. Incorporating many of the procedures suggested in the German proposal of June 7, 1923, but going beyond these in terms of stringent international controls, the plan did not set a fixed reparations sum but laid out an initially ascending payment schedule and called for an international loan of 800 million gold mark, secured by a mortgage on Germany's railroads, to provide the necessary stabilization for the German currency and the German economy. It was to be considered for adoption at a conference in London during July and August.

Adoption was by no means a foregone conclusion. Germany's

right-wing nationalist parties publicly aired their displeasure with the committee even before its report appeared and predicted a "second Versailles," in which unacceptable conditions and controls would be forcibly imposed on Germany. Stresemann countered these arguments not only with an appeal to realism but with a clear statement of his expectation that the participation of the United States on the committee would lead to results acceptable to Germany. Citing the conclusion of the German-American trade treaty as an example of mutually beneficial cooperation between the two countries, he told the Reichstag: "I believe we can only regard it with satisfaction that such a great country and such a great people have now shown an interest in the settlement of European questions, and are not following those who once believed that all of American policy could be summed up with the expression 'No European troubles.' "[20] The German government thereupon accepted the Dawes recommendations in principle, even in the midst of a bitter election campaign from which the right-wing parties were to emerge with sizable gains. It did so on the basis of assurances received from both American diplomats and American bankers and in accordance with a formula whose wording had been decided in conversations between officials of the Foreign Office and Ambassador Houghton.

The United States, in fact, played the decisive mediating role in the formulation and acceptance of the Dawes Plan. Hughes greeted warmly the announcement of the committee's recommendations, and President Calvin Coolidge lent official American approval in a speech to an Associated Press luncheon on April 22. When the secretary of state visited Paris unofficially as president of the American Bar Association during the summer, he privately but pointedly told Poincaré: "Here is the American policy. If you turn this down, America is through."[21] Officially, the American government acted with greater circumspection but with no less decisiveness. Britain duly invited the United States to participate in the forthcoming London conference on the grounds that "the [Dawes] report was framed under the direction and stimulus of a citizen of the United States" without whose "moral authority and technical experience" it might

20. Gustav Stresemann, Reichstag speech of February 28, 1924, in *Ursachen und Folgen: Vom deutschen Zusammenbruch 1918 und 1945 bis zur staatlichen Neuordnung Deutschlands in der Gegenwart*, 26 vols., ed. Herbert Michaelis and Ernst Schraepler (Berlin, 1959[?]–1979), 6: 66.

21. Hughes, quoted in Merlo J. Pusey, *Charles Evans Hughes*, 2 vols., (New York, 1951), 1: 591.

never have been agreed upon, and that "the success of the scheme outlined by General Dawes must depend predominantly on the flotation of the contemplated loan, the subscription for which will inevitably have to come largely from the United States of America." Hughes, after discussions with Coolidge, expressed "the Administration's desire to do all that it properly can without the assumption of objectionable obligations on the part of the Government," and instructed the ambassador to Great Britain, Frank B. Kellogg, and the "unofficial observer" with the Reparations Commission, James A. Logan, "to attend the conference in London on July 16 for the purpose of dealing with such matters as affect the interests of the United States and otherwise for purposes of information."[22]

That "the interests of the United States" were to be widely interpreted and that the American government, despite its official posture of noninvolvement, intended to take a hand in substantive decisions was made clear in Hughes's subsequent instructions to Kellogg:

> It is important that representatives of the United States should do nothing by which it would be made to appear that this Government is participating in imposition on Germany of unduly onerous conditions. In the view of this Government the objective of the forthcoming conference is the promotion of economic recuperation and recovery of just claims against Germany in such a manner as will render unnecessary imposition of sanctions as have been imposed in the past. It is important that no misconception of the position of this Government should obtain currency.[23]

In short, the United States intended to work at the conference for a plan that Germany would be able to accept and to fulfill.

Although Germany's primary concern was for an arrangement that would result in the evacuation of occupied German territory and the stabilization of the country's economy, while the United States's first priority was worldwide economic recovery, the interests of the two nations ran remarkably parallel on specific issues. The U.S., like Germany, sought a truly negotiated settlement that would insure German compliance and thus insisted on Germany's participation as an equal in the London conference. Moreover, the United States shared with the Germans an interest in restoring Germany's territo-

22. Frank B. Kellogg to Hughes, June 24, 1924, and Hughes to Kellogg, June 25, 1924, in *Foreign Relations, 1924*, 2: 30, 31–32.
23. Hughes to Kellogg, June 27, 1924, in ibid., 33.

rial and thus economic integrity and in taking out of the hands of the French-dominated Reparations Commission the right to decide when the imposition of sanctions might be required.

Fully aware of the German position on these questions through discussions between German officials and Houghton, Logan, and others, the United States persuaded the Berlin government to maintain a low profile and to rely on American efforts to work toward an acceptable plan. The degree to which Germany was prepared to place its trust in the United States is revealed in the fact that Stresemann followed this course even after the London conference began without German participation and without any official word that an invitation would be forthcoming. By the time Germany was invited on August 2, the activities of the Americans in London—a group that at various times included not only Kellogg and Logan but also Houghton, Young, Herrick, Treasury Secretary Andrew Mellon, and even Hughes, in his "unofficial" capacity as president of the American Bar Association—had resulted in a series of compromise solutions that approximated American wishes and, to a substantial degree, those of Germany as well.

With leverage provided by the repeated assertion that terms unacceptable to "the American public" would make it impossible to float the required loan in the United States, the Americans succeeded in securing not only German participation in the conference but also the agreement by France to a scheme whereby the Ruhr would be evacuated within a year of the acceptance of the Dawes Plan. Possible future sanctions were to require the agreement of an "American Citizen Member of the Reparations Commission," the American chairman of an arbitration commission, or, in the first instance, the general agent for the Dawes Plan, who was also to be an American.

The success in obtaining agreement on an essentially American solution to the reparations problem which would also improve the situation of Germany can be attributed largely to the skill and tenacity of the negotiators and to the financial pressure that they could bring to bear. It owed something as well, however, to the fact that the international constellation had changed appreciably during the previous year. The Labour government of Ramsay MacDonald, which had taken office in January 1924, was more amenable to such a solution than its predecessor, and May elections in France brought Edouard Herriot to the premiership, as replacement for the more fervently nationalistic Poincaré. Together with the earlier emergence of Stresemann, these changes in leadership produced a greater spirit of accommodation at the London conference than had been observable at any international meeting since the World War.

Nevertheless, the successful outcome of the conference was in doubt to the very end. Under pressure from the nationalist opposition at home and from a number of key industrialists, Stresemann fought vigorously for immediate evacuation of the Ruhr and categorically opposed new trade concessions demanded by France as a quid pro quo for evacuating at all. Again it was the United States that produced an end to the impasse. In conversations on August 14 with Stresemann and with the German ambassador to London, Kellogg left no doubt that everything possible had been achieved on these issues and that further German objections could only lead to another ultimatum. The result was agreement on August 16.

In urging the Reichstag to adopt the legislation necessary to implement the Dawes Plan, Stresemann not only gave full credit to the United States but reiterated his belief that only continued cooperation with America would assure German revival. "The unexpectedly far-reaching change in American policy," he told the members, ". . . toward active involvement with the European problem under the banner of the Dawes Report threatens to fail if the banner of this new line of march, that is, the report itself, were rejected by one of the main participants in Europe. . . . If we again sever the threads that were tied in London, . . . the consequences, particularly for the position of the United States on whom Europe's economic fate depends, are incalculable."[24] Stresemann's efforts to secure approval from members of the nationalist opposition, whose votes were crucial, were ably seconded by Houghton, who had discussed these matters with leaders of the Deutschnationale Volkspartei since May, and even by Hughes during his unofficial visit to Berlin in early August. At the same time, the administration did its utmost to persuade some reluctant American bankers, among them J. P. Morgan, who still doubted that France would really evacuate the Ruhr or that Germany would carry out the promised economic changes, to underwrite the Dawes Plan loan.

On August 29, with the help of forty-eight members of the DNVP, the Reichstag approved the necessary legislation, and on the following day the Treaty of London, which formalized the conclusions of

24. Declaration by the Government, August 23, 1924, in *Ursachen und Folgen,* 6: 102.

the earlier conference, was signed by the Allies and Germany. On October 14 the Dawes Plan loan was floated in New York by J. P. Morgan & Co. More than half the total, $110 million, was subscribed within fifteen minutes. Hughes was delighted with this outcome, in which an American solution had been obtained without any formal commitment on the part of the American government. Stresemann was equally delighted and gave full credit to the United States. "The United States," he told the Reichstag, "is that nation from which emanated the most important efforts directed toward the reconstruction of the economy and, beyond that, the pacification of Europe. For no country can these efforts be more welcome than for Germany. It gives me great satisfaction to be able to determine that our relations with the United States are satisfactory in every way. The far-reaching credits that American financiers have granted to portions of German industry during the past months have been of the greatest importance for our anemic economy. But even aside from that, all signs point to a gratifying increase in the understanding for Germany's situation in the great republic beyond the seas. . . ."[25]

Economic Linkage and Political Cooperation

The adoption and implementation of the Dawes Plan, for which Undersecretary of the Treasury S. Parker Gilbert became general agent, marked the full-fledged entry of the United States as an economic—though by careful design not as a political or military—force into the affairs of Europe. It was, at the same time, the first decisive step in the economic and political revival of Germany. The Dawes Plan was clearly predicated on the assumption that Germany as a "going concern" was essential to the security of all European states and to the economic well-being of the world. The general acceptance of this principle led to the almost complete rehabilitation of Germany in the second half of the 1920s. Through skillful maneuvering by Stresemann, an expanded version of the "Rhine Pact" proposal of 1922 became the Locarno Agreement of December 1, 1925, and Germany was not only admitted to the League of Nations in September 1926 but given one of the permanent seats on the council. Partly because at Locarno Germany had specifically accepted demilitarization of the Rhineland, the evacuation of Allied troops from the area

25. Stresemann, speech of May 18, 1925, in *Verhandlungen des Reichstags*, 3d election period (Berlin, 1925–1928), 385: 1870.

began in 1925 and was completed by 1930, fully five years before the date stipulated in the Versailles treaty. The Allied Military Commission, which was to assure German compliance with the disarmament provisions of the Versailles settlement, was withdrawn in January 1927.

In all of this the United States played no direct role, although Houghton for one continued to urge Germany and France to settle the "security issue." America had withdrawn its troops from the Rhineland at the beginning of the Ruhr occupation in 1923, its services as "trustee" were no longer required under the Locarno agreements, and it remained as far removed as ever from membership in the League of Nations. Nonetheless, the American endeavor to produce the Dawes Plan and the continued, if unofficial, American actions to insure its fulfillment—including behind-the-scenes efforts to encourage the Locarno meetings and pressure on Germany to modify its conditions and to join the League—made all of these developments possible. Quite in accordance with the intentions of both the Harding and the Coolidge administrations, American leverage continued to be almost exclusively economic, and the specific American contribution almost entirely in the form of private capital.

The precise amount of American capital that flowed into Germany in the late 1920s is impossible to determine, but there is no question that it exceeded the total of reparations payments made by Germany during these years and contributed greatly to a major economic revival. Between 1925 and 1931 Germany paid approximately $2.5 billion in reparations under the Dawes and Young plans, of which over $100 million went to the United States. During approximately the same period, the value of long-term loans floated in the United States to German banks, industries, utilities, religious and social organizations, and national, state, and local government units reached nearly $1.25 billion. In addition, the amount of short-term American credits outstanding in any given year averaged approximately $800 million. These totals do not include private loans by American to German companies, American purchases of German bonds issued outside the United States, American mortgages on German real estate, or American deposits in German banks. Neither do they include the direct American investments in Germany, which by 1930 totaled well over $200 million. In all, approximately two-thirds of the foreign capital that passed to and through Germany in the second half of the 1920s came from the United States and amounted to 18 percent of all American capital exports during these years.

The economic ties between the United States and Germany which this capital forged were supplemented by a flourishing trade and ever closer ties between German and American industry. The exchange of goods had an average annual value of $645 million, 7.1 percent of America's total foreign trade and 10.7 percent of Germany's, until the worldwide depression brought a decline in 1930. German and American companies cooperated freely. Where strength was either evenly divided or on the German side, as in the chemical, electrical, and optical fields, this cooperation took the form of joint enterprises, cartel arrangements, "gentlemen's agreements," and the like. Dow, Dupont, Ford, Standard Oil of New Jersey, and the Aluminum Company of America made various arrangements with IG Farbenindustrie, Bausch & Lomb with Carl Zeiss, and General Electric with Krupp and with Germany's two major producers of electrical equipment, Siemens and AEG. America's leading auto manufacturers, Ford, Chrysler, and General Motors, who had far outstripped their German rivals, built assembly plants in Berlin, Cologne, Hamburg, and other cities, and General Motors bought out Germany's largest automobile producer, Adam Opel Werke A.G., in spring 1929.

The growing economic ties made Germany more dependent on the continued goodwill of the United States, even while its own economy was prospering, and converted the American interest in German recovery from a general to a specific one. They thus contributed to the good relations between the two countries which prevailed during the late 1920s. This was true even though the economic relationship produced problems of its own, both in the form of increased competition for American producers from German firms and of a continuously, if decreasingly, negative trade balance on the part of Germany with the United States. It remained true even though the long-range expectations of the two countries were fundamentally different.

For the United States, the Dawes Plan was an economic measure designed to stabilize the European economies. America would benefit, in general from the elimination of threats of war and revolution and the substitution of peaceful competition, in particular from the growth of capital exports, a return to the gold standard, and increased trade. Germany's leaders, by contrast, saw the Dawes

Plan in political as well as economic terms. For them it was merely the first step in a general revision of the Versailles settlement which would restore Germany's international influence, regain its military parity with its neighbors, and, in time, even return some of its lost colonies and eastern borderlands. Although the United States shared none of these political aims, this fundamental difference did not cloud the relationship between the two countries so long as Germany acted moderately and with due regard for the sensibilities of other nations.

The shifts in diplomatic personnel which took place early in 1925 reinforced the prevailing attitudes of friendship and cooperation. The resignation of Hughes led to the appointment as secretary of state of Frank B. Kellogg, who had formed a most favorable impression of Stresemann during the London conference. Kellogg in turn was replaced in London by Houghton, who through his service in Berlin had become more than ever Germany's friend. To replace Houghton, Coolidge chose the sixty-nine-year-old ambassador in Peking, Jacob Gould Schurman. A distinguished academic who had been president of Cornell and had studied at Heidelberg, Göttingen, and Berlin, Schurman continued the tradition of Germanophile ambassadors which, with notable exceptions, extended back to the days of Bancroft. At the same time, the Germans replaced Wiedfeldt in Washington with one of their most skillful diplomats, Baron Ago von Maltzan. Maltzan had been a key figure in the formulation of Germany's policy in eastern Europe and, less than a year after his appointment, assured "his friends" in the State Department that Germany regarded the United States as "a faithful and dependable friend."[26]

Aided by the attitudes of these men and by the sympathetic posture assumed by Coolidge, German-American relations weathered a series of potential storms undamaged. The nomination and subsequent election of Hindenburg as successor to Ebert in the German presidency in 1925, for example, logically resulted in a revival of world war antagonisms in the United States. In mid-April, Maltzan reported that American public opinion regarded the possibility of the old field marshal's election as "fateful for the internal consolidation of Germany, for economic cooperation with America, and for the

26. Ago von Maltzan to Foreign Office, December 26, 1925, in *Akten zur deutschen auswärtigen Politik, 1918–1945* (Baden-Baden and Göttingen, 1950–   ), Series B, 1, no. 2: 88 n. 4.

already begun and here welcomed pacification of Europe."[27] After
the election, however, the efforts of the ambassador and of the
highly regarded Stresemann soon allayed such fears. Within days
Coolidge had confidentially and without solicitation informed Maltzan that he was not worried about the continued development of
sympathetic German-American relations and believed that Hindenburg would be a positive force in creating the necessary inner unity
of Germany.

By the same token, the Treaty of Berlin, which in the following
year reconfirmed and even expanded the arrangements formulated
at Rapallo between Germany and the Soviet Union, caused little
concern in the United States. Germany had feared, with reason, that
this "new Rapallo" would again raise the specter of bolshevism and
cast doubt on Germany's commitment to fulfillment of the Versailles
treaty and to European security. When the Foreign Office sounded
out Schurman just before the signing of the treaty, however, the
ambassador showed himself to be sympathetic and volunteered that
his studies of Bismarck's policies had convinced him that Germany
would be wrong to allow its ties with Russia to lapse. When Maltzan
informed the State Department the following week, he reported
back that the news had been received "without a sign of astonish-
ment or surprise and altogether sympathetically and favorably."[28]
After the treaty had been signed, and despite an unfortunate leak
that had allowed both the London *Times* and the *New York Times* to
raise a number of embarrassing questions, the German ambassador
could be even more reassuring. In conversations with "authoritative
personalities," and particularly with Vice-President Dawes, he had
"met with full understanding for the Russian treaty and had nowhere
found any signs of concern."[29]

In effect, the increasing signs of American trust in Germany's
intentions arose from a growing conviction, encouraged by Houghton and Schurman and fully shared by Kellogg and Coolidge, that
the Dawes Plan had stabilized the situation in Germany and that in
Stresemann a leader had been found who genuinely followed a policy of fulfillment and of peaceful change. Stresemann, who con-

27. Maltzan to Stresemann, April 12, 1925, in Robert Gottwald, *Die deutsch-
amerikanischen Beziehungen in der Ära Stresemann* (Berlin-Dahlem, 1965), p. 120.
28. Maltzan to Foreign Office, April 12, 1926, in *Akten zur deutschen auswärtigen
Politik*, B, 2, no. 1: 333.
29. Maltzan to Foreign Office, April 26, 1926, in ibid., 3: 229.

tinued to believe "that the decision regarding Europe's future lies primarily in the hands of the United States,"[30] encouraged such a belief in large and small ways and showed remarkable sensitivity to American concerns. He refrained, for example, from appointing a naval attaché in Washington when informed by Maltzan that such an appointment would awaken memories of Boy-Ed and Papen, whose world war exploits had already returned to public view through the activities of the Mixed Claims Commission.

Germany yielded on many points raised by the commission itself in hopes of forestalling legal actions that might cause wartime memories to lessen present cooperation. Giving the clearest of all indications that Germany believed the realization of even its ultimate objectives to depend on the goodwill of the United States, a Foreign Ministry official wrote: "For our whole policy, which aims at the elimination of the Dawes Plan and of the Versailles treaty, the willingness of the United States to support us financially is a precondition; and this willingness will disappear for years if public opinion in the United States is whipped up against us and the nature of our conduct of the war is painted for the mass of the people in blackest colors."[31] Germany yielded too on the sensitive question of the transfer of reparations funds to the United States, adopting in this respect a position that differed radically from an earlier insistence on legal niceties.

On a more important issue, Germany went to great pains to clear with Washington its membership in the League of Nations, offering, perhaps speciously, to refrain from joining if this would save the United States embarrassment or, alternatively, "to represent at Geneva such ideas as correspond to American ideals." "Such a policy," the Foreign Office was certain, "would lead to closer ties and a strengthening of mutual relations." An inquiry as to relevant American ideals was sent to Maltzan in Washington.[32] In a similar vein, when conversations between Stresemann and French Premier Aristide Briand at Thoiry on September 17, 1926, foreshadowed a Franco-German agreement that would involve new financial obligations for the United States and might undermine American efforts to reach a settlement with France on the war debt question, the Ger-

30. Stresemann to Maltzan, April 7, 1925, quoted in Link, *Stabilisierungspolitik*, p. 348.

31. Walter de Haas memorandum, November 16, 1926, in *Akten zur deutschen auswärtigen Politik*, B, 3: 459.

32. Bülow note, January 19, 1926, in ibid., 142.

man foreign secretary was quick to denounce any impression "that we would be prepared to join with France against America." "On the contrary," he insisted, "we can, in view of the decisive practical importance of the United States, act only in closest understanding with them."[33] When this understanding proved impossible to achieve, and when opposition to the scheme also developed in England, Germany, and France, the matter was simply dropped.

At the same time, Germany consistently and even ostentatiously lent support to American foreign policy initiatives. This support was particularly evident in the field of disarmament, where the Reich had little to loose and a great deal to gain. But it was also apparent with respect to international arbitration, where a German-American treaty was signed on May 5, 1928, despite the fact that Germany's traditional reluctance to trust to such arrangements had been reinforced by its postwar experience. Germany's cooperative intent was most strikingly displayed in the banning of war as an instrument of national policy, where Kellogg sought and received strong and perhaps decisive support from Stresemann.

When Briand proposed on April 6, 1927, the tenth anniversary of American entry into the First World War, a "mutual engagement" that would "outlaw" war between France and the United States, the State Department's reaction was anything but positive. Aside from the novelty of the language, which incorporated a phrase current in the American peace movement and had been formulated under the influence of James T. Shotwell of the Carnegie Endowment for International Peace, the proposal seemed little more than a new attempt by the French to engage the United States in their painfully constructed security system. Kellogg was reluctant, however, to turn down a "peace proposal" that had the support of an important segment of public opinion and that demonstrated its even wider appeal after Lindbergh's flight had reawakened feelings of Franco-American amity. He therefore procrastinated in a variety of ways. Only in December, at the renewed insistence of the French ambassador, was an official American response made. At that time, the head of the Division of Western Affairs, William R. Castle, indicated to Ambassador Paul Claudel that while a bilateral agreement posed problems for the United States, a multilateral one that all nations could sign was possible. Since both Claudel and Castle realized that

33. Minutes of meeting of the Thoiry committee, October 14, 1926, quoted in Gottwald, *Beziehungen*, p. 80.

a multilateral pact, whatever its psychological impact, would have little if any practical significance, they were fully prepared to drop the entire matter. Indeed, Claudel so recommended to his government.

Kellogg meanwhile underwent a change of heart. Impressed by the degree of support that the idea of "outlawing war" was gaining in press and public and urged on by influential members of Congress, including Senator Borah, chairman of the Foreign Relations Committee, the secretary of state emerged from a meeting of that committee on December 22 determined to push for a multilateral agreement. On December 28, just minutes before the announced arrival of a French note that would have withdrawn the Briand proposal, Kellogg officially offered to join the French "in an effort to obtain the adherence of all principal powers of the world to a declaration renouncing war as an instrument of national policy."[34] Despite immediate objections from Paris, the text of this proposal was published on January 4. It was now Briand's turn to be embarrassed. Though he was no more interested in Kellogg's proposal than Kellogg had been in his, he could no more than the American secretary of state publicly reject an idea whose intention it was to further the cause of peace. In the months of often strained negotiations which followed, an important, perhaps even crucial role was to be played by Germany, which both by circumstance and design emerged as the major supporter of American initiatives.

The German government's reaction to the American proposal was positive from the beginning. The Foreign Office welcomed this new sign of American interest in European problems and was particularly delighted that it represented a clear rejection of the special relationship between the United States and France which Briand had obviously sought to establish. Although German diplomats informally discussed the proposed pact with their American counterparts both in Washington and Berlin, and the German press expressed approval, no formal German reply was either requested or forthcoming. Negotiations between Washington and Paris continued meanwhile without bringing agreement appreciably closer.

For Kellogg, the issue of the "peace pact" had now become a matter of great importance with which his personal prestige was involved and on which his place in history depended. He therefore

34. Kellogg to Paul Claudel, December 28, 1927, in *Foreign Relations, 1927,* 2: 626–627.

moved with new vigor to secure its conclusion. His primary tactic was to involve other powers in the discussions, and he hoped to hasten their approval by first gaining Germany's. Accordingly, he called in the new German ambassador, Friedrich von Prittwitz und Gaffron, on April 4, 1928—Maltzan had been killed in an airplane crash the previous September—expressed his disappointment with new French counterproposals, and showed him the draft of a message to Schurman in which the American ambassador was to be asked to request Germany's formal support of a multinational antiwar pact. Prittwitz, a convinced democrat who believed strongly in German-American cooperation, cabled this information to Berlin with the recommendation for a positive reply. In full accord with the views that had guided German foreign policy for most of the 1920s, he wrote: "Not only would a new confirmation of our policy of peace find a strong echo in public opinion here, our position in relation to that of France with respect to the questions of disarmament, of evacuation [of German territory], and, in the final analysis, of reparations, would be appreciably strengthened."[35]

The actual American note was delivered in Tokyo, Rome, London, and Berlin on April 13, and Stresemann gave provisional approval to the American proposal on the same day. Despite considerable pressure from France and Britain, and to a lesser extent even from Japan, that Germany's final reply be coordinated with that of the other powers, Stresemann proceeded to hand an independent and positive reply to Schurman on April 27. In view of the German interest in new reparations revisions, the foreign secretary believed Germany could not afford to align itself with the major League of Nations powers in opposition, however slight, to American wishes. By becoming the first nation to approve Kellogg's plan, moreover, Germany would strengthen its ties to the United States, especially if, as was to be the case, its action would hasten the actual conclusion of a peace pact.

The favorable reaction of the American press and the appreciative comments of Kellogg demonstrated that German calculations in this respect were not mistaken. Indeed, American appreciation of Germany's action was carried to embarrassing heights by Schurman. In his speech of acceptance of an honorary doctorate from the University of Heidelberg, he declared that in their efforts to obtain a pact

35. Friedrich von Prittwitz und Gaffron to Foreign Office, April 4, 1928, *Akten zur deutschen auswärtigen Politik,* B, 8: 457.

outlawing war, Germany and the United States "were marching forward together in a noble venture for the civilization of mankind."[36] France immediately and formally lodged a protest against this formulation. When further negotiations brought various revisions in the American proposal, it was once again Germany that became the first country to signify its final approval on July 11 and thus to forestall possible further delay.

In a sense, the negotiations that led to the formal signing of the Kellogg-Briand Pact in Paris on August 27—at a ceremony in which Stresemann, the first German statesman to appear in France after the world war in a role other than that of a defeated enemy, played a central part—marked the high point of German-American cooperation after the war. The ultimate test of that relationship and the definition of its limits was to come, however, in the new reparations negotiations that took place in 1929.

The Germans, of course, had always regarded the Dawes Plan as an interim solution, and in the absence of a final determination of the reparations total it could be little else. Nonetheless, the other nations, including the United States, originally believed that the financial arrangements concluded in 1924 would remain workable for a decade and more, and they certainly did not share the German desire to secure revisions for essentially political reasons. By 1928, however, it became clear that soon after the Dawes installments reached their ultimate level, German foreign exchange would no longer suffice to make the annual payments without endangering the payments of interest and principal on outstanding German loans, primarily to the United States. As a result, a specific American interest in the revision of the Dawes Plan quickly developed. As early as 1927, Maltzan had reported from Washington that "well-meaning Americans" had advised him that with respect to such revision the best course for Germany was "not to make the suggestion itself, but to leave it, if possible, to the creditor side and better yet to the reparations agent, Parker Gilbert."[37] Germany carefully followed this advice, and it was Gilbert who in December 1927 first raised the question officially. Subsequent discussions in Geneva led to the authorization for a new committee of experts on which Bel-

---

36. Jacob Gould Schurman, quoted in Gottwald, *Beziehungen*, p. 97.
37. Maltzan to Foreign Office, April 18, 1927, in *Akten zur deutschen auswärtigen Politik*, B, 5: 206.

gium, France, Germany, Great Britain, Italy, and Japan were to be represented.

In the extensive and complex behind-the-scenes discussions that followed, the United States and Germany successfully pursued their common aim of bringing American experts into the committee and of leaving the committee full freedom of action. Unlike four years earlier, it now seemed possible to remove the Reparations Commission entirely from the process, and joint German-American efforts in this direction were also crowned with success. "Without American participation," the Foreign Office reasoned, "a sensible and impartial settlement . . . is unthinkable," and the State Department noted happily that the Germans "are fully alive to the necessity for American good will and cooperation and that is one of the principal factors determining their current policy."[38]

Increasing trust and close cooperation between the United States and Germany thus led to the formation of a new committee of experts. They met under the chairmanship of Owen D. Young from February 11 to June 7, 1929, and produced still another "final solution" to the reparations problem. Yet, as the progress of the discussions within the committee showed, that cooperation and trust did not rest on a true identity of interests. While the Germans wanted a settlement based solely on what they could readily pay without damaging their own economic development, the Americans, who despite their theoretically "unofficial" status were prodded repeatedly by both Mellon and Secretary of State Henry L. Stimson, insisted that primary emphasis be placed on the legitimate claims of the former Allies. Insistence that these claims were wholly independent of the war debts owed the United States complicated matters further. The final version of the Young Plan, though considerate of German views, was based largely on the American concept, and as a result payments were set at a higher level than Germany considered fair. Even more important, the United States had no sympathy whatever for German insistence that proper fulfillment of its reparations obligations depended on certain territorial adjustments. It therefore rejected out of hand the proposition put forward by the chief German expert, Hjalmar Schacht, that any final settlement should allow for future German participation in colonial enterprises and for the possible return of the Polish Corridor.

38. Gerhard Köpke to Prittwitz, September 21, 1928, and Dewitt Poole to A. N. Young, October 21, 1928, quoted in Link, *Stabilisierungspolitik*, pp. 436, 445.

Without support from the United States, Germany had little choice but to yield on these issues at that time. Indeed, Stresemann specifically called off Schacht's initiative on the territorial issue when American opposition became obvious. In the end, the Young Plan reduced the German annuities by more than 20 percent, set 1988 as the final year for German payments, removed most international controls from the German economy, and eliminated the possibility of future sanctions through the Reparations Commission. It did not, in the final analysis, meet Germany's expectations. Nevertheless, the plan was yet another instrument by which Germany, with American assistance, lightened the burden imposed by the Versailles treaty and by which the United States expected to further its goal of achieving worldwide economic stabilization.

At a conference in The Hague in late August, the Young recommendations were approved without difficulty and without further American participation. Stresemann, moreover, was able to persuade France, Great Britain, and Belgium to end what remained of the Rhineland occupation on the basis of the new arrangement. This troop withdrawal in turn helped the plan to survive a Nazi-inspired referendum held on December 22, which would have declared any minister affixing his signature to it guilty of treason. Only 13.8 percent of the voters approved. The Young Plan was officially signed on January 20, 1930, and, although the vote in the Reichstag was relatively close, went into effect on May 17. One month later, a separate debt agreement between the United States and Germany provided for the final settlement of the financial obligations arising out of wartime claims and reparations costs. On July 12 a new extradition treaty was concluded between the two countries.

In view of such results, the Young Plan discussions could be regarded as an additional example of fruitful German-American cooperation. Both nations could see them as reflecting the success of their policies and as a harbinger of even closer ties. Still, the course of the discussions had clearly suggested that if Germany were to regain sufficient economic and political strength or see its dependence on America lessened in other ways, the excellent working relationship between the two countries might well come to an end. The full implementation of the Young Plan, which would have brought Germany both greater strength and greater independence and which promised, in a special memorandum never signed by the American experts, a reduction in Germany's overall obligations if the United States lowered its war debt demands, might itself have been a step in that direction.

The world economic crisis triggered by the New York stock market crash of September/October 1929, though it made the carrying out of the Young Plan impossible, also made the end of the close German-American relationship a near certainty, however. By drastically weakening the American economy, the crisis fatally undermined the laboriously constructed postwar arrangements in which Germany, both as object and as subject, had played a key role. It led in time to far-reaching economic and political changes in both countries, and to an ever sharper divergence in the courses they were to follow. Under the new circumstances, the successors to Stresemann, who died in October 1929, lacked both the skill and the will to continue the policy of fulfillment and peaceful change, while in the United States the policies of the Harding-Coolidge-Hoover years fell increasingly into disfavor. Under the impact of these developments, the relations between the United States and Germany entered yet another phase.

Chapter 7

A PARTING OF THE WAYS:
THE NEW DEAL
AND THE THIRD REICH

*

The End of Reparations—and of the Weimar Republic

The change in the German-American relationship brought on by the world economic crisis was gradual. Though strains of increasing severity made their appearance, the pattern established in the 1920s was maintained through conviction and inertia until well after the accession of Adolf Hitler to the chancellorship on January 30, 1933. Only when the bases for the earlier course had been completely eroded by the new economic conditions and when the divergence in the aims of the two countries revealed both economic and ideological dimensions did a fundamental alteration take place.

The American stabilization policy, which included the revival of Germany, had, ironically, been erected on an extremely unstable foundation. The revitalization of the German economy produced the uninterrupted flow of reparations after 1924, which aided the economic development of France and the other European states, led to an increase in world trade and Allied war debt payments, and thus contributed to the maintenance of peace and order. But all of this depended in the final analysis on the continuing flow of capital from the United States to Germany. This flow in turn depended on continued growth in the American economy, a condition still assumed to exist when the Young Plan was formulated in 1929. The onset of the Great Depression in the autumn of that year showed that assumption to be in error, threw the entire process into reverse, and led to rapid destabilization not only in the economic, but also in the political, sphere.

The drying up of American sources of credit, foreshadowed even before the stock market crash and graphically illustrated by the difficulties encountered in floating the Young Plan loan, resulted almost at once in an economic downturn in Germany, which, owing mainly to rising unemployment, had major social and political repercussions. What proved to be the last genuinely parliamentary government of the Weimar Republic, the coalition headed by Socialist Herrmann Müller, was defeated on March 27, 1930, largely because of its inability to devise an economic policy to meet the crisis which could win support of at least the moderates from both the left and the right. Its successor, a minority cabinet headed by Heinrich Brüning, depended almost entirely on President Hindenburg for its continuance. Brüning was even less able than his predecessor to win parliamentary approval for an economic program, and his effort to implement one by invoking Article 48, the emergency-powers provision of the constitution, was also defeated in the Reichstag. In clear violation of the spirit of the constitution, but with the authorization of Hindenburg and in the hope that a new conservative coalition would somehow emerge, Brüning dissolved the parliament and called for new elections. The result was disaster.

In the elections held on September 14, 1930, major gains were recorded by extremist parties that were contemptuous of the democratic process and opposed the entire governmental structure. The Communists raised their representation from 54 to 77, while Hitler's National Socialists increased their seats from 12 to 107 and became the second largest party in the Reichstag. All possibility for effective parliamentary action was now at an end. No agreement could be obtained on any government policy, yet no antigovernment majority emerged either, since the Socialists and other democratic elements feared that any further change could well bring the Communists or the Nazis to power. The outcome of the elections, moreover, shocked foreign investors, increased the flight of capital from Germany, and thus worsened the economic situation. Within months the Reichsbank lost nearly 1.3 billion mark in gold and foreign exchange, over a third of its holdings.

Despite these developments, however, American policy toward Germany did not change perceptibly. The economic crisis in both

Germany and the United States made it all the more important to safeguard American investments and increased American concern for German economic stability. The forces of the moderate right, which Brüning represented, seemed to offer the best available hope for achieving this. Moreover, the policies that Brüning implemented through emergency decrees corresponded closely to the ideas of the Hoover administration, which could equally well be described as of the moderate right. In essence, these policies sought to reverse economic decline through curtailment of government expenditures and general deflation. A longer range aim of the Germans was to lighten the burdens on their economy by ending reparations payments, or at least ajusting them to the new realities, but Brüning believed this could not be done unless his government first demonstrated what both he and the United States regarded as "fiscal responsibility."

The general American approval of Brüning's economic, though not his political, efforts was heightened by the good opinion that Secretary of State Henry L. Stimson formed of the chancellor both before and during his visits to Europe and by the positive reports of the new American ambassador, Frederic M. Sackett, a former Kentucky senator and Louisville business leader who replaced Schurman in Berlin in 1930. Sackett, indeed, was convinced that Brüning represented the best available guarantee against a Communist takeover, which would mean financial disaster for American investors. Though Sackett recognized that the German government had become "semi-dictatorial" or even "a veiled dictatorship"[1] and duly communicated this to Washington, both Stimson and Hoover agreed with his further assessment that this change in no way precluded continued German-American cooperation. Such cooperation, in fact, manifested itself in the last years of the Weimar Republic not merely in yet another reparations revision, which led to their effective end, but also in the disarmament field, where Stimson strongly supported the idea of lifting most of the military restrictions placed upon Germany by the Versailles treaty, albeit within the context of a general scheme of arms reduction.

Faced with increasing pressure from the left and the right, which expressed itself in mass rallies and street violence, and committed to an unpopular economic policy that caused hardship to the average

1. Embassy memorandum, January 5, 1932, and Frederic M. Sackett to Stimson, August 17, 1932, in *Foreign Relations of the United States: Diplomatic Papers, 1932*, 2: 280, 311.

German, Brüning sought to strengthen his position through positive achievements in the area of foreign policy. His most immediate aim became progress toward new reparations revisions leading to their cancellation. Not only would success here undercut the popular appeal of the right, but the chances for success seemed reasonable if the other powers could be convinced that continued reparations payments aggravated Germany's economic difficulties and thereby the world crisis. Precisely this position was advanced by Schacht during his American tour in October 1930 and in his book *The End of Reparations,* which appeared both in Germany and the United States in 1931.

As a first step, the German government considered asking for a moratorium under the terms of the Young Plan or the unilateral declaration of such a moratorium if all else failed. In a conversation with Sackett on December 19, Brüning also endorsed a proposal for a world economic conference to be called by Hoover. When the American president proved unresponsive to the conference idea, Germany continued to develop its plans for a moratorium. Since any public announcement was certain to increase the loss of capital and thus to worsen the German economic picture, discretion prevailed for the time being. Sackett, however, was kept reasonably well informed of German thinking, and the possibility of a moratorium also provided much of the substance of discussions that Brüning and Foreign Minister Julius Curtius held with their British counterparts at the prime minister's country estate at Chequers in early June.

Even before the end of the Chequers conference, however, increasing pressure on the Brüning government had led to the decision to take a public stance. The collapse of the Creditanstalt, Austria's largest bank, on May 11 had further weakened the precarious financial structure of Central Europe, both Communists and National Socialists had made new gains in provincial elections, and the attempt to launch an Austro-German customs union, which Brüning had pursued as a possible alternative means for diverting nationalist dissatisfaction, faced certain defeat by the League of Nations. At the same time, mounting budget deficits in Germany had led to a new emergency decree raising taxes and cutting pensions and doles. To offset the negative reaction to that decree and to improve its own nationalist credentials, the government issued a manifesto on June 6.

Characterizing Germany's obligations under the Versailles treaty as "tribute payments," the manifesto declared that "the premises on which the Young Plan was based have proved to be erroneous," that the plan had "failed to give the German people the relief which according to the intentions of all concerned it was meant to give," that "the limit of privations which we can impose on our people has been reached," and that "the extremely precarious economic and financial situation of the Reich imperiously requires Germany's relief from unbearable reparation obligations."[2] Despite these strong words, which were intended primarily for home consumption, Brüning still believed that no action toward a moratorium would be required during 1931 and most certainly not before discussions could be carried on with Stimson during the secretary of state's visit to Europe in July.

Meanwhile Hoover had formulated plans of his own. He was increasingly alarmed by Sackett's reports about economic conditions in Germany and worried about the effects of possible defaults on the weakened American economy and on the world situation. Hoping, moreover, to restore his own tarnished political image, Hoover had cast about since early May for a possible move by the United States which would not only bring practical relief but have psychological impact as well. By May 20 his thoughts had turned to a moratorium on both war debts and reparations. This idea, which had been favorably discussed in financial circles for some time, would represent a sharp about-face for the American government, since it would explicitly recognize a linkage that every president since Wilson had gone to great lengths to deny. On June 5, by which time the State Department had rallied to the idea of a moratorium, Hoover discussed his plan with leading cabinet members, and over the next twelve days even Treasury Secretary Mellon became convinced of its feasibility. On June 20, 1931, a startled world heard the announcement of the one-year Hoover Moratorium.

Clearly, the president sought to win a psychological victory over the depression at home and abroad. He also hoped, however, to forestall defaults by the former Allies, which would raise unpleasant political problems, and by the Germans, which would put further strains on the American economy. Unilateral action seemed preferable to a conference because it was more in keeping with an "independent" foreign policy and because it was unlikely that unwanted negotiations on war debts could be avoided at an international meet-

2. George A. Gordon to Stimson, June 8, 1931, in *Foreign Relations, 1931*, I: 9, 10.

ing. The key to Hoover's action undoubtedly was Germany. "He laid before us," Stimson reported, "a very serious situation which he feared would come out of the German situation and laid before us a plan which he had in mind."[3] In his own remarks justifying the moratorium, originally prepared for a radio address scheduled for June 23, Stimson stated the situation more clearly:

> The immediate purpose of President Hoover's proposition for a debt suspension of one year was to relieve the financial panic which was in progress in Germany. . . . In her position in the center of Europe, Germany in good health would be a bulwark of strength against instability and communism, while if she were allowed to fall the disaster would not be confined to her but would certainly involve other nations and would greatly affect the financial systems of all the principal nations of the world, including our own.[4]

When protracted negotiations with France stalled implementation of the moratorium and caused further financial difficulties for Germany, which could not meet payments due on July 15, Hoover intervened once more. He asked the British government to call an immediate conference for the purpose of stabilizing Germany's short-term debt and, to emphasize his view of the gravity of the situation, sent both Mellon and Stimson to London to participate. "The essence of the problem," he told the delegates, "is the restoration of confidence in Germany's economic life, both in Germany and abroad."[5] The conference adopted the American plan for a "standstill agreement" on July 23.

Brüning expressed his gratitude for the American initiatives to Sackett and in a radio speech on June 23. In economic terms, he indeed had reason to be grateful, for Hoover's actions had relieved Germany of the necessity for immediate payment of $400 million in reparations and assured it of the maintenance of private credits amounting to more than $1.3 billion. Politically, however, the surprise moves by the United States prevented Brüning from gaining credit for having forced modifications of the Versailles settlement, and thus failed to strengthen his government's position. As a result, he turned ever more fervently to attempts not only to secure the final

3. Stimson diary, June 5, 1931, in Henry L. Stimson Papers, Yale University Library, New Haven.
4. Stimson to James W. Collier, December 16, 1931, in *Foreign Relations, 1931*, I: 240, 242.
5. Castle to Ray Atherton, July 19, 1931, in ibid., 280.

end of all reparations but, more immediately, to obtain an end to Germany's military disabilities. On the latter score, he once more received encouragement from the United States.

The permanent limitation on Germany's armed forces imposed by the Versailles treaty had served as both a practical and a psychological disability and had continued to undermine the country's security and pride. Germany had circumvented these limitations in a variety of ways during the 1920s with the help of the Soviet Union and even of the United States, which trained German officers in the use of weapons systems prohibited to them by the Versailles treaty. But the lifting of the restrictions themselves had remained a German aim from the beginning. Since the economic crisis made any serious increase in Germany's armed forces impossible for financial reasons, its renewed demands for parity with its neighbors could be linked convincingly to proposals for disarmament which would reduce the armies of these neighbors, particularly of France. In this context the Germans could count on the assistance of the United States, which had not only taken the lead in various disarmament efforts during the 1920s but was increasingly inclined to make a connection between the financial difficulties of the former Allies, including their problems in meeting war debt payments, and their expenditures on weapons of war.

The opportunity for Germany to present its demands for parity was to come at the General Disarmament Conference, for which preparatory work had been going on for years and which was scheduled to take place in Geneva early in 1932. Stimson, during his visit to Berlin in July 1931, strongly encouraged German expectations by assuring Brüning "that in view of the statement of the Allies and the United States to Germany in 1919 in respect to signing the Versailles Treaty as a step towards general disarmament, Germany had an absolutely unimpeachable case before the moral opinion of the world" and that "we would be at the conference and would do our best to help." At an embassy dinner for Germany's highest officials two days later, he was even more expansive. "I told them," he reported, "that in my opinion Germany has a perfect case for the General Disarmament Conference unless she spoiled it by something that gave other nations a chance to draw a red herring across the trail."[6]

Stimson lived up to his promises. He had himself appointed to

6. Memorandum of Stimson conversations with Brüning, July 23, 1931, and with members of German Government, July 25, 1931, in ibid., 548, 552.

head the prospective delegation and sought funds from Congress with the same rationale he had used with the Germans. Norman Davis, a veteran of the disarmament negotiations, seconded the analysis of his chief and sought to convince the Foreign Affairs Committee of the House of Representatives on January 6, 1932, that a disarmed Germany surrounded by armed neighbors created an intolerable situation. "Germany," he insisted, "can not be kept indefinitely waiting under an implied moral obligation without maintaining a constant atmosphere of nervousness and instability which is today affecting the credit and financial structure of the world."[7] In April the secretary of state traveled to Geneva, where the conference was in progress, and attempted to bring Brüning together with French Premier André Tardieu in order to work out a means through which German demands for parity and French concerns for security could both be accommodated within a new disarmament formula proposed by Hoover. Tardieu's illness prevented Stimson from carrying out his plan, but Stimson believed he had worked out in conversations with Brüning an approach the French could accept. The German chancellor fully shared this assumption. Both men were mistaken, however, and the Geneva conference dragged on into July without notable progress.

By that time, the political situation in Germany had worsened again. On May 30 the newly reelected and nearly eighty-five-year-old Hindenburg was persuaded by a small group of his closest advisers to drop Brüning and to appoint Franz von Papen chancellor. The replacement of a man with whom Stimson had been able to exchange wartime reminiscenses by the alleged instigator of the Black Tom explosion and other First World War sabotage acts in the United States could not fail to affect German-American relations adversely. The fact that Papen had even less parliamentary support than Brüning and that his appointment owed much to the intrigues of General Kurt von Schleicher, who became the new army minister, contributed to the change as well. Sackett reported at once that "the personnel of the new Cabinet is strongly indicative of a military dictatorship in close cooperation with nationalist groups having monarchical sympathies," and Stimson judged its appointment to be a victory for "the most reactionary elements in Germany."[8]

7. House Foreign Affairs Committee, *General Disarmament Conference: Hearings*, 72d Cong., 1st sess., 1932, 32.
8. Sackett to Castle, June 1, 1932, in *Foreign Relations, 1932*, 2: 294; Stimson diary, June 1, 1932.

The cooling of the German-American relationship was not yet apparent, however, at the Lausanne conference which after various postponements was convened on June 16 to take up the reparations issue once again. The United States was still amenable to a further scaling down of Germany's obligations in the interest of economic stabilization, though vigorously opposed to outright cancellation for fear that such a step would inevitably lead to default on war debt payments and thus be accomplished totally at the expense of the American taxpayer. Maintaining the pretense of nonparticipation in "purely European affairs" but working assiduously behind the scenes, the American "observers" at Lausanne were able to secure an arrangement whereby, after a further moratorium of three to five years, Germany would make a final payment of 3 billion mark. The Germans accepted this as a step in the right direction and as the best resolution then attainable, even though Britain was prepared to agree to their demand for complete cancellation. The Germans supported yet another key American proposition by refusing to have the final arrangement made contingent on the success of war debt renegotiations. America's war debtors thereupon concluded a "Gentlemen's Agreement" to that affect among themselves, but this only soured their own relationship to the United States and kept Germany blameless when the inevitable defaults on war debt payments occurred.

Even at Geneva the change in German-American relations was gradual. The rightward swing in the German government had obviously alarmed the French even further and made acceptance of any formula for arms parity virtually impossible. The American delegates still took essentially the German side, however, and Norman Davis told his French counterpart as late as June 24, that "if the conference broke up without any real achievement it would only be a matter of time before Germany denounced the military clauses of the Versailles Treaty *and in this she would have a good deal of sympathy from public opinion in the United States* and Great Britain."[9] In order to avoid such a denouement in the face of continued French recalcitrance, the United States found no better solution than to push for acceptance of the Hoover proposal principles, without any reference to Germany's future status. But when such a plan was adopted on July 23 the new German government, ignoring

9. Hugh Gibson to Stimson, June 25, 1932, in *Foreign Relations, 1932,* 1: 235. Emphasis added.

American pleas for patience for the first time in many years, not only voted no but declared its refusal to participate in further disarmament discussions until agreement had been reached on removing the military disabilities imposed on Germany at Versailles.

By early fall, the political and economic situation in Germany had deteriorated even further. Papen proved no more capable than Brüning of building parliamentary support, suppressing violence in the streets, or easing the plight of the average German. Like his predecessor, he came to place his hopes in new elections. They were held on July 31, and the results proved even worse than before. With 37.4 percent of the vote, the National Socialists more than doubled their seats to 230, became the largest party in the Reichstag, and elected one of their number, Hermann Goering, as president of that body. With the exception of the Center party and the Bavarian People's party, both Catholic-based, the bourgeois parties were decimated, while the Communists raised their representation to 89. The two most radical parties thus constituted a clear majority and a vote of no-confidence became not only possible but highly likely. Papen's effort to strengthen his position by bringing the Nazis into the government failed on August 13, when Hitler told Hindenburg, as he had already told the chancellor and the German people, that he insisted on "leadership of the government and state for himself and his party to the fullest extent."[10] Within a month still another call for elections had gone out. They were scheduled for November 6.

In the rather forlorn hope of deflating the extremists, the Papen government pushed its insistence for equality of armaments as prerequisite to entering into further disarmament discussions. Germany's more bellicose stance produced a negative reaction in Washington. It was now apparent that the Germans were far more interested in their own rearmament than in general disarmament; and, too, their approach had the character of an ultimatum and was not readily reconcilable with the concept of peaceful change. Castle promptly warned the German chargé-d'affaires, Rudolf Leitner, that in view of America's interest in arms reduction, "the trend of opinion in this country would turn strongly against Germany" in the event that "Germany, by making extravagant demands should break

10. Otto Meissner notes, August 13, 1932, in *Ursachen und Folgen: Vom deutschen Zusammenbruch 1918 und 1945 bis zur staatlichen Neuordnung Deutschlands in der Gegenwart*, 26 vols., ed. Herbert Michaelis and Ernst Schraepler (Berlin, 1959 [?]–1979), 8: 618.

up the Conference and prevent disarmament."[11] The very instability in Germany which had prompted the hardening of its demands was cited by the undersecretary as a reason why these demands were unlikely to be met at this time.

Stimson took an even dimmer view of the German demarche. Annoyed by what he regarded as a deviation from the agreement he believed he had reached with Brüning in April and worried that both the Kellogg-Briand Pact and the Nine-Power Treaty on the Far East would be undermined if revisions of the Versailles settlement were to be brought about by coercion, he refrained from public comment on the justice of Germany's claims. In his official communications he called it "regrettable," however, that the emphasis should be placed on the right to rearm, to whatever degree, "when the question of real importance to all nations concerned, including Germany, is rather the practicable one of securing the greatest general reduction of armaments possible." In addition he stressed the absolute necessity of "having any changes or modifications which may be made in the Treaty of Versailles brought about by methods of conciliation and mutual agreement rather than by threats and precipitate action."[12]

Nonetheless, the United States continued to play a key role in the attempt to find a formula that would accommodate within a general disarmament scheme both the German desire for equality and that of the French for security. Although the lead in calling for new discussions was taken by the British, both Davis and Mellon, now ambassador in London, worked hard to modify the position of France, while Sackett and Chargé George A. Gordon in Berlin preached reasonableness to the Germans.

At a five-power conference in early December at which American delegates played a crucial role, a viable formula was found. Britain, France, and Italy declared "that one of the principles that should guide the Conference on Disarmament should be the grant to Germany, and to the other powers disarmed by the Treaty [of Versailles], of equality of rights in a system which would provide security for all nations. . . ."[13] On the basis of that declaration Germany agreed to resume its place at the disarmament conference.

11. Castle to Walter E. Edge, September 2, 1932, in *Foreign Relations, 1932*, I: 420.

12. Stimson to Edge et al., September 16, 1932, in ibid., 432.

13. Five-Power Declaration, December 11, 1932, in ibid., 527.

Though Germany had threatened withdrawal unless its demands were fully met, the five-power meeting was the last occasion on which the Germans obtained revisions of the Versailles treaty essentially through peaceful compromise. It was also the last example for many years of German-American cooperation, which though already strained had once more played an important role.

New developments now changed the political picture even further in both nations and put an end to their post-Versailles policies. On November 8 American voters chose Franklin D. Roosevelt to replace Herbert Hoover and thus began an interregnum during which a lameduck president with a Congress already controlled by the party of his successor was effectively deprived of the possibility of taking any further action of consequence. Moreover, while the election result was almost entirely a response to the domestic crisis that the promised "New Deal" was intended to alleviate, it was inevitable that the coming change in leadership, as well as the depth of this crisis, would produce modifications in an American foreign policy that had been formulated in the expectation of continued prosperity.

Two days before America's voters made their decision, the Germans held their second parliamentary election within fourteen weeks. Although the Nazi tide receded somewhat, the Communists made new gains and the antigovernment majority thus remained. Papen now proposed scrapping the Weimar constitution altogether and ruling with support of the army until a new, perhaps monarchist, constitution could be adopted. Hindenburg, although inclined to support this move, was fearful of a civil war in which the army might well prove too weak to cope with both the left and the right. He therefore dismissed Papen and appointed the Machiavellian Schleicher to the chancellorship. Schleicher's hopes for governing effectively rested on his presumed ability to split the Nazis by wooing their less nationalist and more socialist elements led by Gregor Strasser and to win at least tacit support from the more conservative of the major trade unions. When all efforts in these directions proved futile and when Hindenburg refused him the unrestricted powers he had earlier denied to Papen, Schleicher resigned on January 28, 1933. Two days later the old field marshal, persuaded both by his son and by Papen, who now hoped to exert a dominating and moderating influence as vice-chancellor, suppressed his personal antipathy to the "Austrian corporal" and appointed Hitler to head a new government.

Whatever moderation had previously remained in German politics was at an end. After the Reichstag building was destroyed by fire on February 27, all civil rights were suspended by decree. New and no longer free elections on March 5 surprisingly gave the National Socialists only 43.9 percent of the vote but with the 8 percent received by their allies, the Deutschnationale Volkspartei, a majority for the government was obtained for the first time in three years. On March 21, with eighty-one Communist deputies under arrest or otherwise excluded and only the Socialists defending constitutionalism and democracy, the Reichstag voted 441 to 94 for an enabling act that removed all restraints from the cabinet. In effect, the Weimar Republic had come to an end and Adolf Hitler was the ruler of Germany. On March 4 Franklin D. Roosevelt had been sworn in as president of the United States.

The Atrophy of Relations

By a remarkable coincidence, the Roosevelt presidency and the Hitler dictatorship lasted for the same span of twelve years, ending with the death of Roosevelt on April 12, 1945, and Hitler's suicide eighteen days later. For the last third of this period, Germany and the United States were once again opponents in war. Although this outcome could hardly have been foreseen in 1933, it was clear almost from the beginning that the new governments acting under changed circumstances would end the friendly relations that had existed between the two countries for most of the previous decade. The German policy of ostensible fulfillment as a means of securing, with American assistance, revisions of the Versailles settlement was not merely anathema to Germany's new leader but was, in fact, no longer feasible. By the same token, the American policy of world stabilization through noncommittal diplomacy and the export of capital, in which the restoration of a viable and prosperous Germany had been a key element, was not only at variance with the views of Roosevelt but impossible in the age of the Great Depression.

The change in American policy was demonstrated most dramatically in Roosevelt's "bombshell" message of July 2, 1933, which effectively broke up the World Economic Conference then meeting in London. American participation in that conference had been agreed to by Hoover, whose only condition had been the traditional one that war debts not be discussed. Had the United States adhered to its policy of the 1920s, it would have listened sympathetically at London to renewed German requests for economic assistance and led the movement there for the revival of trade and the world economies through gold stabilization. In fact, America ignored Germany altogether at the conference, while Roosevelt denounced "old fetishes of so-called international bankers" and "the specious fallacy of achieving a temporary and probably an artificial stability in foreign exchange on the part of a few large countries." To rely on these, the president insisted, would be "a catastrophe amounting to a world tragedy."[14] The drain of gold from the United States which would have resulted from the conference proposal would have been welcomed as a stimulus to trade during the 1920s. It was now seen as weakening the faltering American economy still further. Relief was to be sought by national rather than international means.

If the United States no longer adhered to its earlier stabilization policy, it did continue its support for the cause of disarmament. Indeed, the rise of Hitler, with its threat of further political destabilization, seemed to make it imperative that a future arms race be avoided through restrictions that would impose reasonable limits while satisfying both Germany and France. Roosevelt himself favored disarmament under some form of international control. When Prime Minister MacDonald came forward with a proposal to that effect, the president supported it in principle and allowed Norman Davis to announce at Geneva on May 22 that if a substantive reduction of armaments were effected by international agreement, the United States was prepared "to contribute in other ways to the organization of peace."

> In particular, we are willing to consult the other states in case of a threat to peace, with a view to averting the conflict. Further than that, in the event that the states, in conference, determine that a state has been guilty of a breach of the peace in violation of its international obligations and take measures against the violator, then, if we concur in the judgement rendered as to the responsible and guilty party, we will refrain from any action tending to defeat such collective effort which these states may thus make to restore peace.[15]

14. Franklin D. Roosevelt to Sumner Welles (for Cordell Hull), July 2, 1933, in *Foreign Relations, 1933*, I: 673.

15. Davis, address of May 22, 1933, in U.S. Department of State, *Peace and War: United States Foreign Policy, 1933–1941* (Washington, D.C., 1943), pp. 188–189.

This statement might at an earlier time have gone far toward supplying France with the security guarantee it had long sought and regarded as a sine qua non for its agreement to even theoretical parity for the Germans. The statement was instantly condemned by American isolationists, however, and was in any event no longer sufficient to bring about a resolution. Germany more fervently than ever sought concessions that would allow it at least limited rearmament, while the new secretary of state, Cordell Hull, had already indicated his opposition "to any German effort to increase armaments now, for in effect we ask them to stay as they are and that other nations will reduce to their level by steps."[16] The president had said as much on May 6 to Germany's special envoy Hjalmar Schacht.

Roosevelt's message to Hitler and other world leaders on May 16, which had proposed a four-step peace and disarmament program based largely on the Geneva discussions had, to be sure, drawn a conciliatory response from the German leader, who was still primarily concerned with consolidating his position at home and stepped only cautiously into the arena of foreign affairs. For the first and last time he expressed his government's "warm thanks" for Roosevelt's efforts and declared that "Germany would see in the realization of the American president's magnanimous proposal to bring the mighty United States into Europe as guarantor of peace a great reassurance for those who profess peace sincerely."[17] But the German position on rearmament, which Hitler had given highest priority at a cabinet meeting on February 8, continued to harden. The German police and other paramilitary units were increased in size, French suspicions grew stronger, and possible agreement at the disarmament conference became more remote.

On October 14 Hitler drew his own final conclusions and threw his own "bombshell." Always convinced that Germany could not and should not wait any longer to throw off the military disabilities imposed by Versailles, he now reasoned that the other powers, beset by difficulties at home, would not take effective countermeasures if Germany acted on its own, and that the domestic benefits of a deter-

16. Hull to Davis, April 25, 1933, in *Foreign Relations, 1933,* 1: 107.
17. Hitler, speech of May 17, 1933, in *Verhandlungen des Reichstags: Stenographische Berichte,* 8th election period (Berlin, 1933), 457: 53.

mined stand would far outweigh any possible external losses. In a speech, the English translation of which was ironically entitled "Germany Declares for Peace," Hitler withdrew his country from the disarmament conference and, for good measure, from the League of Nations as well. The era of fulfillment, whether real or pretended, was over.

The results of the World Economic and General Disarmament conferences illustrate the changes in the course of German-American relations foreshadowed by the accession to power of Hitler and of Roosevelt, and reveal the fundamental divergence that was to characterize it thereafter. Both of the new leaders had attained office by castigating the policies of their predecessors and won support because these policies had failed to preserve their countries from disaster. Both saw as their most immediate concern the relief of mass unemployment, and both moved at once to increase the scope and the powers of their respective governments. Yet even these apparent similarities, of which the Nazi press made much and which for a brief time even muted American criticism of the emerging dictatorship in Germany, concealed basic differences of approach. These differences were readily apparent in the priorities that were soon established by the two governments.

For Hitler, the cardinal sin of the Weimar Republic had been its failure to reestablish an economically sound and militarily strong Germany. He attributed this failure to a political structure unsuited to determined action and to a lack of will which had kept Germany dependent on the whims of other states that, by virtue of the ignominious Versailles treaty, dominated the affairs of Europe and of Germany itself. For Hitler, the policy of fulfillment, through which Stresemann and others had hoped to restore Germany to international respectability as a prelude to overturning the Versailles settlement by peaceful means, was not only impossible to carry out successfully but also wrong in principle and humiliating to Germany. His alternative was first to make Germany militarily powerful, then to solve its economic problems partly through the process of rearmament and finally through war and conquest.

Although the new chancellor was not ready to challenge the world before his regime was fully established at home, his priorities were clearly stated from the beginning. Just nine days after assuming office, he told his cabinet that "for the next five years Germany would have to dedicate itself to making the German people capable of bearing arms again. Every publicly promoted measure for creating employment would have to be judged from the standpoint of its necessity for this restoration of military power. This thought would always and everywhere have to be in the foreground." Five days earlier, he had already told the commanders of the army and the navy:

> The buildup of the armed forces is the most important precondition for the attainment of the goal: regaining [international] political power. . . . How is this political power to be used when it is won? [It is] not yet possible to say. Maybe fighting for new export possibilities, maybe—and certainly better—conquest of new *Lebensraum* in the East and its ruthless Germanization. It is certain that only through political power and battle can present economic conditions be changed. All that can be done now . . . is makeshift.[18]

Hitler's starting position thus ruled out further meaningful cooperation with the United States on the question of disarmament and on economic policy as well. The subordination of all questions of trade and economic development to that of rearmament led inevitably to trade discrimination, a managed economy, and a striving for autarchy. All of this would have been anathema to American policy makers in the 1920s and became that to an even greater degree in the depression decade. To be sure, Roosevelt had harshly criticized the economic policies of the Harding-Coolidge-Hoover era during his election campaign and proceded to change them after assuming office. His major strictures, however, were directed against the notion that prosperity would somehow "trickle down" if priority were given to the encouragement and support of business, and against the idea that the expansion of foreign trade could be permanently financed by American loans even in the face of high tariffs that did not allow other countries to increase their supply of available dollars. Although he devoted his initial efforts to internal economic measures and the independent manipulation of the American currency, Roosevelt never lost sight of the goal of expanding trade by loosening restrictions on it as a means of reinvigorating both the American and the world economies. "I shall spare no effort," he

18. Vogel minutes of cabinet meeting, February 8, 1933, and Liebmann minutes of meeting with commanders, February 3, 1933, in *Akten zur deutschen auswärtigen Politik, 1919–1945* (Baden-Baden and Göttingen, 1950–), Series B, I, no. I: 34, 35.

declared in his inaugural address, "to restore world trade by international economic readjustment, but the emergency at home cannot wait on that accomplishment."[19] With Roosevelt aiming for expanded world trade through a reduction of barriers and Hitler managing trade in the interest of rearmament, conflict in the economic sphere was bound to ensue.

The dimensions of this conflict became readily apparent in 1934, when Congress enacted Cordell Hull's long-sought Reciprocal Trade Agreements Act on June 12, and Germany issued the first of its ordinances implementing Schacht's "New Plan" on September 4. The Reciprocal Trade Agreements Act provided for the mutual lowering of tariffs on selected items through bilateral agreements and extended the unconditional most-favored-nation principle to these arrangements, at least in theory. Germany, which had already circumvented the same principle through the imposition of various quota arrangements, based its "New Plan" on bilateralization of all trade and payments balances, on import limitation and planning in accordance with national priorities, and on the encouragement of exports on a barter basis.

The United States had protested against the quota system from the beginning and claimed that it violated the trade treaty of 1923. It had watched with mounting dismay as Germany, through restrictions on the transfer of foreign currencies, had throttled American imports and curtailed payments on foreign debts. The State Department now took the hopeful if unrealistic position that it was "not likely that current German commercial policy can last for any considerable period of time," but recognized that if this judgment should prove erroneous, "it is clear that any trade relations with Germany are of little value."[20] The Germans meanwhile had had scant luck in concluding barter arrangements with the United States and none whatever in their efforts to persuade Hull to enter into reciprocal trade arrangements with them which would inevitably improve the German balance of payments and hurt the American one. On October 13, 1934, the first day on which it was legally possible, they gave notice of their intention to terminate the unconditional most-

19. Roosevelt, Inaugural Address, March 4, 1933, *The Public Papers and Addresses of Franklin Delano Roosevelt*, 13 vols., ed. Samuel I. Rosenman (New York, 1938–1951), 2: 14.

20. Memorandum by Special State Department Committee on Proposed American Policy with Respect to Germany, October 12, 1934, in *Foreign Relations, 1934*, 2: 453. The quoted position was specifically endorsed by Hull.

favored-nation provisions of their trade treaty with the United States.

The differences that thus developed were by no means the result of instant antipathy between the two regimes. Although the change to the New Deal and the Third Reich appeared in retrospect to be abrupt and even revolutionary, there were in fact sufficient elements of continuity to obscure this fundamental shift for a time. Genuinely democratic government had ceased in Germany by 1930 and been followed by the rule by decree, a device Hitler at first simply extended. Demands for ending the military restrictions of Versailles, for moratoriums on debt payments, or for a new German "place in the sun" were not really novel either, even though they were now expressed with more vigor and with less concern for the sensibilities of other nations. Moreover, the change in the government of Germany was not immediately reflected in the personnel of the Foreign Office. The retention of Konstantin von Neurath as foreign secretary, in particular, was taken as an indication that, whatever internal adjustment Hitler might bring about, relations with the outside world would not be dramatically altered.

Hitler himself, though his views about the United States were vague, confused, and even contradictory, was by no means prepared to look on America as an enemy. Indeed, he was initially fond of pointing to the alleged parallels between his own "revolution" and the course being pursued by Roosevelt. Not only were such sentiments repeatedly reflected in the columns of the semiofficial Nazi party newspaper, the *Völkischer Beobachter,* but the chancellor communicated them directly to the president as late as March 1934. He congratulated Roosevelt "for his heroic efforts in the interests of the American people" and expressed his "accord with the President in the view that the virtue of duty, readiness for sacrifice, and discipline should dominate the entire people." "These moral demands which the President places before every individual citizen of the United States," Hitler continued, "are also the quintessence of the German state philosophy. . . ." In reply, Roosevelt somewhat guardedly expressed his appreciation, as well as the hope "that Germany's efforts toward economic restoration may be entirely successful and so contribute to that universal recovery from which all alike will benefit."[21]

If Germany initially sought no drastic alteration in its relationship

21. Hull to John C. White, March 28, 1934, in ibid., 419.

to the United States, Washington shared that sentiment. The State Department was, at the beginning, prepared to believe that Hitler would either be unable to maintain himself in power for very long or at least be compelled to moderate his more strident views. It was widely held that, even if neither of these developments occurred, the changes in Germany would largely be internal and would not fundamentally alter its foreign policy stance. Given the continued American economic stake in Germany, it appeared to be the course of both prudence and wisdom to avoid picking a quarrel with the new regime and to try to maintain intact the existing relatively good relationship.

In addition, it seemed initially that Germany had by no means become impervious to American wishes. Not only did the Foreign Office go to considerable pains to avoid conflict with the United States over the World Economic Conference, it postponed implementation of a partial transfer moratorium that had already been approved by Hitler himself when Roosevelt declared that he was "profoundly shocked" and Hull called it "the strangest possible course and one calculated greatly to check and undermine American efforts to restore domestic business conditions."[22] On April 7, 1933, Roosevelt went so far as to invite Hitler to Washington for discussions to parallel those already scheduled with British Prime Minister MacDonald and French ex-Premier Herriot. When the chancellor declined because of other commitments and the internal political situation and sent Schacht instead, the president greeted this emissary with full fanfare and ostentatious friendliness. The newly reappointed president of the Reichsbank reported to Berlin that Roosevelt had shown "doubtless sympathy for the personality of the Chancellor," had expressed the hope for a face-to-face meeting with him, and had even quipped that "when it comes to the rapid implementation of governmental measures, there were not everywhere such capable overseers as (literally) Mussolini, Hitler, and Roosevelt."[23]

The basic interest of both nations in carrying on "business as usual" was also demonstrated in the exchange of new ambassadors. Prittwitz, to whom the turn of events in Germany had come as a great shock, tendered his resignation on March 6, explaining to Neurath five days later that his dedication to "a libertarian concept

22. Hull memorandum, May 9, 1933, in State Department Decimal File 862.51/3988 1/2, RG 59, NA.
23. Schacht to Foreign Office, May 6, 1933, *Akten zur deutschen auswärtigen Politik*, B, 1, no. 1: 390.

of the state and to the basic principles of the republican Germany" made it impossible for him to represent the new government, which had condemned both.[24] His successor, however, was no disciple of Hitler but rather Hans Luther, a former chancellor, finance minister, and president of the Reichsbank, who represented both continuity and respectability. The Republican Sackett, whose last dispatches from Berlin catalogued the events of the Nazi seizure of complete power and concluded both that "democracy in Germany has received a blow from which it may never recover" and that the "form this Third Reich will finally take is not yet clear in these critical days of political confusion and uncertainty,"[25] also submitted his resignation. Roosevelt, after some political maneuvering, replaced him with yet another veteran academician who had studied in Germany, William E. Dodd, a University of Chicago historian. Although the appointment of Luther was less a gesture of friendship for the United States than a stratagem for removing the new ambassador painlessly from the presidency of the Reichsbank and from the country, and Dodd's Jeffersonian principles and romantic recollections of his student days at Leipzig placed him quickly at odds with Germany's new rulers, the intention in both cases was to emphasize continuity, not change, and to preserve the basically friendly relations between the two countries.

The establishment of the Third Reich, however, also reintroduced into the German-American relationship an ideological element that had lain dormant since the days of William II, but that quickly assumed astonishing proportions. Within days of the Nazi takeover, the embassy in Berlin began reporting to Washington acts of discrimination, persecution, and outright physical violence directed against Jews. The embassy was informed by Stimson that these actions had produced "apprehension and distress," and by Hull that they were "causing deep concern and even alarm to a large section of our population." In early May, Roosevelt took up the matter personally with Schacht and stressed the danger it posed for German-American relations, not necessarily because of American sympathy for the Jews, "but out of the old Anglo-Saxon sense of chivalry toward the weaker."[26]

24. Prittwitz to Konstantin von Neurath, March 11, 1933, in ibid., 145.

25. Sackett to Hull, March 9, 1933, in *Foreign Relations, 1933*, 2: 209.

26. Stimson to Sackett, March 3, 1933, and Hull to Sackett, March 21, 1933, in ibid., 320, 327; Schacht to Foreign Office, May 6, 1933, in *Akten zur deutschen auswärtigen Politik*, B, 1, no. 1: 388.

By this time, the seizure and destruction of the Socialist trade unions had taken place, and the reorganization of the Evangelical church into a virtual agency of the state was well under way. Conflict with the Catholic church, which had been muted somewhat after the concordat of June 29, surfaced again in December, when Dodd reported the arrest of a number of priests and former leaders of the Catholic Center party. The end of freedom for German universities and the purging of their faculties and student bodies of Jews and of all liberal elements, the dissolution of political parties other than the National Socialists, and revocation of the German citizenship of persons charged with disloyalty toward the new order contributed to a rising feeling in the United States that Hitler's regime was not just another repressive German government but a deadly enemy of liberalism and democracy everywhere.

By late July reports of mounting arrests and imprisonment in concentration camps of political opponents, including well-known leaders of the Weimar Republic, began to appear regularly and were denied only in part by the German government. Large-scale book burnings occurred during the summer, and on December 4 the establishment of the Reich Chamber of Culture, to which the eminent composer Richard Strauss lent his support, brought music, literature, film, theater, broadcasting, creative arts, and the press under direct government control and gave even broader meaning to Hitler's concept of the "total state." These developments took up an increasing proportion of the diplomatic reports from Berlin and were widely and critically reported in the American press. Edgar Ansel Mowrer of the Chicago *Daily News* was forced out of the presidency of the Association of Foreign Press Correspondents in Berlin and out of Germany itself in August for such reporting.

Predictably, public protests began to be organized by Jewish organizations, but even the first of these, a mass rally in New York's Madison Square Garden on March 27, 1933, was addressed by such non-Jewish notables as Mayor John P. O'Brien of New York, Senator Robert F. Wagner, William Green of the American Federation of Labor, and Bishops William T. Manning and Francis J. McConnell. Attempts to organize a boycott of German goods in retaliation for the boycott of Jewish firms proclaimed by the German government were launched almost at once, and before the Senate had even confirmed Dodd, the respected majority leader and 1928 vice-presidential candidate, Senator Joseph E. Robinson of Arkansas, told his colleagues it was "sickening and terrifying to realize" that the Germans were yielding to "impulses of cruelty and inhumanity which . . . will have lowered German civilization in the opinion of all peoples with whom Germany must have social and commercial relations." "Regardless of the origins of this persecution," declared Republican Senator Jesse H. Metcalf of Rhode Island, "it has become a disquieting factor to the peace and economic welfare of the world."[27]

When Congress reconvened the following January, Senator Millard E. Tydings of Maryland introduced a resolution calling for the restoration of civil and political rights to Germany's Jews, and Representative Samuel Dickstein of New York proposed an investigation into the nature and extent of Nazi propaganda in the United States. The Dickstein Resolution was approved on March 20, and the House Special Committee on Un-American Activities was thus launched on its long and often inglorious career. A mock trial of Adolf Hitler, which the American Federation of Labor helped stage on March 7, 1934, drew more than twenty thousand persons to Madison Square Garden. Chaired by Wilson's last secretary of state, Bainbridge Colby, it featured such varied speakers as New York's ex-governor Al Smith, Mayor Fiorello La Guardia, Harry W. Chase, chancellor of New York University, and Edward McNeary of the National Executive Committee of the American Legion.

Neither such demonstrations of American opposition to the "New Germany" nor repeated German protests against this alleged interference in the country's internal affairs led at the outset to a policy of confrontation between the two countries. Instead, the relationship that had flourished during the 1920s simply atrophied. Hitler could not and did not expect American support for his efforts to strengthen the position of Germany in Europe and focused his foreign policy instead on trying to win either acquiescence or support from the European powers. He particularly sought an agreement with Great Britain on plans for rebuilding Germany's navy.

The United States reacted to the economic crisis at home and to increasing turmoil abroad by reducing its international involvement and avoiding commitments more consistently than ever. After Roosevelt's failure to achieve international agreement on disarmament and his earlier lack of success in obtaining Congressional au-

27. June 10, 1933, *Congressional Record*, 73d Cong., 1st sess., 5539.

thorization to halt possible aggression through a selective embargo
on American arms exports, the United States adopted an even lower
profile in world affairs and sought to insulate itself against possible
future wars. This policy took the form of so-called neutrality legislation, which was formally enacted in 1935, 1936, and 1937, but which
was clearly foreshadowed by April 12, 1934, when Congress passed
the Johnson Act prohibiting loans to countries in default—for all
practical purposes all nations except Finland—and, at the same
time, set up the Nye Committee to investigate the munitions industry. Both actions were regarded, at least in part, as steps toward
keeping America out of a possible future war.

If the shift in German foreign policy, including the virtual elimination of the United States as a serious factor in its formulation,
reflected primarily the new priorities established by Hitler, the
American shift seemed to be dictated more by the changed economic conditions and the general disillusionment that accompanied
them. Roosevelt was by temperament more of an internationalist
than any of his immediate predecessors but, for the time being,
subordinated his world concerns to domestic needs and accommodated himself, more or less willingly, to the rising tide of isolationism. Given the enormous problems produced by the depression
at home, it seemed no more than common sense to put America first
and to show caution with respect to problems arising elsewhere.
Moreover, the end of the era of prosperity, had undermined faith in
the business leadership, which had spearheaded American world
involvement in the 1920s and was increasingly held responsible for
American entrance into the First World War. The rise of Hitler,
coupled with the activities of Japan, was taken as evidence that, far
from making the world safe for democracy, America's earlier intervention had fostered dictatorship and brought new threats of war.
The weakened position of the United States also contributed much
to destroying the traditional confidence in America's ability to influence the course of world events.

Under these circumstances, the establishment of the Third Reich
did not catalyze a determination to counter the new threat it posed
to world order, even when that threat began to become apparent.
Instead, it heightened American interest in cutting those ties that
might involve the country in new and dangerous difficulties. As the
issues of disarmament and of war debts and reparations, which had
provided much of the substance for German-American relations dur-

ing the twenties, became increasingly moribund, the two nations moved into a brief period of sometimes pained coexistence during which no substantial relationship of any kind was maintained between them.

In the political realm, this absence of significant interaction was clearly manifested when Germany announced on May 9, 1935, the existence of an air force and reintroduced conscription a week later. Britain, France, and Italy responded to these moves by calling a conference at Stresa which, while producing no agreement on a course of action, at least condemned this open breach of the Versailles treaty. The Council of the League of Nations passed a resolution of censure on April 17. The United States, however, did not even protest what were also obvious violations of its own 1921 peace treaty with Germany. Although a mild note was prepared in the State Department, it was not sent. Instead, conscious of the strength of isolationist sentiment in Congress, which had resulted in the defeat on January 29 of the proposal to have the United States join the World Court, Roosevelt met with the Nye Committee on March 19 and encouraged it to come forth with neutrality legislation. "We are naturally much concerned here over the result at Stresa and the events of the next few months," he lamely wrote to Dodd soon thereafter. "As I told you, I feel very helpless to render any particular service to immediate or permanent peace at this time."[28]

The lack of official American reaction in no way indicated approval of Germany's course. Noting that the government in Washington was "depressed and angry" about recent events, Luther reported correctly that "animosity, especially in the State Department is directed primarily against us."[29] But it did reflect an increasing tendency to let Europe solve its own problems. Accordingly, the Anglo-German naval agreement that followed in June was greeted in Washington as a step in the right direction, although in retrospect it was clearly a major British blunder that split the shaky Stresa front, legitimized Germany's rearmament, and helped the German economy by providing thousands of new jobs. Luther, who in April had still warned that "the far-reaching anti-German tendencies and the deep-seated anger over our economic and financial policies . . .

28. Roosevelt to Dodd, April 16, 1935, in Elliott Roosevelt et al., eds., *F.D.R.: His Personal Letters*, 2 vols. (New York, 1950), 1: 475.
29. Hans Luther to Foreign Office, April 8, 1935, in *Akten zur deutschen auswärtigen Politik*, C, 4, no. 1: 26.

might, as once before, bring the immeasurable economic power of
this continent . . . into play against us," now reported a "calmer
judgment of political events in Europe and a more objective attitude
toward our foreign policy." "In the final analysis," he concluded,
"one respects the restoration of Germany's military power as a fact
about which other nations can, in effect, do nothing."[30]

In the United States, between 1934 and 1936 the belief grew that
nothing could be done about Germany's drive for greater power and
that Hitler would, for better or worse, have to be accepted as a
significant factor on the international scene. This sentiment became
particularly strong after the führer's position was enormously
strengthened by the success of the "Blood Purge," which on June
30–31, 1934, eliminated dissident elements within the Nazi party, by
his assumption after Hindenburg's death on August 2 of the positions of head of state and commander-in-chief of the armed forces,
and by the Saar plebiscite of January 13, 1935, in which 90 percent of
the voters of that region chose reunion with Germany.

When German forces reentered the Rhineland on March 7, 1936,
the United States rejected a specific request from the French foreign
minister, Pierre-Etienne Flandin, that the action be condemned on
moral grounds. The U.S. justified its failure to take any stand by
pointing to the fact that it was party neither to the Locarno agreements of 1925 nor to the Rhineland provisions of the Versailles
treaty, both of which had clearly been violated by Hitler's unilateral
action. Ten days earlier, Roosevelt had indicated that "in view of the
essentially European aspects of the Germany Navy" any attempt to
bring Germany to subscribe to the British-French-American "Gentlemen's Agreement" on further naval limitation, which was to be
the only result of the London naval conference then in progress,
should be left entirely to Great Britain.[31] At the same time, the
administration quietly accepted a new neutrality act, which not only
extended the mandatory arms embargo already enacted in 1935, but
required that this embargo be applied to countries intervening in
wars already under way and thus to those who might possibly join in
collective action to halt aggression.

When Hitler moved on July 25 to provide aircraft, supplies, and
eventually even troops to the forces of General Francisco Franco,

30. Ibid., 28; Luther to Foreign Office, June 18, 1935, in ibid., 315.
31. Hull to Davis, February 29, 1936 in Foreign Relations, 1936, 1: 83.

who had launched his revolt against the republican government of Spain a week earlier with the aid of Italy, the United States did not, however, embargo arms sales to either Germany or Italy. Instead, the administration placed a "moral" embargo on such sales. It secured Congressional approval of a legal embargo on January 6, 1937, but one applicable only to the Spanish government and to the insurgents. Germany's hypocritical pledge not to contribute militarily to the war in Spain, made as a member of the British-sponsored International Nonintervention Committee, was not challenged officially by the United States or the other powers. No American protest against obvious violations was made even after Germany's Condor Legion the following April provided, by its bombing attack on the small Basque town of Guernica, a graphic preview of what much of Europe was to experience later. Neither did the United States react in any way when Mussolini, whose own war of conquest against Ethiopia, though widely condemned, had merely produced a series of efforts to prevent American involvement, spoke for the first time of a Rome-Berlin "axis" on November 1, 1936 (Neurath and the Italian foreign minister, Count Ciano, had signed secret protocols on October 23). Nor was there any American reaction when Germany and Japan on November 25 concluded their Anti-Comintern Pact, an agreement widely though wrongly believed to contain secret military clauses.

In the economic sphere also, German-American relations approached a state of suspended animation. The Germans persisted in trying to secure a new trade treaty that would improve their payments balance and provide them with the strategic raw materials their rearmament effort required. The United States diligently sought to secure modifications in Germany's transfer policies to protect the rights of American bondholders and protested the effects of Germany's new commercial legislation on American firms doing business in the Reich. But no agreement on these matters was ever reached. The German notice of termination of the 1923 trade treaty, which had been given in the hope of negotiating a more favorable one, simply resulted in the exclusion of Germany from the unconditional most-favored-nation provisions of America's reciprocal trade agreements. In turn, Germany struck the United States from its most-favored-nation list and through this procedure continued to discriminate not only against American trade, but also against foreign exchange payments to bondholders that it now regulated through its commercial agreements.

As a result, German-American trade, which had flourished during the 1920s but had been greatly reduced by the onset of the depression, did not share in the general revival of American foreign trade which followed the inauguration of the New Deal. By 1935 exports to Germany amounted to less than 20 percent of what they had been in 1927 and 1928, while imports reached barely a third of those levels. In the following year, Germany accounted for only 3.7 percent of an American foreign trade that totaled only half as much as during the twenties, while the United States supplied only 5.5 percent of Germany's imports and bought 3.6 percent of its exports. The announcement in September 1936 of the first German "Four-Year Plan," with its emphasis on the acquisition of secure sources for needed materials, reduced even further the realistic possibilities for German-American trade. Because Germany was unwilling to accept the "open door" aims inherent in the reciprocal trade agreements program and the United States rejected Germany's ideas of managed bilateralism, the two countries moved increasingly out of each other's economic orbits.

That no actual economic warfare ensued was due, on the one hand, to Germany's continuing need both for dollars and American products and, on the other, to the American realization that investments in Germany and the continuing favorable payments balance gave the United States more to lose than it could hope to gain in any trade war. When in July 1936, at the urging of Treasury Secretary Henry Morgenthau, Jr., the United States nevertheless briefly raised its tariff on German goods through the imposition of countervailing duties intended to offset German export subsidies, the State Department, which had opposed this measure all along, protested along with the Germans. The duties were removed again in August, when Germany ostensibly eliminated the subsidies but in fact changed only its bookkeeping. When the duties were restored in March 1939, the German-American relationship was undergoing a change that had little to do with economic questions. In the meantime, though some discussion was carried on in both countries and numerous notes were exchanged, economic relations had reached their lowest point since the days of the world war.

Such was not the case, to be sure, with respect to private relations between American and German firms. The ties formed in the early years of the century and enormously expanded during the 1920s were broken neither by the establishment of the Third Reich nor by the progressive integration of German industry into the German state and party apparatus. Under the terms of various privately negotiated cartel agreements, American and German firms continued to set prices and export quotas, exchange patent and production information, and divide world markets. Such arrangements still tied the giant IG-Farbenindustrie to Standard Oil, Alcoa, Dupont, and other American firms and kept General Electric, Eastman Kodak, Westinghouse, and Curtiss-Wright, among others, in business in Germany. General Motors, through its Opel subsidiary, at one point even accounted together with Ford for half of Germany's tank production. Indeed, in their effort to safeguard the investments that the American government could no longer protect effectively, American companies cooperated more closely than ever before with their German counterparts, and Germany's prohibition of currency transfers led to the reinvestment of their profits in Germany and thus to an increase in the stake of American industry there.

Such activities, however, can hardly be regarded as symptomatic of American policy. Not only was their full extent unknown to America's policy makers, their effect, to the extent that they aided German rearmament, was clearly contrary to the intentions of the government almost from the beginning. Unlike the 1920s, when American capital investments in Germany had been actively promoted in Washington as a stabilizing factor, in the 1930s such investments became an undesirable by-product of a deteriorating situation.

By early 1937 the official German-American relationship had thus declined to a state of relative insignificance. Tensions clearly existed in both the political and economic realms, but the United States made no move vigorously to oppose Germany's new policies, and Germany largely ignored America while pursuing its interests in Europe and Asia. Nevertheless, the basic divergence in the aims of the two countries had become apparent. The likelihood that they could continue largely to ignore each other for long, even officially, was not great, and actual conflict between them lay just over the horizon. Increasingly frustrated by what he now regarded as a lack of measures to counter the threat posed by Nazi Germany, and more and more isolated and ineffective in Berlin because of his ill-concealed antipathy to Hitler, Dodd asked in March to be relieved of his post by fall. He secured Roosevelt's approval on April 5 and hoped that a strong proponent of collective security measures would succeed him. In May an equally frustrated Luther was recalled from Washington, largely at the instigation of Hans Heinrich Dieckhoff, the Foreign Office's underutilized America expert, who hoped to succeed him and make one final effort to revive German-American relations.

Ideological Conflict and Security Concerns

Despite Dieckhoff's optimistic ambitions, the improvement of Germany's international position and Hitler's growing self-confidence kept America near the periphery of Germany's foreign policy concerns. In the United States, however, these same factors moved the Third Reich at least somewhat closer to the center of those concerns. Moreover, the degree of American recovery from the effects of the depression, which by fall 1937 led Roosevelt at least temporarily to cut back government spending on relief programs, allowed both the administration and the public to pay more attention to events beyond America's borders. Buoyed by his overwhelming reelection victory, the president could devote more of his time and energy to foreign affairs, particularly after the end of the Supreme Court battle in July, when he was assured that key elements of the New Deal program would no longer be declared unconstitutional.

The "New Germany" had not improved its image in the United States by turning the 1936 Olympic Games in Berlin into a giant propaganda carnival, and unfavorable American press reports on the continuing persecution of Jews, the harassment of Christian religious organizations, and the increasingly systematic assumption of control of all aspects of German life by the state drew a more negative response than ever. Neither was the cause of Germany in America aided by the establishment of the Amerikadeutscher Volksbund (commonly called the German-American Bund), which adopted the swastika flag as its official emblem, organized itself on the model of the Nazi party under an American führer, and put its members into uniforms and gave them paramilitary training.

On March 3, 1937, New York's Mayor La Guardia publicly called the real führer "that brown-shirted fanatic who is now menacing the peace of the world," and two months later the respected archbishop of Chicago, George, Cardinal Mundelein, himself of German descent, used even less restrained language at the quarterly diocesan conference. He referred to Hitler as "an Austrian paperhanger and a poor one at that," and denounced "loud-mouthed German propagandists" in general and "the crooked Minister of Propaganda" in particular. Mundelein's remarks were publicly applauded by the president of the Chicago Rabbinical Conference and by the Episcopal bishop of Chicago and prominent labor leaders such as William Green and George Meany.

Such sentiments were also fostered by the growing number of émigrés from Hitler's Germany, who found at least a temporary home in the United States. Since this group included a substantial number of individuals prominent in the scientific and cultural spheres, the very fact of their emigration reflected discredit on the Third Reich, and their activities in the United States contributed to the shaping of American attitudes. What, after all, could be said for a regime that had no use for Albert Einstein, Thomas Mann, Erich Leinsdorf, Otto Rank, Kurt Weill, Hajo Holborn, Hans Morgenthau, or a plethora of other distinguished persons? When Ambassador Dodd returned to the United States on August 4 and handed reporters waiting in Norfolk a statement asserting that "a basic objective of some powers is to frighten, even destroy, democracy everywhere," no one doubted to whom he referred. The Germans vigorously protested against such undiplomatic remarks.[32]

The responses from Washington, however, remained for the time being far more cautious and restrained. Tentative feelers from British Prime Minister Neville Chamberlain regarding a more active American role were met by Roosevelt with an invitation for a visit, but no more. Mussolini, who tried to sound out the president's interest in sponsoring another disarmament conference, did not receive even that. But as the year wore on the drift of world events became ever more ominous. On July 7, Chinese and Japanese troops clashed near the Marco Polo Bridge on the outskirts of Peking, and this "incident" soon led to a full-scale, if undeclared, Sino-Japanese war. On September 4, Mussolini announced an impending visit to Berlin, and three weeks later he was received there with full pomp and circumstance. The enormous display of Germany's new military

32. *New York Times*, March 4, 1937, p. 25, col. 4; May 19, 1937, p. 9, col. 3, p. 11, col. 1; May 20, 1937, p. 1, col. 3; May 26, 1937, p. 6, col. 3; August 5, 1937, p. 3, col. 3.

and industrial might, intended to impress Il Duce, impressed the rest of the world as well. If Germany, Italy, and Japan were to draw closer together, as now seemed likely, world peace and the security of the United States were certain to be threatened.

It was this combination of circumstances which led Roosevelt to deliver his so-called Quarantine Speech in Chicago on October 5. Although the president had not yet evolved any program for action, and no immediate change in American policy followed, the speech proved to be a significant indicator of future policy directions. Roosevelt denounced "the present reign of terror and international lawlessness" and distinguished between "those nations of the world which seem to be piling armament on armament for purposes of aggression" and the 90 percent who were "peace-loving." He also insisted that the treaty violations that had occurred were "a matter of vital interest and concern to the people of the United States," and were "creating a state of international anarchy and instability from which there is no escape through mere isolation or neutrality."[33] Although Dieckhoff accepted Undersecretary of State Sumner Welles's assurances that the primary thrust of the speech was the promotion of peace and informed his superiors in Berlin that the strictures against aggressors referred primarily to Japan and perhaps to Italy, he concluded unequivocally and prophetically: "If a world conflict should break out in which Great Britain becomes involved, the United States will not stand aside for long. In that case we will have to count on the fact that the weight of the United States will be thrown, either at the beginning of the conflict or soon thereafter, on the British side of the scale."[34]

Roosevelt himself played down the significance of the statement and allowed Hull to dissuade him from following Welles's suggestion to issue a call for a world peace conference at a November 11 meeting of all ambassadors accredited to the United States. But the idea that the U.S. could no longer remain inactive in the face of mounting agression was clearly strong in his mind. Moreover, it is virtually certain that even at this date Roosevelt saw the greatest potential danger as emanating not from Japan or Italy but from Hitler Germany. The United States had condemned the Japanese

33. Roosevelt, address of October 5, 1937, in State Department, *Peace and War*, pp. 384, 385, 386.

34. Dieckhoff to Foreign Office, October 15, 1937, in *Akten zur deutschen auswärtigen Politik*, D, 1: 524.

attack in China, as it had the earlier Italian one in Ethiopia, and ostentatiously retained its marines in Shanghai. Roosevelt had refused to invoke the neutrality act because he assumed such a step would help Japan in the conflict. But it was Japan's tie to Germany which was seen as converting a problem in Asia into a worldwide threat, and the president clearly assumed that a solution to the problem must first be sought in Europe. Therefore, when a major reorganization of the State Department had been undertaken in July, the emphasis had been not on the Far Eastern or Mediterranean sections, but rather on increasing the number of "German experts" in responsible positions. Accordingly, the minister to Switzerland, Hugh R. Wilson, had been appointed assistant secretary of state, as had George S. Messersmith, who had been consul general in Berlin at the time of the Nazi takeover and more recently minister in Vienna.

On October 11 Messersmith communicated his view of the world situation to Hull, who immediately showed the memorandum to the president. "The central thought I should like to emphasize in this memorandum," the new assistant secretary wrote, "is that the crux of the major problem which concerns the world and ourselves is still Germany. With the German problem settled and a Government there with which we and other countries could deal in a normal way, the questions in the Far East and in the Mediterranean as well as the general European question would permit of fairly ready, gradual and reasonable settlement." The issue, moreover, was not a simple clash between "haves" and "have nots" which might be resolved by economic concessions and minor colonial adjustments but "an even more basic clash of ideologies." "The final aim of the dictatorships, under the subtle leadership of the present Government in Germany, is the disintegration of the British Empire, the consequent weakening of England in Europe and the opening of the way to attack on the United States."[35] Within a month, Roosevelt expressed dismay at the success of "the German-Italian-Japanese combination" as well as the hope "that the Polish government will not find itself compelled to do things which would be regarded by the democratic nations as yielding to Germany." The basic danger, he told his ambassador in Warsaw, was the spread of fascism throughout the world.[36]

Roosevelt's attitude clearly precluded any meaningful relation-

35. George S. Messersmith to Hull, October 11, 1937, in *Foreign Relations, 1937,* I: 140, 142.
36. Roosevelt to Anthony Biddle, November 10, 1937, in ibid., 154.

ship with Germany at all. Whatever sympathy had once existed for Germany's plight under the terms of the Versailles treaty had vanished in the face of mounting evidence that Hitler's aims went far beyond treaty revision. The führer had, in any event, "withdrawn" Germany's signature in January 1937 and declared the treaty ended. Neither did the administration really share the belief, which Chamberlain was to hold for nearly two more years, that some form of accommodation with the Third Reich might be achieved through negotiation. "There were certain countries with which Germany had good relations," Goering, now minister for aviation, noted somewhat ruefully, "and certain countries with which Germany had bad relations; but with the United States, Germany had no relations at all."[37]

What Germany did have by the end of 1937 was the growing hostility of the United States. This hostility had not yet been translated into an actual American policy—in September 1937 and again in 1938 the United States accepted Hitler's invitation to send a diplomatic representative to the Nuremberg Congress of the Nazi party, and the new American ambassador in Berlin, Hugh R. Wilson, was more sympathetic to German aims than Dodd had been. But the time was clearly not far distant when it would be. The perspicacious Dieckhoff, observing the situation from Washington, was well aware of that fact. Recognizing that he had made no progress in his efforts to improve relations, he blamed the increasing antipathy toward Germany on "American public opinion, on which both the President and the Congress depend." The key elements fostering this antipathy, he reported, were Germany's closer association with Italy and Japan and the resulting fear that "these three 'aggressor states' " would permanently threaten world peace, the sharper emphasis on ideological differences "(here democracy—there totalitarian state; here alleged liberty—there alleged despotism; here alleged Christianity—there alleged neopaganism, etc.)", and the growing impression that Germany was trying to export fascism to the United States. "One can perhaps take the position," he concluded, "that we can be indifferent to American public opinion of Germany. But I believe we should remember that the development of American public opinion against us was fatal for us once before, and that only twenty years ago."[38]

37. Memorandum attached to letter, Bullitt to Hull, November 23, 1937, in ibid., 173.
38. Dieckhoff to Ernst von Weizsäcker, December 20, 1937, in *Akten zur deutschen auswärtigen Politik*, D, 1: 537–538.

Dieckhoff's catalogue makes no mention of economic strains underlying the American attitude and that omission is not only justified but also very revealing. The ambassador's major effort at improving German-American relations had been directed toward the negotiation of a new treaty that would increase trade between the two countries. Under other conditions, this effort would have been welcomed at least by Hull, who regarded the expansion of trade as the major assurance of future peace and who, with Roosevelt's approval, had made this the cornerstone of his entire foreign policy. The State Department failed to respond favorably to German overtures, however, as it had failed to respond to Italy's after that country's adherence to the Anti-Comintern Pact on November 6, 1937. The lack of favorable response resulted not from pique against Germany's trade practices but rather from concern over its long-range political and military goals. "It would appear," the department's economic adviser, Herbert Feis, argued successfully, "that the German Government should not be easily encouraged at the present time when there seems to be a real possibility that within the near future the enlarged military establishment of Germany will be used for the furthering of political ends possibly directed in consonance with, even if not in actual alliance with Japan, thereby threatening the ultimate security both of this country and the British Empire."[39]

The issue of security and the ideological factors surrounding it assumed ever greater dimensions as Hitler's expansionist plans were put into practice in earnest in 1938. At the start of the year, Roosevelt had still tried to revive Welles's world conference idea with a message to Chamberlain seeking British support. But even if the prime minister had not initially rejected this overture as conflicting with his own plans for bilateral "appeasement," it was clearly too late for such a move. At the beginning of February Hitler took personal command of Germany's armed forces, replaced Neurath, the last feeble link to the foreign policies of the Weimar Republic, with the ambitious and unscrupulous Joachim von Ribbentrop, and, though the world did not yet know it, decided to proceed with the annexation of Austria. On March 12 Hitler and his troops entered Vienna in triumph.

This so-called anschluss inaugurated an eighteen-month period of almost constant crisis which culminated in the German invasion of

39. Herbert Feis memorandum, January 20, 1938, in State Department Decimal File 611.6231/1006, RG 59, NA.

Poland and the subsequent declarations of war against Germany by Great Britain and France. America responded with renewed verbal outrage, though still unaccompanied by useful or effective action. "I do not know," Dieckhoff wrote to his friend Ernst von Weizsäcker, "whether in other parts of the world the reunification with Austria has produced such a fantastic hate campaign by the press as the one which made itself felt here for the last eight days." To the Foreign Office he reported the "anger in the State Department," the "totally reserved" attitude of Hull, Welles's expression of "hate-filled obstinacy," and his conclusion that even with the continued existence of the neutrality act, "there is no such thing as a true neutrality of the United States."[40]

Nevertheless, the United States took no action likely to impress Hitler. It did insist that Germany honor Austria's debt agreements and, when this was refused, ostentatiously struck Austria from the list of most favored nations. Roosevelt also permitted the secretary of the interior, Harold Ickes, to win his quixotic battle to bar the sale of helium to Germany on the grounds that it might be used for military purposes. Moreover, he pushed through Congress the Vinson Naval Expansion Act, which in May 1938 authorized the expenditure of a $1 billion over the following decade in order to create a fleet presumably strong enough to offset the combined navies of Germany, Italy, and Japan. Of these actions, only the last could possibly have been meaningful, and that only if there had been even the slightest indication that America was prepared to resort to force, if necessary, to stop further German expansion. Instead, all outward signs continued to suggest the contrary.

The very absence of meaningful German-American relations by the summer of 1938 sharply limited American options in dealing with the growing German threat. Since trade remained at low levels and investments were no longer desired or forthcoming, economic pressure was impossible to apply. Informal contacts among German and American officials, even where they still existed, were no longer useful since Hitler paid little heed to his bureaucrats. American businessmen, who had exercised some influence on German policies during the 1920s, had clearly lost it. Thus the only real alternative that remained was a credible threat of force to be applied in conjunc-

40. Dieckhoff to Weizsäcker, March 22, 1938, and Dieckhoff to Foreign Office, March 15 and 30, 1938, in *Akten zur deutschen auswärtigen Politik*, D, 1: 556, 493–494, 570.

tion with the European democracies. That alternative, however, was politically impossible to adopt even if the president had been inclined to do so. To be sure, Roosevelt had speculated for some time about the possibilities of blockades against Germany as well as Japan and about other measures involving the use of force. But there is nothing to suggest that these were more than visible outbursts of frustration.

The United States had traditionally insisted on acting unilaterally in its foreign relations and even during the twenties had intervened in Europe only as an ostensibly impartial mediator acting through nominally independent private citizens. In the 1930s the onset of the depression, coupled with the possibility of a new war, had turned America inward and made the avoidance of war the major foreign policy goal. The experience of the First World War, moreover, had convinced most Americans that war could be avoided only if entanglements were eschewed, and this belief clearly ruled out commitments of any kind to other countries. Even when it became apparent that the neutrality legislation, which was the clearest expression of such sentiments, might well aid potential aggressors and thus increase the possibility of a major war, it seemed preferable to leave the prevention of war to others and to seek safety in at least relative isolation. Roosevelt would have found little public or Congressional support for a policy that rested, in the final analysis, on the willingness of the United States to intervene militarily in Europe and Asia. As a good politician, he did not seek such support or pursue such a policy until Germany appeared as a plausible threat not merely to world peace and order but also to America's physical security.

During the summer of 1938, when the world seemed at the edge of war over Hitler's new demand that the Sudeten districts of Czechoslovakia be "reunited" with the Reich, American policy therefore remained cautious and essentially noncommittal. In May and again in August Hitler rejected the contention of the chief of the general staff, General Ludwig Beck, that a war over Czechoslovakia was impossible in part because the United States would in all probability put its vast war potential on the side of Britain and France. The führer was obviously right. Roosevelt certainly was not as sanguine as Chamberlain that negotiations with Germany, which the prime minister undertook, would either be successful or truly serve the cause of peace, but he had no practical alternative to offer. In a conversation with the British ambassador shortly before the Munich conference, he did express the fear that even if Hitler's demands were met in this case, others against Poland, Denmark, and Roumania would inevitably lead to war. He also talked once more of the alternative of a blockade of Germany by the Western powers. But Roosevelt made clear, as he had to Chamberlain and to French Premier Edouard Daladier earlier, that he could neither send troops to Europe nor supply arms and ammunition if hostilities ensued.

When the president decided on September 26 to intervene directly in the crisis by sending an appeal to Hitler, he took no stand on the issues at all but simply pleaded for continued negotiations. The German leader replied with a tirade about self-determination and the sufferings of the Sudeten Germans—the American minister in Prague correctly called it "a mixture of half-truths and misstatements of fact"—and concluded that the latest German proposals had exhausted the possibilities for further discussion and that it rested "with the Czechoslovakian Government alone to decide whether it wants peace or war." Roosevelt thereupon sent a second message in which he expressed the belief that the German-Czech differences "could be settled by pacific methods" and suggested "a conference of all nations directly interested in the present controversy" if "present negotiations" proved unsuccessful. "The Government of the United States," he was quick to add, "has no political involvements in Europe, and will assume no obligations in the conduct of present negotiations."[41] At the same time he urged Mussolini to use his influence to bring about a peaceful settlement. The Czechs meanwhile had been told by Pierrepont Moffat of the Division of European Affairs that the United States was unwilling to advise them "either directly or inferentially" as to whether or not they should fight. Hull, who was fully aware of the solution proposed by Chamberlain, added that the United States could not say what it would do if the crisis resulted in a war to which Britain and France would also become parties because "we do not undertake to discuss theoretical questions. . . ."[42]

Though Roosevelt had earlier described the settlement to be imposed on Czechoslovakia as "the most terrible remorseless sacrifice" ever demanded of a country, he greeted the Munich agree-

41. Hitler to Roosevelt, September 26, 1938; Wilbur J. Carr to Hull, September 28, 1938; and Roosevelt to Hitler, September 27, 1938, in *Foreign Relations, 1938*, 1: 673, 689, 685.

42. Pierrepont Moffat memorandum, September 20, 1938, and Hull memorandum, September 27, 1938, in ibid., 626, 676.

ment with a sense of relief that peace had been preserved. That sentiment was shared by Hull and by most other State Department officials. But the enormity of what had been done to Czechoslovakia—ironically to the most democratic state to have been created by the Versailles treaty—and the arrogance of Germany, which was only fed by this new triumph, produced sober second thoughts. Within a month, Roosevelt warned the American people that "peace by fear has no higher or more enduring quality than peace by the sword,"[43] and the renewed outbreak of anti-Jewish violence in Germany two weeks later produced the first clearcut sign of an impending German-American confrontation. During the so-called Crystal Night of November 9, Jewish stores were smashed and synagogues torched throughout Germany. Immediately thereafter, German Jews were barred from trade, one of the very few occupations still left open to them, and collectively fined one billion mark. The move produced an immediate outcry in the United States, with which a wide variety of public figures associated themselves, and it resulted in Roosevelt's ordering home "for consultation" the American ambassador in Berlin "You should sail on the first available non-German ship," Hull telegraphed. Four days later, Dieckhoff was similarly called home to report on "the peculiar attitude toward internal German events as expressed in the various statements of Roosevelt and other influential personages of the United States."[44]

Although these actions did not constitute a break in diplomatic relations nor even, "technically," as Roosevelt put it, a formal recall of ambassadors, the two men never returned to their posts and no replacements were appointed. More than three years before American entry into the Second World War, therefore, diplomatic relations between the United States and Germany had been downgraded to the chargé level. A full break at this time was considered only by Germany, however, and rejected not merely because of possible undesirable economic consequences but also in the belief that such a break would strengthen the domestic position of Roosevelt, enough, perhaps, to bring him his "longed-for third term." That in turn would allow the president, who was according to the political division of the Foreign Office "a docile pupil of Wilson's," to succeed with his current "anti-German agitation and thus to create in the American

43. Roosevelt, radio address of October 26, 1938, in *Public Papers,* 7: 564.
44. Hull to Wilson, November 14, 1938, and Gilbert to Hull, November 18, 1938, in *Foreign Relations, 1938,* 2: 399, 402.

people a psychic willingness to accept every anti-German measure of the government, even if these lead finally to American military involvement." It would even allow him to act out his "Saviour complex," which he again allegedly shared with Wilson, "in order to bring the large European democracies into the anti-dictator front" designed to make the world safe for "beatific liberalism."[45]

Although the Foreign Office overestimated both Roosevelt's willingness to espouse measures that would clearly lead to war and the degree of support he might have gained for such measures at home, its reasoning placed the United States definitely among the Reich's potential enemies. But whereas Hitler believed that enmity to be of little consequence to his future plans, the hostile activities of Germany were viewed in America increasingly as a threat. In his State of the Union message on January 4, 1939, Roosevelt stressed the attacks on religion, democracy, and international good faith—"three institutions indispensable to Americans, now as always"—and warned that these institutions had to be defended against acts of aggression "which automatically undermine all of us." While still rejecting any armed intervention by the United States, he stressed the "many methods short of war, but stronger and more effective than mere words, of bringing home to aggressor governments the aggregate sentiments of our own people."[46] Chief among those methods mentioned were greater military preparedness and the revision of restrictive neutrality legislation that encouraged aggressors. As a result of that speech, Ribbentrop ordered members of the German foreign service henceforth to refuse invitations from the American embassy or embassy staff in Berlin and no longer to extend invitations of their own. For the first time a violent German press campaign against Roosevelt and his policies ensued.

The president followed up the speech with a budget request to raise military spending by more than 30 percent to over $1.3 billion and for good measure added a supplementary request for the purchase of aircraft amounting to $500 million. Near the end of January he acknowledged that arrangements had been made to sell planes to France—the first orders had actually been placed the previous June—and at the same time told the Senate Foreign Relations Committee that there were "fifteen or sixteen independent nations in

45. Notes on Political Consequences, November 20, 1938, in *Akten zur deutschen auswärtigen Politik*, D, 4: 566, 568.
46. Roosevelt, Annual Address, January 4, 1939, in *Public Papers*, 8: 1, 3.

Europe whose continued independent political and economic existence is of actual moment to the ultimate defense of the United
States," particularly against "German and Italian aggression in the
future."[47] He did not literally say that America's frontier lay on the
Rhine, but his meaning was clear enough.

On March 14 Hitler openly violated his pledge given at Munich
only five months before and annexed what remained of Czechoslovakia. That aggression was followed with the demand on Lithuania
that Memel be surrendered and with rumblings about the return of
Danzig and the Polish Corridor. Even Chamberlain now abandoned
appeasement and pledged Britain to aid Poland in case of war. The
State Department condemned both the destruction of Czechoslovakia and Mussolini's invasion of Albania the following month as
"wanton lawlessness,"[48] products of Bohemia and Moravia were
taken off the most-favored-nations list on March 18 and countervailing duties of 23 percent imposed on all German imports. Two days
later legislation was introduced in effect to repeal the arms embargo
by placing all trade with belligerents on a cash-and-carry basis.

On April 14 Roosevelt sent a new message to the European dictators. Unlike his September 1938 appeal for continuing negotiations, this one asked for formal pledges that thirty-one specified
countries in Europe and the Middle East not be attacked for at least
ten years. If such assurances were given, he proposed the participation of the United States in a world conference dealing with disarmament and equal access to markets and raw materials. No formal
reply to this message was received, but Hitler was clearly angered
by it, and Goering told Mussolini it might be evidence of "an incipient brain disease."[49] The führer did respond in a Reichstag speech
on April 28, in which he derided the president's words almost line by
line, justified all of his earlier actions, and indicated that he had
polled the countries mentioned and that none felt the need for the
guarantee suggested by Roosevelt. (On April 17 the Foreign Office
had in fact requested such statements from most of these states.)
For good measure, Hitler declared null and void both the Anglo-
German naval agreement and the nonaggression pact with Poland. If

47. Roosevelt to John Cudahy, March 4, 1939, in Roosevelt et al., *F.D.R.: Personal Letters* 2: 862.
48. Welles statement, March 17, 1939, and Hull statement, April 8, 1939, in State
Department, *Peace and War*, pp. 454–455.
49. Note on Goering-Duce conversation, April 16, 1939, in *Akten zur deutschen
auswärtigen Politik*, D, 6: 215.

any further proof of the führer's contempt for the United States and of the impossibility of "doing business with Hitler" had been needed, it had now been provided. The last basis for meaningful and effective relations between the two countries had been removed.

Unlike the period before the outbreak of the First World War, when relations between the two countries had been outwardly serene and when normal contacts continued well into the wartime period itself, Germany and the United States were thus plainly at odds with each other and maintained only the most strained, diminished relations by spring 1939, when the world was still nominally at peace. Contacts at the ambassadorial level had ceased, trade had shrunk to an annual rate of less than $100 million, barely 1.8 percent of America's total, and the ideological conflict was open and undisguised. The prophecies of Dieckhoff were surely approaching fulfillment.

Chapter 8

PEACE AND WAR

*

A Different Neutrality

During the late spring and summer of 1939 the world was definitely heading for war. Unlike the European democracies who had to decide whether to yield further to Hitler's expansionist ambitions or prepare to fight, the United States had the margin of safety provided by the oceans. It could thus still afford to discuss the alternatives of insulation or further involvement that might eventually lead to war. As Germany stepped up its campaign against Poland, the Roosevelt administration did no more than try to remove the most serious shackles imposed on it by the neutrality act and to encourage the newfound determination of Britain and France to hold firm on the Polish question. Although most Americans and a clear majority of the Congress still preferred insulation, doubt about its practicality was widespread. Moreover, the alternative of aid and preparedness was made more palatable by the comforting, widely held belief that Britain and France would be able to defeat Italy and Germany, if war came, without direct military assistance from the United States. Still, Congress refused to change the neutrality legislation even by summer, though it did approve sharply higher appropriations for the army and navy.

American concern about the direction of world events, continued to grow, however. The outright military alliance, the "Pact of Steel," which Hitler and Mussolini signed on May 22, and the ever greater demands made by Germany on Poland increased the fear that the two dictatorships, together with Japan—whose war with China continued and whom Hitler was anxiously, if as yet unsuccessfully, wooing—sought world domination and thus posed a direct threat to the interests of the United States. Even if actual conquest of America was not yet on the agenda of the aggressors, it was argued, a world dominated by the three would bring economic hardship and an end to democracy. Such conclusions were drawn not merely by proponents of American intervention such as former secretary of state Henry L. Stimson, but also by the embassy in London, which was still headed by the far more cautious and essentially isolationist Joseph P. Kennedy.

Stimson, calling for "farsighted affirmative action," warned, in a letter to the *New York Times* which received front page coverage, that if the United States stood idly by while China, Britain, and France were forced to submit either militarily or diplomatically to the aggressors, "our own hemisphere might become economically so affected and militarily so endangered that it would be neither a safe nor happy place to live in, for a people with American ideals of life."[1] Kennedy drew a scenario of the results of a similar submission. He speculated that the United States would lose 50 percent of its exports and 75 percent of its foreign investments, see its standard of living decline, be forced to arm massively even to survive, and in the process take on all the characteristics of a fascist state. "In short," the memorandum concluded, "America, alone in a jealous and hostile world, would find that the effort and cost of maintaining 'splendid isolation' would be such as to bring about the destruction of all those values which the isolation policy had been designed to preserve."[2]

Although arguments for some sort of American intervention were phrased more and more often in economic terms, and concern about trade, jobs, and living standards was justified, the essential issues remained the ideological and potentially military ones. The trading practices of the dictatorships were seen as threats not primarily because they provided competition for markets and raw materials or discriminated in various ways against the United States, but because

1. Stimson letter, *New York Times,* March 7, 1939, p. 1, col. 6 and p. 16, cols. 2–6.

2. Joseph P. Kennedy memorandum, March 3, 1939, quoted in Detlef Junker, *Der unteilbare Weltmarkt: Das ökonomische Interesse in der Aussenpolitik der U.S.A., 1933–1941* (Stuttgart, 1975), pp. 212–213.

these practices were fostered through military coercion and conquest and enforced by antidemocratic and antiliberal regimes with whom negotiation and a "normalization" of intercourse were deemed impossible. It was the growing conviction that attempts to deal effectively with the dictatorships even on the economic level would require the United States itself to move toward a form of dictatorship. And that conviction transformed public perception of the impending world conflict from that of a "foreign war" to one of attack on the American way of life.

Hitler's Germany was the chief villain in this scenario. As early as May, the German chargé in Washington, Hans Thomsen, predicted that Roosevelt would win his battle with Congressional isolationists, and that, in case of a war between Germany and England, the president would soon make the British cause his own. Referring repeatedly to the "unbridled hatred of the totalitarian powers" on the part of the president and his advisers, he concluded melodramatically: "The leitmotif of Roosevelt's policy is the participation of America in a new war of annihilation against Germany."[3]

The president did indeed hate at least one of the dictators and probably hoped for his annihilation, but he clearly still preferred avoidance of war over American participation. When Britain and France finally entered into serious discussions with the Soviet Union over the possibility of a joint guarantee to Poland and other potential victims of Nazi aggression, Roosevelt signified his approval. He urged the Russians to cooperate, sending messages through the Soviet ambassador, who was going home for a vacation, and through Laurence Steinhardt, who had just been appointed to the Moscow post. Roosevelt's aim was obviously not to bring about the destruction of Germany but to deter Hitler from his expansionist course and to prevent war from breaking out. When the Franco-British-Russian negotiations foundered nonetheless and were followed on August 22 by the startling announcement that Ribbentrop would go to Moscow to sign a German agreement with the Soviet Union, the president still did not abandon this hope entirely.

The apparent Russian somersault had, of course, made war more likely by virtually guaranteeing the success of a German attack on Poland. On the day that the Ribbentrop invitation was announced,

3. Hans Thomsen to Foreign Office, May 17, 1939, in *Akten zur deutschen auswärtigen Politik, 1918–1945* (Baden-Baden and Göttingen, 1950–), Series D, 6: 436, 439, 441.

Premier Daladier told the American ambassador in Paris, William C. Bullitt, that such an attack would surely come within eight days or less, that France would honor its commitment and declare war, and that a major conflict was thus imminent. He urged Roosevelt to make a final appeal for peace. The president responded positively, initially with a message to King Victor Emmanuel of Italy, in which he reiterated his earlier request for nonaggression guarantees and his promise to discuss disarmament and freer trade at a subsequent conference. The idea that Mussolini might serve as a moderating influence on Hitler had not yet entirely lost its persuasiveness.

On the following day Roosevelt also communicated with Hitler and with Ignaz Moscicki, the president of Poland. He urged both to settle the differences between their countries through direct negotiation, through impartial arbitration, or through the procedure of conciliation. His message to the führer also carried a reminder of the president's April plea and Hitler's failure to respond, as well as a clear condemnation of what Germany for all practical purposes had already decided to do.

> The people of the United States are as one in their opposition to policies of military conquest and domination. They are as one in rejecting the thesis that any ruler, or any people, possess the right to achieve their ends or objectives through the taking of action which will plunge countless millions of people into war and which will bring distress and suffering to every nation of the world, belligerent or neutral. . . .[4]

When the Polish government accepted direct negotiations or conciliation "through a third party as disinterested and impartial as Your Excellency," Roosevelt forwarded this acceptance to Hitler with a new plea that "you and the Government of the German Reich will agree to the pacific means of settlement accepted by the Government of Poland."[5]

There is no evidence that these messages had any effect on Hitler, who wavered even briefly in his decision only because of concern over what Italy and England might do and, in the end, ignored even that. Certainly he never answered Roosevelt. Receipt of the messages was merely acknowledged on August 26, when German

---

4. Roosevelt to Hitler, August 24, 1939, in U.S. Department of State, *Peace and War: United States Foreign Policy, 1933–1941* (Washington, D.C. 1943), pp. 477–478.
5. Roosevelt to Hitler, August 25, 1939, in ibid., 479, 480.

mobilization had already been ordered and war was a certainty. Nevertheless, Germany had no wish to offend the United States needlessly and, foreshadowing the course that was to be followed for some time, on August 31 Ribbentrop had Thomsen express his appreciation to the State Department for the president's efforts and place the blame for war on the recalcitrance of the Polish government. Within hours the Wehrmacht launched its attack. When Great Britain and France thereupon honored their commitments and on September 3 declared war on Germany, Roosevelt made clear America's stand. Like Woodrow Wilson in 1914, he promptly announced that "this nation will remain a neutral nation," but unlike his predecessor he did not call for neutrality of thought. "Even a neutral," he observed, "has a right to take account of facts. Even a neutral cannot be asked to close his mind or his conscience."[6] The Second World War thus began for the United States on a different note from the one that had been struck under similar circumstances twenty-five years before.

Two Roads to War: The United States

The period from the outbreak of war in Europe to the entrance of the United States into that war proved to be only slightly shorter than it had been in 1914–1917, but the German-American relationship in the interval bore little resemblance to the earlier one. Unlike Wilson, Roosevelt was convinced from the outset that the interests of the United States required support of the Allied cause with all necessary means, though he too hoped and for a time even expected that military intervention could be avoided. The circumstances leading to the outbreak of war, moreover, had already produced considerable support for this policy in the American public, where, according to the polls, 82 percent blamed the war absolutely on Germany. Conversely, Hitler, unlike Bethmann Hollweg, was confident that the war would be of short duration and therefore worried far less about the attitude of the United States, at least initially. In any event, encouraged both by his own preconceptions of a "mongrelized and Judaicized" America and by the sanguine reports of his military attaché in Washington, he regarded effective

6. Roosevelt, Fireside Chat, September 3, 1939, in *The Public Papers and Addresses of Franklin Delano Roosevelt,* 13 vols., ed. Samuel I. Rosenman (New York, 1938–1951), 8: 463.

American intervention as impossible and any intervention as unlikely, so long as unrestricted submarine warfare and other direct challenges were avoided and so long as Japan confronted the United States with the threat of a two-front war.

Since full diplomatic relations between Germany and the United States had already ceased before the onset of the conflict, their resumption under the new circumstances or the development of any meaningful discussion between the two countries could not be expected. Neither could Roosevelt, whose personal feelings had been clearly expressed, entertain any realistic thought that he might, like Wilson, attempt to mediate the war and bring it to an early conclusion. That is not to say that the president had entirely given up the idea that an international conference dealing with disarmament and economic matters might still be possible at some future time. But he could hardly presume to take an intermediary position between the Allies and the Axis powers.

For all of these reasons, the United States and Germany did not interact significantly from September 1939 to December 1941, but followed separate courses in their attempts to deal with the problems each raised for the other. The U.S. steadily increased its moral and material commitment to the Allied war effort and to the defeat of Germany. The Germans, for their part, attempted to keep America formally out of the war by encouraging antiwar elements and avoiding direct provocations, as well as by cooperating more closely with Japan, who was expected to balance off and neutralize the American factor in Germany's war.

On September 5, Roosevelt duly invoked the still unaltered neutrality act with its arms embargo provision that cut off the supply of war materials to Great Britain and France. To refrain from doing so would have been politically impossible. It was not clear, in any event, what shape the war would take or what aid the allies might require. Britain and France could not intervene in the fighting in Poland and were unprepared to launch an attack on Germany from the west. Their only immediate action, therefore, consisted of the imposition of a blockade, for which no American assistance was required at all. Still, Roosevelt declared a state of limited national emergency on September 8, thus indicating that he wanted the authority to respond effectively to events as the situation developed. The most striking development during September was Germany's speedy conquest of Poland.

Within days of the invasion the Polish air force had been demolished, and the blitzkrieg tactics, which relied on massed armor and the use of the dive bomber as a ground support weapon, proved devastating. By September 17, when Russian troops also entered their country, the Poles had been obviously defeated, and two days later Hitler made a general peace offer on the basis of his territorial gains. This "peace offensive" included a joint Russo-German declaration, on September 28, calling for an end to the war and culminated in Hitler's Reichstag speech of October 6. It drew only a negative response from London, even though the British did not yet know that the führer's plans for an offensive in the west developed almost simultaneously and orders for actual preparations were issued on October 9. The American response was equally negative and underlined the significant difference from the situation that had prevailed in 1914.

Already on September 11, in response to vague peace feelers launched by Goering and to the suggestion by Kennedy that "this situation might crystallize to a point where the President can be the savior of the world," Hull had confidentially informed the ambassador in London that "so long as present conditions in Europe continue" there would be "no opportunity or occasion for any peace move. . . ." The president wanted him to know, Hull continued, that "the people of the United States would not support any move for peace initiated by this Government that would consolidate or make possible a survival of a regime of force and aggression."[7] Now, with Hitler himself talking of peace, albeit on his own terms, Roosevelt's response was less direct but even more negative.

Only two days after the Danzig speech that contained Hitler's peace offer, the president called Congress into special session to modify the neutrality act by repealing the arms embargo. During the following week, Welles persuaded the Pan-American conference meeting in Panama City to declare a three-hundred-mile neutrality zone around the Western Hemisphere (excluding Canada), in which naval operations by belligerents were prohibited. Both actions clearly implied that no early end to the war was envisaged and were, equally clearly, anti-German in intent. The neutrality zone was established on October 3 and the United States Navy was ordered to deploy in it eighty destroyers for patrol purposes. It created an area

7. Kennedy to Hull and Hull to Kennedy, September 22, 1939, in *Foreign Relations of the United States: Diplomatic Papers, 1939*, I: 423, 424.

in which Allied cargo ships would be relatively safe from German submarines and surface raiders and the British navy relieved of the necessity for maintaining patrols. Repeal of the embargo on November 4 allowed American weapons to go to the Allies.

In the meantime, Roosevelt continued to turn a deaf ear to suggestions for peace actions which came from Romania, Belgium, Finland, Spain, and—in unofficial and highly unauthoritative ways, partially again through Goering—from Germany itself. Instead he approved the establishment of a joint Anglo-French purchasing mission in Washington and promised the cooperation of the government on October 18, two weeks before Congress passed the new neutrality act that permitted arms sales on a cash-and-carry basis. The Anglo-French Purchasing Board was officially constituted on November 30. A special committee composed of officials of the War, Navy, and Treasury departments was established to coordinate Allied purchases with American defense needs. The stunning speed of the German victory over Poland, while not eliminating America's desire to remain at peace, thus clearly heightened the perception of a threat to American interests and strengthened the administration's conviction that the danger had to be met.

Although an immediate German attack in the west, which had been widely expected, did not materialize because of intelligence and weather problems and the opposition of some of Germany's military leaders, the invasion of Finland by the Soviet Union on November 30 made the danger appear even greater by raising the specter of a Europe dominated by Hitler and Stalin. Roosevelt, who on October 11 had already appealed to Soviet President Mikhail Kalinin on behalf of the Finns, expressed his horror and anger at "this dreadful rape of Finland" and his concern about "the next Russian plan."[8] Though he balked at providing arms on credit as some now urged, he authorized the use of $10 million for agricultural products that could be traded by Finland to Sweden for war supplies. The Russo-Finnish conflict did not involve the Allies, however, and no military actions against Germany were actually under way. The scope and nature of American assistance thus became increasingly unclear, particularly when the so-called phony war continued into 1940.

Hitler's peace offensive had formally ended on October 24, when

8. Roosevelt to Lincoln MacVeagh, December 2, 1939, in Elliott Roosevelt et al., eds., *F.D.R.: His Personal Letters*, 2 vols. (New York, 1950), 2: 961.

Ribbentrop made a bellicose speech in which he blamed Britain for the war and demanded not only the retention of all conquests but a return of Germany's colonies as the price for ending it. Germany's failure to launch further attacks, however, gave rise to new speculation that a peace settlement might be possible. Moreover, Ribbentrop had spoken well of the United States in his speech, and Roosevelt could hardly promote further aid to the Allies, in the absence of serious fighting and in a presidential election year, without having demonstratively exhausted all possibilities for a peaceful resolution of the conflict. Moved by such considerations and pressed for some kind of action by other neutral states, the president decided late in January to let Undersecretary of State Welles go on a fact-finding mission to Rome, Paris, London, and Berlin.

Unlike Wilson, who genuinely believed the various missions of Colonel House might bring about a negotiated peace, Roosevelt neither expected such a result nor necessarily thought it desirable. The undersecretary nevertheless arrived in Rome on February 25 carrying handwritten personal notes from Roosevelt to Mussolini, Chamberlain, and Daladier—but conspicuously not to Hitler. His mission ended, for all practical purposes, six days later in Berlin.

The Germans had received news of the impending visit without enthusiasm, and Ribbentrop had acidly informed the State Department that he noted "a certain contradiction" between "the recall of the American Ambassador Wilson and the wish of President Roosevelt to inform himself about conditions in Germany." Although Weizsäcker, by now wholly without influence, called Welles "a kind of Colonel House, with the difference that he has learned something and has ability" and speculated on the possibility of a genuine breakthrough, Hitler gave personal instructions on February 29 that the American should be told as little as possible and that all expressions should be avoided "which could be interpreted by the opposing side to mean that Germany has the slightest interest in the discussion of peace possibilities at this time."[9] As a result, Ribbentrop gave Welles a two-hour diatribe, Goering was cheerful but unyielding on Germany's "just" demands, and Hitler, who had prepared himself well for the interview, left the American little hope

9. Ribbentrop to Thomsen (for Welles), February 14, 1940, and notes of the Führer, February 29, 1940, in *Akten zur deutschen auswärtigen Politik,* D, 8: 610, 645; Weizsäcker letter, February 22, 1940, and notes, February 25, 1940, in *Die Weizsäcker Papiere, 1932–1950,* ed. Leonidas E. Hill, (Frankfurt, 1974), pp. 190–191.

that anything could be accomplished. Although the undersecretary continued his trip to Paris, London, and back to Rome, his final verdict might just as well have been reached when he left Berlin.

Hitler in fact had issued orders to prepare for an invasion of Denmark and Norway on the day before he met Welles and was convinced that any talk of peace would be construed as a sign of weakness and make Britain, in particular, less likely to come to terms. He did talk peace and reasonableness to General Motors executive James D. Mooney, whom he met on March 4, but this was merely a maneuver to encourage the isolationist opposition to Roosevelt and thus to keep America out of the war in the west he was now determined to wage. His major concern, arising in part from the Welles mission, was that Mussolini not be lured away but would lend support in the new warfare about to begin. Accordingly, Hitler wrote a long letter to Il Duce on March 8, in which he suggested that Welles's purpose might have been simply to win time for the Allies, and reiterated his intention to fight until the "plutocratic war-criminal clique" in Britain and France had given up its goal of destroying the totalitarian states, including Italy. Ribbentrop was sent to Rome directly after Welles to arrange a meeting between the two dictators. When that took place on March 18, Mussolini showed himself once more to be under the führer's spell and renewed an earlier promise to enter the war in due course. Just two weeks after Welles left for home, Hitler gave the order to begin offensive action in Scandinavia on April 9.

The attacks on Denmark and Norway and the invasion of the Low Countries and of France which followed on May 10 dramatically clarified the situation and simplified the U.S.'s course. Roosevelt now sought to prevent the extension of the conflict to the Mediterranean and, between April 29 and May 30, made four separate appeals to Mussolini to stay out of the war and use his influence for a just and stable peace. Primarily though, he single-mindedly pursued the goal of aligning America ever more directly with the Allied war effort. The wisdom of that course was increasingly apparent as, within weeks, it became clear that France would be defeated, that Hitler would control Europe from the Arctic Circle to the Pyrenees, that Britain might well be successfully invaded, and that a direct military threat to the United States could thereby emerge.

The heightened sense of imminent danger prompted the establishment on May 15 of the Committee to Defend America by Aiding the

Allies and led a subcommittee of the State Department's Advisory Committee on Problems of Foreign Relations to study the economic and political consequences of a possible German victory for the United States. It underlay both the text and the tone of Roosevelt's speech at the University of Virginia, which immediately followed Italy's attack on an already prostrate France on June 10. Not only did the president express America's overwhelming concern "that military and naval victory for the gods of force and hate would endanger the institutions of democracy in the western world," he promised unequivocally that he would "extend to the opponents of force the material resources of this nation."[10] Three days later, as German tanks stood ready to enter Paris, he pledged redoubled efforts to aid France and the other Allies, though he pointedly "did not commit this Government to military participation in support of the Allied Governments." "You well know," he told Winston Churchill, who had assumed the prime ministership on May 10, "that there is of course no authority under our Constitution except in the Congress to make any commitment of this nature."[11]

The commitment to give all possible aid short of war was already firm, however, and over the next three months it was manifested in a variety of ways. On June 17 French assets in the United States were frozen. Germany and Italy were both informed that no transfer of Western Hemisphere territory to them would be recognized. Two days later, what was in effect a coalition cabinet came into being when Roosevelt appointed two prominent Republicans to head the War and Navy departments. Both Henry L. Stimson, Hoover's secretary of state, and Frank Knox, the 1936 vice-presidential candidate, were ardent supporters of the Allied cause and strong opponents of Hitler Germany. Congress meanwhile passed the National Defense Act, increased military appropriations, and provided for the construction of a "two-ocean Navy." On July 30 the Pan-American conference meeting in Havana responded to the Hull's urging and put European colonies in the Western Hemisphere under joint trusteeship for the duration of the war, thus keeping Germany out.

10. Roosevelt, address at University of Virginia, June 10, 1940, in *Public Papers*, 9: 261–262, 264.
11. Roosevelt to Churchill, June 14, 1940, in *Roosevelt and Churchill: Their Secret Wartime Correspondence*, ed. Francis L. Loewenheim, Harold D. Langley, and Manfred Jonas (New York, 1975), p. 103.

The degree to which these actions represented not merely the wishes of the president but a developing American consensus was dramatically revealed at the Republican national convention in late June. Meeting under the impact of the surrender of France, the Republicans rejected the party's established leaders, all of whom were identified with isolationism, and chose a political novice, Wendell Willkie, to head their ticket. Willkie's domestic views differed from Roosevelt's, but he energetically supported both national preparedness and aid to the Allies. Thomsen correctly reported to the Foreign Office that the nomination was "unpleasant for us," that neither Willkie's membership in the still isolationist American Legion nor his "pure German descent" had altered his pro-Allied stance, and that in the realm of foreign policy, the differences between Roosevelt and his challenger were "at most over methods, not over conception."[12] Roosevelt's own renomination, despite the traditional opposition to a third term, was yet another indicator of public sentiment.

On August 18 the president met with the Canadian prime minister, Mackenzie King. Plans were laid for the disposition of the British fleet in case of German conquest of England, and the meeting resulted in the establishment of the Joint Defense Board with a country already at war with Germany. In September, while the air battle over Britain was at its height, the United States, with Willkie's full approval, concluded the "destroyer deal" that sent fifty overage American warships to Great Britain in return for leases on future air and naval bases on British territory in the Western Hemisphere. The intended long-range result of the "deal" was to strengthen American defensive capabilities enormously, and the transaction was legal for that reason. Its immediate purpose, however, was to enable the British to convoy supplies from America without stripping their naval defenses against "Operation Sea Lion," Hitler's expected invasion attempt.

When, at the end of that month, economic pressure against Japan was further intensified by the imposition of an embargo on sales of scrap iron and steel and when an additional loan was extended to China, the main target was still Germany. American "acts and utterances with respect to the Pacific area," Hull informed the British ambassador, "would be more or less affected as to time and extent

12. Thomsen to Foreign Office, June 28, 1940, in *Akten zur deutschen auswärtigen Politik*, D, 10: 41–42.

by the question of what course would, on the part of this Government, most effectively and legitimately aid Great Britain in winning the war."[13]

The apparent threat to the United States which prompted these actions grew even stronger on September 27, 1940, with the signing of the Tripartite Pact. This treaty bound Germany, Italy, and Japan into a defensive alliance "when one of the three contracting parties is attacked by a power at present not involved in the European War or in the Sino-Japanese Conflict." Since the agreement also stipulated that none of its terms would "in any way affect the political status which exists at present between each of the three Contracting Parties and Soviet Russia,"[14] and small nations were hardly perceived as a factor by the Axis powers, the point of the treaty was clearly to intimidate the United States. Far from being intimidated, however, Roosevelt became more determined than ever to counter Axis designs, particularly after his own position was strengthened by reelection on November 5.

A key test of that determination came early in December, when Churchill forwarded a long list of Britain's material needs for the coming year and pointed out that "the moment approaches when we shall no longer be able to pay cash for shipping and other supplies" as required by the neutrality act. "If, as I believe," the prime minister concluded, "you are convinced, Mr. President, that the defeat of the Nazi and Fascist tyranny is a matter of high consequence to the people of the United States and to the Western Hemisphere, you will regard this letter not as an appeal for aid, but as a statement of the minimum action necessary to the achievement of our common purpose."[15]

Roosevelt was indeed convinced. Reemphasizing that "the best immediate defense of the United States is the success of Great Britain," he proposed to "get rid of the silly, foolish old dollar sign" by providing not money but actual supplies to the Allies. His homely analogy of lending a garden hose to a neighbor whose house was on fire suggested the identity in his mind of American and British interest in the defeat of Germany. In his fireside chat on December 29, he

13. Hull memorandum of conversation with Lord Lothian, September 30, 1940, in State Department, *Peace and War*, p. 575.
14. Translation of Tripartite Pact, September 27, 1940, in State Department Decimal File 763.9411/136, RG 59, NA.
15. Churchill to Roosevelt, December 7, 1940, in *Roosevelt and Churchill* p. 125.

insisted that "the Nazi masters of Germany have made it clear that they intend . . . to dominate the rest of the world." He projected an attack on the Western Hemisphere if Britain were defeated and urged that "Democracy's fight against world conquest" must be aided "by the rearmament of the United States and by sending every ounce and every ton of munitions and supplies that we can possibly spare to help the defenders who are in the front lines. . . . We must be," he concluded, "the great arsenal of democracy."[16] No more definite commitment, short of actual fighting, was imaginable.

Throughout 1941 the United States moved to meet this commitment. The lend-lease bill was introduced into Congress on January 10 and was signed into law on March 11. The first $7 billion in aid was appropriated sixteen days later. On April 10 Roosevelt increased the chances that such aid would actually reach the beleaguered British by extending the American neutrality patrol to longitude 25 degrees west, far out in the Atlantic and clearly beyond the accepted confines of the Western Hemisphere. Denmark's Greenland was occupied by American troops at the same time.

Meanwhile, British-American staff talks, which had begun on January 29, had concluded with the adoption of ABC-1, a plan outlining "the best methods by which the armed forces of the United States and the British Commonwealth . . . could defeat Germany and the Powers allied with her, should the United States be compelled to resort to war." The significance of this contingency plan lay less in its speculation on future American military intervention than in the agreement that "since Germany is the predominant member of the Axis powers, the Atlantic and European area are to be the decisive theater."[17] Regardless of the future scope of the war, Germany and Italy would be defeated before Japan was to be dealt with. That view represented American as much as British thinking. It had already formed the basis for an earlier American contingency plan, RAINBOW 5, which was now also officially adopted. Within weeks permanent military missions were exchanged between Washington and London. By the end of May arrangements had also been made for the training of British pilots in the United States. Roosevelt still hesitated to order the convoying of British vessels by American

16. Roosevelt, press conference, December 17, 1940, and Fireside Chat, December 29, 1940, in *Public Papers*. 9: 604, 607, 634, 641, 643.
17. Joint Committee for the Investigation of the Pearl Harbor Attack, *Hearings*, 79th Cong., 1st. sess., 1945, pt. 15, 1487, 1491.

destroyers but extended his ability to provide further aid by declaring a state of unlimited national emergency.

When Hitler launched his attack against Russia on June 22, the president immediately released previously frozen Russian credits and promised assistance. His primary concern, again, was not the defense of the Soviet Union but extension of support to a new, if somewhat uncomfortable, ally who might contribute significantly to the destruction of Hitler's power. Welles, while denouncing both the "communistic" and Nazi dictatorships, declared the real issue to be the defeat of Germany. "In the opinion of the Government," he told a press conference, ". . . any defense against Hitlerism, any rallying of the forces opposing Hitlerism, from whatever source these forces may spring, will . . . redound to the benefit of our own defense and security."[18] On July 7 American troops occupied Iceland, thus establishing a military presence beyond the limits of the hemisphere and squarely astride the North Atlantic shipping lanes.

One month later, Churchill braved these shipping lanes to meet secretly with Roosevelt in Placentia Bay off Newfoundland. There the two leaders reviewed the problems of the war in Europe, Africa, and the Far East, as well as the need for further American aid. The American position at this time was defined both by the fact of the meeting itself and by the resulting joint press release, grandiloquently called the Atlantic Charter, which was to have future significance far beyond any either imagined or desired by its authors. In this document, the still theoretically neutral United States in effect proclaimed joint war aims with a belligerent British Empire and, although these aims were worldwide in scope, made "the final destruction of the Nazi tyranny" the major prerequisite for their attainment. On the day following the release of this statement, moreover, Roosevelt and Churchill sent a message to Stalin suggesting a conference in Moscow for the purpose of "planning the program for the future allocation of our joint resources" with the aim of securing "the defeat of Hitlerism."[19]

Two Roads to War: Germany

While the United States thus moved ever more clearly and publicly into the ranks of the enemies of the Reich, Germany exercised re-

18. Press conference, June 23, 1941, in State Department, *Peace and War*, p. 684.
19. Atlantic Charter, August 14, 1941, and Roosevelt-Churchill to Stalin, August 15, 1941, in *Public Papers*, 10: 315, 318.

markable restraint in its policy toward America. On September 12, 1939, Weizsäcker had suggested that high priority be given to "preventing the United States from throwing its weight into the scales on the side of our foes" and urged doing "everything to keep it in the group of the neutral powers. . . , despite its hostile sentiments."[20] He even suggested that an ambassador be sent to Washington regardless of whether or not the gesture were reciprocated. Ribbentrop was by no means prepared to go that far, but great pains were taken to avoid offending the United States. Criticism of Roosevelt and American policy virtually ceased in the German press immediately after the outbreak of war on direct orders from the Ministry of Propaganda, and care was even taken to avoid giving public support to Roosevelt's American opponents. As the ultimate token, the social boycott of American embassy personnel that had been in effect for a year was lifted in November. This policy was modified as time went on, and the administration's more obviously anti-German utterances and actions eventually drew strong adverse comments in the press and produced some direct attacks on Roosevelt and his alleged links to Jews and Freemasons. But such outbursts remained consciously reactive and were rarely encouraged.

German espionage and sabotage efforts in the United States also remained far below the level achieved in the First World War, and the Foreign Office worked hard to restrain the military authorities in this respect. Thomsen, for example, noted some sabotage activity in May 1940 and protested to Berlin that "this activity is the surest way to bring America actively to the side of our enemies and to destroy the last remaining sympathies for Germany." The Foreign Office thereupon took up the matter with the military authorities and assured the attaché in Washington that while certain kinds of "information gathering" in the United States were essential "for urgent military reasons," "the expressed political misgivings of the Foreign Office and the Embassy with regard to sabotage activity in the U.S.A. are fully shared by the OKW [Supreme Armed Forces Command] and have always been considered."[21]

Even German propaganda efforts in the United States remained relatively muted. The only direct governmental attempt by the Germans to influence opinion in America was the publication on March 28, 1940, of the White Book, *Documents on the Events Preceding*

20. Weizsäcker memorandum, September 12, 1939, in *Akten zur deutschen auswärtigen Politik*, D, 8: 41.

21. Thomsen to Foreign Office, May 22, 1940, and Weizsäcker to Embassy, June 2, 1940, in ibid., D, 9: 336, 403.

the Outbreak of the War. Consisting of captured Polish documents, the book was intended to embarrass the Roosevelt administration and weaken it at home by demonstrating that the United States had encouraged Poland to provoke war with Germany. Although the allegations were promptly denied by all of the participants, the White Book did produce a sensation in the United States, and arrangements were promptly made for an English translation and its wide distribution. Whatever effects the documents might have had, however, were quickly overshadowed by the German attack on Denmark and Norway. German shortwave broadcasts to the United States were given high priority for a time but were poorly designed to win an American audience. More ambitious projects, such as a proposed "Goebbels Hour," were never launched.

The embassy in Washington did, of course, conduct various propaganda operations. It provided financial support for the German Library of Information, the American Fellowship Forum, the Flanders Hall publishing house, and similar pro-German or anti-British organizations, and also worked through the American branches of the German Railway Office and Transocean Cable Agency. Its most ambitious maneuvers consisted of the promotion of isolationist activity and the publication of "useful" books, preferably by well-known and respected Americans. Embassy funds were secretly used to promote the attendance of antiwar personages at both the Republican and Democratic national conventions in 1940 and to distribute the speeches of Hamilton Fish, Rush Holt, Charles A. Lindbergh, and other prominent isolationists. The funds were also used to subsidize the publication and distribution of books by such diverse authors as Theodore Dreiser, John T. Flynn, Burton Rascoe, Sylvia Porter, and Kathleen Norris, at least some of whom were clearly ignorant of the source of their support. Nonetheless, the moneys expended for these purposes were relatively small, and great pains were taken to conceal such activities lest American sentiments against Germany grow even stronger.

The clearest evidence of Germany's interest in avoiding provocation of the United States was provided by Hitler's naval policies. The cutting edge of America's anti-German stance from 1939 to 1941 was the swelling flood of war materiel which crossed the Atlantic, and Germany's most obvious recourse was to conduct an energetic campaign against this traffic both with submarines and surface raiders. From the very beginning, however, Hitler opposed the repeated

requests of his admirals and insisted that all such activities be conducted with due consideration for the sensitivities of the United
States.

On September 9, 1939, in the first of his military orders dealing
with naval matters, Hitler stipulated that U-boat warfare was to be
conducted according to the rules of cruiser warfare. He thus met in
advance the demand that Woodrow Wilson had made of Bethmann
Hollweg in 1914 and 1915. Three weeks later he reiterated this order
as well as its corollary that passenger liners were not to be attacked
at all. Again drawing on a lesson from World War I dealings with
America, he agreed at a conference with the chief of the naval staff
that "the notorious expression 'unrestricted submarine warfare' "[22]
was to be avoided at all cost. The first incidents involving Americans
were treated in accordance with this policy. Hitler was concerned
when he learned that the sinking of the British liner *Athenia,* with
the loss of twenty-eight American lives, in the first hours of the war
had actually been the work of a German submarine commander and
had the offending officer dismissed from the service—at least temporarily. The American cargo vessel *City of Flint,* which was captured by the surface raider *Deutschland* on October 9 while en route
to England, was allowed to return home.

Though Hitler in fact permitted attacks on American vessels in
declared combat zones where their sinking could be blamed on British mines, his concern for producing incidents remained undimmed.
On February 23, 1940, he refused Admiral Erich Raeder's request to
send two submarines with mines and torpedoes to operate off
Halifax "in view of the psychological effect on the U.S.A."[23] In
June, when he theoretically granted "operational freedom" to the
navy, Hitler specifically limited it to the combat zones that American ships could not legally enter. Despite growing American shipments to Great Britain and the increasingly unneutral conduct of
American vessels, which had begun to radio the positions of U-boats
they encountered for the benefit of the British, Hitler steadfastly
refused to heed the ever louder pleas of his admirals for permission
to take effective counteraction. He even refused permission for attacks on American vessels engaged in clearly unneutral activities.

22. Notes from the Führer, naval conference, September 23, 1939, in *Brassey's
Naval Annual, 1948* (New York, 1948), p. 42.
23. Report of the Commander-in-Chief, Navy, to the Führer, February 23, 1940, in
ibid., p. 81.

Although the führer's attitude stemmed in part from his consistent failure to appreciate the full significance of the navy as an instrument of war, it rested too on his conviction that nothing should be done which would bring the United States formally into the war. This conviction grew firmer as the failure of Britain to respond to peace feelers after the fall of France and the inability of Germany to mount an invasion of the British Isles raised the prospect of a drawn-out war. Indeed, Hitler's first directive dealing with future cooperation with Japan, which was issued on March 5, 1941, assigned to the navy the task of planning "the swift conquest of England *in order to keep the United States out of the war.*"[24]

German policy with respect to Japan was in fact largely the result of the importance that Hitler assigned to continued American non-belligerence. Although earlier moves to convert the Anti-Comintern Pact into a military alliance may well have been aimed at keeping the Soviet Union from interfering with German plans for conquest in the east, the reopening of negotiations for such an alliance in September 1940 was obviously designed to prevent the United States from providing similar interference. Hitler regarded some propaganda efforts and the avoidance of incidents as necessary for the achievement of that purpose, but believed, as always, that intimidation would prove even more effective. Ribbentrop accordingly proposed to Tokyo the "joining together of Germany-Italy-Japan for the purpose of neutralizing America" and stressed that "Germany does not want the present conflict to develop into a world war," "particularly wants the United States to stay out," and wishes "to have Japan play the role of restraining and preventing the U.S. from entering the war, by all means."[25] Hitler described the proposed alliance to Mussolini in the same terms a week later.

The Tripartite Pact thus concluded actually backfired and, far from intimidating the United States, spurred it to greater efforts to frustrate German ambitions both in Europe and in the Far East. Hitler continued nevertheless to adhere both to the strategic concept and the immediate aim that underlay the treaty. If the German-Japanese alliance brought about the defeat of the Soviet Union, for which he gave the initial order on December 18, 1940, and at the

24. Directive No. 24, March 5, 1941, in *Hitlers Weisungen für die Kriegsführung, 1939–1945,* ed. Walter Hubatsch (Frankfurt, 1962), p. 104. Emphasis added.
25. Embassy in Tokyo to Foreign Office, September 10, 1940, in *Akten zur deutschen auswärtigen Politik,* D, 9, no. 1: 49.

same time deprived Britain of Singapore and other bastions of its empire, the United States would not dare to interfere. Even if it tried to do so, it would find itself facing an impregnable Axis-controlled Eurasian land mass, against which all its efforts would be in vain.

Throughout the early months of 1941 the Germans urged Japan to enter the war by moving southward toward Singapore. They argued not only that this action would be the best way to bring about the defeat of England, "the main enemy one encountered in the creation of the new order," but also that it would prevent "that America enters actively into the war or pursues its [policy of] aid to England too actively." When the Japanese expressed doubt that these two aims were compatible and concern that an attack on British territory would in fact bring the United States into the war, Hitler reassured them. He promised that Germany would "intervene immediately in case of a Japan-American conflict," not because he wanted such a war, but "because the strength of the three pact powers lay in their following a common course." That course was to defeat Great Britain and the Soviet Union, and to keep the United States out of the war.[26]

Consistent with this strategic concept, the Germans, after their own invasion of Russia, urged the Japanese to attack Vladivostok and to move southward as well, but warned them not to attack the Philippines. They strongly opposed the Japanese-American negotiations that were launched in the summer of 1941. Such negotiations, they believed, would undermine the Tripartite Pact, weaken its presumed intimidating impact on the United States, and thus make America's undesired entry into the war far more likely. "The truth of the situation is," Ribbentrop advised Tokyo, "that the Americans will be the more careful, the more categorically the determination of Japan to stand by the Tripartite Pact is expressed, while every yielding in this respect will encourage Washington to take further steps in the direction of American entry into the European war and thus lead, through this aggressive action, to precisely the situation that the Japanese Government wishes to avoid." As a last resort in trying to maintain the concept of the pact, the Germans urged Japan to make unmistakably clear to the American government that "further moves by Roosevelt along the road of aggression against the Axis Powers" would lead not only to war with Germany and Italy but

26. Notes on Ribbentrop-Matsuoka conversations, March 27, 1941, and Hitler-Matsuoka conversations, April 4, 1941, in ibid., 13, no. 1: 314, 376.

would bring "the immediate entry of Japan into such a war against America."[27]

How seriously the führer still clung to his belief that the United States could be kept out of the war in this way is graphically demonstrated by his fantasizing during September and October that the collapse of Russia would lead to a compromise peace with England. A new British government, he believed, would eventually come to the realization "that Germany's mission is the ordering of Europe against the Mongol flood from the East," and that "Germany and England finally will have to stand together *against the United States*."[28] Unrealistic as such a vision may have been, it was not entirely illogical. But any possibility for its fulfillment depended absolutely, even in its own terms, on keeping America from entering the existing war on the side of Britain.

Hitler meanwhile continued to restrain his admirals. He was disturbed when a U-boat sank the American freighter *Robin Moor* in the South Atlantic in May and no happier when he learned that another submarine had followed the battleship *Texas* for more than 150 miles on June 19 and 20, failing to attack only because of the zigzag course and unfavorable weather. Again and again he told Raeder that incidents had to be avoided, at least for the time being. The American decision at the end of August to have vessels of the U.S. Navy escort British convoys as far as Iceland made incidents more likely, however. On September 4 the destroyer *Greer* encountered a German submarine, followed it for some time, and radioed its position to British patrol vessels. Eventually the two ships opened fire—which fired first remains in dispute—and though both missed, the first armed encounter of the Second World War between Germany and the United States had thus taken place. Roosevelt used the occasion to declare in a speech on September 11 that German and Italian vessels entering American patrol zones would henceforth do so at their own peril, and two days later the navy received orders to "shoot on sight."

Even then Hitler did not authorize substantial changes in the naval orders. Neither the torpedoing of the *Kearney* on October 17, with the loss of 11 American lives, nor the sinking, two weeks later,

27. Ribbentrop to Embassy, July 19, 1941, and September 13, 1941, in ibid., 151, 413.

28. Weizsäcker notes, October 21, 1941, in *Weizsäcker Papiere*, p. 274. Emphasis added.

of the *Reuben James,* in which 155 men, including all the ship's officers, were killed were intentional attacks on American vessels. Both destroyers were engaged in convoy duty, and the submarine commanders could not clearly determine the nationality of either. Neither did the repeal on November 17 of key sections of the neutrality act, including the prohibitions against the arming of merchant ships and entry into declared combat zones, alter the picture. Though anticipating that change, Hitler's directives still put first priority on the effort to "lessen the possibility of incidents with American forces."[29] Permission to disregard the American "neutrality zone," which by now extended almost indefinitely eastward, was still refused on December 2.

By that time, however, the United States had moved so far from even the semblance of neutrality that, except for sending troops, all possible aid to the British had been legitimized. American supplies in unprecedented amounts were proceeding across the North Atlantic under escort of American destroyers who brought them as far as Iceland; American warplanes were being flown by Pan-American Airways across the South Atlantic and across Africa for delivery to British forces in Egypt. Since November 7, over twenty thousand men of the British Eighteenth Division had been en route to the Middle East aboard American navy transports. The concept of "all aid short of war" had thus been pushed to the very edge of belligerency itself, and it is doubtful that German restraint could have prevailed for much longer.

Nevertheless, it is at least equally doubtful that Hitler would actually have declared war in the foreseeable future, no matter how far beyond the bounds of neutrality American conduct would advance. His consistent strategic aim remained the securing of the Eurasian land mass for the Axis powers under the leadership of Germany, and war against the United States could contribute nothing to the realization of that aim. Neither is it clear when, if ever, the United States would have reached the point of actually declaring war on Germany. The logic of the American position required a declaration if aid short of war proved insufficient to prevent a British defeat. But in December 1941 such defeat was not imminent. Hitler had failed to invade Britain and failed, despite claims to the contrary, to defeat the Soviet Union. What the future would hold could not be clearly fore-

29. Report of the Commander-in-Chief, Navy, to the Führer, in *Brassey's,* p. 239.

seen. Germany and the United States had thus reached the brink of war with each other but might well have teetered on that brink for months or even years to come.

As it happened, however, the issue of the future of German-American relations was resolved by the Japanese attack on Pearl Harbor on the afternoon of December 7. That attack followed the breakdown of Japanese-American negotiations, which Germany had vigorously opposed and in which the United States had remained unyielding at least in part because of the commitments it had already assumed to the defense of the Allied countries and the defeat of Germany. That the war in which the United States thus became engaged was not a separate conflict but part of the struggle already in progress was made unmistakably clear when Britain declared war on Japan even before America had the chance to do so. Japan, in turn, declared war on both Britain and the United States on December 8. At the White House, Stimson and others suggested that America respond to the attack with a declaration of war not only against Japan, but against Germany as well. While Roosevelt vetoed that suggestion, his mind, too, was not entirely in the Pacific. "I think that all of us believed," noted presidential adviser Harry Hopkins, "that in the last analysis, the enemy was Hitler and that he could never be defeated without force of arms."[30]

The führer now saw matters the same way. He had had no more advance warning of the Pearl Harbor attack than had the United States, though the Foreign Office had known for some weeks that Japan wanted a formal promise of German support if its "tactical moves" led to war with the United States. At this point he did not hesitate at all. Hitler had assured the Japanese as early as April that Germany would join them if they became involved in a new armed conflict. In response to a specific Japanese request on December 2, he had authorized the formal though secret response that "in case a state of war should arise between Japan and the United States of America, Germany and Italy for their part will also consider themselves to be in a state of war with the United States. . . ." On the morning of December 8, he simply converted the contingency to reality. Still in secret, the Foreign Office cabled to Tokyo a revised text that now read: "Germany, Italy and Japan will jointly wage the war forced upon them by the United States of America and En-

30. Hopkins notes, in Robert E. Sherwood, *Roosevelt and Hopkins* (New York, 1948), p. 431.

gland. . . . ."[31] The public announcement lagged by a few days only because Hitler wanted to wait for a Japanese commitment that they, too, would not conclude a separate peace, to arrange the necessary withdrawal from Washington and, above all, to assure maximum impact with a speech from Berlin.

Hitler had always regarded himself as leader of the Axis alliance and was not inclined to relinquish that leadership—or that of the postwar order he was still confident the alliance would fashion—by remaining aloof now. Neither would his pride allow him to wait until the United States declared war on Germany. In any event, the führer believed that he no longer had anything to lose by such a declaration. The United States would surely turn its attention primarily to the Pacific and the naval commanders could take care of what would remain of America's efforts in the Atlantic. If the plan to keep America out of the war had been overtaken by events, the alternative of isolating it in the Western Hemisphere and rendering its assistance to Great Britain ineffective had been furthered by the destruction of the Pacific fleet in Hawaii and by the immediate successes of the Japanese in Malaya, Hong Kong, Thailand, and the Philippines.

On December 9 German submarine commanders received orders to begin immediate attacks on American ships. On December 10 Ribbentrop asked Thomsen to deliver a declaration of war to Hull on the following day, which read in part:

> Although Germany has, on its part, adhered strictly to the rules of international law with respect to the United States during the entire course of the present war, the Government of the United States has finally proceeded from initial breaches of neutrality to open acts of war against Germany. . . . The Government of the Reich is therefore breaking diplomatic relations with the United States and declares that under these circumstances brought about by President Roosevelt, Germany also regards itself, as of today, in a state of war with the United States of America.[32]

Hitler, whose Reichstag speech announcing the new war included a bitter personal attack on Roosevelt, expressed his relief that clarity

31. Ribbentrop to Embassy in Italy, December 5, 1941, and Ribbentrop to Embassy in Japan, December 8, 1941, in *Documents on German Foreign Policy, 1919–1945* (Washington, D.C., 1949–1966), Series D, 13: 958, 983.
32. Ribbentrop to Embassy, December 10, 1941, in *Akten zur deutschen auswärtigen Politik*, D, 13, no. 2: 813.

had been produced in German-American relations. In a meeting with the Japanese ambassador he boasted that he would now send his submarines even into American harbors. Five U-boats did indeed arrive off the American coast in mid-January, and before the end of that month had sunk 143,000 tons of U.S. shipping. But although in a moment of euphoria in July Hitler had told the same ambassador that Germany and Japan would jointly destroy both Russia and the United States, he really had no plan for the latter enterprise. "How one defeats America," he told Hiroshi Oshima, "[I do] not know yet."[33]

Toward Unconditional Surrender

In 1917 the United States had entered a war in which both sides were near exhaustion. The essential area of combat had been reduced to a single, well-defined area—the western front—in which American troops could be brought into action almost at once. In 1941, by contrast, only Germany of the countries remaining in the war had even mobilized fully, and only Germany and the Soviet Union had engaged in substantial land warfare. Except for the eastern front, where American forces could not be employed for political as well as logistical reasons, the only military contact between the Allies and Germany was the mobile desert warfare in North Africa, in which more tanks and not more troops were initially the key requirement. The Allies' first contacts with Japan were entirely determined as to time and place by Japanese military planners. The momentum of the war, moreover, lay clearly with the Axis powers. It is hardly surprising, therefore, that the first months of America's belligerency witnessed a series of military disasters that this country was powerless to prevent.

The situation differed from that of the First World War in other ways as well, however. Despite the shock of the Pearl Harbor attack and the losses suffered both there and in the subsequent fighting in the Philippines, the United States was far better prepared for war, both psychologically and militarily, than in 1917. Moreover, the scruples against alliances had been sufficiently overcome so that America fought not as an "associated" power jealous of its indepen-

33. Minutes of Hitler-Oshima meeting of January 3, 1942, in *Staatsmänner und Diplomaten bei Hitler*, 2 vols., ed. Andreas Hillgruber (Frankfurt, 1967 and 1970), 2: 41.

dent status, but as a full-fledged ally. In the Declaration of the United Nations of January 1, 1942, the U.S. formally joined with twenty-five other nations in a pledge "to employ its full resources, military and economic, against . . . members of the Tripartite Pact . . . and not to make a separate armistice or peace with the enemies."[34] With Great Britain this alliance was to reach a degree of closeness unparalleled in history, and the United States, contrary to Hitler's expectations, adhered faithfully to the "Europe first" strategy that had been developed before the Japanese attack.

The United States, in fact, began planning for a frontal assault on Germany through France as early as February 1942, and by May Roosevelt expressed the hope that it could begin before the end of that year. He agreed only reluctantly, and against the advice of both the army chief of staff, General George C. Marshall, and the chief of naval operations, Admiral Ernest J. King, to yield to Churchill's insistence that the operation be postponed in favor of the invasion of North Africa, and then only after it had been agreed that an American, General Dwight D. Eisenhower, would command the attacking forces. So anxious was the president that the United States enter into active fighting against German forces as soon as possible that he insisted that American troops constitute the bulk of the invasion force. Thereafter he steadfastly pushed for the frontal attack at the earliest possible moment, resisted attempts by Churchill to pursue instead an enveloping strategy through the Mediterranean and Scandinavia, and expressed profound disappointment when no landings in France proved possible even in 1943. Moreover, though the staging area for the cross-Channel invasion was Great Britain, Eisenhower was in charge of the preparations almost from the beginning and in December 1943 was appointed Supreme Allied Commander for the final assault of "Fortress Europe," which ultimately was launched on June 6, 1944. Thus the United States, unlike in 1917, played the key military role in the struggle against Germany in the West.

Two additional factors not immediately apparent were also to be of decisive importance to wartime relations between Germany and the United States. The first was that the war reached its turning point less than a year after American entry. The battle of Midway on June 4–7, 1942, put an end to Japanese offensive actions, restored

34. Declaration of the United Nations, January 2, 1942, in State Department, *Peace and War*, p. 851.

the balance of naval power in the Pacific, and made possible the American landings on Tulagi and Guadalcanal in the Solomons on August 7–8, which inaugurated the island-hopping campaigns westward. The decisive British victory over the German Afrika Korps at El Alamein on October 23–29, and the successful landings in Algeria and Morocco by American and some British troops under Eisenhower's command on November 8, led to Allied control of North Africa and left Italy open to invasion. In the meantime, the Red Army had stopped the German advance at Stalingrad on October 1, and by November 22 had succeeded in encircling the entire Sixth German Army there. On February 2, 1943, the remnants of that army of three hundred thousand men, including twenty-five of its generals, surrendered. The ultimate question of the war thus became not its outcome but only the time that would still be required to secure the Allied victory that now seemed certain.

If the outcome of the war was not long in doubt, neither was the manner in which it would be concluded. Unlike the First World War, when both sides had talked to the very end about a negotiated peace and thus about the terms under which such a peace might be concluded, the Second was from its inception a fight to the finish. For Hitler this meant the destruction, and indeed the colonization, of the Soviet Union and of Eastern Europe, the permanent elimination of France as a truly independent state, and the relegation of the United States and what would remain of the British Empire to isolation and impotence. For the Allies it was soon to mean the unconditional surrender of at least Germany and Japan, a policy formally announced after the conclusion of the Casablanca conference on January 24, 1943.

The idea of "unconditional surrender" was inherent in the ideological nature of the conflict and in the repeated assertions by Roosevelt and others that Germany in particular, but also Italy and Japan, had become outlaw nations with whom any negotiations were impossible. It drew its main strength, however, from the widely held conviction that the failure to obtain the unconditional surrender of Germany in 1918 had hampered the work of the Versailles conference, led to a generally unsatisfactory postwar settlement, and even encouraged the myth that Germany had never been really defeated. That myth, in turn, was deemed to have contributed greatly to the failure of the Weimar Republic, to the rise of Hitler, and to the German drive toward a new war.

"Unconditional surrender" was formally advanced in this context in a memorandum entitled "The Armistice Negotiations, 1918," which Grayson Kirk presented to the security and armament group of the Council on Foreign Relations on April 8, 1942. It was immediately forwarded to the State Department, where it formed part of the basis for the initial discussion in the Subcommittee on Security Problems of the Advisory Committee on Post-War Foreign Policy. The subcommittee reached agreement by early May that nothing short of unconditional surrender should be accepted in the case of Germany and Japan. When Norman Davis, the subcommittee's chairman, so informed Roosevelt on May 20, he gained the impression that the president's thoughts ran along similar lines. Certainly Roosevelt's announcement at Casablanca was neither a whim nor an inspiration of the moment, though he himself characterized it as such at the time. The Joint Chiefs of Staff had been informed of the formula before the president left Washington and Churchill given notice early enough to consult the War Cabinet, which, far from raising objections, was so committed to the idea that it suggested its application to Italy as well.

The unconditional-surrender formula was a war measure and not a peace plan. It was an attempt to reassure all of the Allies that none of their individual war aims would be sacrificed in the process of bringing the conflict to a close. It was intended to preclude the necessity for reconciling possibly divergent aims, a process that might well have weakened the alliance and prolonged the war. In short, the formula simply sought to avoid the mistakes of the First World War, when the vanquished had been left in doubt as to their fate and the victors divided by secret commitments on the shape of the postwar world.

As such, the formula was firmly adhered to by Roosevelt even when in the closing months of the war it came to be regarded by some of his military and civilian advisers as a tactical liability that strengthened the German will to resist. Its espousal showed once more how central to the president's thinking the issue of Germany was. Not only was the experience with Germany after the 1918 armistice taken as a lesson in what not to repeat, it was the reappearance of Germany as the primary foe which made this lesson particularly relevant. Thus unconditional surrender was seen as the necessary precondition for demilitarization, denazification, and democratization, and for a future peace that could be arranged among the major Allies without the advice and consent of a defeated Germany.

Nevertheless, neither the fact that eventual victory was virtually certain by early 1943 nor the primacy of Germany in American eyes resulted in the development of a specific policy for Germany's future. Postwar planning committees that debated that future had existed in the State Department as early as February 1942 and in the War Department since April 1943. The Interdepartmental Working Security Committee, initially composed of representatives of the State, War, and Navy departments, entered the discussions in December 1943, and the Treasury Department became involved at all levels in August/September 1944. These bodies conducted endless studies and discussions and produced a variety of proposals concerning Germany's future, but no actual American policy emerged until after Allied troops had already crossed the Rhine. Even then, the policy was stated only in broad and frequently contradictory terms, and those charged with its implementation were left largely to find their own way between rhetoric and reality. At the same time, the United States played by far the smallest role in the Anglo-American-Russian discussions on the future of Germany at various wartime conferences and showed the most reluctance to seek agreement on the issues that were raised.

For this state of affairs Roosevelt bore the major responsibility. The president clearly gave much thought to Germany, discussed the subject frequently with advisers and friends, and, over the course of the war, developed some definite ideas of his own. He came to favor partition and especially the segregation of Prussia from the rest of Germany, long-term disarmament, the internationalization of the Kiel Canal, and, for a time, even the imposition of reparations (though only in the form of labor and equipment). All this together fell far short of representing a coherent plan, however much it suggested a preference for a Carthaginian peace and the punishment of Germany. Roosevelt recognized this and in fact provided no guidelines at all for the planning that was going on in the various departments. At the same time, he rejected the results of such planning when it disagreed with his own preferences.

A State Department recommendation of September 23, 1943, opposed the breakup or even the forced decentralization of Germany. Rather it called for "the fostering of moderate government in Germany . . . [through] a program looking to the economic recovery of

Germany, to the earliest reconciliation of the German people with the peace, and to the assimilation of Germany, as soon as would be compatible with security considerations, into the projected international order."[35] The recommendation had been modified greatly, however, by the time Hull brought it to the Moscow conference the following month. Now included in a larger memorandum entitled "Basic Principles Regarding German Surrender," its more moderate proposals were contradicted by strident calls for the admission of total defeat, submission to three-power occupation, denazification, total demobilization, and the surrender of war criminals. The question of partition was left in abeyance. Moreover, the memorandum was handed by Hull to Molotov with the explanation that "this is not a formal United States proposal but something to show a slant of mind. It is just a personal suggestion you and I can talk about."[36]

The document presented at Moscow revealed not only the divergencies in American thinking about the manner in which Germany was to be treated but also the unwillingness of Roosevelt to commit himself to a definite course at all. The president remained convinced that attempts to engage in concrete postwar planning were potentially divisive, that the exact conditions that would prevail at war's end could not be accurately foreseen, and that, in any event, the question could be more readily resolved in high-level discussions when the time arrived. In keeping with his conviction that Wilson's Fourteen Points had been a mistake because they raised expectations on the one hand and produced needless disputes on the other, Roosevelt steadfastly adhered to a policy of postponement, in which the winning of the war remained his primary focus and the future of Europe was left for determination after victory had been won.

In accordance with his general view that the postwar world was to be shaped by agreements among the "Big Four"—the United States, China, Great Britain, and the Soviet Union—and that Europe would become the primary responsibility of the latter two, Roosevelt sought no more than to establish where necessary his own position as mediator between Churchill and Stalin. The Moscow conference did set up the European Advisory Commission to consider "Euro-

35. "The Political Reorganization of Germany," in *Postwar Foreign Policy Preparation, 1939–1945,* Department of State Publication 3580 (Washington, D.C., 1949), p. 559.
36. Cordell Hull, *Memoirs,* 2 vols. (New York 1948), 2: 1285.

pean questions connected with the termination of hostilities," but, for the United States at least, referral of matters to the EAC became simply another means of postponing decisions. None of the plans eventually adopted by the commission were originated by the U.S., and the work actually undertaken by the group was continually hampered by the lack of specific instructions from Washington to John G. Winant, the American representative.

At the first meeting of Roosevelt, Churchill, and Stalin at Teheran, which began on November 28, 1943, the lack of a specific American policy for Germany and the unwillingness to establish one were even more graphically demonstrated. Stalin for the first time gave an indication of what the Soviet Union expected, expressing concern both about future German aggression and the possibility that the United States and Britain would prove too lenient. He proposed dismemberment, annexation of portions of East Prussia to the Soviet Union, the reduction of Germany's industrial capacity, the transfer of large amounts of German machinery as well as of at least 4 million laborers to Russia, and the liquidation—perhaps literally—of the German General Staff.

Roosevelt, unencumbered by State Department officials with quite different ideas and anxious to establish a close working relationship with Stalin to complement the one he already had with Churchill, countered with a proposal to place the Ruhr, the Saar, the port of Hamburg, and the Kiel Canal under international control (perhaps that of the future United Nations), and to divide the rest of Germany into five self-governing areas. But he repeatedly made it clear "he had reached no final conclusions,"[37] and steadfastly refused to make any commitments, not even regarding the western boundary of Poland, on which near agreement had already been reached at Moscow. Torn by his own anti-German biases, the moderate views that prevailed in both the State and War departments, and uncertainty of what the postwar power position would actually be, Roosevelt preferred to put off the difficult decisions until after unconditional surrender. Hull was not even informed of the drift of the Teheran discussions, and Winant, who had been at the conference, came away with no sense that he had received any guidance for the work of the European Advisory Commission.

Nonetheless, as the moment of victory drew closer with the inva-

37. Matthews memorandum, April 22, 1944, in *Foreign Relations: The Conferences at Cairo and Tehran, 1943*, p. 879.

sion and surrender of Italy in September and October 1943, the landings in the Gilbert Islands in the central Pacific in November, and the success of the Soviet winter offensive in December, which at one point pushed the Germans back to the prewar borders of Poland, the EAC felt compelled to reach at least some agreement on postwar issues. Indeed, the British and Winant hoped that "not only the treatment of Germany and other enemy countries with respect to frontiers, military occupation, disarmament, reparation, decentralization, as well as armistice terms and controls [would be considered], but also numerous questions connected with the liberated territories." In short, the British at least hoped to engage in meaningful decision making. Hull repeatedly voiced his annoyance at this fact, insisting that "this view was definitely not shared by the Russians and ourselves," and informed Winant that "the President expressed to me his own anxiety lest the European Advisory Commission might tend to arrogate to itself the general field of postwar organization."[38] The EAC therefore confined its activities to developing an instrument of surrender for Germany and the outlining of prospective zones of occupation. Even in this process, the United States followed the principle of postponing difficult decisions.

The idea that Germany would have to be occupied for a time was readily accepted by the United States on the basis of military considerations and the conviction that such a step was necessary to bring home the reality of defeat to the Germans and make a peaceful reordering of Europe possible. That some decision would consequently have to be reached on the areas to be occupied by each of the Allies was clear, particularly because many American experts still believed in 1944 that the Russian and American armies would eventually meet, not on the Elbe, but on the Rhine, and that without previous planning the Soviet Union would occupy all of Central Europe and gain the preponderant influence on future planning. Roosevelt himself had toyed with a map of Germany on his way to the Teheran conference, and had sketched a large American zone in northwestern Germany, a smaller British one to the south of it, and a still smaller Soviet one east of Berlin.

But the president, who as late as November 1944 told Churchill "that after Germany's collapse I must bring American troops home

38. John G. Winant to Hull, January 4, 1944, and Hull to Winant, January 9, 1944, in *Foreign Relations, 1944*, I: 2, 11, 12.

as rapidly as transportation problems will permit"[39] and even at Yalta, three months later, contended that Congress would never approve the maintenance of an appreciable American force in Europe for more than two years, clearly believed that occupation was a short-term issue. Any British proposal for zones of occupation which was acceptable to the Soviet Union was therefore acceptable to the United States, and one was eventually adopted on June 21. To be sure, Roosevelt continued to demand for several months thereafter that the United States and not the British be assigned the northwestern area. His adamancy on this question had nothing to do with the future of Germany or of Europe, however, but simply reflected his desire for easier lines of supply—and withdrawal—and America's unwillingness to assume the responsibility for policing France.

On the issue of the surrender document, the lack of an American plan and the unwillingness to decide on one were even clearer. "I understand," Roosevelt wrote to Churchill, "that your staff presented a long and comprehensive document—with every known kind of terms—to the European Advisory Commission, and that the Russians have done somewhat the same. My people here believe that a short document of surrender should be adopted." Indeed, the American proposal consisted of little more than a statement of unconditional surrender and sweeping generalization declaring the right of the Allies to reorganize German political and economic life. The final compromise, prepared by the British, went far to meet Roosevelt's desire for the postponement of decisions. It merely provided for German disarmament and the assumption of supreme political authority by the Allies. "In the exercise of such authority," it continued, "they will take such steps, including complete disarmament and demilitarization of Germany, as they deem requisite to future peace and security . . . [and] present additional political, administrative, economic, financial, military and other requirements arising from the surrender of Germany."[40]

Roosevelt's failure to develop a definite policy for postwar Germany provided Treasury Secretary Henry Morgenthau, Jr., with the opportunity to enter the fray. Dismayed by what he learned of the

39. Roosevelt to Churchill, November 18, 1944, in *Roosevelt and Churchill*, p. 602.
40. Roosevelt to Churchill, February 29, 1944, in ibid., pp. 456–457; "Unconditional Surrender of Germany," July 25, 1944, in *Foreign Relations: The Conferences at Malta and Yalta, 1945*, p. 117.

discussions in the State Department and the European Advisory Commission, appalled by the moderate tone of the *Handbook for Military Government in Germany,* which the hundred fifty English and American staff planners of the so-called German Country Unit had prepared for General Eisenhower, and aware that the president had expressed a preference for much harsher treatment, Morgenthau came forward in mid-August with his celebrated "Plan." Prepared by the secretary and his special assistant, Harry Dexter White, the proposal that Morgenthau now urged on Roosevelt called for Germany to lose substantial amounts of territory to France, Denmark, Poland, and the Soviet Union, to be stripped of most of its industry, and to be divided into two predominantly agricultural states. The Ruhr and Saar regions, also largely deindustrialized, were to be placed under some form of international control, and their German population eventually replaced by French, Belgian, Dutch, and other workers.

The Morgenthau Plan was both an economic and a political monstrosity—the heavily urbanized Germany could not support its population without industry, and the vacuum created in Central Europe would be an open invitation to Russian expansion. But the idea of punishing the Germans and eliminating for all time their war-making potential held emotional appeal for Roosevelt. He too had found the *Handbook* "pretty bad" and had ordered its withdrawal. He now set up a cabinet committee on Germany under the chairmanship of Harry Hopkins, which was to draw up new proposals based on the recommendations of the State, War, and Treasury departments. Though Hull was inclined to compromise somewhat with the Treasury Department's views for tactical reasons, Stimson was adamant on the folly of the Morgenthau proposal, and no agreement was reached before the Anglo-American Quebec conference of September 11–16.

At that conference, however, the secretary of the treasury scored a victory that, although only partial and in a formal sense temporary, was to leave a lasting impress at least on American policy statements. After considerable discussion involving not only the future of Germany but also the respective zones of occupation and additional lend-lease aid, in all of which Morgenthau played a key role, Churchill drafted a memorandum that both he and Roosevelt initialed and which incorporated key elements of the Morgenthau Plan. The two leaders agreed on the elimination of the war-making industries in the Ruhr and Saar, in part through the removal of their machinery to the Soviet Union and other devastated countries, and the placing of these regions under the aegis of a world organization. In the most celebrated phrase of the document, they indicated that they were "looking forward to converting Germany into a country primarily agricultural and pastoral in character."[41]

The Quebec memorandum did not support the dismemberment of Germany which Morgenthau had advocated; neither was it clear to what degree the country was in fact to be pastoralized. Nonetheless, the first American policy toward postwar Germany to be adopted at the highest level clearly envisioned a situation much further removed from the status quo ante than had previously even been seriously discussed. Its impact was immediate and resulted by September 22 in a new directive intended for Eisenhower, prepared by the Working Security Committee, on which Treasury Department representatives sat together with those of the State Department and the War Department, and by the War Department's Civil Affairs Division.

Although the supreme commander, Allied Expeditionary Force, was to be informed that his "objectives must be of short term and military character, in order not to prejudice whatever ultimate policies may be later determined upon," he was also instructed that "Germany will not be occupied for the purpose of liberation but as a defeated enemy nation" and that his aim, while not oppression, was to be "to prevent Germany from ever again becoming a threat to the peace of the world." To that end he was to take complete control of the schools, the press, and all political activity, to promote decentralization, and to "take no steps looking toward the economic rehabilitation of Germany."[42] It was the first version of "JCS 1067," the directive intended to guide the first phase of the American occupation of Germany.

Despite this apparent determination of a policy, however, Roosevelt almost immediately retreated from the position he had taken. Not only did he assure Hull on September 29 that "no one wants to make Germany a wholly agricultural nation again" and that it was still too early to talk with the British or the Russians about

41. Roosevelt-Churchill memorandum, September 15, 1944, in *Foreign Relations: The Conference at Quebec, 1944*, p. 467.

42. Postdefeat memorandum to Supreme Commander, Allied Expeditionary Force, September 22, 1944, in *Foreign Relations: The Conferences at Malta and Yalta, 1945*, pp. 143, 153.

levels of German industry, he added three weeks later that "speed on these matters is not an essential at the present moment." "I dislike," he informed his unhappy secretary of state, "making detailed plans for a country which we do not yet occupy. . . . Much . . . is dependent on what we and the Allies find when we get into Germany—and we are not there yet."[43] In subsequent campaign speeches, the president adopted a moderate stance and on December 4, after his reelection to a fourth term, he informed his new secretary of state, Edward R. Stettinius—Hull had resigned because of ill health—that he was opposed to reparations and that Germany should be allowed to come back industrially to meet her own needs. The period of divided counsels and postponed decisions was thus not yet over.

It persisted, in fact, to the Yalta conference, by which time Allied troops had liberated all of France and reached the German border, Soviet forces were preparing to invade Pomerania, and the U.S. First Cavalry had retaken Manila. At Yalta, Roosevelt agreed to give the Allied military commanders supreme authority in their respective zones and to establish an Inter-Allied Control Council, composed of these commanders, for the purpose of setting all-German policies. But he agreed to nothing else regarding Germany. The briefing documents that the State Department had prepared for the president again reflected rather moderate views and represented a retreat from the immediate post-Quebec period. Roosevelt himself had come to appreciate more fully the advantages a totally destroyed Germany would offer the Soviet Union. Thus he did not accept the Russian proposals that all German territory east of the Oder and the Neisse rivers be turned over to Poland or that Germany be required to pay reparations in goods and services in the amount of $20 billion. A decision on both matters was once again postponed, as was the question of dismemberment.

Stalin strongly urged acceptance of the principle of dismemberment, but both Roosevelt and Churchill were now uncertain of the results of such a move. The president would go no further than to suggest to Stalin that "permanent treatment of Germany might grow out of the question of the zones of occupation, although the two were not directly connected." And the foreign ministers, charged with working out a mutually acceptable formula, qualified the dis-

43. Roosevelt to Hull, September 29 and October 20, 1944, in ibid., pp. 155, 158, 159.

memberment phrase to be added to the surrender document by calling for its implementation by the Allies only "as they deem requisite for the future peace and security." Stalin was to conclude from this, as he told Hopkins three months later, that "the proposal in regard to dismembering had really been rejected at the Crimea Conference."[44]

When American troops entered Germany in force in late February and early March, therefore, the long-range policy goals they were to pursue in their occupation had not been defined at all. In a broad sense, of course, their actions were supposed to further the general aims for the postwar world which had been set forth in the Atlantic Charter and in Roosevelt's "Four Freedoms" pronouncement. In a somewhat narrower sense, they were to eliminate the remains of militarism and National Socialism and to take the first necessary steps toward assuring that Germany would not again threaten the peace of the world. But none of the hard questions that lay behind these generalities had yet been answered.

Reduced to their least common denominator, these questions defined the two alternatives presented on the one hand, by the State and War departments plans and on the other, by the Morgenthau Plan and Roosevelt's more immoderate suggestions. The American objective could be either the restoration of a democratized and economically viable Germany, at least after the general reorganization of postwar Europe by agreement among the victorious Allies, or the permanent destruction of Germany as a political and economic factor in world affairs. Deciding this question had been deliberately postponed, partly because both alternatives were tempting in various degrees, partly because a clear definition of American objectives would have brought conflict with the other Allies and thus weakened the war effort, and partly because Roosevelt, as a pragmatic statesman, believed to the end that such matters could best be decided after the situation had been fully clarified by the surrender of Germany.

As late as March 12 the president approved a State Department memorandum that called neither for dismemberment nor for the destruction of much of Germany's heavy industry and envisioned the integrated treatment of Germany by an all-powerful Allied Con-

44. Bohlen minutes of second plenary meeting, February 5, 1945, and protocol of proceedings, February 11, 1945, in ibid., pp. 612, 978; Bohlen memorandum, May 28, 1945, in *Foreign Relations: Conference of Berlin (Potsdam), 1945*, I: 50.

trol Council. When Morgenthau protested, Roosevelt once more asked the State, War, and Treasury departments to iron out their differences, a process certain to result only in further ambiguity. JCS 1067, the policy directive to the commander-in-chief of the U.S. forces of occupation, was not finally prepared until April 1945, when Roosevelt was already dead, the rudiments of an American military government had been set up at Frankfurt, and Russian and American troops were meeting on the Elbe. It was not formally issued to Major General Lucius D. Clay, who was eventually to head the American Military Government, until after the German surrender.

Even that document did not constitute a coherent blueprint for Germany's future. As in the original draft of the previous September, JCS 1067 still proclaimed that it was not intended as the ultimate statement of American policies concerning the treatment of Germany in the postwar world. Nazism, militarism, and Germany's war-making capacity were to be destroyed and the Germans made aware that chaos and suffering were the inevitable result they had brought upon themselves. Beyond that, the ambiguities remained. On the one hand, virtually all aspects of German political, economic, and even social life were to be brought under military government control, no steps toward the economic rehabilitation of Germany were to be taken, the standard of living was not to be permitted to rise above the level of that in the neighboring Allied states, and both political and economic decentralization were to be promoted. On the other hand, the directive clearly considered Germany as a single unit, decreed that levels of production sufficient "to prevent starvation or such disease and unrest as would endanger the [occupying] forces" were to be maintained, and listed one of the major aims of the occupation as "the preparation for an eventual reconstruction of German political life on a democratic basis."[45] If the shadow of the Morgenthau Plan was thus clearly discernible, so too was an alternate policy of reconstruction and reintegration.

In the dying moments of the Third Reich, while Heinrich Himmler and some German generals were desperately trying to arrange for surrender to the Americans, Hitler, in consonance with his often proclaimed intention to fight to the bitter end, ordered his retreating troops to destroy all industrial, transportation, communication, and other facilities in Germany which might be of value to the enemy. In

45. Directive (JCS 1067), April 1945, in *Germany, 1947–1949*, Department of State Publication 3556 (Washington, 1950), p. 23.

his last message to his troops on April 15, three days after Roosevelt's death, he still held out the hope for a reversal in Germany's fortunes, "in this moment, in which fate has removed the greatest war criminal of all times from this earth."[46] But on April 30, with Russian troops at the gates of Berlin, he appointed Admiral Karl Dönitz as his successor and then took his own life in a bunker under the Reichschancellery. On May 7, the Germans surrendered unconditionally to the Western Allies at Eisenhower's headquarters in Reims. They repeated the process on the following day at the Soviet headquarters in the suburbs of Berlin. On May 23, the Dönitz government was officially dissolved and its members taken prisoner at Flensburg on Eisenhower's orders. The war with Germany was over, and that country, devastated by war and without civil or military administration, lay at the mercy of the victorious Allies. As subsequent events were soon to make clear, the time for postponement had ended.

46. Führer order, April 15, 1945, *Hitlers Weisungen*, p. 311.

Chapter 9

ALLIES OF A KIND

*

The American Occupation of Germany

In 1945 the Allied armies entered Germany in triumph. No wartime planner had foreseen a decade of occupation by hundreds of thousands of American soldiers and civilians. None could predict that the United States would commit itself to permanent political, economic, and military roles in Europe, or that two German states would be established for which the U.S. and the Soviet Union would serve at least as godparents. The Second World War so effectively destroyed the world of the 1930s that none of the schemes for post-war order that had been considered proved applicable.

The United States had expected that the unconditional surrender of Germany would lead to agreement among the victors and, after a brief interlude during which American troops might be used for policing operations, to a peace treaty. Such a treaty would bring Allied withdrawal from a denazified, demilitarized, democratized, and economically viable Germany, and would in other respects restore the ante bellum status quo. Thereafter, America's role in Europe would be exercised within a great power consortium whose members would work collectively to maintain peace and restore prosperity. Only the United States and the Soviet Union survived the war as genuine powers, however. Divergencies in the aims and perceptions of these countries, as well as mutual distrust rooted deeply in history and experience, ruled out genuine cooperation between them. Thus no agreement could be achieved, and expectations of collective management proved illusory.

The almost total destruction of Germany, not simply as a military power but also as an area with a functioning government and the ability to support its population, helped shatter the thin cement that had held the wartime alliance together. Moreover, the utter misery and chaos that reigned in Germany in 1945 did not allow any of the occupying powers the luxury of simply preventing military resurgence while possibly compatible long-range plans were hammered out. Instead the situation required prompt action leading to some kind of reconstruction. In the day-to-day exercise of their roles in the defeated country the powers determined the future of Germany and, to an extent, of Europe and the world as well. America's postwar policy toward Germany thus grew not out of wartime planning or postwar hopes but out of the realities of the occupation and differences with the Soviet Union, differences that in this context became ever more difficult to resolve.

The perceptions of the men who became the temporary rulers of the various parts of Germany considerably influenced the policies of the occupying nations. In no case was this influence more far-reaching than in that of the American general Lucius D. Clay who, first as Eisenhower's deputy and then as his successor, headed the American Military Government. Clay became aware as soon as he reached Germany that earlier discussions in Washington had limited relevance to the task before him. "I think that too much of our planning at home," he wrote to James F. Byrnes, who was soon to become secretary of state, "has envisaged a Germany in which an existing government has surrendered with a large part of the country intact. In point of fact, it looks like every foot of ground will have to be occupied. Destruction will be widespread, and government as we know it will be non-existent."

The immediate issue thus became restoring a semblance of order and self-sufficiency. "Several years will be required," Clay was certain, "to develop even a sustaining economy to provide a bare minimum standard of living." A week later he expressed himself even more specifically to the assistant secretary of war, John J. McCloy, who was in time to become the American high commissioner for Germany:

> I think that Washington must revise its thinking relative to destruction of Germany's war potential as an immediate problem. The progress of the war has done that. . . .
> Similarly we should not be too hasty in listing specific reparations.

They too could make it impossible to bring order back into Germany. . . .

It is going to take all we can do to reestablish government services and a semblance of national economy for many months. This much must be done if only to make it possible to govern Germany with comparatively small occupational forces.

"In solving the short-range problem," he had assured Byrnes, "we should find the answer to the long-range problem, if at the same time we develop unanimity of action among the Allies."[1]

Clay's views were soon shared by his political adviser, Robert Murphy, by Byrnes, Stimson and McCloy, and by the new president, Harry S Truman. These views expressed a scale of priorities which was adhered to with only minor variations, and which guided the American occupation far more than did specific provisions of JCS 1067. First, Germany was to be made governable by the restoration of order and of a working economy; the future was to be left to inter-Allied agreement. But if this restoration were carried out separately in the various zones, it would undoubtedly assume various forms, and future agreement would become even more difficult to attain. In the absence of the "uniformity of action" stipulated in the Allied postsurrender agreement,[2] the short-term programs would go far to determine the long-range results.

At the final meeting of the Big Three at Potsdam between July 16 and August 2, 1945, the lack of uniformity was already in evidence and contributed to the ensuing virtual stalemate. Of the wartime leaders, only Stalin remained. Truman had succeeded Roosevelt in April, and British elections during the conference brought Clement Atlee to the prime ministership as head of a new Labour government. Both Atlee, who had served in the war cabinet and played a key role in postwar planning, and Truman, who had little time to acquaint himself with the basic issues, were in theory determined to follow the policies of their predecessors, but some changes, at least in the American approach, were evident almost at once.

Truman of necessity relied more than Roosevelt had on the State Department and was more readily influenced by the moderate views

1. Clay to James F. Byrnes, April 20, 1945, and Clay to John J. McCloy, April 26, 1945, in *The Papers of General Lucius D. Clay,* 2 vols., ed. Jean Edward Smith (Bloomington, Ind., 1974), 1:6, 8.

2. Statement by the Governments of the United Kingdom, the United States, the U.S.S.R., and the Provisional Government of the French Republic on Control Machinery in Germany, June 5, 1945, in *Documents on Germany under the Occupation, 1945–1954,* ed. Beate Ruhm von Oppen (London, 1955), p. 36.

concerning the treatment of Germany which prevailed there. That influence was all the more apparent after he appointed Byrnes secretary of state for domestic political reasons and accepted Morgenthau's resignation on July 5, rather than take the more militant treasury secretary with him to Potsdam. The new president, moreover, differed from his predecessor in personality, and America's dealings with the Allies underwent a change of style. Nonetheless, Truman went to the conference to carry forward the Roosevelt policy of reaching broad agreement with the Soviet Union and fitting a denazified, demilitarized, and democratized Germany, stripped of much of its industrial potential, into a new European order that Great Britain and the Soviet Union would jointly supervise.

By July 1945, however, Truman had also confronted the chaos in Germany, the presence of the Red Army in the heart of Central Europe, and the necessity of removing the bulk of American troops to carry on the war against Japan. Already suspicious of the behavior of the Russians, he was determined to do nothing that would further strengthen the Soviet position in Europe. That determination was shared by Atlee and by the new British foreign secretary, Ernest Bevin, both of whom were worried that Britain's role in the future Europe would be sharply curtailed if Russian dominance were permitted to grow. At the same time Stalin was intent on maximizing the physical security of the Soviet Union by building up a massive buffer zone and was more mistrustful than ever of his wartime allies.

The various differences came into sharpest focus in discussions about reparations. The Soviet Union regarded reparations as essential, not merely for weakening Germany but also for rebuilding the devasted regions of western Russia, and was particularly anxious to dismantle and acquire a share of the substantial industrial resources of the Ruhr. The United States and Britain were convinced that Germany was already economically weaker than was necessary. Both nations also controlled zones that (unlike the Soviet Union's) were not capable of producing sufficient food to sustain themselves. Consequently America and Britain saw reparations from their zones as drains on their own economies and, in effect, as a subsidy for the Soviet Union. Moreover, while the Russians counted on dismantled German equipment for reconstruction at home, the United States was already considering the output of a restored German industry as essential to reconstruction in Western Europe.

The issue was skirted in a compromise, proposed by Byrnes, that coupled reparations with other matters in dispute. It gave Poland "administrative control" over large parts of Pomerania and Silesia which lay east of the Oder and Neisse rivers, allowed Italy to join the United Nations, and placed limits on reparations. The Russians were granted, beyond what they could extract from their own zone, only 25 percent "of such usable and complete industrial capital equipment . . . as is unnecessary for the German peace economy," of which two-fifths was to be exchanged for agricultural and mineral products. Not only was the definition of "unnecessary" left for all practical purposes to the Western zonal commanders, it was specifically provided that "payment of reparations should leave enough resources to enable the German people to subsist without external assistance." As to political matters, the conference adopted a version of JCS 1067, with all its ambiguities intact, including the agreement to "prepare for the eventual reconstruction of German political life on a democratic basis and for eventual peaceful cooperation in international life by Germany."[3]

At Potsdam, Germany was specifically defined as a single economic unit and even treated, over the protests of the French, as a single, though decentralized, political unit. Nevertheless, the earlier agreements that gave the zonal commanders authority to act in all cases where no agreement had been reached by the Allied Control Council permitted the occupying powers to follow their own courses. The Potsdam agreement, in short, granted the Soviet Union the boundaries in Eastern Europe which could not have been denied it in any case, left much of the reparations settlement—and the future of German industry—to the Western powers who controlled the Ruhr and Saar, and tacitly allowed all the occupying powers to tailor policy in their zones to their own needs. It is hardly surprising, therefore, that separate "Germanies" began to emerge almost at once.

To be sure, Clay remained convinced at least until November 1946 that cooperation with the Soviet Union was possible. He felt that the United States had much to gain from "the true unification of Germany under quadripartite control" and that a major effort to reach agreement should continue to be made. Byrnes still expressed optimism in January of the following year "that we can achieve a just

3. Protocol of proceedings, August 1, 1945, in *Foreign Relations of the United States: Conference of Berlin (Potsdam), 1945*, 2:1485–1486, 1482.

peace by cooperative effort if we persist with firmness in the right as God gives us to see the right," and the Russians might well have said the same thing, albeit without reference to the deity.[4] But neither such hopes and assumptions nor endless negotiations about reparations, economic unity, "levels of industry," all-German elections, and a possible German peace treaty did anything to alter the fact that, in the absence of a basic agreement among the victorious nations, the Soviet Union constructed a communist state out of its occupation zone, and the United States, with the cooperation of the British and the reluctant agreement of the French, a democratic-capitalist one out of the Western zones.

Indeed, the only example of successful East-West cooperation on more than a minor scale in the year following the end of the war was the International Military Tribunal, which conducted the trials of twenty-two surviving "major Nazi war criminals" at Nuremberg between November 20, 1945, and October 1, 1946. Although the Russians had at first been reluctant to join even in this American-inspired endeavor and were less interested in legal niceties than in the liquidation of the offenders, the ten-month trial was a genuinely cooperative effort. It resulted in the conviction of nineteen of the defendants, twelve of whom were to be hanged, and the acquittal of three. Further it succeeded at least to a degree in condemning the Nazi regime as a criminal conspiracy and in establishing the principle that political and military leaders bear responsibility for criminal acts performed as part of a national policy. It was also the only instance since their surrender when the defeated Germans faced the united front of the victorious Allies.

But the Nuremberg trials involved denazification and demilitariation—the only areas of even proximate agreement between the Western powers and the Soviet Union—and they were an attempt to liquidate the past, not to construct the future. Where even denazification impinged directly on future plans, that is, at the lower and local levels, it too became an area of disagreement among the powers. "During an arduous and exacting year," a contemporary observer noted, "the representatives of the four Powers worked harmoniously together and for the most part of that time Nuremberg was the only place where they worked harmoniously together."[5]

The early steps along the road to division were certainly clear.

4. Clay for Byrnes, November 1946, in *Clay Papers*, 1:284; Byrnes, speech of January 11, 1947, in *Department of State Bulletin*, 16 (January 11, 1947): 88.

5. Peter Calvocoressi, *Nuremberg* (New York, 1948), p. 116.

The Soviet Union allowed the reestablishment of "antifascist" political parties and "free" trade unions on June 10, 1945, and set up German Central Administrations—that is, ministries—in such fields as transportation, industry, education, and the like, the following month. The Russians plainly hoped, and for a brief time expected, that these institutions would acquire an all-German character and provide the basis for a single German state acceptable to the Soviet Union.

Such hopes were unrealistic. Not only did the French veto in the Allied Control Council all steps to reconstitute Germany, but the restrictions that Soviet authorities imposed on the parties and unions, the support they gave to militantly Communist groups and leaders, and the initial policies that the German Central Administrations were compelled to carry out presaged the Sovietization of the Russian zone of occupation. By nationalizing all banks, promoting a land reform under which estates larger than two hundred fifty acres were confiscated, converting some ten thousand private businesses into "People's Enterprises" (VEB) or "Soviet Joint Stock Companies" (SAG), and staffing their Central Administrations largely with Communist functionaries (some of the leading ones newly returned from exile in Moscow), the Russians made it unlikely at best that their model would find acceptance in the West.

There the process of restoring some form of responsibility to the Germans was proceeding more slowly and less systematically. Political parties made sporadic appearances at the local level only in the late summer of 1945. German administrators—among them Fritz Schaeffer and Konrad Adenauer—were appointed and then dismissed for reasons reflecting no clear lines of policy. Major reforms were not immediately instituted. Nevertheless, the individuals appointed to office or permitted to participate in the formation of political parties, as well as the policies promoted in order to shape future German political and economic development, conformed to a very different model from that of the Russians. The results of this process were evident by the early months of 1946.

On April 21 of that year, the Soviet Union formalized the forced merger of the Social Democratic and the Communist parties in its zone into the Communist-dominated Socialist Unity party (SED). Under the guidance of Moscow this party was henceforth to bear responsibility for the political development of Eastern Germany. Clay, with the subsequent approval of Byrnes, in May ordered the suspension of reparations deliveries from the U.S. zone. On June 30 the Russians formally closed the boundaries between their zone and the three Western ones and moved officially to take reparations from current production in their zone. On July 12 Byrnes asked the other powers to unite their zones economically with the American one and received a positive reply from Great Britain. That combination of actions, whatever their intended purposes, made it virtually certain that there would be separate economic and political development in East and West Germany. The creation of a bizonal economic structure, which followed rapidly in the West, required ever greater administrative participation by Germans and thus offered, as a contemporary observer correctly noted, "the platform on which a German *political* organization, crossing state and zonal boundaries, could be created—even if it were in the provisional form of a rump polity."[6] In the East, economics and politics were indivisible in any case.

The speech by Byrnes at Stuttgart on September 6, which has generally been interpreted as signaling the revision of America's postwar policy toward Germany, merely expressed what had already begun in the American and British zones, had its counterpart in the Russian, and would start in the French as well. As the secretary of state told his listeners:

> Germany is part of Europe and recovery in Europe, and particularly in the states adjoining Germany, will be slow indeed if Germany . . . is turned into a poor house.
>
> We favor the economic unification of Germany. If complete unification cannot be secured, we shall do everything in our power to secure the maximum possible unification. . . .
>
> It is the view of the American Government that the German people throughout Germany, under proper safeguards, should be given primary responsibility for the running of their own affairs.[7]

The further implementation of such policies led directly to the formation of two German states by 1949.

If the German Democratic Republic was both the creation and the client of the Soviet Union, the Federal Republic of Germany had a similar relationship to the United States. The American government, of course, sought and ultimately obtained the assistance of

6. Fritz Rene Allemann, *Bonn Ist Nicht Weimar* (Cologne, 1956), p. 51. Original emphasis.

7. Byrnes, Stuttgart speech; restatement of policy on Germany, September 6, 1946, in *Documents on Germany*, pp. 156, 155, 157.

Great Britain and France, and of the West Germans themselves, in setting up the new state. But given its dominant economic and military position, its promotion of European economic recovery in the face of a perceived Soviet threat, and its belief that a Germany tied to the West was essential to this recovery, the United States remained the prime mover.

Within six months of Byrnes's speech, the Truman Doctrine in effect renounced hope of early accommodation with the Russians anywhere in the world. And the fourth conference of foreign ministers, meeting in Moscow, underlined the impossibility of basic agreement on Germany, not merely with the Soviet Union but also with France. "The recovery of Europe has been far slower than had been expected," lamented the new secretary of state, George C. Marshall, after listing the points of disagreement. "The patient is sinking while the doctors deliberate. So I believe that action cannot await compromise through exhaustion."[8]

The announcement of the Marshall Plan for Western European recovery through economic cooperation and infusions of American aid—intended both to forestall Russian expansion and to allay French fears—followed within six weeks. So did the invitation to the three Western occupation zones in Germany to participate. On July 12 representatives of fifteen western European nations meeting with those of the United States in Paris agreed that "in order for European cooperation to be effective, the German economy should be integrated into the European economy." One day earlier, JCS 1067 had been replaced by JCS 1779, a new directive that informed a less than surprised General Clay that "as a positive program requiring urgent action the United States Government seeks the creation of those political, economic and moral conditions in Germany which will contribute most effectively to a stable and prosperous Europe."[9]

The creation of a West German state entered its final phase the following April when, in the aftermath of the Communist coup in Czechoslovakia, representatives of the United States, Britain, France, and the Benelux countries (Belgium, the Netherlands, and Luxembourg) met in London to plan the transformation of an expanded Bizonia, the newly merged British and American occupation

8. Marshall, extracts from radio broadcast, April 28, 1947, in ibid., pp. 226–227.

9. Paris protocol, quoted in André Piettre, *L'économie allemande contemporaine (Allemagne Occidentale), 1945–1952* (Paris, 1952), p. 475; JCS 1779, July 11, 1947, in U.S. Department of State, *Germany 1947–1949: The Story in Documents,* Publication 3556, European and British Commonwealth Series 9 (Washington, 1950), p. 34.

zones, into a political entity. On June 4, 1948, they announced agreement on unifying all three Western zones under a constitution to be devised by the Germans and on bringing the new "Germany" fully into the European Recovery Program. Two weeks later, they decreed a currency reform designed to make economic recovery possible in West Germany.

The Soviet Union made every effort to stop these developments. It quit the Allied Control Council on March 28, continued to apply strong diplomatic pressure on the West, and threatened the Germans with permanent division. None of these actions proved effective, however, and the most serious and most dramatic of them was wholly counterproductive. On June 24 the Russians cut off all land and water access to the city of Berlin, thus virtually blockading the city and exposing the 2.5 million residents of its western sectors to economic ruin and even starvation. The move also threatened the American, British, and French garrisons, and was designed to force their withdrawal. The Allied response came in the form of an airlift, which over a ten-month period carried 275,000 plane loads of food, coal, machinery, and raw materials into the city, and large quantities of commercial exports out of it.

The airlift not merely foiled the Russian blockade attempt, but greatly strengthened the support of the Western Allies in Germany. Not only were the Berliners thoroughly converted to opposition to the Soviet Union and support for the United States and Britain, but many of West Germany's emerging leaders were also impressed by the strength and reliability of the Allies and more prepared than before to consider a rump Germany tied to the West. In any event, the minister-presidents of the German states that lay in the Western occupation zones were "authorized" on July 2, just five days after the airlift began with the delivery of eighty tons of supplies, "to convene a constituent assembly to be held no later than 1 September . . . to draft a democratic constitution which will establish for the participating states a governmental structure of the federal type. . . ."[10] After approval by the military governors, the constitution was to be submitted to the voters for ratification.

This call for the creation of a West German state reflected primarily the needs and desires of the United States, the center-piece of whose Cold War strategy it had become. Great Britain, whose economic weakness and disintegrating empire dictated ever greater re-

10. Directives Regarding the Future Political Organization of Germany, dated July 2, 1948, in State Department, *Germany 1947–1949*, pp. 315–318.

liance on American protection of its international interests, supported the idea in principle if not always in detail, while France was a most reluctant partner in the enterprise. Despite growing external and internal Communist threats to their own stability, only the promise of massive Marshall Plan aid, the assurance that the economic revival of the Ruhr and Saar regions would be shared by France, and the American commitment to a North Atlantic Alliance—the security pact France had sought in vain for thirty years—led the French to overcome their fear that any German state would sooner or later pose an economic and military danger.

German leaders were equally reluctant. Only a handful outside the Communist and Socialist parties in the Soviet zone favored an eastward orientation for a revived Germany, but a substantially larger number held that a neutral Germany functioning as a bridge between East and West was the only alternative that would restore German unity and permit free development. Even pro-Western leaders showed little genuine enthusiasm for a step that might well seal the permanent division of their country. Their reluctance was clearly demonstrated by various delaying tactics against which Clay repeatedly marshalled his persuasiveness and his power. It was equally evident in the Germans' insistence that a government rather than a state be established, that they draft a "basic law" rather than a constitution, and that the "provisional" nature of the entire enterprise be emphasized by avoiding a popular referendum, in which even this *Grundgesetz* might have failed of adoption.

American policy initiatives not only led to the establishment of a West German state, they also defined its contours. The United States insisted on a federal structure—complete with checks and balances and a system of judicial review—because its own experience led it to equate such a system with democracy. Moreover, the U.S. regarded centralization, whether under the kaiser or under Hitler, as the key to German militarism and aggression. The French, for their part, preferred a weak confederation as the best safeguard against German resurgence. Great Britain's Labour government, and the Germans themselves, accepted a federal structure but envisioned a central government with far greater powers, particularly in the social and economic spheres, than the American model provided.

In the final analysis, the United States prevailed with respect to the form of the new state and to its economic system as well. Left to their own devices, the Germans undoubtedly would have provided in their "basic law" for substantial government ownership and control of major industries. Great Britain favored such a course as consistent both with earlier German experience and with British postwar expectations. Clay, however, had for all practical purposes already vetoed socialization in the state of Hesse, which had written it into its 1947 constitution with 71 percent voter approval. He had "postponed" not only the socialization measures adopted in Berlin, but also those—involving much of West Germany's coal and steel industries—that the British had supported in the newly created state of North Rhine–Westphalia in their zone. The United States had promoted economic development for Bizonia on a free-market basis over British objections and those of the leadership of the German Social Democratic party (SPD). It now successfully insisted that the new federal constitution make no provision for socialization and bestow no powers that would make it readily possible. Clearly, "American concepts structured the framework in which bourgeois democracy developed in West Germany."[11]

The Federal Republic as Client State

The Federal Republic of Germany, which thus came into existence in September 1949, remained for a considerable time America's client state. Under the terms of the original occupation statute the United States, Great Britain, and France reserved "supreme authority" to themselves and specifically retained supervisory control over such fundamental matters as foreign trade and exchange, demilitarization, restrictions on industry and, above all, "foreign affairs, including international agreements made by or on behalf of Germany." More than that, they reserved the right "to resume, in whole or in part, the exercise of full authority if they consider that to do so is essential to security or to preserve democratic government in Germany *or in pursuit of the international obligations of their governments.*"[12] As one of the occupying powers—and certainly the strongest one—the United States could thus readily dominate the German-American relationship.

11. Stanley H. Sisson, "Chronological History in Regard to Socialization Program in Hesse," December 13, 1948, Office of Military Government Economics Division file, box 2403, RG 260, NA; Ernst-Otto Czempiel, "Die Bundesrepublik und Amerika: Von der Okkupation zur Kooperation," in Richard Löwenthal and Hans-Peter Schwarz, eds., *Die zweite Republik* (Stuttgart, 1974), p. 561.
12. Draft Occupation Statute Defining the Respective Powers and Responsibilities of the Future German Government and the Allied Control Authority, April 8, 1949, in *Documents on Germany*, pp. 375–377. Emphasis added.

The circumstances of the creation of the Federal Republic and the perceived needs of the United States nevertheless made a degree of mutuality and cooperation likely from the outset. Konrad Adenauer, who served as chancellor during the first fourteen years of the new state's existence, had risen to his position of leadership in the Christian Democratic party (CDU), in the Parliamentary Council, and then in the government in no small measure because of his effectiveness in dealing with the Americans, and with at least tacit American support. Ludwig Erhard, who served as economics minister during these years, had earlier been handpicked by the Americans to serve as director of the Bizonal economic administration. Because these dominant figures in the West German government, and most of the lesser ones as well, shared many of the ideas of their counterparts in Washington—not the least of which were fervent anticommunism, commitment to European integration, and devotion to the principles of the free market economy—the larger aims expressed by the two nations were not in serious conflict, and the relations between them showed a remarkable degree of cooperation and agreement.

For the Federal Republic, of course the primary aim after 1949 was to regain full sovereignty and, as after 1919, to restore its economy and international respectability. Beyond that, the new state sought to insure its own security, for which the closest possible ties with the West constituted at least a practical option. While France and other adjoining countries could never quite banish their fears that the fulfillment of these aims would create a dangerous neighbor, and Great Britain worried about restoring an economic rival, the United States, operating from greater strength, found these aims wholly compatible with its own.

Like thirty years before, a healthy and prosperous Germany— even a rump Germany—was now regarded in Washington as essential to the recovery of Western Europe—and that recovery was made all the more important by the growing conflict with the Soviet Union. America, moreover, had no interest in maintaining indefinitely its role as an occupying power and regarded European integration with German participation as the ideal solution to the problem of future European security. Also, since the United States, unlike in 1919, had confidence in the German leadership that had emerged, the decade after 1949 became one of extraordinarily close cooperation between the two countries.

The meshing of interests was illustrated, shortly after the formation of the new West German government, by the Petersberg Agreement, which set the stage for the end of the occupation, the rearmament of Germany, and its integration into NATO. In April 1949 the United States had joined Britain, France, and the Benelux countries in establishing an international authority to control the production and distribution of the output of the Ruhr region. "Germany," which thereby had been deprived of control over its major coal, iron, and steel producing area in order to assuage the fears of its neighbors, had without consultation been included in the authority and given three of the fifteen votes. These were to be cast as a bloc by a representative of the occupation authorities "until the Occupying Powers concerned determine that the [still nonexistent] German Government . . . has assumed the responsibilities placed upon Germany by the present Agreement."[13]

In November the newly installed Chancellor Adenauer offered to assume such responsibilities and thus to surrender future claims to full control over Ruhr production. He further agreed to bring the Federal Republic into the Council of Europe, a consultative body dealing with general European problems. In sum, he expressed West Germany's willingness to cooperate fully in the process of European integration, which was promoted by the United States and at least partly supported by other countries as a means of preventing German resurgence.

Adenauer's willingness to take these steps was not shared by his political opponents at home, who denounced the concession of German sovereignty over the Ruhr and the voluntary ties with the West which were likely to hinder reunification. The chancellor, however, was aware that he could expect significant concessions in return— concessions that clearly served West Germany's interests. Dean Acheson, Marshall's successor at the State Department, had persuaded his colleagues at a Paris meeting two weeks before to loosen somewhat the strings of the occupation and had paid his respects to Adenauer in unprecedented fashion during a visit to Bonn. By the Petersberg Agreement that followed, dismantlement was virtually stopped and West Germany was permitted to increase its shipbuilding activity, to enter into a bilateral agreement with the United States concerning economic assistance, and, most significant, to resume commercial and consular relations with other countries.

13. Draft Agreement for the Establishment of an International Authority for the Ruhr, signed April 28, 1949, in ibid., p. 448.

West German economic recovery was thereby accelerated, and the beginnings of the "economic miracle" *(Wirtschaftswunder)* both pleased the United States and muted opposition to Adenauer's policies at home. Although West Germany still pledged "to maintain demilitarisation of the federal territory and to endeavor by all means in its power to prevent the re-creation of armed forces of any kind,"[14] the United States was already considering German rearmament and NATO participation.

Even while Adenauer and the high commissioners were negotiating, General Clay discussed "a composite military force drawn from the nations of Western Europe, including Germany" with a reporter in Boston. Adenauer was not slow in taking up the theme. On December 3, he talked to an American reporter about "German armed forces . . . under a European command," and six days later insisted at a regional CDU meeting "that West German manpower be included in a European striking force against Russia."[15]

The Adenauer government and the American military leaders thus almost simultaneously mentioned the unmentionable in public. German demilitarization had been, along with denazification, the most unshakable of the Allies' aims, and German rearmament was repugnant to them as well as to most Germans. The logic of NATO, however, demanded the utilization of German troops. Without them, the anti-Soviet military alliance was unlikely to provide the necessary manpower, Great Britain and the United States would be required to maintain ever greater troop strength on the continent, and Germany itself could not be defended.

At the same time, West Germany could assure its own security vis-à-vis the Russians and the German Democratic Republic, whose *Volkspolizei* already constituted a sizable force of at least paramilitary character, only by rearming to some degree. It could, moreover, enhance its international standing most readily by making a military contribution to the defense of Western Europe and win sovereignty as the price for making that contribution. American interests and those of the Federal Republic thus ran parallel, although the idea of rearmament aroused widespread opposition in both Germany and the United States and understandable fears, particularly in France.

14. Protocol of Agreements Reached between the Allied High Commissioners and the Chancellor of the German Federal Republic at the Petersberg, November 22, 1949, in ibid., p. 439.

15. *New York Times,* November 20, 1949, p. 5; December 4, 1949, p. 23; December 10, 1949, pp. 1, 2.

The outbreak of the Korean War in June 1950 greatly strengthened the case for rearmament. Not only did the conflict reduce the ability of the United States to protect Western Europe, it raised the specter of Germany as a second Korea, with the German Democratic Republic as prospective Soviet surrogate in an invasion westward. By late summer, Acheson had become convinced of the necessity of German participation in European defense, and discussions concerning the nature of such participation were well under way. On August 29 Adenauer dispatched two memoranda to the Allied high commissioners, memoranda that dealt with the creation of a German federal police, a possible German "defense contribution," and the revision of the Federal Republic's relation to the occupying powers.

By early September the United States had formulated a policy for achieving all of these things, and Acheson promoted it at a conference with his British and French counterparts in New York. Though Bevin agreed only reluctantly, and France's Robert Schuman remained opposed at least to rearmament, the final communique of the conference proposed the ending of the state of war with Germany and modification of the occupation statute. Declaring that "the three Governments consider the Government of the Federal Republic as the only German Government freely and legitimately constituted and therefore entitled to speak for Germany . . . in international affairs," the foreign ministers agreed to increase the powers of the Bonn government by permitting, among other things, the establishment of a ministry of foreign affairs and of "mobile police formations" for purposes of "internal security." Furthermore, they agreed to study "the participation of the German Federal Republic in the common defense of Europe."[16] Both the United States and West Germany had reason to be pleased.

The road to German rearmament and the achievement of German sovereignty proved to be a rocky one, however, and the results were not always those envisaged in 1950 by either the United States or the Federal Republic. But the ultimate dependence of Western Europe on American economic and military resources, and the skill and determination of Konrad Adenauer, proved decisive. On March 6, 1951, the Occupation Statute was formally amended, a German

16. Extract from communique issued by the foreign ministers of Great Britain, the U.S., and France, September 19, 1950, in *Documents on Germany*, pp. 517–519.

ministry of foreign affairs established (with Adenauer as foreign minister), and the powers of the high commissioners greatly reduced. The Federal Republic could henceforth conduct its own foreign policy—though not yet with the occupying powers—and no longer needed prior approval for internal legislation. By May 1952 the Occupation Statute was replaced by five conventions that regulated West Germany's relations with its "allies," thus establishing the fledgling state more nearly as an independent power.

Three more years were to elapse before West German sovereignty became a reality, as France struggled mightily to prevent actual German rearmament. Its original Pleven Plan of 1950 had sought to limit any German military contribution to battalion-size units serving in an integrated European army. Under the European Defense Community (EDC) treaty, which was actually signed in 1952, such units could be of division strength, but the French remained adamant that no specifically Germany army or German general staff would ever be created again, and in the end vetoed even the EDC that they had themselves proposed.

The debate over these issues served, however, to strengthen German-American cooperation. Reminiscent of the situation after the First World War, the United States, contrary to the wishes of the French, supported Germany's insistence on equality of treatment, but this time the American engagement was full and direct. President Dwight D. Eisenhower, who took office in January 1953, and his secretary of state, John Foster Dulles, enthusiastically embraced plans for West European economic and military integration— including that of West Germany—and Dulles and Adenauer developed a particularly close relationship fostered by mutual admiration.

In one of its first moves, the new American administration invited Adenauer to a well-publicized twelve-day visit to Washington in April 1953, a visit designed not merely to impress the French and Russians, but also to strengthen the position of the chancellor in the upcoming German elections. Subsequent messages from both the president and the secretary of state hinting at new East-West negotiations and other steps leading to German reunification were intended to serve the same purpose, and in September Dulles went so far as to state publicly that defeat for Adenauer would have disastrous consequences. "The resonance which came from America to Germany was one of Adenauer's greatest aces in the campaign," a

German official noted, "because the Germans realized that the United States were putting their money, were so to speak betting on Konrad Adenauer."[17]

In the elections on September 6, the CDU scored a substantial victory, receiving 45.2 percent of the vote, versus only 28.8 percent for the opposition SPD. The outcome assured the continuation of a German government committed, as was the United States, to West European integration, to the raising of German military units, and to the Western alliance system. These policies were thus furthered and ultimately brought to fruition. In October 1954, after the French had scuttled the EDC, the foreign ministers of the United States, Britain, France, and the Federal Republic agreed to the end of the occupation and to the admission of West Germany to the Western European Union (WEU), originally designed to thwart German resurgence. Convinced now that the United States was determined to push for German rearmament and might pull its own ground troops out of Europe if that were not agreed to, the French accepted a proposal by the British prime minister, Anthony Eden, to convert the WEU into the framework for a "German defense contribution." On May 5, 1955, the occupation ended and the Western powers formally recognized German sovereignty. Four days later, the Federal Republic gained NATO membership.

Economic and Political Mutuality

The establishment of the Federal Republic as an independent state completed yet another transformation in the German-American relationship. The power imbalance between the two countries remained for some time far greater even than it had been in the 1920s and left West Germany almost wholly dependent on the United States. More important, the new German state conformed in large measure to the American democratic-capitalist model. That fact was both confirmed and strengthened in November 1959, when the Social-Democratic party (SPD), which opposed most of the foreign and domestic policies of the Adenauer government (and thus the plans for German redevelopment promoted by the United States), adopted its "Godesberg Program."

Concerned with the failure of the party to achieve electoral suc-

17. Felix von Eckhardt interview, Dulles Oral History Project, quoted in Roger Morgan, *The United States and West Germany, 1945–1973* (London, 1974), p. 42.

cess in a country in which the American model had taken firm root, the Socialists consciously sought to change their image from that of Marxist "worker's party" to that of a more centrist "people's party." They gave up their demands for the large-scale socialization of industry, dropped their antireligious position, and accepted a strong national defense. By June 1960, SPD spokesmen publicly applauded German membership in the Western alliance. Their electoral successes promptly increased. By 1966 they were invited to share in the government as part of a "Grand Coalition" with the CDU, and three years later their leader, Willy Brandt, was elected chancellor. The combination of German dependence and convergent political and economic systems brought the mutuality of interest between the United States and Germany to their highest point.

That mutuality was characterized by several major elements. In the first place, the Federal Republic operated under numerous restrictions imposed by the World War II victors, and two hundred fifty to three hundred thousand American troops remained in Germany—as allies, if no longer as occupiers. Moreover, the world situation and the overall power constellation remained the same as that which had led to the creation of the two Germanies. The perceived threat from the Soviet Union was not attenuated even when Moscow recognized the Federal Republic in September 1955, and German security continued to depend on the strength of the American commitment. Beyond that, the economic ties between the United States and the new state had become very strong. German internal stability and economic development were effectively bound to American aid, investments, and trade.

American economic aid had been a major factor in the creation of the Federal Republic, had made possible much of the work of reconstruction, and had provided the seed money for the *Wirtschaftswunder*. It was no accident that the very first matter of foreign policy taken up by the new Bundestag in 1949 had been the European Recovery Program Agreement concerning "economic cooperation" between the United States and the Federal Republic. Between 1946, when shipments of foodstuffs, primarily to Germany, began under the GARIOA (Government and Relief in Occupied Areas) program, through 1952, West Germany was the recipient of well over three billion dollars in American aid, nearly half of which came in four years under the Marshall Plan. Combined with the billion dollars in counterpart funds which this aid generated and which were developed into five billion dollars through expert German management by 1967, American aid played a major role in Germany's economic growth.

While dependence on American aid declined as the German economy flourished from the mid-fifties on, the economic ties between the two countries grew even stronger. Direct American capital investment climbed steadily after 1950 and reached a book value of over a billion dollars by 1960. At that point more than 3 percent of all American foreign investments were in West Germany. By the 1970s, the value of these investments at times exceeded $8 billion, approximately 7 percent of the U.S. total. In 1975, American firms owned or controlled 495 major companies in West Germany. Moreover, by then the stream of investment had ceased to be unidirectional. Beginning in the late 1950s a modest flow of German capital to the United States had begun, and this flow swelled in the decade after 1968. In 1975 German direct investments in the United States had reached over $1.25 billion, about 15 percent of the reverse flow. At the same time, the two countries were closely connected through trade.

Between 1950 and 1960, when American exports to Germany rose from an annual value of less than DM 1 billion to nearly DM 6 billion they constituted, on the average, over 14 percent of German imports. The percentage remained at about 12.5 for the succeeding decade. Only the spectacular rise in oil prices after 1972 brought America's percentage of Germany's imports into the single digit range. By that time, however, American exports to Germany approached an annual value of DM 15 billion.

German exports to the United States were initially on a more modest scale. Even in 1950, however, 5.2 percent of Germany's exports went to the United States, leaving a negative trade balance of nearly DM 1 billion. As the German economy expanded, the volume of exports grew rapidly, and by 1968, when the volume of trade between the two countries amounted to approximately DM 10 billion in each direction, Germany achieved a positive trade balance with the United States for the first time. At that point approximately 10 percent of the Federal Republic's exports went to the United States, where they constituted about 8 percent of total imports.

The increasing closeness of economic ties, the German dependence on the United States for its security, and the initial mutual admiration shown by Adenauer and Dulles provided the cement for a de facto German-American alliance and at times created a situation in which each nation regarded the other as its most dependable ally. Nevertheless, there were built-in strains in the relationship which manifested themselves almost as soon as the Federal Republic achieved sovereignty and which became more serious as German and even European problems became less central to the United States. The major issues that revealed these strains involved the German military contribution and its cost, and the Western powers' long-range relationship with the Soviet Union, which soon came to involve the possibility of détente.

In an effort to maximize the value of their potential military contribution and thus to gain sovereignty, the Germans had promised to raise an army of 500,000 men within two years and to make it available to NATO. For financial and other reasons this promise proved impossible to fulfill. Only 67,000 men had been raised by the end of 1956, even after Dulles had prodded Adenauer by appealing to the chancellor's concept of German self-interest. "A nation that does not possess adequate military forces of its own," the secretary of state had asserted, "cannot count as fully sovereign, but at best as a protectorate, which cannot speak with full voice in matters of foreign policy."[18] Only 120,000 German troops existed by 1957 and no more than 230,000 by the end of 1959.

At issue was more than a question of manpower. Cost early entered the discussion and soon became the major point of contention. The Germans initially adopted a three-year defense plan that provided for the establishment of military forces and projected a budget deficit. Since the raising of a German army had more support from NATO, and particularly from the United States, than it did from the Germans themselves, there was an initial expectation that the U.S. might offer to cover the deficit. Washington made clear that it had no such intention and insisted that the Germans pay not only for their own troops but, at least in part, for the American troops stationed in Germany.

As time went on and America's balance-of-payments deficit escalated sharply, the United States increased its insistence that Germany relieve it of some of the financial burdens. A request for $600 million in annual payments which Treasury Secretary Robert Anderson carried to Bonn in 1959 was turned down by Foreign Minister

18. Konrad Adenauer, *Erinnerungen*, 4 vols. (Stuttgart, 1965–1968), 3:164.

Heinrich von Brentano for what he termed "political and psychological reasons." Not until 1961 was an at least moderately satisfactory agreement reached, under which Germany offset some of the American costs by purchasing large amounts of American military equipment. Though the controversy had served as an irritant to German-American relations, and indeed continued to be one, this temporary resolution actually tied the two countries even more strongly together by assuring the permanent dependence of Germany's armed forces on weapons made in America.

Differences over military and financial matters were overshadowed by apparent shifts in America's global strategy. As early as 1956, the Radford Plan—Admiral William Radford was chairman of the Joint Chiefs of Staff—proposed a reduction in the conventional troop strength of the United States and greater reliance on nuclear deterrence. While this plan made some sense with respect to a general Western defense against the Soviet Union, it clearly suggested a strategy that did not include the defense of German territory and, indeed, threatened to turn Germany into a nuclear battlefield.

Adenauer protested vehemently, if somewhat disingenuously against such plans, insisting that they not only undercut the rationale on which the Germans had accepted rearmament—that is, that German troops were necessary to the defense of Germany—but also gave aid and comfort to the Social Democratic opposition and thus threatened both German stability and its commitment to the West. Even after the Radford Plan itself was shelved, the Germans argued strongly against American support for an independent British nuclear capability and acquiescence in a French one, unless the Federal Republic were also brought into the nuclear club.

Adenauer's concern intensified during 1957 and 1958 when various proposals surfaced which looked toward "normalization" of the situation in Central Europe through some sort of recognition of the German Democratic Republic and the ultimate neutralization of a reunified Germany. Such ideas were proposed not only by British Opposition Leader Hugh Gaitskell and Polish Foreign Minister Adam Rapacki, but also by George Kennan in his Reith Lectures at Oxford. Even Dulles seemed to give some support to the notion of recognizing the East German state, at least as "agent" of the Russians. Eisenhower, on a visit to Bonn, pushed for exchanges of persons between the two German states as a step leading toward eventual negotiations. Coupled with the secret talks conducted between Eisenhower's disarmament adviser, Harold Stassen, and the Russians, this initiative by the secretary of state seemed to presage a shift in American policy which might well undermine the security and even the existence of the Federal Republic.

The problem was heightened by Soviet Premier Nikita Khrushchev's Berlin ultimatum of November 27, 1958, which demanded either the incorporation of West Berlin into the German Democratic Republic or the reconstitution of all Berlin into a "free city." Further, it threatened a treaty with East Germany within six months which would allow annexation of all Berlin and the cutting off of access from the West if these demands were not met. The Western powers, of course, rejected the ultimatum but, over Adenauer's objections, offered to discuss the Berlin matter with the Soviets in the broader context of the "German question" and the issue of European security. The chancellor saw his policy so threatened that he made overtures to French General Charles de Gaulle by telling him that "he had had differences with Dulles over American policy toward Russia." In addition, Adenauer launched his abortive attempt to secure the German presidency "for reasons of state necessity, to ensure the continuity of our policy."[19] The simultaneous retirement of the mortally ill Dulles provided Adenauer no reassurance at all.

Neither did it help matters when the Western powers agreed to a new conference of foreign ministers at Geneva in the summer of 1959, at which representatives of both Germanies would be present as "advisers." The Herter Plan, which was presented by the United States at Geneva—Christian Herter had succeeded Dulles in April—did reiterate the earlier American position that German reunification through free elections was a precondition for any negotiations on political or military disengagement. And such negotiations as did actually take place in Geneva produced no visible result. Nevertheless, the very idea that accommodation with the Soviets would now be sought through negotiations in which the interests of the Federal Republic per se were not of central concern sharply illustrated that German and American aims, however closely related, were not identical.

The United States had worked to create the Federal Republic both to ensure the containment of the Soviet Union in Europe and to

19. Ibid., 429–435; Adenauer to Dulles, April 15, 1959, in John Foster Dulles Papers, Catalog 2 (Correspondence), Princeton University Library, Princeton, N.J.

eliminate the "German problem" by tying the new state firmly into a Western European framework. Under Adenauer's leadership, the West Germans had embraced this scheme as promoting their own security, their economic recovery, and their political rehabilitation, all believed to be useful for making eventual reunification possible. Although these aims resulted in virtually identical policies through the mid-fifties and produced the short-term results desired by both countries, the basic rationales of the two nations were different. Once its initial plans for Germany were realized, the United States could explore alternate ways of dealing with the Soviet Union, so long as those alternatives did not threaten to create a new German problem. On the other hand, any alternative that did not contribute to strengthening the West German position or that suggested, however faintly, that the existence of two Germanies must be accepted as a fait accompli was regarded by the Federal Republic as contrary to its interests.

The tensions that arose periodically between the United States and the Federal Republic in the two decades after the end of the occupation are, without serious exception, explainable in these terms. As the world changed in the 1960s and immediate postwar priorities were replaced by new and pressing concerns, the original parameters of the German-American relationships became less and less relevant. The relationship nonetheless remained a remarkably friendly and stable one. That is attributable to the firm economic and political ties that had developed between the two countries and to the fact that the Federal Republic, despite spectacular economic successes and gratifying international acceptance, remained in fundamental ways dependent on the United States. In the final analysis, the Federal Republic even accepted the new American priority of détente and, after Adenauer's departure from the scene, embarked on its own "Ostpolitik."

Détente and Ostpolitik

By the early 1960s the political and economic stabilization of Europe, the rough nuclear balance between the United States and the Soviet Union, the multiplication of newly independent "third world" countries, and the Sino-Soviet rift had given the cold war a far less Eurocentric character. Under those circumstances it was scarcely surprising that at least superficial cracks in German-American cooperation should appear.

The new American president, John F. Kennedy, recognized more clearly than his predecessors had that the realistic interests of the United States required, at least as a first step toward greater stability and peace, the maintenance of the world balance that had been achieved, and that maintenance required both the strengthening of American capabilities and efforts to reach some form of accommodation with the Soviet Union. Although circumstances initially compelled him to respond, on an ad hoc basis, to a series of crises in Cuba, Laos, the Congo, and Berlin, the new approach became visible in Berlin, as well as in the final abandonment of Dulles's doctrine of "massive retaliation." In place of that strategy—always more rhetorical than real—came the notion of "flexible response," proposed by General Maxwell Taylor, who became chairman of the Joint Chiefs of Staff, and ardently espoused by Defense Secretary Robert McNamara and the president himself. For the Federal Republic, however, such an approach presaged both the weakening of America's "nuclear umbrella"—which West Germany regarded as essential to its own survival and in which it clearly wanted a share—and an arrangement with the Soviet Union which would in all likelihood make the division of Germany permanent.

Both of these elements emerged clearly in Kennedy's response to the Berlin crisis. In his meeting with the president in Vienna in June 1961, Khrushchev had reiterated in no uncertain terms his determination to sign a peace treaty with the German Democratic Republic, Such a treaty would terminate Western rights in Berlin unless one with "the two German states" could be concluded which would make Berlin a "free demilitarized city."[20] Kennedy rejected this threat not only verbally but with actions designed to shore up the military position of the United States in Europe. Although the president was adamant about preserving Western rights in West Berlin, however, the "three essentials" he was determined to uphold did not include Western rights in all of Berlin, a key precondition for a reunited Germany. The Federal Republic thus found itself in opposition to the implications of the American actions, while depending on these actions to maintain even a foothold in Berlin.

Khrushchev read the American position correctly and permitted the East Germans to build their "wall" across Berlin on August 13. The barrier not only halted the drain of German minds and labor to

20. Khrushchev memorandum for Kennedy, June 3, 1961, in *Germany and Eastern Europe since 1945*, Keesing's Research Report (New York, 1973), p. 171.

the West; it gave the division of Germany a new physical reality. As he expected, the Western response, though outraged and firm, consisted of nothing more than a reaffirmation of Western rights in *West* Berlin. Mayor Willy Brandt poignantly appealed to Kennedy that "after accepting a Soviet step that is illegal and has been called illegal, and in view of the many tragedies that are now taking place in East Berlin and the Soviet Zone, we cannot avoid the risk of extreme resoluteness" with respect to Germany as a whole.[21] But his plea fell on deaf ears.

Insistence on German reunification now would threaten all that had been gained and make any accommodation with the Soviet Union all but impossible. When Khrushchev in November postponed indefinitely the signing of a peace treaty with East Germany, the wisdom of Kennedy's course seemed confirmed. The West German assumption that the establishment of the Federal Republic would create conditions conducive to eventual reunification, though dubious from the beginning, was, however, a cornerstone of the new state. Its abandonment now came hard and pushed German-American relations to a low point in the late spring and summer of 1962.

In April the United States and the Soviet Union were conducting multilevel negotiations in both Moscow and Washington. The U.S. sought a settlement of the only partially defused Berlin crisis within the framework of a general European settlement. The secret working papers for these discussions were routinely passed on for comment to America's allies, including the Federal Republic. One paper, calling for nonaggression declarations between the Warsaw Pact and NATO, a pledge by the U.S. and the U.S.S.R. not to give nuclear weapons to third parties, and the establishment of all-German committees to deal with technical issues arising between the two existing German states, was unceremoniously leaked to the press by Heinrich von Brentano, the CDU/CSU Parliamentary Group chairman in an effort to undercut scheduled negotiations between Secretary of State Dean Rusk and the new Russian ambassador in Washington, Anatoly Dobrynin.

The indiscretion was due in part to the Germans' pique at having been given a mere twenty-four hours to respond to the proposal. More basic, however, was their fear that they—and NATO—would

21. Brandt to Kennedy, August 16, 1961, in Peter Rassow, ed., *Deutsche Geschichte im Überblick*, 3d ed. (Stuttgart, 1973), pp. 799–800.

forever be excluded from control of the nuclear weapons on which
their security depended and that all-German committees meant tacit
recognition of the German Democratic Republic. A strong American
protest of the German action in turn led Adenauer, in early May, to
make a series of speeches in which he condemned American policy
in general and negotiations with the Russians in particular, and, in
the words of one observer, "smashed as much alliance-policy porce-
lain as he could."[22] Immediately thereafter, Germany's ambassador,
Wilhelm Grewe, was recalled at Washington's request.

This diplomatic tempest, though it involved issues of fundamental
concern to Germany, had calmed by the end of the year, for a
variety of reasons. First, Adenauer's position was weakening, for he
had retained the chancellorship after the elections of 1961 only on
condition that he resign within two years. Also responsible were the
succession of the pro-American Gerhard Schröder to the foreign
ministry and the resignation after a domestic scandal of the hard-
lining defense minister, Franz Josef Strauss. In part, also, the end of
the dispute resulted from the success of the America policy of seeking meaningful negotiations with the Russians—a success particularly evident after Khrushchev's retreat in the Cuban Missile Crisis
of October 1962 led him to drop the threat of an East German peace
treaty altogether and to consider seriously the banning of nuclear
testing.

Fundamentally however, the reestablishment of cordial cooperation between the United States and Germany issued from the Germans' realization that their interests had ultimately to be maintained
and promoted within the parameters of world policy established by
the United States. Adenauer's long-cherished alternative—the alliance with France—though formalized in a treaty of friendship on
January 22, 1963, was no alternative of all. If the United States was
no longer fully committed to German reunification, France had
never been. America could at least maintain the security of the
Federal Republic, while France, despite de Gaulle's now independent nuclear *force de frappe,* could not. The period of American
hegemony was not yet over.

Though the Federal Republic was still not ready to recognize the
existence of two Germanies or to concede that the postwar territorial arrangements, in particular the setting of the Polish border at the

22. Herbert von Borch, "Anatomie der Entzweiung," *Aussenpolitik* 13, no. 6
(1962): 360.

Oder-Neisse line, were permanent, modest moves toward a rapprochement with Eastern Europe and even with the German Democratic Republic (DDR) became apparent by 1963. Schröder negotiated a trade agreement with Poland in March of that year, followed by similar pacts with Romania in October, Hungary in November, and Bulgaria in March 1964. The signing of these agreements was followed by the establishment of West German trade missions in these countries and thus by at least an implicit retreat from the so-called Hallstein Doctrine, under which the Federal Republic had declined to maintain diplomatic relations with any country that recognized its East German counterpart.

At the same time, an agreement was reached to allow citizens of West Berlin to pay a Christmas visit to East Berlin. It was an agreement that, despite the face-saving formula agreed to by both sides, represented more of an acknowledgement than the Federal Republic had been prepared to make earlier that two separate states existed in Germany. The road was thus opened which was to lead to the resumption of diplomatic relations with the Eastern European countries, beginning with Romania and Yugoslavia in 1967. This road also led, although no German leader was as yet prepared to say so publicly, to the recognition of the German Democratic Republic, on December 21, 1972.

Germany's new Ostpolitik was built on the initiatives taken by Schröder and carried to its logical conclusion by Brandt, as foreign minister in the "Grand Coalition" government from 1966 to 1969 and as chancellor from 1969 to 1974. The German policy meshed in significant ways with that of détente—foreshadowed by Kennedy, promoted by Lyndon Johnson between 1963 and 1969, and carried to fruition by Richard Nixon and his secretary of state, Henry Kissinger, from 1969 to 1974. In combination, these policies led to the European peace settlement that had eluded the world since the end of World War II and thus formally decided the future of Germany.

By the so-called Eastern Treaties with Poland and the Soviet Union, the Federal Republic accepted both the Oder-Neisse line and the border between itself and the German Democratic Republic. Through its various treaties with the DDR, culminating in a final "Basic Treaty," it formally recognized the existences of two separate German states. The United States meanwhile achieved agreement with the Soviet Union on a nuclear nonproliferation treaty and on SALT I, and it settled permanently, through a four-power treaty on September 3, 1971, the status of Berlin. Neither set of accomplishments would have been possible without the other. One year after the Federal Republic had done so, the United States established diplomatic relations with the German Democratic Republic.

In the process of achieving exit from the impasse into which both American and West German policies had fallen by 1960, the two states moved into a new phase of cooperation with each other. If the United States remained the senior partner in the alliance, the initiatives taken by the Federal Republic gave it both greater stature and greater independence. As a result, disagreements between the now more equal allies increased. Continued controversy over offset payments and over Germany's sharing the costs of the American military presence escalated as the Vietnam War raised the United States's balance-of-payments deficit. Washington at times tried hard to put a brake on Brandt's dealings with the Soviet Union, lest in his anxiety to further his Ostpolitik Brandt be tempted in the direction of another Rapallo. And the Federal Republic fought strenuously against the terms of the nuclear nonproliferation treaty.

But in the final analysis, the matter of burden-sharing was substantially settled by an agreement in 1971. Brandt remained true to the Western alliance in his dealings with the Soviet Union, and the fate of the nuclear nonproliferation treaty illustrates how basically firm the alliance had become.

The signing of this treaty in 1968 was the major step on the road to détente by the Johnson administration. The Federal Republic strenuously objected to the treaty not only because it would permanently deny the West Germans access to the nuclear weapons they believed they needed for their own defense, but also because the treaty called for inspection by the International Atomic Energy Agency, which they believed would be used by the Soviet Union for industrial espionage. Even more important, the West German government feared that the expected accession by the German Democratic Republic would imply diplomatic recognition by the other signatories, and thereby undercut its own Ostpolitik. The Soviet Union, for its part, refused to ratify the agreement unless the Federal Republic, whose rearmament remained Russia's bête noire, signed first.

Through controversy developed between Washington and Bonn, the Nixon administration chose not to bring pressure on the Germans. Instead, it successfully persuaded the Soviet Union that simultaneous ratification by the U.S. and the U.S.S.R.—or at least the appearance of it—would induce the Germans to sign. The two powers duly announced that their ratification procedures were completed in November 1969. Brandt in his turn recognized that, under the circumstances, refusal to sign would drastically weaken his position in future dealings with the Soviet Union. The German signature was quietly appended. Both Washington and Moscow then permitted the Germans to defer their final ratification until the complete settlement of European matters was in place early in 1973. Clearly the Federal Republic had become a full partner in the Western alliance, which the United States continued to lead. Clearly that view was accepted in Moscow. And it prevailed in Bonn—and in Washington.

Continuity and Change

Late in 1974, John Sherman Cooper became the first American ambassador in thirty-six years to take up residence in Berlin, now the capital of the German Democratic Republic. His arrival there did nothing to alter the essential fact that, for the United States, the successor state to Hitler's Third Reich was the Federal Republic that America had helped to create, just as that Reich had been, through several removes, the successor to eighteenth-century Prussia, whose capital of Berlin had received John Quincy Adams in 1799.

For nearly two centuries the two countries had had substantial impact on each other, and their relationship had been a factor of consequence in international affairs. The ties of spiritual kinship, which loomed so large in the thinking of Americans about Germany in the first half of the nineteenth century, were as unrealistic as the demonic image of the Germans entertained in America during the two world wars of this century. And the German counterviews were no more firmly grounded. Nevertheless, the record of the relationship between the two countries over a period during which both went through profound and sometimes cataclysmic changes is one in which basic continuities, when properly understood, outweigh the more obviously apparent shifts.

The United States consistently supported the development of a more or less united, democratic, and economically viable Germany and maintained that position against the contrary views of, in particular, the French and the Russians in both the nineteenth and twentieth centuries. America turned against Germany only when such aims were not shared by Germany's rulers, whether William II or Adolf Hitler. The Germans, for their part, with two brief though notable exceptions, sought cooperation with and assistance from the United States. From Bismarck's drive for German unity, William II's courtship of Theodore Roosevelt, the policy of "fulfillment" of the 1920s, through Adenauer's quest for European integration, to Brandt's Ostpolitik, the Germans looked to the United States for support in an often unfriendly world. By the mid-1970s, with both countries for the first time endowed with comparable political, economic, and even social institutions, such continuities appeared unlikely to be broken.

Bibliographical Essay

A large number of archival sources and a vast secondary literature in a variety of fields shed at least some light on the history of the relations between the United States and Germany over the span of nearly two centuries. No attempt is made here to enumerate all of these materials (although that would be a service of great value to historians), or even to list all that have been consulted during the preparation of this volume. What follows is merely an indication of where the most important archival material may be found, and what books (and, on occasion, articles) have proven of special value in dealing with the American-German relationship. Many works that provided useful information but had only a tangential relationship to the focus of this study have been omitted without prejudice.

ARCHIVAL MATERIALS

In the United States

By far the most comprehensive collection of materials dealing with the relations between the United States and Germany reposes in the National Archives in Washington, D.C. Record Group 59, General Records of the Department of State, contains despatches from U.S. ministers to the German States and Germany from 1799 on and despatches from consular officials beginning in 1790. Also included are instructions to U.S. ministers to Germany after 1835, and notes to and from the legations of the German States and Germany beginning in 1834 and 1816 respectively. After 1906, when the Department of State adopted the practice of filing incoming and outgoing correspondence by subject, the various files were consolidated under the heading of German-American relations, which, with the adoption of a decimal system of subject classification in 1910, became File 711.62. Additional American documents appear in Record Group 76 (documents relating to the agreement concerning Samoa in 1899 and to the post–World War I Mixed Claims Commission, for example), and in Record Group 84, which contains the papers of the U.S. legation (later embassy) in Germany from 1835 to 1913.

Because the Allies took possession of most official German records, including the files of the Foreign Office, after World War II, transported them to Great Britain and copied them, the National Archives also contains over thirty-seven thousand microfilm rolls of German documents in Record Group 242. The originals were returned to the Federal Republic beginning in 1958. Included in this collection are the archives of the German embassy in Washington from 1867 to 1929, files on relations with the United States, 1886–1920, the files of some German ambassadors to the United States, and the general Foreign Office files, 1918–1945.

In Germany

In Germany, the diplomatic archives since 1867 are housed in the Politisches Archiv des Auswärtigen Amtes in Bonn. They include the returned records, documents that escaped capture, as well as the records of the Foreign Office of the Federal Republic. Access is generally limited to materials before 1945. In addition, the Archiv includes an impressive collection of the papers of key Foreign Office officials, such as Brockdorf-Rantzau and Stresemann. The records of the Reichskanzlei for 1919–1945 are in the Bundesarchiv in Koblenz. Most of the Prussian diplomatic correspondence prior to 1867 which was not destroyed in World War II is now in the Zentrales Staatsarchiv in Merseburg, German Democratic Republic. A smaller collection is in the Geheimes Staatsarchiv Deutscher Kulturbesitz in West Berlin.

PUBLISHED DOCUMENTS

American

On the American side, a good deal of the diplomatic correspondence or summaries thereof, and, at least for the later period, relevant supporting materials have been published in *Foreign Relations of the United States: Diplomatic Papers,* the State Department series that now covers the years from 1861 to 1954. Several of the special supplements to this series, especially *The Lansing Papers, 1914–1920,* 2 vols. (1939–1940), *The World War, 1916–1918,* 6 vols. (1929–1933), *The Paris Peace Conference, 1919,* 13 vols. (1929–1933), *The Conferences at Malta and Yalta, 1945* (1955), *The Conference of Berlin (The Potsdam Conference), 1945* (1960–1961), and *The Conferences at Cairo and Teheran, 1943* (1961), contain valuable materials bearing on German-American relations. So do the State Department's *Peace and War: United States Foreign Policy, 1931–1941* (1941), and *The Axis in Defeat, A Collection of Documents on American Policy toward Germany and Japan* (1945). For the later period not covered by the *Foreign Relations* volumes, *American Foreign Policy, 1950–1955: Basic Documents,* 2 vols. (1957) and the annual *American Foreign Policy, Current Documents 1956–* (1959–) provide at least some documentation.

In the post–World War II period both the State Department and the U.S. Congress published several document collections dealing specifically with Germany. The most important of these are *Occupation of Germany: Policy and Progress, 1945–1946* (1947), *Germany, 1947–1949* (1950), and *The United States and Germany, 1945–1955* (1955), all in the European and British Commonwealth Series, and *Documents on Germany, 1944–1961* (1961), published for the Senate Foreign Relations Committee. Particularly for the nineteenth century, *Opinions of Attorneys General, Decision of Federal Courts, and Diplomatic Correspondence Respecting the Treaties of 1785, 1799, and 1828 between the United States and Prussia* (Washington, D.C., 1917), published by the Carnegie Endowment for International Peace, and both James D. Richardson, *A Compilation of the Messages and Papers of the Presidents, 1789–1902,* 9 vols. (Washington, D.C., 1903), and Fred L. Israel, ed., *The State of the Union Messages of the Presidents, 1790–1966,* 3 vols. (New York, 1966), contain some materials not readily found elsewhere.

German

On the German side, few documents for the preunification period have been published. A notable exception is *Die auswärtige Politik Preussens 1858–1871*, 10 vols. (Oldenburg, 1932–1945), most of which was lovingly compiled by the Reichsinstitut für Geschichte des neuen Deutschlands, but which contains little of importance for German-American relations. By contrast, the Foreign Office's *Die grosse Politik der europäischen Kabinette, 1871–1914*, 40 vols. (Berlin, 1922–1927), despite substantial omissions, is invaluable even for matters relating to the United States. A most useful gloss on German policy during these years by an "insider's insider" is provided in Norman Rich and M. H. Fisher, eds., *The Holstein Papers*, 4 vols. (Cambridge, 1955–1963).

Published documentary sources for the 1914–1918 period are somewhat less rich, although the rather eclectic *Official German Documents Relating to the World War*, translated under the supervision of the Carnegie Endowment for International Peace, 2 vols. (New York, 1923), has now been joined by André Scherer and Jacques Grunewald's splendidly edited *L'Allemagne et les problèmes de la paix pendant la première guerre mondiale*, 4 vols, (Paris, 1962–1978). For the period 1918–1945, extensive portions of the Foreign Office papers have been published. The American English-language version, *Documents on German Foreign Policy* (Washington, D.C., 1949–1966), comprises all 13 volumes of Series D (1937–1941) and 5 volumes of Series C (1933–1937). The German version, *Akten zur deutschen auswärtigen Politik* (Baden-Baden and Göttingen, 1950–), which will eventually be completed, currently consists of 15 volumes of Series B (1925–1933), which carry the documents to September 1930, the same 5 volumes of Series C, which go to October 1936, and the complete set of 8 volumes of Series E (1941–1945). Broader documentation, which draws on more than the official record and is also more widely concerned with internal German developments, can be found in *Ursachen und Folgen: Vom deutschen Zusammenbruch 1918 und 1945 bis zur staatlichen Neuordnung Deutschlands in der Gegenwart* 26 vols., ed. Herbert Michaelis and Ernest Schraepler (Berlin, 1959[?]–1979). This collection dates through 1950. The invaluable *Führer Conferences on Matters Dealing with the German Navy* was published by the State Department (Washington, D.C., 1946–1947), and some of the key documents therefrom in *Brassey's Naval Annual, 1948* (New York, 1948). Hitler's war directives are collected in Walther Hubatsch, ed., *Hitlers Weisungen für die Kriegsführung, 1939–1945* (Frankfurt, 1962). The Akten der Reichskanzlei are being published, though only a few volumes on the Weimar Republic are as yet available. Key documents for the post–World War II occupation period have been collected in Beate Ruhm von Oppen, *Documents on Germany under the Occupation, 1945–1954* (London, 1955).

MEMOIRS AND SECONDARY WORKS

1770–1870

For the period before 1871, the literature bearing on American relations with any of the German states is sparse indeed. Of what does exist, Henry M. Adams, *Prussian-American Relations, 1775–1871* (Cleveland, 1960), and the opening chapters of Otto, Graf zu Stolberg-Wernigerode, *Deutschland und die Vereinigten Staaten im Zeitalter Bismarcks* (Berlin, 1933), translated by Otto E. Lessing as *Germany and the United States of America during the Era of Bismarck* (Reading, Pa., 1937), are the most generally useful. The fascinating and quite original work by Horst Dippel, *Germany and the American Revolution, 1770–1800* (Chapel Hill, N.C., 1977) deals largely with political thought in Germany and the United States. John A. Hawgood dealt more prosaically with the period of the German revolution in *Politische und wirtschaftliche Beziehungen zwischen den Vereinigten Staaten von Amerika und der deutschen provisorischen Centralregierung zu Frankfurt am Main, 1848–1849* (Heidelberg, 1928), but the period is put into a broader and far more suggestive perspective in Günter Moltmann, *Atlantische Blockpolitik im 19. Jahrhundert: Die Vereinigten Staaten und der deutsche Liberalismus während der Revolution von 1848/49* (Düsseldorf, 1973), as well as in Eckhart G. Franz, *Das Amerikabild der deutschen Revolution von 1848/1849* (Heidelberg, 1958). There are two studies of the Civil War period which offer some help. The rather dated Ralph H. Lutz, *Die Beziehungen zwischen Deutschland und den Vereinigten Staaten während des Sezessionskrieges* (Heidelberg, 1911), has however, been largely superseded by Baldur Eduard Pfeiffer, *Deutschland und der amerikanische Bürgerkrieg, 1861–1865* (Mainz, 1971).

John G. Gazley, *American Opinion of German Unification, 1848–1871* (New York, 1926), though pedestrian, offers some useful clues, as does some of the published work on George Bancroft. Mark A. DeWolfe Howe, *The Life and Letters of George Bancroft*, 2 vols. (New York, 1908), and Russel B. Nye, *George Bancroft* (New York, 1944), are helpful, as is Henry Blumenthal, "George Bancroft in Berlin: 1867–1874," *New England Quarterly*, 37 (June 1964): 224–241. Henry A. Pochmann's exhaustive *German Culture in America: Philosophical and Literary Influences, 1600–1900* (Madison, Wis, 1957), and Carl Diehl's interesting *Americans and German Scholarship* (New Haven, 1978) are suggestive of other relationships, as are the studies in German immigration, including the pioneering one, Albert B. Faust, *The German Element in the United States*, 2 vols. (Boston, 1909), and Mack Walker, *Germany and the Emigration, 1816–1885* (Cambridge, Mass., 1964). Useful as well are the essays by Walter D. Kamphoefner, Günter Moltmann, James M. Bergquist, La Vern J. Rippley, and Otfried Garbe in Hans L. Trefousse, ed., *Germany and America: Essays on Problems of International Relations and Immigration* (New York, 1980).

1871–1900

For the period between the formation of the German Empire and the Spanish-American War, the two older works which carry the story to the World War, Jeannette Keim, *Forty Years of German-American Political Relations* (Philadelphia, 1919) and Clara Eve Schieber, *The Transformation of American Sentiment toward Germany, 1870–1914* (Boston, 1923), though dated and in many ways superficial, remain useful. So, of course, does Stolberg-Wernigerode's study cited above.

The early chapters of Ilse Kunz-Lack, *Die deutsch-amerikanischen Beziehungen, 1890–1914*, add some materials of importance, as does Herman Leusser, *Ein Jahrzehnt deutsch-amerikanischer Politik, 1897–1906*, Supplement 13 of *Historische Zeitschrift* (Munich and Berlin, 1928). Alfred Vagts, "Hopes and Fears of an American-German War, 1870–1915," *Political Science Quarterly*, 54 (December 1939): 514–535, and 55 (March 1940): 53–76, is intriguing but, at least for the early part of the period, not overly convincing. Primarily economic relations are detailed in George M. Fisk, *Die handelspolitischen und sonstigen völkerrechtlichen Beziehungen zwischen Deutschland und den* Vereinigten Staaten von Amerika (Stuttgart, 1897), now also substantially out of date. More specialized, but also more helpful, are two articles by Louis L. Snyder, "The American-German Pork Dispute, 1879–1891," *Journal of Modern History*, 17 (March 1945): 16–28, and "Bismarck and the Lasker Resolution, 1884," *Review of Politics*, 29 (January 1967): 41–64.

On the Samoan imbroglio, the standard work is George H. Ryden, *The Foreign Policy of the United States in Relation to Samoa* (New Haven, 1933). Some additional information is provided in Paul M. Kennedy, *The Samoan Tangle: A Study in Anglo-German Relations, 1878–1900* (New York, 1974), and the final settlement is discussed both in Joseph W. Ellison, "The Partition of Samoa: A Study in Imperialism and Diplomacy," *Pacific Historical Review*, 8 (September 1939): 259–288, and Edward Younger, *John A. Kasson: Politics and Diplomacy from Lincoln to McKinley* (Iowa City, Iowa, 1955). The latter work devotes considerable space to Kasson's service as minister to Germany in general.

For the period surrounding the Spanish-American War, Alfred Vagts's monumental *Deutschland und die Vereinigten Staaten in der Weltpolitik*, 2 vols. (New York, 1935), though unflaggingly tendentious, is invaluable, in part because at least some of the documents that are lovingly explicated either have been destroyed or are generally inaccessible. Lester B. Shippee provides some additional material in "Germany and the Spanish-American War," *American Historical Review*, 30 (July 1925): 754–777, and the classic refutation of the "Manila myth" remains Thomas A. Bailey, "Dewey and the Germans at Manila Bay," *American Historical Review*, 35 (October 1939): 59–81. A more recent and more detailed treatment is in William R. Braisted, *The U.S. Navy in the Pacific, 1897–1909* (Austin, Texas, 1958). A German counterpoint is provided in Holger Herwig's valuable *Politics of Frustration: The United States in German Naval Planning, 1889–1941* (Boston, 1976). The German perception of the resulting transformation of sentiment can be found in Ernst von Halle, "Deutschland und die öffentliche Meinung in den Vereinigten Staaten," *Preussische Jahrbücher*, 107 (1902): 189–212, and Justus Hashagen, "Zur Geschichte der amerikanisch-deutschen Beziehungen, 1897–1907," *Zeitschrift für Politik*, 16 (1927): 122–129.

Three relatively recent interpretive American studies of late nineteenth-century foreign relations, Ernest R. May, *Imperial De-*

mocracy: The Emergence of America as a Great Power (New York, 1961), Walter LaFeber, *The New Empire: An Interpretation of American Expansion, 1860–1898* (Ithaca, N.Y. 1963), and Milton Plesur, *America's Outward Thrust: Approaches to Foreign Affairs, 1865–1890* (DeKalb, Ill., 1971), not only provide valuable insights but deal specifically with various aspects of German-American relations. Erich Eyck, *Das persönliche Regiment Wilhelms II* (Zürich, 1948) is the best and most suggestive study of the kaiser, whose earlier speeches are lovingly collected in Wolf von Schierbrand, ed., *The Kaiser's Speeches* (New York, 1903). Michael Balfour, *The Kaiser and His Times* (Boston, 1964), adds some useful information. Among the more interesting memoirs are Kurd von Schlözer, *Amerikanische Briefe* (Stuttgart, 1927), and Andrew D. White, *The Autobiography of Andrew Dickson White*, 2 vols. (New York, 1905), to which a recent biography, Glenn C. Altschuler, *Andrew D. White: Educator, Historian, Diplomat* (Ithaca, N.Y., 1979) adds relatively little of value for this study. The early portions of Henry Cabot Lodge, *Selections from the Correspondence of Theodore Roosevelt and Henry Lodge, 1884–1918*, 2 vols. (New York, 1925), and, of course, also of Elting E. Morison et al., eds., *The Letters of Theodore Roosevelt*, 8 vols. (Cambridge, Mass., 1951–1954), are enormously valuable.

1901–1913

The period from the turn of the century to the outbreak of the First World War, particularly the presidency of Theodore Roosevelt, has attracted considerable scholarly attention. The books by Balfour, Braisted, Eyck, Herwig, Keim, Kunz-Lack, Lodge, Roosevelt, Schieber, von Schierbrand, and Vagts, as well as the articles by Hashagen and Leusser, all previously cited, provide useful information, albeit to varying degrees. Directly concerned with this period are the Germanophilic John W. Burgess, *Germany and the United States* (New York, 1913), and two German works, Bernhard Kostmann, *Präsident Theodor Roosevelt und Deutschland* (Emstetten/Westphalia 1933), and Evelene Peters, *Roosevelt und der Kaiser* (Leipzig, 1936), both of which overstate the "cooperation" between Roosevelt and William II. The outstanding American work, though with a much broader focus, remains Howard K.

Beale, *Theodore Roosevelt and America's Rise to World Power* (Baltimore, 1956). Beale's energetic defense of Roosevelt's truthfulness in talking of an ultimatum to Germany in 1903 misses the essential point that what the president may have regarded as an ultimatum was not seen as that by Germany. The same theme, with an ingenious though fanciful explanation, is taken up in Frederick W. Marks, III, *Velvet on Iron: The Diplomacy of Theodore Roosevelt* (Lincoln, Neb., 1979).

The overall literature on Roosevelt's diplomacy is very extensive. Most relevant to relations with Germany are Howard C. Hill, *Roosevelt and the Caribbean* (New York, 1927), and Dana G. Munro, *Intervention and Dollar Diplomacy in the Caribbean, 1900–1921* (Princeton, N.J., 1927), with respect to the Venezuela crisis; Eugene N. Anderson, *The First Moroccan Crisis, 1904–1906* (Chicago, 1939), Oron J. Hale, *Germany and the Diplomatic Revolution, 1904–1906* (Philadelphia, 1931), and, with reservations, Luella J. Hall, *The United States and Morocco, 1779–1956* (Metuchen, N.J., 1971), concerning the events surrounding the Algeciras Conference; John A. White, *The Diplomacy of the Russo-Japanese War* (Princeton, N.J., 1964), Raymond A. Esthus, *Theodore Roosevelt and Japan* (Seattle, 1967), and, though now superseded, Tyler Dennett, *Roosevelt and the Russo-Japanese War* (Garden City, N.Y., 1925), for contacts with the kaiser induced by the Russo-Japanese War; and John G. Reid, *The Manchu Abdication and the Powers, 1908–1912* (Berkeley, Calif., 1935), with reference to a possible Sino-American-German alliance. See also Manfred Jonas, "The Major Powers and the United States, 1898–1910: The Case of Germany," in Jules Davids, ed., *Perspective in American Foreign Policy* (New York, 1976), and Hans W. Gatzke, "The United States and Germany on the Eve of World War I," in Immanuel Geiss and Bernd Jürgen Wendt, eds., *Deutschland in der Weltpolitik des 19. und 20. Jahrhunderts* (Düsseldorf, 1974).

There is some interesting material in Stephen Gwynn, ed., *The Letters and Friendships of Sir Cecil Spring-Rice*, 2 vols. (London, 1929), and in Alfred von Tirpitz, *Politische Dokumente*, 2 vols. (Berlin, 1924–1926). The book by the former ambassador to Germany, Charlemagne Tower, *Germany of Today* (New York, 1913), offers an unusual perspective, as does Emil Witte, *Aus einer deutschen Botschaft* (Leipzig, 1907).

1914–1920

For the period surrounding the First World War, Arthur Link's *Wilson*, 5 vols. (Princeton, N.J., 1947–1965), particularly volumes 3, *The Struggle for Neutrality, 1914–1915* (1960), 4, *Confusions and Crises*, 1915–1916 (1964), and 5, *Campaigns for Progressivism and Peace, 1916–1917* (1965), remain indispensable. Volumes 32 et seq. of *The Papers of Woodrow Wilson*, ed. Arthur Link et al. (1966–   ) fill in some gaps. Ernest May, *The World War and American Isolation* (Chicago, 1959), deals in considerable detail with the diplomacy prior to U.S. entry. Some of the same ground was covered earlier in James B. Scott, *A Survey of International Relations between the United States and Germany, 1914–1917* (New York, 1917), supplemented by James B. Scott, ed., *Diplomatic Correspondence between the United States and Germany, August 1, 1914–April 6, 1917* (New York, 1918). Reinhard Doerries, *Washington-Berlin, 1908–1917* (Düsseldorf, 1975) details the activities of Ambassador von Bernstorff and there is useful information in Konrad H. Jarausch, *The Enigmatic Chancellor: Bethmann Hollweg and the Hubris of Imperial Germany* (New Haven, 1973). Martin Kitchen, *The Silent Dictatorship: The Politics of the German High Command under Hindenburg and Ludendorff, 1916–1918* (New York, 1977), is crucial to an understanding of the situation in Germany.

The U-boat controversy and other aspects of German-American friction are discussed in Gabriel Alphaud, *L'action allemande aux Etats-Unis de la mission Dernburg à l'incident Dumba* and *Les Etats-Unis contre l'Allemagne du rappel de Dumba à la déclaration de guerre* (Paris, 1915 and 1917); Karl E. Birnbaum, *Peace Moves and U-Boat Warfare* (Stockholm, 1958); Arno Spindler, ed., *Der Handelskrieg mit U-Booten*, 5 vols. (Berlin, 1932–1941), and Barbara Tuchman, *The Zimmermann Telegram* (New York, 1958).

An interesting perspective on the years preceding American entry into the war is offered in Laurence W. Martin, *Peace without Victory: Wilson and British Liberals* (New Haven, 1958), while Arno J. Mayer, *Political Origins of the New Diplomacy, 1917–1918* (New Haven, 1959) puts the Fourteen Points into a broader context. Of the memoirs and letters, Johann Heinrich, Graf von Bernstorff, *Deutschland und Amerika: Erinnerungen aus dem fünfjährigen Kriege* (Berlin, 1920; an English version appeared as *My Three*

Years in America, New York, 1920), and *Erinnerungen und Briefe* (Zurich, 1936; translated as *Memoirs of Count Bernstorff,* New York, 1936); James W. Gerard, *My Four Years in Germany* (New York, 1917), and *Face to Face with Kaiserism* (New York, 1918); Theobald von Bethmann Hollweg, *Betrachtungen zum Weltkriege,* 2 vols. (Berlin, 1919–1921); and despite very careful editing, Edward M. House, *Intimate Papers,* 4 vols., ed. Charles Seymour (Boston and New York, 1926–1928), are the most consistently helpful. The previously cited Tirpitz memoirs are also of help, if not entirely reliable, as is volume 2 of Karl Helfferich, *Der Weltkrieg, Vom Kriegsausbruch bis zum uneingeschränkten U-Bootkrieg* (Berlin, 1919).

On preparations for the peace conference, Lawrence E. Gelfand, *The Inquiry* (New Haven, 1963), is definitive. Klaus Schwabe's thorough and perceptive *Deutsche Revolution und Wilson Frieden* (Düsseldorf, 1971) adds much to our understanding of German-American interaction in ending the war and at the peace conference. Some of the essential points are repeated in Schwabe's contribution to Manfred Knapp et al., *Die U.S.A. und Deutschland, 1918–1975: Deutsch-amerikanische Beziehungen zwischen Rivalität und Partnerschaft* (Munich, 1978). David F. Trask, *The United States in the Supreme War Council: American War Aims and Inter-Allied Strategy, 1917–1918* (Middletown, Conn., 1961), provides the American perspective prior to the Armistice. Alma Luckau, *The German Delegation at the Paris Peace Conference* (New York, 1941), remains helpful, as is the opening chapter of Klaus Epstein, *Matthias Erzberger and the Dilemma of German Democracy* (Princeton, N.J., 1959). The reparations issue is discussed in Philip M. Burnett, *Reparations at the Paris Peace Conference from the Standpoint of the American Delegation,* 2 vols. (New York, 1940), and Peter Krueger, *Deutschland und die Reparationen 1918–1919* (Stuttgart, 1973). A recent assessment of America's opportunity at Versailles can be found in Arthur Walworth, *America's Moment: 1918* (New York, 1977), and any evaluation of the Paris conference must consider the evidence and conclusions in Arno J. Mayer, *Politics and Diplomacy of Peace Making: Containment and Counterrevolution at Versailles, 1918–1919* (New York, 1967). There is some interesting material in the fourth volume of W. K. Hancock and Jean van der Poel, eds., *Selections from the Smuts Papers,* 4 vols. (Cambridge, 1966).

1921–1938

The literature of American relations with the Weimar Republic is growing steadily. The pioneering and impressionistic work of Sidney Brooks, *America and Germany, 1918–1925* (New York, 1925), and the more narrowly specialized Erich Biber, *Die Entwicklung der deutsch-amerikanischen Handelsbeziehungen nach dem Kriege* (Frankfurt am Main, 1928), have been more than superseded by Lloyd E. Ambrosius, *The United States and the Weimar Republic,* University Microfilms (Ann Arbor, Mich., 1972), Robert A. Gottwald, *Die deutsch-amerikanischen Beziehungen in der Ära Stresemann* (Berlin-Dahlem, 1965), and the enormously detailed and impressive Werner Link, *Die amerikanische Stabilisierungspolitik in Deutschland, 1921–32* (Düsseldorf, 1970). Peter Berg, *Deutschland und Amerika, 1918–1929,* Historische Studien, 385 (Lübeck and Hamburg, 1963), examines German attitudes toward the United States, as does Ernst Fraenkel, *Amerika im Spiegel des deutschen politischen Denkens* (Cologne, 1959), which is also useful for both the earlier and later periods.

Hans Ronde, *Von Versailles bis Lausanne* (Stuttgart, 1950), and Hans W. Gatzke, *Stresemann and the Rearmament of Germany* (Baltimore, 1954), provide useful insights. American involvement with the reparations issue is treated in Dieter B. Genscher, *Die Vereinigten Staaten von Nordamerika und die Reparationen 1920–1924* (Bonn, 1956), Eckhard Wandel, *Die Bedeutung der Vereinigten Staaten von Amerika für das deutsche Reparations-problem, 1924–1929* (Tübingen, 1971), and Stephen A. Schuker, *The End of French Predominance in Europe: The Financial Crisis of 1921 and the Adoption of the Dawes Plan* (Chapel Hill, N.C., 1976). These works can be profitably augmented with Herbert Feis, *The Diplomacy of the Dollar, 1919–1932* (New York, 1966), and Joan Hoff Wilson, *American Business and Foreign Policy, 1920–1933* (Lexington, Ky., 1971). Karl Obermann added a stridently Marxist-Leninist interpretation in *Die Beziehungen des amerikanischen Imperialismus zum deutschen Imperialismus in der Zeit der Weimarer Republik, 1918–1925* (Berlin, 1952).

Other foreign policy aspects are dealt with in Keith L. Nelson, *Victors Divided: America and the Allies in Germany, 1918–1923* (Berkeley, Calif., 1975); Robert H. Ferrell, *Peace in Their Time: The Origins of the Kellogg-Briand Pact* (New York, 1952), and *Ameri-*

can *Diplomacy in the Great Depression: Hoover-Stimson Foreign Policy, 1929–1933* (New York, 1957); Edward W. Bennett, *Germany and the Diplomacy of the Financial Crisis, 1931* (Cambridge, Mass., 1962); and Louis P. Lochner, *Herbert Hoover and Germany* (New York, 1960). See also Manfred Jonas, "Mutualism in the Relations between the United States and the Early Weimar Republic," and Klaus Schwabe, "America's Contribution to the Stabilization of the Early Weimar Republic," both in the Trefousse volume cited above, and Kenneth Paul Jones, "Alanson B. Houghton and the Ruhr Crisis: The Diplomacy of Power and Morality," and John M. Carroll, "Owen D. Young and German Reparations: The Diplomacy of an Enlightened Businessman," both in Kenneth Paul Jones, ed., *U.S. Diplomats in Europe, 1919–1941* (Santa Barbara, Calif., 1981).

The perspective of the last Weimar ambassador in Washington is provided in Friedrich von Prittwitz und Gaffron, *Deutschland und die Vereinigten Staaten seit dem Weltkrieg* (Leipzig, 1934), and in his memoirs, *Zwischen Petersburg und Washington: Ein Diplomatenleben* (Munich, 1952).

For the early years of the Third Reich, the literature is as yet somewhat sparser. Of great value, however, are Arnold Offner, *American Appeasement: United States Foreign Policy and Germany* (Cambridge, Mass., 1969), despite its overplaying of the appeasement theme; Hans-Jürgen Schroeder, *Deutschland und die Vereinigten Staaten, 1933–1939* (Wiesbaden, 1970), even though it tends to downgrade World War II to a trade war; and the more balanced and thoughtful Detlef Junker, *Der unteilbare Weltmarkt: Das ökonomische Interesse in der Aussenpolitik der U.S.A., 1933–1941* (Stuttgart, 1975). Of substantial use too are Alton Frye, *Germany and the American Hemisphere, 1933–1941* (New Haven, 1967), and James V. Compton, *The Swastika and the Eagle* (Boston, 1967). A more thorough analysis of German policy toward the United States can be found in Gerhard Weinberg, *The Foreign Policy of Hitler Germany, 1933–1936,* and *The Foreign Policy of Hitler Germany: Starting World War II, 1937–1939* (Chicago, 1971 and 1980), and in Hans-Adolf Jacobsen, *Nationalsozialistische Aussenpolitik, 1933–1938* (Frankfurt and Berlin, 1968). Joachim Remak's unpublished dissertation, "Germany and the United States, 1933–1939" (Michigan, 1955), remains helpful. Joseph E. Heindl, *Die diplomatischen Beziehungen zwischen den Vereinigten Staaten von Amerika von 1933 bis 1939* (Würzburg, 1964), is brief and superficial.

The first third of Robert Dallek, *Franklin D. Roosevelt and American Foreign Policy, 1932–1945* (New York, 1979) deals with various aspects of relations with Germany, as do some of the documents in Edgar B. Nixon, ed., *Franklin D. Roosevelt and Foreign Affairs, 1933–1937*, 3 vols. (Cambridge, Mass., 1969). William L. Langer and S. Everett Gleason, *The Challenge to Isolation, 1937–1940*, the first volume of their *The World Crisis of 1937–1940 and American Foreign Policy* (New York, 1952), remains invaluable, and Francis L. Loewenheim, "The Diffidence of Power: Some Notes and Reflections on the American Road to Munich," *Rice University Studies*, 58 (fall 1972): 11–79, is thoughtful and persuasive. Of substantial value too are Nancy H. Hooker, ed., *The Moffatt Papers* (Cambridge, Mass., 1956), which offers the thoughts of one of the State Department's most careful observers; the recollections of the American ambassador, William E. Dodd and Martha Dodd, eds., *Ambassador Dodd's Diary, 1933–1938* (New York, 1941); and Robert Dallek's biography, *Democrat and Diplomat: The Life of William E. Dodd* (New York, 1968). Some insight into the views of Dodd's successor may be gained from Hugh R. Wilson, *A Career Diplomat, the Third Chapter: The Third Reich*, ed. Hugh R. Wilson (New York, 1961). For the activities of Wilson's counterpart in Washington, see Manfred Jonas, "Prophet without Honor: Hans Heinrich Dieckhoff's Reports from Washington," *Mid-America*, 47 (July 1965): 222–233, and Warren E. Kimball, "Dieckhoff and America: A German's View of German-American Relations," *The Historian*, 27 (1965): 218–243. Dieckhoff's own account, *Zur Vorgeschichte des Roosevelt-Krieges* (Berlin, 1943), was written as a polemic designed to gain him advancement.

1939–1945

For the period from the outbreak of World War II to the Pearl Harbor attack, the work by Langer and Gleason cited above, as well as their second volume, *The Undeclared War, 1940–1941* (New York, 1953), has not been surpassed. Günter Moltmann, *Amerikas Deutschlandpolitik im zweiten Weltkrieg* (Heidelberg, 1958), focuses specifically on Germany and carries the story to 1945. The Frye volume previously cited deals with part of the same period. The most incisive study focusing on Hitler's policies and actions is Saul Friedländer, *Hitler at Les Etats-Unis* (Geneva, 1963), translated as

Prelude to Downfall, (New York, 1967); the Junker volume cited above analyzes the American position. Of considerable value too are Hans L. Trefousse, *Germany and American Neutrality* (New York, 1951), and, to a lesser degree, Norman Rich, *Hitler's War Aims,* 2 vols. (New York, 1973), which pays relatively little attention to the United States. There is important relevant material in Johanna M. Meskill, *Hitler and Japan: The Hollow Alliance* (New York, 1966), and Paul Schroeder, *The Axis Alliance and Japanese-American Relations, 1941* (Ithaca, N.Y., 1958).

Hitler's overall strategy and his plans for the United States are brilliantly analyzed in Gerhard L. Weinberg, *World in the Balance* (Hanover, N.H., 1981), which reaches conclusions differing in emphasis but not in substance from the present work. On the same theme, there is much of value in Andreas Hillgruber, *Hitlers Strategie: Politik und Kriegsführung, 1940–1941* (Frankfurt am Main, 1965), and Jochen Thies, *Architekt der Weltherrschaft: Die "Endziele" Hitlers* (Düsseldorf, 1976). The view from Nazi Germany is expressed in Friedrich J. Berber, *Die amerikanische Neutralität im Kriege, 1939–1941* (Essen, 1943); that from Communist Germany in Gerhart Hass, *Von München bis Pearl Harbor* (Berlin, 1965), a study drawn largely from IG-Farben records and archives in Potsdam and Warsaw. A recent detailed study of Pearl Harbor and the prelude thereto is Peter Herde, *Pearl Harbor, 7. Dezember 1941,* Impulse der Forschung, 33 (Darmstadt, 1980).

For the period during which the two countries were at war, little exists on the German side. Roosevelt's policies are discussed both in Dallek's *Roosevelt,* cited previously, and in James MacGregor Burns, *Roosevelt: The Soldier of Freedom* (New York, 1970). Enormously useful as well is Herbert Feis, *Churchill, Roosevelt, Stalin: The War They Waged and the Peace They Sought* (Princeton, N.J., 1957). The heart of an immensely revealing interchange of messages is contained in Francis L. Loewenheim, Harold D. Langley, and Manfred Jonas, eds., *Roosevelt and Churchill: Their Secret Wartime Correspondence* (New York, 1975). The postwar revisionist view is detailed in Gabriel Kolko, *The Politics of War: The World and United States Foreign Policy, 1943–1945* (New York, 1968).

More directly focused on problems relating to Germany are John L. Snell, *Wartime Origins of the East-West Dilemma over Germany* (New Orleans, 1959), Daniel J. Nelson, *Wartime Origins of the Berlin Dilemma* (University, Ala., 1977), Anne Armstrong,

Unconditional Surrender: The Impact of the Casablanca Policy upon World War II (New Brunswick, N.J., 1961), Raymond G. O'Connor, *Diplomacy for Victory: FDR and Unconditional Surrender* (New York, 1971), and Warren F. Kimball, *Swords into Ploughshares? The Morgenthau Plan for Defeated Nazi Germany, 1943–1946* (Philadelphia, 1976).

Wartime planning for Germany's future is more fully described both in Department of State, *Postwar Foreign Policy Preparation*, written by Harley Notter (Washington, D.C., 1950), and Robert S. Knox, *High Level Planning in the United States regarding Germany, 1941–1946* (Washington, D.C., 1949). The Treasury Department's involvement in this process is indicated in John M. Blum, *From the Morgenthau Diaries: Years of War, 1941–1945* (Boston, 1967). The issue of breaking up the Reich is discussed in John H. Backer, *The Decision to Divide Germany* (Durham, N.C., 1978), Bruce Kuklick, *American Policy and the Division of Germany: The Clash with Russia over Reparations* (Ithaca, N.Y., 1972), and Tony Sharp, *The Wartime Alliance and the Zonal Division of Germany* (Oxford, 1975). Robert E. Sherwood, *Roosevelt and Hopkins* (New York, 1948) is always useful, and one side of an ongoing debate is expressed in Henry Morgenthau, Jr., *Germany Is Our Problem* (New York, 1945).

1945–1973

The entire period is surveyed in Alfred Grosser, *L'Allemagne de notre temps* (Paris, 1970), translated as *Germany in Our Time* (New York, 1971), and more specifically concerning German-American relations in Roger Morgan, *The United States and West Germany, 1945–1973: A Study in Alliance Politics* (London, 1974), and the concluding essay in the previously cited volume by Manfred Knapp et al. Hans W. Gatzke, *Germany and the United States: A "Special Relationship"* (Cambridge, Mass., 1980), though reaching back to 1776 devotes all but seventy-five pages to the period after 1933 and half of the book to what follows World War II. W. R. Smyser, *German-American Relations*, The Washington Papers, 8, no. 74 (Beverly Hills, Calif., 1980), is a highly suggestive brief essay.

For the American occupation of Germany, the standard work for the crucial early period remains John Gimbel, *The American Occupation of Germany: Politics and the Military, 1945–1949* (Stanford,

1968), to which should be added the two publications by Lucius D. Clay, *Decision in Germany* (Garden City, N.Y., 1950), and *The Papers of General Lucius D. Clay*, 2 vols. ed. Jean Edward Smith (Bloomington, Ind., 1974). For the whole of the occupation, Harold Zink, *The United States in Germany, 1944-1955* (Princeton, N.J., 1957), and the impressionistic and highly critical Eugene Davidson, *The Death and Life of Germany: An Account of the American Occupation* (New York, 1959), have been largely superseded by Edward N. Peterson, *The American Occupation of Germany—Retreat to Victory* (Detroit, 1978). Some more specialized aspects are treated in Earl F. Ziemke, *The U.S. Army in the Occupation of Germany, 1945-1949* (Washington, 1975); John H. Backer, *Priming the German Economy: American Occupational Policies, 1945-1948* (Durham, N.C., 1971), Herbert C. Mayer, *German Recovery and the Marshall Plan, 1948-1952* (New York, 1969), W. Phillips Davison, *The Berlin Blockade: A Study in Cold War Politics* (Princeton, N.J., 1958), and the highly intriguing John Gimbel, *The Origins of the Marshall Plan* (Stanford, 1976). There are some useful essays in Carl J. Friedrich et al., *American Experiences in Military Government in World War II* (New York, 1948), and Hans A. Schmitt, ed., *U.S. Occupation in Europe after World War II* (Lawrence, Kan., 1978).

The broader aspects of American policy toward Germany are treated in Henry L. Bretton, *United States Policy toward Germany* (Minneapolis, 1955), and Robert W. Miller, comp., *Die amerikanische Deutschlandpolitik, 1945-1955* (Frankfurt am Main, 1956), and the question of reunification in Robert F. Smith, "The Policy of the United States toward Political Unity in Germany" (Ph.D. diss., University of Chicago, 1955). More impressionistic and interpretive are Harold C. Deutsch, *Our Changing German Problem* (Chicago, 1956), Otto Butz, *Germany: Dilemma for American Foreign Policy* (Garden City, N.Y., 1954), and Wilhelm Cornides's wide-ranging *Die Weltmächte und Deutschland, 1945-1955* (Tübingen, 1957). The founding of the Federal Republic itself is detailed in Hans-Peter Schwarz, *Vom Reich zur Bundesrepublik* (Neuwied and Berlin, 1966), Peter H. Merkl, *The Origins of the West German Republic* (New York, 1963), and John F. Golay, *The Founding of the Federal Republic of Germany* (Chicago, 1958). Interesting relevant essays may be found in Edgar McInnis et al., *The Shaping of Post-War Germany* (New York, 1960), and Richard

Löwenthal and Hans-Peter Schwarz, eds., *Die zweite Republik* (Stuttgart, 1974). An intriguing comparative perspective is provided in John D. Montgomery, *Forced To Be Free: The Artificial Revolution in Germany and Japan* (Chicago, 1957), and an East German one in Max Seydowitz, *Deutschland zwischen Oder und Rhein* (Berlin, 1960).

For the years after the end of the occupation, the literature is less rich, though some of the works already cited carry over. The Adenauer policies are discussed in Richard Hiscocks, *The Adenauer Era* (Philadelphia, 1966), Terence Prittie, *Konrad Adenauer, 1876–1967* (Chicago, 1972), and in more detail in Waldemar Besson, *Die Aussenpolitik der Bundesrepublik* (Munich, 1970), and Wolfram Hanrieder, *West German Foreign Policy, 1949–1963* (Stanford, 1967), and *The Stable Crisis: Two Decades of German Foreign Policy* (New York, 1970). Narrower issues are treated in Robert McGeehan, *The German Rearmament Question* (Urbana, Ill., 1971) and Jack M. Schick, *The Berlin Crisis, 1958–1962* (Philadelphia, 1971). Heinrich von Siegler, ed., *Wiedervereinigung und Sicherheit Deutschlands, 1944–1967,* 2 vols. (Bonn, 1967–1968), provides some useful documentation. The Détente-Ostpolitik combination is considered in Karl Kaiser, *German Foreign Policy in Transition: Bonn between East and West* (New York, 1968), Philip Windsor, *Germany and the Management of Détente* (New York, 1971), and Kenneth A. Myers, *Ostpolitik and American Security Interests in Europe* (Washington, D.C., 1972). The economic aspects of that policy are examined in Angela Stent, *From Embargo to Ostpolitik: The Political Economy of West German-Soviet Relations, 1955–1980* (Cambridge, 1981).

Among the memoirs, also useful in addition to those of Clay are James F. Byrnes, *Speaking Frankly* (New York, 1947), and *All in One Lifetime* (New York, 1958), Robert Murphy, *Diplomat among Warriors* (Garden City, N.Y., 1964), and the first volume of Konrad Adenauer, *Erinnerungen,* 4 vols., (Stuttgart, 1965–1968), translated as *Memoirs, 1945–1953* (Chicago, 1966). Dean Acheson, *Present at the Creation* (New York, 1969), though long and often detailed, is highly reticent on the things that matter most. John Foster Dulles, *Our Policy for Germany* (Washington, D.C., 1954) provides some useful insights, as do Willy Brandt, *A Peace Policy for Europe* (New York, 1969), and *People and Politics: The Years 1960–1975* (Boston, 1978). Helpful in varying degrees are Harry S Truman, *Memoirs,* 2 vols. (Garden City, N.Y., 1955–1956), Dwight D. Eisenhower, *The White House Years*, 2 vols. (Garden City, N.Y., 1963–1965), Wilhelm G. Grewe, *Deutsche Aussenpolitik der Nachkriegszeit* (Stuttgart, 1960), Lyndon Baines Johnson, *The Vantage Point: Perspectives on the Presidency, 1963–1969* (New York 1971), Richard M. Nixon, *RN, the Memoirs of Richard Nixon* (New York, 1978), and Henry M. Kissinger, *White House Years* (Boston, 1979).

Index

William I, kaiser, 40; as arbitrator in U.S.-
Canada dispute, 29, 33; friendship
with U.S., 26; policies, 21
William II, kaiser: abdication, 134, 136; alliance with Russia, 83; bellicose attitudes, 63; gestures of friendship,
40–41, 68, 72–73; and Morocco, 78;
personal regime, 41, 67; policy of
power, 41, 50, 63; and Theodore
Roosevelt, 67–68, 74, 75, 76, 80, 89–
90; weakness, 127, 133; and World
War I, 96, 99, 109, 114–115, 127
Willkie, Wendell, 247
Wilson, Woodrow: domestic concerns, 95,
137; fear of Germany, 98, 108–109,
110, 131, 138; foreign policy, 94, 96,
112, 113, 136, 138, 149; as peacemaker, 99, 115–116, 118–121, 122, 126,
133, 137, 244; at Versailles, 137–139,
140–142, 144–147; and the world order, 112–113, 124, 129, 130, 137, 141,
147. *See also* Fourteen Points; League
of Nations
Winant, John C., 266, 267
Wirth, Joseph, 158, 160; government of,
167, 168
World Economic Conference, 206, 207,
209, 213
World War I
and Germany: 99–100, 105, 107, 109–
110, 119; constitutional reform, 134;
internal chaos, 134, 136; misunderstanding of Wilson's role, 136–138;
peace efforts, 115–118, 120, 122;
peace negotiations with Russia, 128–
129; Supreme Army Command, 127,
128, 129; war aims, 127. *See also* submarine warfare
U.S. policy in: agreement to intervene
113; declaration of war, 123–124, 125;
favoritism to Allies, 98–99, 115, 116;
peace offensives, 115–121, 125, 126,
132, 133; war aims, 125. *See also* Allies
World War II: Allied offensives, 261, 262,
272; battle of Midway, 261; declaration, 240, 259; German offensives,
240, 241–242, 243, 245, 250; German
surrender, 262, 263–264, 274, 275; invasion and fall of France, 245, 247;
U.S. aid to Allies, 241, 242–243, 245–
250, 257; U.S. entry into, 258. *See
also* peace offensives; postwar planning

Yalta conference, 271
Young, Owen D., 176, 191
Young Plan, 191, 193, 194, 198; conse-
quences, 182; provisions, 192
Yuan Shi-kai, General, 88, 89

Zimmermann, Arthur, 96, 100, 101, 120,
121; telegram, 122

Library of Congress Cataloging in Publication Data

JONAS, MANFRED.
    The United States and Germany.

    Bibliography: p.
    Includes index.
    1. United States—Foreign relations—Germany.
2. Germany—Foreign relations—United States.   I. Title.
E183.8.G3J66   1984   327.73043   83-15278
ISBN 0-8014-1634-5